Nineteenth-Century

NINETEENTH-CENTURY

Richard W. Bailey

Ann Arbor

THE UNIVERSITY OF MICHIGAN PRESS

Copyright © by the University of Michigan 1996
Published in the United States of America by
The University of Michigan Press
Manufactured in the United States of America
⊗ Printed on acid-free paper

1999   1998   4   3   2   1

A CIP catalog record for this book is available from the British Library

Library of Congress Cataloging-in-Publication Data

Bailey, Richard W.
    Nineteenth-century English / Richard W. Bailey.
       p.   cm.
    Includes bibliographical references and index.
    ISBN 0-472-10750-X (alk. paper)
    1. English language—19th century—History.   2. English language—
Great Britain—History—19th century.   3. English language—United
States—History—19th century.   I. Title.
PE1085.B35   1996
420'.9'09034—dc20   96-43417
                                                        CIP

ISBN 0-472-08540-9 (pbk : alk. paper)

In Dickens's *Bleak House* (1853), Mrs. Jellyby is a practitioner of "telescopic philanthropy," so preoccupied with the needs of people in faraway lands that she takes little notice of her own surroundings. Historians of English have likewise practiced telescopic *philology* and have peered myopically at the dim outlines of a distant past while the unruly language has been changing all around them. Thus twelfth-century English has been more intensely studied than nineteenth-century English on the assumption that the conquest of England by speakers of Norman French produced revolutionary change, while the industrial revolution stimulated little change at all.

In 1888, one of the most discerning of contemporary observers felt obliged to invite readers to turn the telescope around in order to see the present. In his preface to the first volume of the *New English Dictionary*, James Murray pointed out what might be discovered in the entries he had compiled for the letter *B*.

> For B contains many illustrations of the fact, which has of late years powerfully impressed itself upon philological students, that the creative period of the language, the epoch of "roots," has never come to an end. The "origin of language" is not to be sought merely in a far-off Indo-European antiquity, or in a still earlier pre-Aryan yore-time; it is still in perennial process around us. (Quoted in Raymond, vii)

Nonetheless, alluring visions of "yore-time" continued to occupy the imaginings of people alert to the language, and even today the remarkable evolution of nineteenth-century English has too seldom been "powerfully impressed" on historians of the language (despite Michel Foucault's observation that nearly everything changed in the nineteenth century).

Linguistic periods, like all historical eras, are blurred at the edges. Some sounds, words, and syntactic structures fell into disuse during the nineteenth century; of the others that emerged, a few acquired social meaning of large consequence—for instance, the initial *h* sound in southern England or the use of first *an't* and then *ain't* in North America, both of which were seen to have horrific consequences for the socially aspiring and to express the unalterable brutishness of the lower classes. Mere sounds, yet mighty and serious.

Studying English during the nineteenth century is made easy by the era's unprecedented linguistic self-consciousness. More than ever before, observers commented on the state of English— sometimes finding in it signs of cultural superiority of English speakers, more often construing language change as evidence of bad manners, bad morals, and bad expression. Despite their vigilance and scrutiny, however, even the most zealous pedants failed to notice—and thus failed to celebrate or condemn—many of the innovations taking place around them. Then as now, English was constantly changing, shifting the means of expression in some ways that are patterned and predictable, in others that are unsystematic and unsuspected.

Reading the English of the nineteenth century is not made difficult by problems of intelligibility. The danger of misreading lies rather in the apparent familiarity of the language, lulling modern readers into imagining that this English is much like our own, when it is not. Newly minted grammar, like "the house is being built," seems to twentieth-century readers entirely familiar, and the hysterical condemnation that formerly surrounded sentences of this sort is difficult for us to understand. The vocalization or disappearance of the *r* sound before consonants and at the ends of words is now an established feature of the prestige dialect of southeastern England. When it first appeared in the speech of the educated in the early nineteenth century, it was thought to be a blemish to be resisted with all possible effort—not only because it produced such spurious forms as *mashmallow* from *marshmallow* (Savage, 18) but also because it was aesthetically displeasing.

At the beginning of the century, overseas varieties of the language were barely distinguishable from those of Britain; by the end of it, they had become independent and distinct standards for English. There was more English and more voices speaking it as population increased and as linguistic assimilation took place. Discontented with the arrogance of linguistic authorities, these speakers claimed for their language its own merits and their own right to respect.

English-speaking culture was transformed during the century by urbanization, by technology, by travel, and by rich new opportunities for communication. These cultural transformations had linguistic consequences to which the following chapters are devoted. In them, I assume that no single linguistic center has priority over the others; London, Edinburgh, Dublin, Toronto, New York, Charleston, Kingston, San Francisco, Durban, Hong Kong, and Sydney were all centers of English-speaking culture, and, taken together, they constitute a whole society. English is a single language full of variety, and I believe that no speaker is beneath notice and no single one has exclusive rights to represent "the language." Models assuming metropolis and hinterland, capital and colony, standard language and dialect have little to offer except fragmentation and prejudice. In applying this principle I have set a difficult task for myself, but I hope not an impossible one. With the abundance of evidence provided by nineteenth-century observers, a comprehensive view is certainly possible. I hope to have achieved a beginning here.

In treating the several domains of English, I have placed change in its cultural context in the belief that ideas about English are as much a part of its history as the bare facts of sound, syntax, and vocabulary. Our language is our most nuanced social gesture, and, by understanding how people behaved and what they believed, we can gain a more profound knowledge of the past and acquire an illuminating perspective on the present.

Aside from the great interpreters of the language of their own day—Otto Jespersen and James Murray, especially—authors who have addressed this subject recently have provided me with a foundation upon which to build. I am happy to acknowledge in particular the important books by Hans Aarsleff, J. F. Burrows, Kenneth

Cmiel, Linda Dowling, Lynda Mugglestone, K. C. Phillipps, and Dennis Taylor. Work on this book was begun during the tenure of a fellowship from the National Endowment for the Humanities supplemented by funding from the University of Michigan. To both institutions I am very grateful. Now that both are under assault by discontented legislators, I am eager to acknowledge that the work reflected in this book is built upon public investment, not only in me but in the sources upon which I have depended. Readers will see throughout the results of inquiry that could only be carried out by searching immense computer databases of English, most especially the *Oxford English Dictionary* and the novels by Austen, Dickens, Hardy, and Twain quoted here. I am grateful to the person mainly responsible for making these resources available to me: John Price-Wilkin of the University of Michigan Library. Others at the University of Michigan Library have been unfailingly helpful, especially Thomas C. Burnett, Judith C. Avery (who drew my attention to the many voices of Sojourner Truth), and Barbara Beaton, who, in addition, provided encouragement and friendship. Other libraries have provided me with valuable information, both through on-line catalogs, and through the old books upon which this new book is based. I mention with particular gratitude the library of the Athenæum Club (London), the Beinecke Library at Yale, the British Library, and the Library of Congress. For assistance of varied kinds, I am grateful to Charles A. Huttar, Joy Culbertson Huttar, Jonathan Evan Lighter, the late R. H. Super, Martha Vicinus, and Robert A. Weisbuch. Readers of earlier versions of this work have provided meticulous and invaluable counsel, particularly Jacqueline Anderson, Anne Curzan, Manfred Görlach, Dennis Taylor, and Bernard van't Hul. My family has provided love and unflagging support, particularly C. A. S. Bailey and Julia Huttar Bailey.

This book owes its origin to my mother, Elisabeth Weld Bailey (b. 1897). When asked about changes in her lifetime—a regular conversational strategy when addressing the very old—she said that on the whole not much had changed. It was her grandmother, Delia Thayer Parmalee Phelps (1837–1935), who had seen the world transformed. In the way of mothers, she was exactly right.

CONTENTS.

List of Illustrations.

INTRODUCTION

SINCE ENGLISH WAS RECOGNIZED as a distinct language some fifteen hundred years ago, it has undergone such wholesale changes that the early stages are hardly discernible in the later ones. Former historians of the language dwelt on those early stages, attempting to find an ideal past to confirm their idea of the present. For some, Old English (A.D. 450–1150) provided an ideal of a "pure" language later spoiled by massive borrowings from Norman French after the conquest of England in 1066. For others, the Middle English period (1150–1475) demonstrated the "cosmopolitan" quality of the language and a willingness of its speakers to draw riches from other languages in the form of adapted vocabulary. Still others regarded the Early Modern period (1475–1700) as "the wells of English undefiled" (as Samuel Johnson called the era before 1660), "the pure sources of genuine diction." All of these characterizations located the era of excellence somewhere in the past and reflect, in varying degrees, a discontent with the present.

Curiosity about the remote past accompanied a desire to emphasize the antiquity of English and, consequently, to endow the present with the riches of a language long treasured. Thus it is that writers about English often viewed themselves as *custodians,* bearing the heavy responsibility for maintaining past glory against present shame. Focus on the remote past inevitably drew attention away from the recent past, and, given this long antiquarian tradition, it is no wonder that there is no thorough treatment of a most transforming century for English, the nineteenth century.

Because nineteenth-century English is superficially like our own, its differences have been overlooked. No modern reader needs a grammar to read Jane Austen (though one is obliged to study one to comprehend *Beowulf*), nor is a special dictionary required to understand Herman Melville (while glossaries and footnotes are needed to support the reading of Chaucer and Shakespeare). Yet it is undeniable that English grew explosively in the nineteenth century, both in vocabulary and in numbers of speakers. Rapid change so transformed the century from 1801 to 1900 that a person born at the beginning of it would hardly recognize life at the end. Inventions, education, communication, and travel all had an impact on English. It is usual to call the early part of the century the "industrial revolution," but that term gives undue weight to only one aspect of the transformation that took place. What had been discovered was *progress.*

Early in the century, *progress* was used as a verb to celebrate social improvement. "Our country . . . is fast progressing in its political importance and social happiness," wrote George Washington in anticipation of the century to come. British critics found little to celebrate in American progress and derided the use of *progress* as a verb. In fact, *to progress* was old in English but, in Britain, it had fallen out of use. The *Oxford English Dictionary,* the monumental testimony to progress in English, provided this analysis.

> Common in England *c* 1590–1670. . . . In 18th c[entury] obs[olete] in England, but app[arently] retained (or formed anew) in America, where it became very common *c* 1790. . . . Thence, readopted in England after 1800; but often characterized as an Americanism, and much more used in America than in Great Britain.

Nineteenth-century Britons continued to deplore *progress* used as a verb, and few of them were sympathetic to the *idea* of progress applied to English. For most of them, the past provided a high ideal against which to measure the misery of the present. For others, however, progress made demands on English for new vocabulary (and new ways of making new words) and for new genres of expression. English was compelled to change—along with everything else.

In unprecedented ways, nineteenth-century writers believed

that the language must be *codified*, that is, reduced to a *code* 'a systematic collection'. (Equally emblematic as Washington's use of *progress* is Jeremy Bentham's invention of *codify* in 1800, for the nineteenth century saw completion of earlier attempts to codify English.) Dictionaries and grammars had long existed in the English-speaking world, but not until the nineteenth century did the idea emerge that everyone ought to consult them. Educated people with the leisure for hobbies often took to philology for recreation. Some of them collected words and expressions of interest, and, one way or another, many published their discoveries. Like most accumulators, they developed an affection for the curiosities they amassed. Perhaps among the half dozen most important such collectors was Henry Bradley, the second editor of the *OED*. Writing in 1904, he counseled optimism about the future.

> We may rest assured that wherever worthy thought and feeling exist, they will somehow fashion for themselves a worthy medium of expression; and unless the English-speaking peoples have entered on a course of intellectual decline, there is no reason to fear that their language will on the whole suffer deterioration. In the daily increasing multitude of new forms of expression, even though it may be largely due to the unwholesome appetite for novelty, there must be not a little that will be found to answer to real needs, and will survive and be developed, while what is valueless will perish as it deserves. It is therefore perhaps not an unfounded hope that the future history of the language will be a history of progress, and that our posterity will speak a better English—better in its greater fitness for the uses for which language exists—than the English of today. (239–40)

Apprehension and disapproval were slowly replaced by caution and, sometimes, as in Bradley's case, carefully qualified optimism even in the face of changes arising from "the unwholesome appetite for novelty."

Cultural change and linguistic change interact in complicated ways, as present-day sociolinguistic studies so amply reveal. Societies celebrating progress and embracing change do not necessarily experience language change; those with static institutions and well-preserved traditions may find language shifting in unanticipated directions. In the nineteenth century, cultural changes transformed both anglophone societies and the English language. Some of the most important of these cultural changes are sketched below as an introduction to the linguistic history in the chapters that follow.

Increase in Population

In 1800, English was spoken in Britain (though by no means exclusively) and in a handful of fledgling colonies and states along the Atlantic seaboard of North America. By 1900, English was celebrated by its speakers as a "world language." From 1801 to 1900, Britain's population tripled (to 38 million). The number of people in the United States multiplied almost fifteen times (to 76 million). In the second half of the century, Canada doubled its population to 5.4 million (with an increasing share of that growth taking place in English-speaking Canada). In 1801, there were only a handful of English-speakers in the seaports of southern Africa; by 1900, there were more than a million, both on the coast and in newly built cities in the interior. In 1801, Australia was primarily a penal colony with some 5,000 English-speakers; by 1858, the population had reached a million and by 1900 it stood at 4 million. From even smaller beginnings, New Zealand gained an anglophone population of 770,000 by 1900. Viable outposts of English had been settled in many parts of south Asia and in both East and West Africa. Of English-speaking countries, Ireland alone experienced population decline, the result of emigration and starvation. In 1841, before the famine, there were 6.5 million people in Ireland; by 1900, the population had fallen to 3.2 million.

Taken together, these figures suggest that English, over the course of the century, increased in mother-tongue speakers from 26 million to 126 million. At the beginning, English was a language concentrated in a few unimportant places; at the end, it had been introduced nearly everywhere.

Dispersion of English Speakers

The growth of colonial empires, both British and American, stimulated the idea of English as a world language. Perhaps no episode better represented the nineteenth-century spread of English than the meeting of Henry Morton Stanley and David Livingstone in central Africa in 1871. Stanley, acting on instructions from the New York newspaper that employed him, penetrated "darkest Africa" and greeted Livingstone with the famous words, "Dr. Livingstone, I presume." Thanks to Stanley's flair for publicity, this elaborately phrased courtesy became a byword, suggesting that English and English manners had arrived in what was then the region of the world least explored by curious Europeans.

At the very end of the century, the United States became a colonial power by subduing the Philippines and immediate / exporting teachers to bring English to its new possession. According to a report in 1900, "The introduction of English, wherever made, has been hailed with delight by the people, who could hardly believe that they were to be encouraged to learn the language of those in authority over them" (E. Yule, 112).

Before 1800, English speakers had made only the most tentative explorations in Africa and Asia; by the end of the century, English-medium schools were established across the vast reaches of British and American expansion.

INCREASE IN BILINGUALISM

During the century, the idea arose that Britons were not especially skilled at learning other languages. (This view was exactly contrary to the seventeenth-century opinion that English people were wonderfully adept in learning other tongues [Camden, 40].) Being politically powerful, agents of the British Empire were in a position to compel others to learn English, and, indeed, subject people were eager to learn English so they might share in the power and wealth that flowed, however inequitably, with empire. As a result, the use of English increased dramatically in commercial centers around the world.

Missionary efforts likewise brought English into formerly remote districts. When British traders in the second half of the eighteenth century attempted to open trade with China, for instance, they were repulsed by the emperor, who declared: "We in

$25. # REWARD **$25.**

Twenty-five dollars reward for sufficient evidence to convict any person of

Removing or Cutting

Any timber on these premises.

This Land is for Sale at a very Low Price on Terms that suit everybody. For particulars call on or write to

F. C. PARKER,

24 E. Ann St., ANN ARBOR, MICH.

$25. ## Belohnung. **$25.**

Eine Belohnung von $25 wird offerirt für genügende Beweise, welche irgend eine Person der Schuld überführen

Holz abgehauen oder ausgegeben

zu haben, auf diesem Eigenthum.

Dieses Land ist zum Verkauf zu sehr niedrigen Preisen und Bedingungen, welche für Jedermann annehmbar sind. Wegen Näherem wende man sich, oder schreibe an

F. C. PARKER,

24 E. Ann St., ANN ARBOR, MICH.

By the end of the century, local printers had accumulated a great variety of typefaces and styles, often combined in unpredictable ways. In this example, printed in 1897, three logotypes are used for the dollar sign; serif, sans serif, and gothic faces are promiscuously employed. Printing, in this case, was done on cotton cloth to allow the notices to be tacked to trees. (In the collection of the author.)

China do not attach great importance to strange or clever objects, and we have no need of your manufactured products" (Li, 42–43). By the early years of the nineteenth century, however, Anglo-Chinese trade began to flourish, and by the end of the century even distant villages in China were endowed with mission stations where English was fostered. (Representative of English-speaking triumphalism was the view of a New England divine writing in 1849 that God had ordained natural resources as well as revealed truth: "Coal, like the English language, like freedom, general intelligence, or piety, is protestant" [H. Read, 49].)

Full bilingualism involving English and other languages became widespread, but partial bilingualism led to English-based pidgins and creoles, especially in the seaports of West Africa, where Krio developed and eventually became the national language of Sierra Leone. In Asia, a different trade language developed, Pidgin English. Aboard merchant vessels, *lascars*—ordinary seamen, usually of south Asian origin—were employed as stokers and as deck crew. These workers (and the officers appointed to direct them) sustained a form of maritime pidgin English that extended a long-established tradition of shipboard multilingualism. (When in 1906 Parliament outlawed the employment of merchant seamen who did not have "a sufficient knowledge of the English language," *lascars* were explicitly exempted [6 Edward 7.c.48].) Indian newspapers in English appeared, written and read by Indian bilinguals, and Indian English was established among those eager to assist in carrying out the duties of empire.

In Britain, these new kinds of English were not sympathetically received. Pidgin English was treated with haughty amusement by Charles G. Leland in *Pidgin-English Sing-Song; or, Songs and Stories in the China-English Dialect* (1876), and Arnold Wright cruelly lampooned Indian English in *Baboo English as 'Tis Writ* (1891).

By the end of the century there was not only more English, there were more kinds of English than ever before.

EXTENSION OF LITERACY

The newly organized United States was ahead of other English-speaking areas in establishing schools at public expense, but the education most children received in them was rudimentary. In Britain, only a minority of working-class children attended school before 1870 (when attendance became compulsory). Even the statistically minded Victorians were unable to determine just what counted as literacy and to count how many of Victoria's subjects lacked it. One estimate suggested that as many as 40 percent of the people in England and Wales were illiterate in the 1840s, with slightly lower figures for Scotland and considerably higher ones in Ireland. Grinding poverty, exhausting toil, and a lack of artificial lighting conspired to discourage reading; only at the end of the century were these conditions much improved. In North America, schooling was increasingly available, and public higher education was established for large numbers of students, but these new institutions barely kept pace with the increase in population, and resources were taken from poor immigrants, African-, Asian-, and Hispanic-Americans to invest in the education of the majority population.

From the earliest times for which reliable estimates exist, women had lagged behind men in literacy with a gap of 15–20 percent at the beginning of the century. However, literacy rates increased dramatically for both women and men, and, by the end of the century, women equaled men as literates (see Schofield).

Literacy became both wider and deeper. Readers had more to read, and they read more. Newspapers flourished; magazines multiplied; books cheapened; and lending libraries came into existence, even in isolated areas. Children's literature, which had been virtually nonexistent in 1800, became a flourishing genre, with many books later considered "classics" available in richly illustrated and inexpensive editions. Some publishers, especially in Britain, produced special editions of books to be awarded as school prizes for clever pupils. Writers attuned to the popular taste became wealthy and were seen as illustrious figures, often taken to be wise interpreters of cultural value.

At the beginning of the century, literacy was enjoyed by only a minority, and for most workers there was no economic advantage in learning to read and write (see Laqueur). Recreational literacy, particularly in the realm of fiction, exploded in popularity, with

YOU have thoughts that you wish to communicate to another through the medium of a letter. Possibly you have a favor to bestow. Quite as likely you have a favor to ask.

In either case you wish to write that letter in a manner such as to secure the respect and consideration of the person with whom you correspond.

The rules for the mechanical execution of a letter are few; understanding and observing the rules already considered for composition, the writer has only to study perfect naturalness of expression, to write a letter well.

Style and Manner.

The *expression* of language should, as nearly as possible, be the same as the writer would speak. A letter is but a talk on paper. The *style* of writing will depend upon the terms of intimacy existing between the parties. If to a superior, it should be respectful: to inferiors, courteous; to friends, familiar; to relatives, affectionate.

Originality.

Do not be guilty of using that stereotyped phrase,

Dear Friend:
I now take my pen in hand to let you know that I am well, and hope you are enjoying the same great blessing.

Be original. You are not exactly like any one else. Your letter should be a representative of yourself, not of anybody else. The world is full of imitators in literature, who pass on, leaving no reputation behind them. Occasionally originals come up, and fame and fortune are ready to do them service. The distinguished writers of the past and present have gone aside from the beaten paths. Letter writing affords a fine opportunity for the display of originality. In your letter be yourself; write as you would talk.

Inexpensive postage and a global network of distribution made letters available to all. (From T. E. Hill, 79.)

women as the principal producers and consumers. "Hawthorne made perhaps $1,500 in his lifetime from *The Scarlet Letter;* Susan B. Warner's tear-jerker *The Wide, Wide World* sold half a million copies in the United States, and was also widely popular in England" (Kenner, 8). At the end of the century, a considerable majority of both men and women were literate, and literacy was perceived as necessary for social advancement.

EMERGENCE OF ENGLISH TEACHING

Though the idea of the grammar school was old in Britain and North America, grammar had served as the foundation for the study of Latin. From the mid–eighteenth century, English grammars were produced with the idea that learning English grammar for its own sake was a worthy and valuable use of time. By 1813, the Belfast Academical Institution had formed an "English department," and the same innovation was introduced in the school in East Hartford, Connecticut in 1834 (Michael, 377–78).

Schoolteaching was driven by high moral purpose, and English became a subject of particular study at the many church-affiliated schools and colleges that were founded in both Britain and North America. Lecturing at one of them, the Diocesan Training School in Winchester, Richard Chenevix Trench declared "that words often contain a witness for great moral truths—God having pressed such a seal of truth upon language, that men are continually uttering deeper things than they know" (1891, 7). Searching for these truths through classes in English linked the subject to the ethical and religious themes that pervaded the curriculum.

Though there had been some earlier attempts to make English a university subject, at the beginning of the century there were only a handful of teachers and few students studying literature or the history of the language. Chaucer and Shakespeare were not read at the universities, nor were more modern writers in English a part of the curriculum. Thanks to the example the Scottish Enlightenment and an explosive demand for educated clergy of many persuasions, rhetoric and belles lettres became focal sub-

PROPER POSITION.   IMPROPER POSITION.

PROPER POSITION.   IMPROPER POSITION.

Dramatic increases in literacy made most young people literate in English by the end of the century. For young men, reading was connected with work; for young women with leisure—illustrated in the furniture used by the readers above. (From Northend, frontispiece.)

jects in higher-education not only in Scotland but also in colonial American colleges.

English as a university subject in England emerged on the model of the study of classical authors, that is, through philological analysis. Elsewhere, literary, linguistic, and rhetorical studies were influenced by the Scottish example, making writing nearly as important as reading. In Britain, Oxford and Cambridge long resisted teaching any of the modern languages, and English studies in England had its beginning in the radically modern curriculum formulated by the founders of the University of London. By the end of the nineteenth century, universities throughout the English-speaking world had created departments of English on recognizably modern lines, with efforts to make composition, language study, and literature (especially that of very early periods) the center of education, not merely (as with the earlier emphasis on rhetoric) professional training for lawyers or clergy. With those developments emerged an international enterprise to create a "science" of language and literature, and by the end of the century many of the modern learned societies had been organized and with them the apparatus of scholarly journals, definitive editions of important texts, and deeply informed accounts of English literary and linguistic history. Progress in knowledge came to be a focal idea, and collaborative works of scholarship, serial publication of "original" ideas, and a sense of accumulating wisdom shaped English teaching as thoroughly as it did other intellectual disciplines.

As the profession of English emerged during the century, enormous investments were made in buildings, libraries, publications, and teachers. All these gave substance and respectability to English in a way never before imagined.

EXALTATION OF STANDARD ENGLISH

Denunciation of this or that "low" expression had long been a staple of comments on English, but nineteenth-century observers organized long lists of "incorrect" usages and found the means to enforce the use of the choices they endorsed. The first volume solely devoted to distinguishing good usages from bad ones had appeared in the last decades of the eighteenth century, but with the spread of literacy such works multiplied. A representative specimen is Walton Burgess's *Five Hundred Mistakes of Daily Occurrence in Speaking, Pronouncing, and Writing the English Language Corrected* (1856). The preface states a rationale that would not have occurred to earlier writers.

> It was prepared to meet the wants of persons—numbered by *multitudes* in even the most intelligent and refined communities—who from deficiency of education, or from carelessness of manner, are in the habit of misusing many of the most common words of the English language, distorting its grammatical forms, destroying its beauty, and corrupting its purity. (iii)

Here persons to be improved were not bumpkins or rustic squires, but multitudes of people whose usage threatened the integrity of English, who were likely by their ignorance or inadvertence to corrupt or destroy its purity. Usage books and dictionaries were no longer simply tools for intellectual interpretation but vehicles for social advancement.

As the doctrine of pernicious and salubrious usage was formulated, errors were treated as a threat and error makers as pariahs. By the end of the century, these ideas led to formal tests of literacy. In the United States, for instance, literacy became a prerequisite in many states for full citizenship, whether for immigrants or for voter registrants. At the beginning of the nineteenth century, such requirements would have seemed to threaten the foundation of democracy and to deny the promises made to Europeans of many languages who were recruited to populate the United States. As the century progressed, English seemed more and more important, and standard English—defined negatively by its absence of solecisms—a requisite for civilized behavior. Conduct books grew increasingly numerous throughout the anglophone world, and such works came to include quite particular recommendations about English usage.

In the course of the nineteenth century, an easy tolerance for linguistic diversity gave way to harsh punishments for those who did not mimic successfully "the best usage."

Errors of Speech.

An unprecedented obsession with correctness shaped nineteenth-century attitudes toward English. (From Meredith, 9.)

ENLARGEMENT OF HISTORY

The beginning of the new century presaged an increasingly
catholic view of history. Thomas Jefferson, among many other
intellectuals, taught himself Sanskrit, and the rage for "oriental"
learning extended the concept of history far beyond the legacy of
classical Greece and Rome. While the most conservative scholars
devoted themselves to minute analysis of classical languages—
Edward Bradley's comic treatment of Oxford included the Master
of Brazenface College, author of the "celebrated 'Disquisition on
the Greek Particles,' afterwards published in eight octavo volumes"—innovators devoted themselves to the great enterprise of
comparative and historical linguistics, an attempt to reconstruct,
from the documentary record and from scientifically based inference, the language of the earliest "Aryan" ancestors of the Indo-
Europeans. In this effort, Anglo-American scholarship was very
much a dependent adjunct to what Noel Annan has called "the
German Renaissance."

> No one can appreciate the nineteenth century, or indeed our own
> times, unless he realizes that we live in the shadow of a Renaissance
> as brilliant and dominating as the Italian Renaissance. . . . [T]he
> explosion of genius which burst in Germany and Austria in the eigh-
> teenth and nineteenth centuries was even more startling than what
> had occurred during the Italian Renaissance: the originality was as
> striking and the political and intellectual influence more profound.
> (165)

Except perhaps for chemistry, no field was more originally conceived by German intellectuals than the enterprise of philology. English scholars worked uneasily in the shadows of their Germanic counterparts. Among the first English scholars to gain a profound understanding of Old English, John Mitchell Kemble, declared in 1834: "had it not been for the industry of Danes and Germans, and those who drew from the well-heads of their learning, we might still be where we were, with idle texts, idle grammars, idle dictionaries, and the consequences of all these—idle and ignorant scholars" (392; see Kennedy).

For these opinions, Kemble became an academic outcast, and resistance to German scholarship continued to flourish in Britain—though, increasingly, with little evidence that the gentlemen amateurs had made "discoveries" equal to those of the German philological "scientists." In *Middlemarch* (1872), George Eliot obviously aligned herself with the character who dismisses the xenophobic insularity of a dreary pedant.

> "I merely mean," said Will in an offhand way, "that the Germans have taken the lead in historical inquiries, and they laugh at results which are got by groping about in woods with a pocket-compass while they have made good roads. When I was with Mr. Casaubon I saw that he deafened himself in that direction: it was almost against his will that he read a Latin treatise written by a German. I was very sorry." (1964, 204)

The more capacious view of linguistic and literary history fostered by the Germans, one designed to demonstrate the racial superiority of Germanic peoples, would be only incidental to the story of English had it not been for the opinion among some Germans that English was merely a highly corrupt dialect of their own language—an idea expressed by Schopenhauer in 1851.

> It is well known that languages, especially from a grammatical point of view, are the more perfect the older they are, and that by degrees they become ever inferior, from the lofty Sanskrit down to English jargon, that cloak of ideas which is patched and compiled from scraps of different materials. (2:565)

Given the Anglo-American idea of linguistic progress, this opinion was anathema, and in response scholars made greater and greater efforts to place English not only within the grand conception of Aryan history but even at the pinnacle of its development. Fortunately for anglophone self-esteem, another German, Jacob Grimm, had a different view of English, also expressed in 1851.

> Of all modern languages, not one has acquired such strength and vigour as the English. . . . Its highly spiritual genius, and wonderfully happy development, have proceeded from a surprisingly intimate alliance of the two oldest languages of modern Europe—the Germanic and Romanesque. It is well known in what relation these stand to one another in the English language. The former supplies the material groundwork, the latter the higher mental conceptions. Indeed, the English language, which has not in vain produced and supported the greatest, the most prominent of all modern poets (I allude, of course, to Shakespeare), in contradistinction to the ancient classical poetry, may be called justly a LANGUAGE OF THE WORLD; and seems, like the English nation, to be destined to reign in future with still more extensive sway over all parts of the globe. (S. H., 125–26)

Unsurprisingly, it was Grimm's opinion, rather than Schopenhauer's, that found favor with British and American readers.

Through the nineteenth century, linguistic history was reshaped in a way that made English far more prominent than it had ever been before. Anglo-American scholarship endeavored to place English in the larger scheme of Aryan superiority and thus justified, on linguistic and cultural grounds, its imposition on others.

GROWTH OF COMMUNICATION

Modern technology begins, effectively, in the nineteenth century. Animal power gave way to machinery, making possible inexpensive travel and population mobility. Steamships, railways, and (at the end of the century) motor vehicles all had a transforming effect on both expectations and behavior. Stable rural and village life—which had sustained local norms for English—was violently disrupted by urbanization and migration.

In the last decade of the eighteenth century, Samuel Pegge wrote a spirited defense of the urban speech of London.

> [T]o shew that the humble and accepted dialect of London, the Londonisms, as I may call them, are far from being reproachable in themselves, however they may appear to us not born within the sound of *Bow-Bell;* nay, further, that the *Cockneys,* who content themselves with the received language and pronunciation which has descended to them unimpaired and unaugmented through a line of ancestry, have not corrupted their native tongue, but are, in general, luckily right, though upon unfashionable principles;—and, moreover, that even those very words which appear to be distorted in pronunciation are, for the most part, fairly and analogically formed. (44–45)

The fact that Cockney needed defending from reproach is itself significant, showing an erosion of linguistic tolerance. As London and other urban centers grew, their local speechways became more and more reprobated as symptoms (or even causes) of urban ills. Stereotypes of English were formed and codified ever more rapidly as mobility of population made Americans familiar in Britain or Irish people in Boston.

Mobility and travel were not the only social changes to affect English, however. Cheap postage and a highly efficient mail distribution system extended the value of written English across social classes and made writing even more common among the wealthy than it had been when letters could be sent only at great cost. (In England and Wales, each person, on average, received four letters a year in 1839; thirty-two in 1871; and sixty in 1900 [Robbins, 156].) Telegraph and, latterly, telephone communication created new communities of interest—most of them, at first, commercial. Transatlantic cable service commenced in 1865, ensuring that written English would have an ever more privileged place. Explosive growth in domestic telegraph services was also important, with a ninefold increase (to 90 million) in messages transmitted annually within Britain between 1870 and 1900.

These technological developments changed the nature of expression and the marketplace for English, particularly in jour-

CLOTH $1.00   PAPER 50 CENTS

CHOICE
DIALECT for
Reading
and Recitation

THE PENN PUBLISHING COMPANY
PHILADELPHIA

National and regional dialects of English were a staple of humor for nineteenth-century audiences at music halls and in vaudeville. Sometimes performers merely exaggerated their usual ways of speaking, but often they delighted in making ethnicity humorous through mimicry. (From Shoemaker, cover.)

nalism, where significant events could be made known to a wide public almost immediately. How far communication had changed in the course of the century can be encapsulated in the spontaneous creation of the verb *maffick* 'riotously rejoice'. In a minor skirmish of the Anglo-Boer War, British forces relieved their garrison in Mafeking in South Africa on May 17, 1900, a Thursday;

news was promptly telegraphed to London, where the public rioted happily (if destructively) on Saturday. On the following Monday, the *Pall Mall Gazette* coined the word *maffick*, whose voguish lexical existence over the next few months was enshrined in the *Oxford English Dictionary*. At the beginning of the nineteenth century, such a rapid sequence of episodes could not have been imagined. Distance and time, by the end of the century, had been drastically foreshortened.

During the nineteenth century, words could be created, distributed, codified, and recorded with unprecedented speed and permanence.

Spread of Democracy

One of the principal cultural changes to sweep the Anglo-American world of the nineteenth century was the extension of voting rights to more and more citizens. Property ownership was abolished as a qualification for voting in Britain, and, after the American Civil War, former slaves were enfranchised. (Women's suffrage, though the subject of intense agitation in both Britain and the United States, was delayed until the twentieth century.)

As more and more people became involved in the political process, a new rhetoric emerged to suit the perceived needs of a majority of voters. American conservatives invented the term *demagoguery* (first attested in 1855 in Kentucky) to deride those whose appeals were based on interests the conservatives did not support. Though *demagogue* (both as noun and verb) had existed in English since the seventeenth century, nineteenth-century Americans made special and frequent use of it to assail the speeches of those ambitious to hold office. Other political vocabulary was created: *Free Soilism* (1847; with *Free-Soilish* 'inclined to the principles of the *Free Soil Party*'); *Know-Nothingism* (1866; from the name of the Know-Nothing Party, 1854); *Silverite* (1886) and *Silverism* (1895; for advocates of silver as a monetary standard).

Especially in the United States, folk stereotypes were created to express political views in a highly colloquial English. These stereotypes emerged from *yarns* (a word first recorded in the nineteenth century and used among members of the London criminal subculture); *yarn-spinners* told tales, often humorously exaggerated, for domestic entertainment, and oral storytelling was the foundation for literary invention. In Canada, Thomas Chandler Haliburton created "Sam Slick," while in New England James Russell Lowell (through "Hosea Biglow") and Frances Whitcher (with the "Widow Bedott") made political and social commentary the focus of humorous narrative. These efforts were closely connected to ideas about English. A sympathetic British reviewer in 1860 praised Lowell's "marked delight in idiomatic terms and forms of speech, as well as quaint and racy thoughts" (F. Stephens, 206). Lowell's satire used the demotic to assault social ills perpetuated by respectable speakers: "the slave-trade, corrupt election practices, stump orators, and other rank growths" (206).

Deliberately nonstandard in their English, such fictional caricatures were granted wide latitude for social criticism. The American fashion for social criticism through vernacular characters even spawned imitators in Britain, most notably William Duncan Latto, whose "Tammas Bodkin" in the Scottish penny press was a particularly vigorous scourge of imperial expansion (see Donaldson); Latto's characters spoke a form of English distinctive to Scotland but accessible to all readers. Colloquial English thus became a strand in the tapestry of democratic eloquence, its nonstandard forms contrasting with respectable English and the interests of its speakers usually opposed to the interests of the governing classes.

While correctness and gentility were increasingly enforced, vernacular English came to be a vehicle for expressing resistance to authority.

Ownership of Information

At the beginning of the century, authorship was a precarious and ill-rewarded profession, but, before the end of it, a star system had emerged by which the most popular authors—for instance, Walter Scott, Charles Dickens, and Mark Twain—were able to amass fortunes through writing and speaking. In order to gain this wealth, however, writers had to secure exclusive rights to their work. Early in the century, copyright in England was construed to give rights equally to American and British authors, and Washington Irving and James Fenimore Cooper were able to profit from the popularity of their books in Britain. In 1842, Parliament established the modern basis for literary ownership, laying the foundation in property rights for the literary epoch for fiction and poetry that almost immediately flowered.

British writers, however, enjoyed no protections in the U.S. market. By 1850, the situation had deteriorated to the point that unscrupulous publishers in the United States were able to bring out cheap (and often inaccurately printed) editions of works by the most popular foreign writers, reducing the income of authors and eroding the authorized publisher's profits. These American publishers were called "pirates," and, like other assertive entrepreneurs in a setting where the title to property was unclear, they prospered. The U.S. government, though providing rights for American authors, held that the prevailing unregulated system made information from abroad cheaply available and thus benefited American society. Despite British agitation, action on international copyright was delayed until 1891. Even so, in the course of the century, authorship could become a means to a livelihood, and a more and more diverse group of authors began to seek opportunities for publication, increasing both the diversity and quantity of English enshrined in print.

Equally important for English was the passage of the Trademark Act by Parliament in 1862. This legislation granted property rights for the commercial use of "any name, signature, word, letter, device, emblem, figure, sign, seal, stamp, diagram, label, ticket, or other mark of any other description" (25 and 26 Victoria 88 at 178). By giving and protecting ownership of words, the government supported a vastly enriched array of advertising English, whose distinctive typefaces and slogans were replacing the rather plainly descriptive advertising earlier in use. Such protection allowed manufacturers to evolve images for products through the appearance, as well as the wording, of the English of their promotional efforts. Copyright and trademark legislation made it possible to own fragments of English. Forms of English became personal, rather than communal, property, and the emphasis on the "personality" of style and authorship came to be more and more emphasized, both in the higher reaches of literary authorship and in the less exalted domains of advertising and vivid popular journalism.

Ownership of information also extended to readers. At the beginning of the century, books were costly, and only a few people had access to libraries. In 1848, one social observer described British household libraries as usually scanty, and even the few books available were treated as family heirlooms rather than read for pleasure or profit (Alec Ellis, 3). Even after elementary education became compulsory in England and Wales, libraries in schools were not common (though the number of schools having libraries increased from 12 percent in 1880 to 40 percent in 1900). Nonetheless, book ownership was seen as socially symbolic, and, aside from religious works, a popular genre throughout the century, self-help books in fields ranging from agriculture to household management were viewed as indispensable sources of information. Owning books meant owning knowledge and the English in which the books were written. Enormous encyclopedias and dictionaries were produced and sold in huge numbers; "sets" of revered authors were peddled to householders; anthologies, etiquette books, and directories were published in ornate styles. As never before, written English flooded the marketplace.

In the course of the century, English was transformed from merely a language to a valuable property, firmly incorporated into capitalist economies. Far more than at any earlier time, English could be bought and sold. It was even possible to earn one's livelihood by working with it.

WRITING

ONLY DURING THE NINETEENTH CENTURY did English come to privileged status as a written language. Before 1800 English for most people was heard rather than seen. Writing and reading the language were activities of the minority, most of them of the highest social classes. The masses had little incentive to read and even less to write.

Before 1800, both British and American cultures were primarily oral societies in which public speaking for both religious and civic purposes was highly developed and valued. For most people, written documents merely gave sanction to mutual obligations—for instance, articles of indenture or property deeds—but there was little need to read these documents, and certainly little purpose in reading them twice. Documents certifying such agreements were elaborately produced, often with attached ribbons and wax seals (both archaic devices still well suited to a chiefly oral culture). Legal forms were produced by job printers, and a list of those available in 1780 from a provincial English printer shows vividly whose interests they served: search warrants, passes for vagrants, assessments for taxes (see Twyman, 4). At least until the end of the eighteenth century, literacy both in Britain and in North America was "stagnant, incomplete, socially hierarchical, and, *en masse,* intellectually passive" (Lockridge, 195). Of course some written English was visibly present to all, but compared to what was to follow, there was little written English encountered in everyday life. Books were uncommon; costly postage made letters expensive; advertising—even signs on shops—barely existed; printed papers seldom fell into the hands of most people.

The air was full of talk. Printed ballads and broadsides were hawked on the streets, and oral entertainment satisfied most of the popular craving for songs and tales. "Patterers" on the streets of London continued to satisfy the demand for scandal involving criminals and politicians, although these street performers often left their auditors in suspense, hoping that they would buy a sheet or pamphlet in which the full details were provided. And while charlatans sold nostrums and prophecies, often accompanied by paper documents to be used as charms to perfect their promises, these traders in talk and writing lived by their skill in the oral culture well into the nineteenth century.

> "We are the haristocracy of the streets," was said to me [Henry Mayhew] by one of the street-folks, who told penny fortunes with a bottle. "People don't pay us for what we gives 'em, but only to hear us talk. We live like yourself, sir, by the hexercise of our hintellects—we by talking, and you by writing." (Mayhew, 1:213)

Sellers of street literature profited from popular curiosity of all kinds, including that aroused by gossip and politics: Clandestine love letters allegedly found in the neighborhood, vivid accounts of shipwrecks, fires, and murders. "The burning of the old Houses of Parliament [in 1834] was very popular among the street-sellers," Mayhew explained (1:230); it was "a source of profit" when embellished by suggestions that the fire had been set by a cabal of politicians or a conspiracy of builders. To buy the full accounts of these tales, purchasers might pool their small coins and then find someone to read the broadsheets aloud. For the first half of the century, and more, people could be satisfactorily informed without taking the trouble to read.

Religious expression did not typically involve very many people in the practice of literacy, and worship services were often ostentatiously oral, particularly in sects where "spontaneous" preaching and prayer were valued over worship "by the book." Bible ownership was common, but it is unlikely that the Bible was very commonly read. Even in middle- and upper-class households, where Bible reading did take place, selections were performed aloud by one person and heard by many, the verses commonly dwelling on proper behavior for children and servants. For most people who owned one, the Bible was merely a text, a talisman, a hallowed place into which could be recorded births, marriages, and deaths—giving the printed text a powerfully iconic value not necessarily accompanied by a desire for silent reading in private. (Life's milestones were often noted on the blank flyleaves at the beginning of the family Bible, linking one's personal genealogy to the biblical begats, and during the century publishers inserted special pages to facilitate such purposes.) Taking a *Bible oath,* though the phrase had appeared in the seventeenth century, continued to be a common practice in the nineteenth, particularly in the United States. Owning a Bible, or swearing by one, manifested lingering faith in the magical properties long associated with writing, but these practices did not often involve active literacy.

Work life emphasized the practical over the theoretical, and even the literate professions like medicine and law did not require frequent resort to written English. Except for landowners who might read new volumes that were beginning to suggest improvements in animal husbandry or farming practices, agricultural workers—by far the majority occupation in both Britain and America—had no need for reading. Literacy was, at the beginning of the century, a personal rather than an institutional responsibility; individuals were primarily self-taught (since most people attended school only a few months a year for a very few years). Persons of unusual curiosity and perseverance might use writing and reading to become experts, erudite in one or even several fields of interest. For most people, however, there was no incentive to learn or to practice literacy until the end of the century. As far as can be determined from the printed matter that survives, there was little demand for written material in the skilled trades (like carpentry or masonry), in resource extraction (like mining or forestry), or in manufacturing (like spinning or pottery making). Books devoted to these subjects did exist, of course, but they were not routinely used on the job nor were they designed to disseminate technical advances in the work. Transport—navigation, railways, and horse power—did sometimes call for record keeping of various kinds, but most people employed in such pursuits had little need to read or write.

Though written English played only a minor part in most

people's work, commercial interests provided an important stimu- lus for literacy during the century as merchants recognized the power of written advertising to attract trade. Before 1800, adver- tising consisted mainly of trade cards designed to attract cus- tomers to shops and services, but, apart from printed sheets dis- tributed or posted in the largest cities, written advertising hardly existed. Few packages had printed labels, and documents later to become commonplace—newspapers, magazines, and leaflets— reached only a few people. In 1800, printers were mostly located in the cities; small towns and villages had little need for such estab- lishments, though the printing industry was soon to be diffused to such places. Signboards on shops continued the long-established practice of representing visually, rather than verbally, the articles for sale—for instance, shoes or hats. In the eighteenth century, descriptive notices, often elaborately worded, began to appear in newspapers and were circulated as flyers. But there was little idea that literacy in the service of commerce would soon flourish. Spec- ulating about the matter in 1759, Samuel Johnson declared: "The trade of advertising is now so near to perfection, that it is not easy to propose any improvement" (1790, 1:169).

Newspapers were an obvious vehicle to reach the literate and leisured minority. In 1792, newspapers in England were small, and only fifteen million copies appeared during the entire year. Not many people read a newspaper, but a great many heard the news. Most people listened to the contents read aloud by someone else, partly because the stamp duty in Britain made newspapers expen- sive and partly because a majority of the audience was not adept with written English. Not until 1855, when the duty was repealed, did newspapers begin to appear in large numbers, and the aboli- tion of the tax on paper in 1861 gave a further stimulus to growth. Papers that had been rented by tavern keepers and newsagents for a penny were now sold at the same price. The *Times* grew larger and longer, and yet, thanks to the reduced taxes and technical innovations in printing, cost less per copy in 1900 than it had in 1800. In 1896, the *Daily Mail* was founded in London and quickly reached a circulation of a million copies each day, supplementing the quality press with entertainment and news for a mass audience.

Scandal and sensation, formerly the domain of patterers in the oral culture of the streets, were suddenly available in written form for solitary reading. Newspapers made readers of more and more people, and they gave immensely increased authority to written words while marginalizing the testimony of speech. Oral culture asserted the authority of a speaker in face to face interaction; print culture, as developed in the nineteenth century, disguised authority in anonymous written English. Patterers like Bristol George, Corporal Casey, and Jemmy the Rake might hold forth in the London streets and maintain "a character for great integrity among the neighbours for many years" (Mayhew, 1:218), even while they were embellishing the scandals and sensations of the day. When the same events were reported in print, the accounts were given an unmerited reputation for fidelity, and journalists who published anonymously (as most did) could not easily be brought to account. Contrary to what might have been expected, oral testimony came to be dismissed as untrustworthy hearsay, while written narratives acquired the authority already vested in contracts, deeds, indentures, and certificates.

To the nineteenth century belongs the idea of the citizen as *consumer* (the modern sense of this word begins to flourish in that era). With the emergence of mass production and brand names came an ever-increasing investment in printed advertising, as traditional street cries like "Spar-row gra-ass" (Mayhew, 1:93) were replaced by placards with the word *Asparagus*. Desire for goods was stimulated with visual imagery accompanied by words. Urban landscapes, as depicted at the close of the eighteenth century, were almost devoid of signs and posters, but very soon advertising began in earnest, most prominently in displays designed to attract patrons to theatrical performances. Bill posting emerged as a clandestine trade, and virtually every accessible wall was coated with overlapping posters. Describing the street scene in midcentury London, Henry Sampson offered a vivid picture of this explosion of written English in public places.

> Never heeding the constant announcement of him to beware, the billsticker cared nothing for the privacy of dead walls, or, for the mat-

ter of that, of dwelling-houses and street doors; and though he was hardly ever himself to be seen, his disfigurative work was a prominent feature of the metropolis. It was also considered by him a point of honour—if the term may be used in connection with billstickers—to paste over the work of a rival; and so the hoardings used to present the most heterogeneous possible appearance, and though bills were plentiful, their intelligibility was of a very limited description. Sunday morning early used to be a busy time with the wandering billsticker. (25)

Advertising, like other aspects of nineteenth-century commercial life, became rationalized, with designated and privately owned *hoardings* (1823) or *billboards* (1851) leased to advertisers for limited periods. The resulting system covered nearly as much space as the unauthorized postings but prevented overlap and regulated competition. Urban scenes blossomed with English, often in elaborate forms. Wagons passed through busy streets carrying towering structures covered with posters. "Board work" became a recognized street trade as advertisers employed itinerant workers to carry huge, lavishly illustrated signs through the busiest districts. Such uses of English associated literacy with informed consumption of goods and services and did much to foster a desire for reading.

While literacy was stimulated by commercial interests, it was discouraged by political forces. Since the introduction of printing in Europe, those in authority had recognized the power of the press to disseminate radical ideas, and, while most Britons approved of the printed Bibles and tracts that had fostered the Protestant Reformation three centuries earlier, they also feared unregulated printing that could threaten the status quo. Certainly the role of tracts and newspapers in fomenting the American Revolution was a vivid and recent memory in Britain at the turn of the century, and an even more present danger was perceived in the role of the radical press in overthrowing the monarchy in France. Although its Constitution had guaranteed press freedom, the United States still wrestled with what such freedom meant in practice, and there remained questions of treason and sedition to be worked out in relation to that freedom. In both Britain and the

United States, the cost of schooling to make children literate
alarmed the taxpayers, adding a financial motive to the ideological
reluctance to support genuinely effective mass literacy. Thus literacy was a hazardous and expensive prospect, and, before English
could emerge in a fully powerful written form, these issues sur-
rounding literacy had to be resolved.

A significant debate over education took place in Parliament
in 1807, when a proposal was introduced to provide schools for
poor children. The leading figures in the debate were well-known
and influential people: Samuel Whitbread (1758–1815), who
introduced the proposal; William Wilberforce (1759–1833); and
Davies Giddy, subsequently surnamed Gilbert (1767–1839). Whitbread, a vocal proponent of civil liberties, had earlier urged,
unsuccessfully, a minimum agricultural wage to relieve the suffering of farmworkers in hard times. Wilberforce, almost universally
admired for his piety, was author of the internationally popular
Practical Christianity (1797) and the leader of the movement to halt
the slave trade (in which campaign he eventually prevailed in
1807). Giddy was scientifically inclined, active in learned societies
concerned with geology and biology, and sufficiently mathematical to be consulted by the leading engineers of the day. In 1827, he
was elected president of the Royal Society. All three represented
important segments of public opinion in Britain at the turn of the
century.

In the parliamentary debate, Whitbread argued vigorously in
favor of his bill to establish schools funded at public expense. In
this effort, he was opposed by Giddy, whose argument raised the
specter of social discord.

> For, however specious in theory the project might be, of giving edu-
> cation to the labouring classes of the poor, it would, in effect, be
> found to be prejudicial to their morals and happiness; it would teach
> them to despise their lot in life, instead of making them good ser-
> vants in agriculture, and other laborious [*sic*] employments to which
> their rank in society had destined them; instead of teaching them
> subordination, it would render them factious and refractory, as was
> evident in the manufacturing counties; it would enable them to read
> seditious pamphlets, vicious books, and publications against Chris-

tianity; it would render them insolent to their superiors; and, in a few years, the result would be, that the legislature would find it necessary to direct the strong arm of power towards them, and to furnish the executive magistrates with much more vigorous laws than were now in force. (Hansard, July 13, 1807, 9:798–99)

Whitbread replied to Giddy and other opponents of the measure. When riotous mobs formed, the illiterate many, he thought, were at the mercy of the literate few: "If one man had knowledge, he would have a much better chance of leading a thousand ignorant creatures to mischief, than if they were all so far informed as to read what might appear on both sides of the question" (803). Wilberforce weighed in with support: "The necessity of instruction among the lower classes in the south and west of England, and in Ireland, was strikingly obvious; in the latter, particularly, he [i.e., Wilberforce] was convinced that on the instructing and enlightening of the people depended the very safety of the empire itself" (July 21, 1807, 9:850–51).

Whitbread and Wilberforce temporized by making their proposal optional, both for taxpayers who might not be inclined to support schools in their neighborhoods and for poor parents who might prefer to have their children at work rather than in school. Despite some interest in the proposal, more than sixty years would pass before primary education became universal in England and Wales. Perhaps the most revealing issue in the debate, however, was the presumption expressed by Giddy (and others on his side of the issue) that written English could lead to social unrest and to the assertion of rights by the disenfranchised.

A parallel in North America can be found in the reluctance of slaveowners to allow African-Americans access to the power of literacy. As Giddy had argued in England, they believed that slaves able to read and write would be discontented and likely to foment unrest. When a slave revolt did take place in 1831, literacy was cited as a cause in the narrative constructed to explain to a horrified white public the reasons for the revolt. The *Confession*, composed by Thomas R. Gray, made Nat Turner, the leader of the insurrection, a child of the Enlightenment, given equally to reading and to scientific investigation.

To a mind like mine, restless, inquisitive and observant of every thing that was passing, it is easy to suppose that religion was the subject to which it would be directed, and although this subject principally occupied my thoughts—there was nothing that I saw or heard of to which my attention was not directed—The manner in which I learned to read and write, not only had great influence on my own mind, as I acquired it with the most perfect ease, so much so, that I have no recollection whatever of learning the alphabet—but to the astonishment of the family, one day, when a book was shewn to me to keep me from crying, I began spelling the names of different objects—this was a source of wonder to all in the neighborhood, particularly the blacks—and this learning was constantly improved at all opportunities—when I got large enough to go to work, while employed, I was reflecting on many things that would present themselves to my imagination, and whenever an opportunity occurred of looking at a book, when the school children were getting their lessons, I would find many things that the fertility of my own imagination had depicted to me before; all my time, not devoted to my master's service, was spent either in prayer, or in making experiments in casting different things made in moulds made of earth, in attempting to make paper, gunpowder, and many other experiments, that although I could not perfect, yet convinced me of its practicability if I had the means. (Gray, 8)

Gray's narrative, selected from many interviews with Turner, might have emphasized the bloodiness of the revolt—sixty whites were killed—and presented the slave leader as a bestial monster, an image with ample precedent in the culture. Instead, Turner is shown to be a "fanatic," but one thoroughly grounded in what literacy offered those who acquired it in his day: a set of biblical quotations useful for guiding conduct, books to aid the "fertility of imagination," and a curiosity about the conversion of raw materials into manufactured goods. Turner was frightening, not because he was so different, but because he held familiar values about freedom and inquiry. The lesson drawn by slaveowners was that literacy must be ever more vigilantly denied and curiosity even more thoroughly suppressed.

In the United States, literacy and the knowledge that would grow with it was presumed to be the birthright of every free-born male citizen. But opportunities for schooling were unequally distributed, even among this minority privileged to vote. In 1787, the Northwest Ordinance provided the legal foundation for settlement of the region north of the Ohio River and westward from New York State. It declared: "Religion, morality and knowledge being necessary to good government and the happiness of mankind, schools and the means of education shall forever be encouraged." (A portion of the public land in each settled area was set aside to provide money for building schools.) The U.S. Constitution, framed the same year and ratified in 1789, made no mention of education or schools as one of the fundamental rights guaranteed to citizens, however, and even within the states where public education was generally established, schools were designed mainly to give rudimentary lessons to children until they were old enough to begin full-time work.

Nonetheless, the ideal of republican government was an active force in promoting literacy in the United States. For the nation to prosper, individuals needed to be literate in order to be full participants in public life. Literacy was initially conceived as a private and personal way for individuals to fulfill themselves politically and spiritually, but this conservative notion was surprisingly overturned by what people did with their ability to read and write. By seizing their power as consumers of printed matter and, less commonly, as writers, they freed themselves from the past. The result, particularly in rural Vermont and New Hampshire, was "moral fervor, Christian republicanism, entrepreneurship, acquisitiveness, mechanical ability, intellectual currency, and cosmopolitanism, personal dynamism, and eccentricity—all notions drawn from a wide variety of reading matter" (Gilmore, 363). Nat Turner, John Brown (the revolutionary abolitionist), Elizabeth Cady Stanton (the crusader for women's rights), and Joseph Smith (to whom the Book of Mormon was revealed on gold tablets and then translated by him into print) were all cut from the same cloth. All became what they were through literacy, and all but Turner relied on literacy for their influence. In an important way, Giddy's prediction for Britain was borne out in New England, where mass literacy rendered a whole culture "factious and refractory," distrustful of

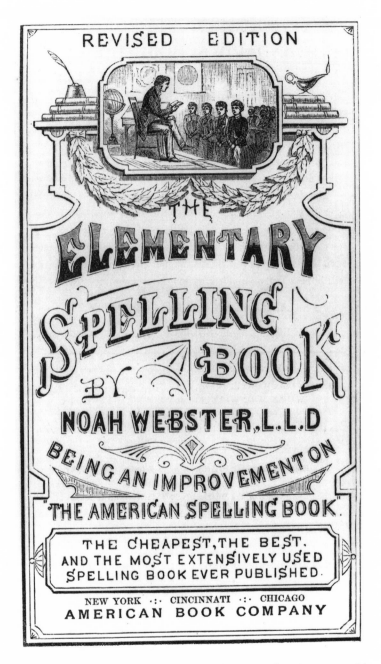

REVISED EDITION

THE ELEMENTARY SPELLING BOOK

BY NOAH WEBSTER, L.L.D

BEING AN IMPROVEMENT ON "THE AMERICAN SPELLING BOOK"

THE CHEAPEST, THE BEST, AND THE MOST EXTENSIVELY USED SPELLING BOOK EVER PUBLISHED.

NEW YORK ·:· CINCINNATI ·:· CHICAGO
AMERICAN BOOK COMPANY

Exuberant title pages helped to market books that were otherwise typographically uninteresting. (From Webster 1880.)

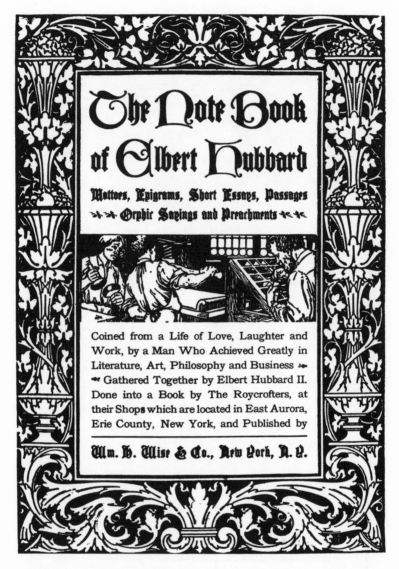

The Note Book
of Elbert Hubbard

Mottoes, Epigrams, Short Essays, Passages
Orphic Sayings and Preachments

Coined from a Life of Love, Laughter and
Work, by a Man Who Achieved Greatly in
Literature, Art, Philosophy and Business
Gathered Together by Elbert Hubbard II.
Done into a Book by The Roycrofters, at
their Shops which are located in East Aurora,
Erie County, New York, and Published by

Wm. H. Wise & Co., New York, N. Y.

At midcentury, revived interest in medieval life expressed itself in poetry, architecture, and crafts. William Morris's Kelmscott Press asserted the medieval aesthetic of individual craft, particularly in the *Kelmscott Chaucer* (1896) with illustrations by Edward Burne-Jones. Elbert Hubbard—"the P. T. Barnum of art"—founded the Roycrofters in East Aurora, New York, to produce Morrisonian goods for the mass market. Hubbard quickly gave up the handpress for the mechanical method and produced "a bastardized rendition of the Kelmscott style, with coarse paper, Morris-like Ornaments, incongruous halftone illustrations, abundant red ink, conventional typefaces, and limp chamois covers" (Peterson, 303; see Blumenthal, 50–52). However distasteful to the critics, Hubbard did much to popularize the Arts and Crafts ideals, and, when he drowned in the sinking of the *Lusitania,* he was deeply mourned.

authority and "insolent" to self-proclaimed superiors. Society was fractured by religious schisms and political partisanship built around narrow self-interest. Cultural diversity increased as never before; utopian societies rethought everything from marriage to economic organization; "fraternal" orders invented new patterns for cooperation and enlightenment. Conservatives were too preoccupied with questions of morality in fiction (particularly the novel) to notice that in consequential matters of morality literacy was transforming their culture.

In early nineteenth-century Britain, literacy was driven by cultural rather than by economic factors. Evangelical Christianity fostered Sunday schools, and a personal engagement with religious texts was believed to be essential for proper spiritual growth. A second important stimulus for literacy arose from the excitement of mechanization that transformed the industrial workplace. At the end of the eighteenth century, John Anderson (1726–96), the professor of natural philosophy (that is, science) at the University of Glasgow, offered a series of lectures on physics for "artisans." On his death, he left an endowment to enlarge this enterprise, and, in 1799, George Birkbeck (1776–1841), another Scot, became Anderson's successor. Having Anderson's successful lectures as a model, Birkbeck determined to make even more ambitious provision for workers.

> I beheld, through every disadvantage of circumstances and appearance, such strong indications of the existence of the unquenchable spirit, and such emanations from "the heaven-lighted lamp of man," that the question was forced upon me—Why are these minds left without the means of obtaining that knowledge which they so ardently desire; and why are the avenues to science barred against them, because they are poor? It was impossible not to determine that the obstacle should be removed; and I therefore resolved to offer them a gratuitous course of Elementary Philosophical Lectures. When the plan was matured, it was mentioned to some of the wise in their generation. They treated it as a dream of youthful enthusiasm, and scarcely condescended to bestow upon it a sneer, for it appeared to them so thoroughly visionary and absurd. They predicted that if invited the mechanics would not come; that if they did come they

would not listen; and if they did listen they would not comprehend. This offer however, was made; they came, they listened, and conquered; conquered that prejudice which would have consigned them to the dominion of interminable ignorance, and would have shut the gates of knowledge against a large and intelligent portion of mankind forever. (Quoted by Hudson, 33–34)

Popular lectures, supported by modest entry and subscription fees as well as by philanthropy, were soon fostered in the other principal cities: Birmingham, Edinburgh, Liverpool, and London. Scientific lectures were often illustrated by demonstrations—for instance, displays of chemical reactions or of optical or mechanical apparatus—and these proved especially popular. By the 1820s, organizations to promote adult education were well established; most of them supported libraries, and many came to own large halls and reading rooms. Conservatives viewed these developments with suspicion, particularly when the meeting spaces were rented to political groups espousing reforms favoring an increased role for working people in public life.

Another Scot joined Birkbeck in the campaign for popular education: Henry Brougham (1778–1868). While still a student at the University of Edinburgh, Brougham had published scientific papers in the *Transactions* of the Royal Society, and he was one of the vigorous writers who made the *Edinburgh Review* a nationally prominent magazine from its founding in 1802. In 1803, Brougham went to London to study law—he later became, for a brief period, lord chancellor—and he joined Whitbread and Wilberforce in advocating abolition of the slave trade. In 1825, he took an active role in the founding of the University of London, and in 1827 was one of the contributors of the influential Society for the Diffusion of Useful Knowledge.

A natural consequence of these "mechanics' institutes" (as they became generically known) was the increase in demand for written English. The Society for the Diffusion of Useful Knowledge published the *Penny Magazine* (1826–46), one of several efforts in Britain and North America to provide reading matter to satisfy the curiosity of adult readers with little schooling. The *Penny Magazine* was directed to a mass audience of workers, and magazines like it anticipated the remarkable growth in literacy in the second half of the century. In England in 1850, 30 percent of men and 45 percent of women were unable to sign their names in the parish register when they were married; the figure was just 1 percent in 1900 for both. People wanted to read and write as never before, and literacy turned from an incidental skill to an ability with economic value.

Brougham's ideas for educating the workers went beyond both the improving lectures of the mechanics' institutes and the uplifting magazines. He was interested in circulating libraries, supported with the pooled resources of their members, and in book publication. For libraries to be intellectually as well as practically accessible, Brougham thought that books must be written in a way that combined erudition with an appealing style. Noting the high cost of labor, Brougham hoped that machinery might soon replace handwork in setting type and printing books, and he urged every expedient that might reduce the unit cost of the published volumes. Like other progressives, he railed against the paper duty as "a tax on knowledge."

> [T]he excise upon paper, of three-pence a pound (including all that is cut to waste), and the absurd duty on foreign books imported, are serious obstructions to the progress of knowledge, especially the former. It prevents many a cheap work from being undertaken, and has caused some excellent ones to be discontinued. It amounts to a heavy burthen upon all cheap books, falling infinitely lighter upon those of a high price. The admirable works, of which thousands are sold to the common people, pay, it is calculated, in the proportion of thirty to forty per cent. upon the prime cost; while the books bought by the rich do not pay above five or six per cent. Can any thing be more absurd, or more iniquitous, than such a duty? (Brougham, 172)

To lower prices, Brougham urged that the page be crowded with type, illustrations omitted, and books issued in parts so that workers with little ready money might be induced to buy books in installments.

Brougham's efforts did not lack critics, and radicals who anticipated civil war during the economic slump of the 1830s decried the reluctance of the Society to engage political questions. Literacy merely temporized, they thought, when more drastic actions were required. Representing the radical forces was John Arthur Roebuck (1801–79), who asserted that the Society's publications were mere diversions designed to thwart popular unrest and to divert it into harmless pastimes.

> Hodge [a personification of the agricultural laborer] with a firebrand in his hand, about to set the standing corn in a blaze, and the Committee for the Diffusion of Useful Knowledge presenting him with various of their treatises, say for example, their ill-digested papers on Heat, in hopes of thereby preventing his dreadful purpose, would form a very instructive, though somewhat ludicrous picture. (376)

As time went on, the Society expanded its scope to include titles designated for the "Library of Entertaining Knowledge" (including *Insect Architecture* [1830] and *The History of British Costume* [1834]) and others intended as a "Library for the Young" (including a two-volume history of Spain and Portugal [1835–36]). However, its managers were unwilling to issue tracts that might raise political passions. No wonder that Frederick Denison Maurice asked: "useful for what?" In fact, the Society was not successful in reaching its intended audience, but it did show that a mass market existed for works of popularization, though this market did not lie among disaffected wage slaves and exploited agricultural workers. It consisted of young people who, often from prosperous families, were spurred by curiosity and supported by recently reformed or newly established schools (see H. Smith).

To an extent that Brougham could hardly have imagined, his efforts helped transform the diffusion of knowledge, though the effects would not become obvious for the half century it took to demonstrate that skills learned from books could better one's life. The marketplace for self-help books and self-improvement was enlarged in Britain by the establishment in 1855 of competitive examinations for government work. Until then, positions had been filled through patronage or purchase or both. The new examinations called for the breadth of knowledge usually gained in schools and universities, but it was permissible for those without much formal education to compete. *Grinders* or *crammers*—terms first recorded in writing in 1813—formed schools to prepare young persons for the tests. The examinations often demanded a knowledge of theoretical matters where the jobs to be filled required only practical skills. Critics of the examination system noted that "it is perfectly possible to get a man who can spell without getting a philologist" (Cecil, 579), but philology was nonetheless part of the test, and, among other things, candidates for appointment were expected to know something about etymology, syntax, and the history of English (stimulating the production of books designed "to supply all the information needed by students in preparing themselves for the Civil Service and other competitive examinations" [Craik, ii]). Private enterprises followed the government's example in putting a new emphasis on educational credentials, and consequently the desire for literacy and education increased, though it was not obvious to everyone that book learning had practical value. So useless was most book learning that Robert Cecil, writing in 1860, thought that the sons of the working class would, "in ninety-nine cases out of a hundred," fail in their attempts to obtain a clerkship and "return sullen and discontented men to the plough-tail" (580). Not until 1867 did a public figure suggest that the national economy in Britain was depressed from too little education; in that year, Lyon Playfair declared that a poor showing at the 1862 Paris Exposition resulted from "inferior educational provisions" (Goldstrom, 187; see Paz). For most people in Britain, there was little in the cultural experience of those raised in the first half of the century to enable them to foresee any economic benefit from schooling and literacy. Books, which had always furnished the mind, would eventually advance careers. Though Adam Smith had coined the expression "nation of shop-keepers" (1776), a more apt description of metropolitan life in the nineteenth century would be a *nation of bookkeepers*—some of those books containing an inventory of profit and loss, others an accumulating wisdom from technology and trade that could be applied to circumstances to produce wealth.

Many of the trends that Brougham had championed in 1825

were already at work with the rapidly increasing demand for printed matter. Only about six hundred book titles were published annually in Britain in the first quarter of the century, but this number increased rapidly. Some indication of the explosive increase in printing of all kinds can be found in the consumption of paper. In 1800, 11,000 tons were produced in Britain; in 1860, 100,000 tons; and in 1900, 652,000 tons (Twyman, 10). Inexpensive paper was not merely the result of increasing volume; before 1804 (when the first, primitive papermaking machine was introduced), it was made by hand from linen rags. Technology quickly displaced hand methods, and inventive minds turned their attention to materials that might replace the rags. German experiments discovered that wood fibers softened by acid made acceptable paper, and paper fell in price. Mechanized presses were introduced slowly, however. Though the *Times* began to print with a cylindrical press in 1814, most book printers continued to use flatbed presses not markedly different from those introduced into Britain from the Continent in the fifteenth century. The only innovations at the beginning of the century were that presses were made out of cast iron (rather than wood) and operated by a lever (rather than a screw); the iron press allowed greater force to be applied to the inked plate and the paper, while the lever hastened the process. The work of printers was virtually unchanged; type was hand-set, and the press was operated by two workers—one to refresh the ink supply and supervise, the other to feed the paper and remove finished sheets for drying. While mechanical presses were progressively improved, typesetting was slow to mechanize, and not until the last quarter of the century did practical typesetting machines come into regular use.

As technology became more efficient, books became increasingly ugly. Paper declined in quality since traces of acid in the wood-fiber paper caused yellowing and brittleness; book design, dictated by cost consciousness, emphasized density of the page; illustrations, until midcentury, were few in all but the most expensive volumes. Thus, books became more accessible but at the same time more forbidding. With mass production of books, fewer typefaces and styles were in use. Many of the ligatures found in eighteenth-century books were dropped from production typecases, partly because many different types increased the cost of setting, particularly when payment was made on a piecework basis. Books were designed with two or more columns on a page, and, often, the columns were surrounded by borders to allow the eye to pick out the lines from the crowded mass of tiny type. The creation of new book fonts became moribund, and the nineteenth century continued to use the designs made in the prior century. The art of printing deteriorated; the business of printing flourished. As John McCreery wrote in his nostalgic poem "The Press" in 1827, "Wher'er we cast our eye, / For steam and cheapness there is one dull cry" (quoted by Handover, 143).

Looking at the first half of the century, historians of printing have declared it was bedeviled by ugliness in book printing: "A tide of bad taste had swept everything before it by 1844" (Updike, 2:196). At least some of the shabbiness of books can be attributed to factors other than bad taste. Piecework payment based on the number of lines set encouraged typesetters to hasten the justification of a line of type by inserting too many blank slugs between words; the result was excessive spacing and, occasionally, the distracting appearance of a ghostly image in white on the densely packed pages. Small types chosen to cram words onto the page were fragile, and, with repeated use, portions of the letters broke off; the damaged type might continue in use because of inattention or indifference. To increase durability, new designs made use of faces with thick verticals; these types were less subject to damage, but the interior portions of the letters were often obscured if the plates were not carefully inked. These characters, especially when set close together, made the page grimly forbidding. As another labor-saving effort, printers ceased to moisten paper before printing, reducing the crispness of the letters. Visually, nineteenth-century books are much more resistant to reading than their predecessors, but economic factors, rather than a lack of taste, are mainly responsible for their shortcomings. Still, connoisseurs have rightly decried "the typical mass-produced volume of the nineteenth century—nastily printed in greyish ink on shoddy, acidic paper" (Peterson, 9).

Not all books were ugly, of course. Scholarly books were often modeled on the lavishly printed volumes sponsored by patrons and subscribers in the prior century. For such books, new fonts might be designed, many of them entirely original (as with Joseph Bosworth's "Anglo-Saxon" font) or an improvement on old types for greater "authenticity" (as with Julian Hibbert's Greek uncial letters carefully imitated from the "best" manuscripts of differing ages). Mechanical methods of folding and gathering printed sheets allowed the production of tiny books; pocket-size Bibles and devotional works were a popular result of this innovation, though perhaps better suited for iconic purposes than for reading.

Printer's ornaments to fill space empty of type took on elaborate and innovative forms, while rules and other devices added decorative art to the better books, both features that successors enamored of a chaste classicism would deplore. Good printing had never been better, but bad printing had seldom been worse. From the viewpoint of legibility and elegance, most nineteenth-century books were avowedly unattractive, not only to later readers but also to such critics of the industrial age as John Ruskin, who especially deplored them. But they were increasingly inexpensive, allowing people with little money the opportunity to assemble a library.

Until the end of the century, book design remained relatively unchanged. Mechanical typesetting by Linotype and Monotype machines developed for practical use in the 1880s, though these devices were designed to imitate hand-set book pages, and many British publishers did not make mechanization a selling point, preferring to allow consumers to believe that they were purchasing "traditional" hand work. American publishers were less squeamish about the use of machinery in printing, but their ordinary books followed British fashions closely.

At the beginning of the nineteenth century there had been no important American contribution to the art or craft of printing; by mid-century, when the industrial revolution had almost transformed printing, there had been many; by the beginning of the twentieth century American invention and engineering had played a leading role in changing printing from handcraft to mechanical mass pro-

January 1885 35

10A.
Quads and Spaces. 38c.   THREE-LINE NONPAREIL IDEAL. $2.85

CUYAHOGA'S SHADY SUMMER GROVE EXCURSIONS

7A   DOUBLE PICA IDEAL. $3.00

SYLVAN TROUT STREAMS PISCATORIAL

5A.   THREE-LINE PICA IDEAL. $4.80

MILD & FAIR ROYAL

Cleveland Type Foundry, Cleveland, Ohio.

6A, 12a.   TWO-LINE PICA SIGNET SHADE. $5.00

DEEP THINKING
Artists Enjoy Odd Conceits
1234567890

4A, 8a.   THREE-LINE PICA SIGNET SHADE. $7.30

RECHERCHE
Exquisite and Grand
1234567

IN COMBINATION.

Leonard National Bank
Received of $

THE H. H. THORP MFG. CO.   22   CLEVELAND TYPE FOUNDRY

THE H. H. THORP MFG. CO.   23   CLEVELAND TYPE FOUNDRY

Late in the century, new technology fostered a renaissance in type design, particularly in display fonts. Often legibility was sacrificed to art, as in these specimens from the Cleveland Type Foundry. (From Annenberg, 35.)

duction. Less significant was America's contribution to aesthetic and design. The nineteenth century cannot on the whole claim a high place in the history of the book for the beauty or the quality of its work. American books, still largely derivative in style, were no better than their models. (J. M. Wells, 330)

Despite their poor quality and because of their low price, books sold widely in Britain and the United States, both in the urban centers and in the hinterlands. In 1798, American firms engaged in printing and publishing were concentrated on the Atlantic coast: 41 in Boston, 56 in New York, 88 in Philadelphia, 19 in Baltimore, and 15 in Charleston. As the functions of printers and publishers diverged, printers set up shops, often devoted mainly to newspaper production, nearly everywhere; publishers appeared in large

**A portion of Press Room of
The Cranbrook Press, Detroit, Mich., U. S. A**

Examining the freshly printed sheet is George G. Booth, the wealthy proprietor
of the Press; inking the plate at the right is Stephen N. Chilton, an elderly com-
positor with experience of handsetting Booth brought out of retirement to revive
handwork in the age of mechanical typesetting. The large pictures show Gutenberg and Franklin; not shown in this view was a similar representation of Caxton.
Smaller portraits below honored the theoreticians and practitioners revered by
the Arts and Crafts movement: Ruskin, Emerson, Carlyle, Morris, Theodore Low
De Vinne, and Elbert Hubbard. (From Booth, frontispiece; see McPharlin.)

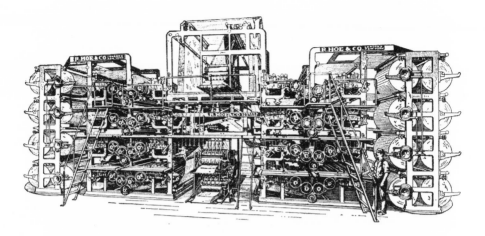

Engineering ingenuity produced ever more complex printing machines. This press, constructed from drawings sent from the United States to Britain, could produce 100,000 copies per hour of a sixteen-page newspaper "printed both sides, cut, folded and counted off in quires complete." (From *Encyclopedia Britannica*, 11th ed., s.v. *printing*.)

numbers but almost exclusively in the cities. From 1820 to 1852, publishers (whether individuals or companies) were distributed with 147 in Boston, 345 in New York, 198 in Philadelphia, 32 in Baltimore, 15 in Charleston, and 25 in Cincinnati (Wroth, 99–100). Thus, Boston, New York, and Philadelphia became highly competitive publishing centers. As new technology became available, publishers in these cities rushed to adopt the innovations that would make them competitive and increase profits.

In the American South, however, book publishers remained few, partly because the population of literate people did not much increase before the 1860s. Cincinnati, however, became a center of schoolbook publishers equipped to meet the ever-increasing demands of frontier communities for books. Even with this concentration of the book business, some publishers managed to thrive in small towns, and many printers remained able to produce books as well as other forms of printed material. Within this setting, fine printing did take place (often under the patronage of a wealthy sponsor), but most people would never see the product of the best presses—except, perhaps, for the large-format "lectern Bibles" on ostentatious display in many churches.

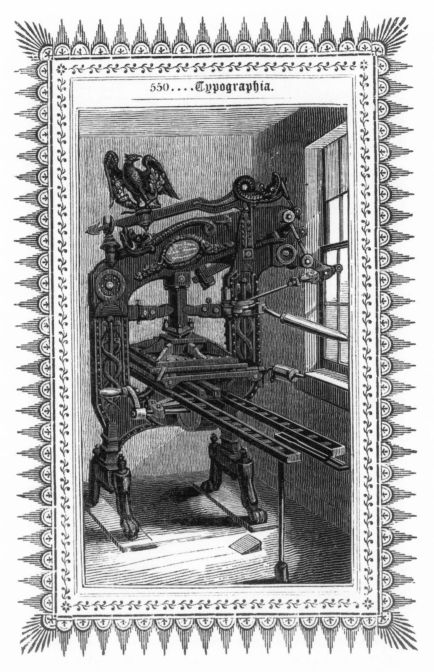

550....Typographia.

Introduced to Britain from the United States in 1814 was the Columbian Press, made ornately from iron and displaying the American eagle holding symbolic arrows and olive branch. Presses of this type continued to be used for poster and proofing work well into the twentieth century, though they were superseded by cylinder presses for books and newspapers. (From J. Johnson, 550, in the collection of the W. L. Clements Library, University of Michigan.)

Good, and occasionally imaginative, printing reached a mass audience in a few domains, especially almanacs, smaller Bibles, and reference works—all books where an attractive appearance might make a difference in a highly competitive marketplace. In both Britain and in North America, publications of these kinds flourished. Harper and Brothers in New York, a leader in introducing technical innovations, profited from books and highly popular magazines. Their illustrated *Bible* (1846) was a splendid example of nineteenth-century book production, marked by the most skillful use of wood engraving. While the typography of this volume is in an unremarkable "modern" face, initial capitals and frequent inset illustrations show nineteenth-century decoration at its most rococo. Such visual images made reading more appealing, not only in the Bible but also in other illustrated works produced with the same technology.

Color illustrations, usually individually hand colored, had appeared in costly books earlier, but by midcentury the development of practical lithography made *chromos* (1869 < [i.e., derived from] *chromolithographs* [1860]) inexpensive and common, both in book and magazine illustrations and in posters and handbills. Demand for pictures spurred alternative technologies including *zincography* (1834) and *algraphy* (1897) where metal plates were used instead of the unwieldy lithographic stones. These methods had the desirable features of durability and speed in the printing of large numbers of impressions. Wars in the Crimea and in the United States increased the demand for pictures. These were often crafted by imaginative illustrators and were far better in quality than the halftones made from photographs late in the century. Illustrations could be vividly realistic; halftones could be merely literal (since slow film speeds required static subjects). The new technologies united book and illustration publishing more intimately than ever before. In the eighteenth century, James Granger had published a *Biographical History of England* (1769) with blank pages provided for portraits and other illustrations that were sold separately; this method of marketing was revived and produced the term *grangerize* (1882) and *extra-illustrated* (1889), encouraging hobbyists to ornament their books with added matter of their

THE CONFUSION OF TONGUES GENESIS. GENERATIONS OF SHEM.

THE TOWER OF BABEL.

be restrained from them, which they have
[e]imagined to do.
7 Go to, [f]let us go down, and there confound their language, that they may [g]not understand one another's speech.
8 So [h]the LORD scattered them abroad from
thence [i]upon the face of all the earth: and
they left off to build the city.
9 Therefore is the name of it called ||Babel,
[k]because the LORD did there confound the
language of all the earth: and from thence
did the LORD scatter them abroad upon the
face of all the earth.
10 ¶ [l]These *are* the generations of Shem:
Shem *was* a hundred years old, and begat
Arphaxad two years after the flood:
11 And Shem lived after he begat Arphaxad five hundred years, and begat sons and
daughters.
12 And Arphaxad lived five and thirty
years, [m]and begat Salah:
13 And Arphaxad lived after he begat Salah four hundred and three years, and begat
sons and daughters.
14 And Salah lived thirty years, and begat
Eber:
15 And Salah lived after he begat Eber four
hundred and three years, and begat sons and
daughters.
16 [n]And Eber lived four and thirty years,
and begat [o]Peleg:
17 And Eber lived after he begat Peleg four

B.C. 2311.
e Ps. 2, 1.
f ch. 1, 26. Ps. 2, 4. Acts 2, 4, 5, 6.
g ch. 42, 23. Deut. 28, 49. Jer. 5, 15. 1 Cor. 14, 2, 11.
h Luke 1, 51.
i ch. 10, 25, 32.
|| That is, *confusion.*
k 1 Cor. 14, 23.
l chap. 10, 22. 1 Chron. 1, 17.
2346.
2311.
m See Luke 3, 36.
2281.
2247.
n 1 Chron. 1, 19.
o Called, Luke 3, 35, *Phalec.*
2217.
2185.
p Luke 3, 35, *Saruch.*
2155.
2126.
q Luke 3, 34, *Thara.*
2056.
r Josh. 24, 2. 1 Chron. 1, 26.
1996.
s ch. 17, 15, & 20. 12

hundred and thirty years, and begat sons
and daughters.
18 And Peleg lived thirty years, and begat
Reu:
19 And Peleg lived after he begat Reu two
hundred and nine years, and begat sons and
daughters.
20 And Reu lived two and thirty years, and
begat [p]Serug:
21 And Reu lived after he begat Serug two
hundred and seven years, and begat sons and
daughters.
22 And Serug lived thirty years, and begat
Nahor:
23 And Serug lived after he begat Nahor
two hundred years, and begat sons and
daughters.
24 And Nahor lived nine and twenty years,
and begat [q]Terah:
25 And Nahor lived after he begat Terah
a hundred and nineteen years, and begat
sons and daughters.
26 And Terah lived seventy years, and [r]be-
gat Abram, Nahor, and Haran.
27 ¶ Now these *are* the generations of
Terah: Terah begat Abram, Nahor, and
Haran: and Haran begat Lot.
28 And Haran died before his father Terah
in the land of his nativity, in Ur of the
Chaldees.
29 And Abram and Nahor took them wives:
the name of Abram's wife *was* [s]Sarai: and

12

Though for much of the century type design was moribund, illustrations became more luxuriant as new technologies became available. *The Bible,* published by Harper and Brothers, New York, in 1846 was a landmark in U.S. publishing, and James and John Harper presided over a huge enterprise with the latest machinery.

own choosing. Nineteenth-century consumers, however, came to expect that books and magazines would combine pictures with text in a single package. Spectacularly illustrated magazines competed for readers, particularly *Punch* (London, 1841–1992, 1996–), *The Illustrated London News* (London, 1842–), *Harper's* (New York, 1857–), and *Puck* (New York, 1877–1918).

Pictures invited readers to read captions, and the captions compelled reading of the text. By allowing reading at several levels of depth, these new publications, whether in book or magazine form, helped to enlarge the scope for literacy and enhance the profit for publishers. The new publications led to a reversal of meaning of the word *scan;* previously, *scanning* a page meant examining it minutely, but by the end of the century *scanning* came to refer to the practice of *skimming*—itself a nineteenth-century word as applied to reading—or looking over a text hastily to grasp the gist. While *browsing* was not a new word, the term *browser,* a usage first attested in 1863, designated readers who read here and there, and the attractive combination of pictures and text did much to encourage it.

Written English was changed as a result of increased literacy and the mass production of reading materials. Many of the changes were cultural rather than linguistic, but the centralization of printing in the cities gave further stability to written English and fixed the standards for good usage far more firmly than at earlier times. With the dispersal of printing shops and their products to provincial towns and villages, urban norms were disseminated and, with increased schooling, enforced. The new technologies were shaping the language itself, as can be seen in English presented for display in posters, handbills, and title pages of books. While the format of such documents had origins in earlier centuries, the nineteenth century developed new ideas about the way English should be read.

Samuel Johnson's *Dictionary* of 1755 has a neoclassical title page typical of serious works of his day. It consisted of a long phrase split apart on the page in a format common in monumental inscriptions.

Lillie.

She faltered by the wayside, and
the Angels took her home.

Darling Freddie.

The Angels called Him.

Hon. M. Randall,

DIED

August 15, 1869. AGED 61 Years.

A Member of the U.S. Congress for 20 Years, he
died as he lived, a pure and upright man.

MINNIE,

INFANT DAUGHTER OF

L. & M. Binninger,

DIED

Sept. 15th, 1873. AGED 1 Mo. & 15 D's.

Beneath this stone, in soft repose,
Is laid a mother's dearest pride;
A flower that scarce had waked to life
And light and beauty, ere it died.

MARY ELLEN,

WIFE OF

Chas. Williamson,

Born at Keene, N. H., Jan. 8, 1805.

Born into Spirit Life Sept. 6th, 1865.

NOT DEAD, BUT GONE BEFORE.

Wm. D. Hubbard,

Dec. 28th, 1873. Aged 92 Y's, 8 M's.

"Farewell to thee, my house of clay !
Long have we two been bound together,
But I forsake thy porch to-day,
And yield thee up to wind and weather.
Sleep, sleep at last ! thy sleep shall be
My rest, my strength, my victory !"

TRUMAN MARTIN,

Aged 60 Years. August 2, 1870.

H. W. Billings.

December 1, 1872. Aged 36 Years.

Our Mother,

Died October 5, 1869. AGED 61 Years.

Harriet Theresa,

WIFE OF

F. D. Stevenson,

AGED 41 Years. Oct. 4, 1872.

"I Fear not Death."

CHARLES H.,

SON OF

Thos. & A. Smith,

DIED

December 25th, 1870. AGED 4 Y'S, 3 M'S & 4 D'S.

MINNIE B. PHELPS,

BORN INTO SUMMER LAND

Sept. 1st, 1872. Aged 19 Y's, 3 M's.

DARLING SISTER ;

" Yet, though thou wear'st the glory of the sky,
We know thou'lt keep the same beloved name ;
The same fair, thoughtful brow and gentle eye,
Lovelier in heaven a sweet climate, yet the same."

Little Johnny,

DIED

November 1st, 1871. AGED 5 Y's & 8 M's.

" 'Tis a little grave, but O, have care,
For world-wide hopes are buried there;
How much of light, how much of joy,
Is buried with a darling boy."

SACRED

to the Memory of

S. K. Mannering,

WHO DEPARTED THIS LIFE

August 10, 1871. Aged 50 Years.

" I go to prepare a place for thee."

Mary L. Palmer,

ENTERED SPIRIT LIFE

September 9, 1872. Aged 38 Y's, 6 M's.

" O land beyond the setting sun !
O realm more fair than poet's dream !
How clear thy silvery streamlets run,
How bright thy golden glories gleam !
For well we know that fair and bright,
Far beyond human ken or dream,
Too glorious for our feeble sight,
Thy skies of cloudless azure beam."

Harvey J. Belden,

CAPT. OF

51st Regiment, Illinois Vols.,

Killed at the Battle of Perryville,
October 8th, 1863.
Aged 51 Y's, 6 M's, 10 D's.

Rev. G. Wells,

BORN, **DIED**,

Sept. 21st, 1841. Nov. 21st, 1872.

He Died as He Lived—a Christian.

Herbie :

The angels called him on a sunny day,
August 15th, 1872.

AGED 5 Y'S, 6 M'S, 4 D'S.

" We shall all go home to our Father's house,
To our Father's house in the skies,
Where the hope of our souls shall have no blight,
And our love no broken ties :
We shall roam on the banks of the River of Peace,
And bathe in its blissful tide :
And one of the joys of our heaven shall be,
The little boy that died."

Many of the new typefaces could be inscribed in stone only with great difficulty;
these above, however, showed some graphic possibilities for serious and ceremonial inscriptions. (From T. E. Hill, 298.)

> A dictionary of the English language: in which the words are deduced from their originals, and illustrated in their different significations by examples from the best writers. To which are prefixed, a history of the language, and an English grammar. By Samuel Johnson, A. M. In two volumes.

In its published form, of course, some words of the title were emphasized by layout and some by type selection. Words centered on the page and presented in the smallest type include *a, of the, in which, and, by, to which are prefixed, and*. Other words are presented in majuscule and in large type—*Dictionary* (36 point) and *English Language* (24 point) are the most prominent. Thus readers had the opportunity for reading the title in depth (with its grammatical apparatus) or superficially (by noticing the most prominent words).

Grammatically "full" and grammatically "empty" title pages continued to compete in the nineteenth century, but the explicit grammar gradually disappeared (beginning, most probably, with the deletion of *by* between the title proper and the name of the author). Printing in which the visual was seen to be more important than the verbal offered the most creative opportunities for imaginative designers. A specimen from early in the century suggests what the visual made possible; the following example is a handbill advertising an excursion.

> Pleasure and packet boats are daily starting from Bath and Bradford, on the Kennet and Avon Canal, in which parties may enjoy a most delightful ride, and beautiful picturesque scenery without the inconvenience of horse exercise or walking. No expense has been spared to render them commodious, and remove every idea of fatigue. Terms and hours of starting may be known at the Boat Office, N. E. side of Sydney Garden, or of Mr. Andras, Milsom-St. (Twyman, 199)

All but three words of this handbill are printed in ordinary book type; printed in immense, bold, display type (occupying nearly the entire sheet) are the words *Pleasure Without Fatigue*. The trick invites two-layered reading: the words printed large lure interest, and the smaller print fleshes out details.

The domain of print having the most significant impact on

A VIEW

OF

UNIVERSAL HISTORY,

LITERATURE,

AND THE SEVERAL

SCHOOLS OF PAINTING;

SYNCHRONISTICALLY AND ETHNOGRAPHICALLY PRESENTED

IN

TWENTY-FIVE ILLUMINATED CHRONOLOGICAL TABLES,

FROM THE PERIODS OF THE EARLIEST RECORDS

TO THE YEAR 1842:

Each Subject in Separate Series,

BEING SYNOPTICALLY ARRANGED

IN COLLATERAL COLUMNS OF NATIONS (OR SCHOOLS);

THE SEVERAL TABLES,

EMBODYING EACH A COMPLETE AND CHARACTERISTIC PERIOD, BEING TERMINATED, NOT BY ANY REGULARLY SPECIFIC NUMBER OF YEARS, BUT, BY THOSE VARIOUSLY SUCCESSIVE EPOCHS OF VAST CHANGE OR EVENTFUL RECOLLECTION WHICH APPEAR THE MOST NATURALLY AND VIVIDLY TO CLASSIFY TIME INTO DISTINCTIVE REGIONS.

BY

MAJOR JAMES BELL,

(EAST YORK MILITIA).

THE HISTORICAL AND LITERARY TABLES ORIGINALLY FOUNDED ON THE GERMAN OF THE LATE HISTORY-PROFESSOR AND PRUSSIAN REGENCY-COUNCILLOR G. G. BREDOW; BUT CONSIDERABLY ENLARGED AND VARIOUSLY ALTERED, ESPECIALLY IN THE BRITANNIC, THE ASIAN, AND THE AMERICAN COLUMNS: AND THE TABLE OF PAINTERS MAINLY DERIVED FROM THE PRIVATE FRENCH NOTES OF SIR MATTHEW VAN BREE.

Fifth Edition,

ENLARGED; GREATLY IMPROVED; AND THE FACILITIES FOR RAPID AND LUCID REFERENCE EXTENSIVELY INCREASED, AS WELL BY VARIETY OF COLOUR, AS BY VARIEGATED FORMS OF TYPE.

LONDON:

PRINTED BY T. C. HANSARD, FOR THE AUTHOR,

AND SOLD BY

ROBERT BALDWIN, PATERNOSTER-ROW.

MDCCCXLII.

Grammatically complete title pages often had densely subordinated syntax, but, through the use of different type sizes, the principal elements could be highlighted. Lithography made the production of vivid illustrations widely available, both for ornament and, in this case, "for rapid and lucid reference extensively increased, as well by variety of colour, as by variegated forms of type." The *View* was issued on paper 18″ × 26″; the sheet was first passed through a handpress, where the inked type was impressed on the paper, then placed on a series of lithographic stones to receive the colors.

English was the most common: newspapers. Though newspaper headlines had been used earlier in Britain—1622 seems to have been the year of the first—they had fallen out of fashion. Both British and North American papers at the beginning of the century typically named sections of the paper for departments of interest, for instance "Foreign News." So the *London Chronicle* for 1792 reported one of the spasms of violence from the French Revolution under the heading "Important News from France."

North American papers led the way in developing the modern system of headlines and subheads, and a particular innovator was the *New York Sun*, founded in 1833; its first issue carried the headline "Attempted Insurrection in the Ohio Penitentiary." The *Sun* evolved a grammar for headlines that would, by the end of the century, prove influential throughout the English-reading world. An example reporting the outcome of the battle of Gettysburg in 1863 shows the *Sun* at its creative best.

> Victory—Invasion Comes to Grief—Lee Utterly Routed—His Disastrous Retreat—All Federal Prisoners Re-Captured—Eighteen Thousand Prisoners Captured—Means of Escape Destroyed

This series of heads (distinguished in descending importance by diminishing type sizes) shows the way in which grammar was reduced to what were perceived to be essentials. Except for the first word, all phrases contain words closely connected to verbs, and all encourage the practice of layered reading (ostensibly inviting the reader—always imagined to be in haste—to read down the headlines to a certain depth of interest. Headlines (and associated display forms of English) produced a grammar of "condensed" English that had not existed previously in print. Deletion of articles (like *a, an,* and *the*), reliance on participles rather than finite verbs (for instance, *routed* and *destroyed*), and use of surnames alone rather than titles or given names (as in *Lee*) are typical features of headline grammar parallel to the handbill "Pleasure without Fatigue." One consequence of these devices was to reduce emphasis on agents and to stress the significance of the things or persons affected—thus, there is no explicit mention of the forces that caused the prisoners to be *captured.*

What makes the Gettysburg headline of particular interest is the use of the present-tense inflection in "Invasion Comes to Grief." This *s*-form in headlines became a typical feature of American journalism, one not adopted in Britain until nearly the end of the century. By 1900, however, the *s*-forms were typical of newspapers in both countries—for instance, a headline reporting the Anglo-Boer War in 1900: "British Patrol Falls in With a Big Force." Present-tense verb forms suggest an immediacy to events—that they are "news"—in a way that past-tense forms or nonfinite forms did not. Thus the headline in the *Times* reporting the demise of William IV in 1837 was "Death of the King," and in 1900, a headline in the *Evening News* still used the old past participles: "Enemy Surprised and Fled in Disorder." Not until the twentieth century did British newspapers begin to employ headlines of the type "Countess Dies" (Straumann, 217, 163). Of course the "dramatic present" (Jespersen's suggested corrective to the traditional term "historic present") had long been in use in English, but nineteenth-century newspaper headlines shifted this aspect of the grammar of oral narrative reports to written convention.

Deemphasis of agency (by means of deverbal nouns and nonfinite verb forms) and use of the dramatic present do not compel changes in conception about events, but these, and other grammatical devices employed in headlines, do invite them. Agency was often seen as part of common knowledge (as in the well-understood assumption that federal troops were the agents to the verbal expressions in the Gettysburg headline); the dramatic present invited the inference that these events were in continuous (or at least recent) motion and hence of lively interest. Competition among newspapers grew intense in urban centers, and headlines with the most arresting—and briefest—expressions served to attract interest from possible purchasers. By the end of the century, news bills (full sheets of newsprint with headlines in bold capital letters) were produced to attract purchasers to street sellers of papers. Through them, the grammar of the poster tradition merged with that of headline writing: "Relief of Mafeking," "Fall of Pretoria," "Kruger Bolts" (Twyman, 228).

While mass literacy increased dramatically over the century,

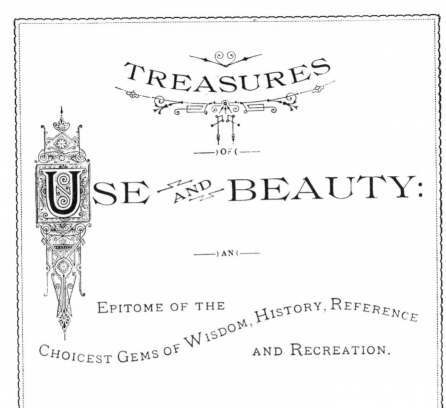

TREASURES

)OF(

USE AND BEAUTY:

)AN(

EPITOME OF THE CHOICEST GEMS OF WISDOM, HISTORY, REFERENCE AND RECREATION.

TWO VOLUMES IN ONE.

PROFUSELY ILLUSTRATED.

BY A CORPS OF SPECIAL AUTHORS.

F. B. DICKERSON & CO., Publishers,

DETROIT, MICH.   CHICAGO, ILL.   CINCINNATI, OHIO.   ST. LOUIS, MO.

1883.

New technology made it possible to vary layout on the printed page, produce asymmetrical designs, and employ curves in place of the rigid horizontals and verticals made necessary by rectangular type-slugs.

printers and publishers made ever more strenuous efforts to locate and increase the number of their readers. Far more than at any earlier time, English became the content, as well as the vehicle, of commerce. Advertising, publishing, and marketing all drew upon innovations in technology to promote economic interests. Each one made English more visually appealing, and each innovation (for instance, color printing on trade cards or embossed lettering on the newly invented greeting cards) stimulated still more innovations, whether in new methods (such as halftone reproductions of photographs) or in making cheaply available the products that were formerly too costly for most consumers (like color illustrations in books).

Literary historians have generally considered William Blake's illuminated books as breaking down barriers between print and script and between visual and verbal. But in the history of English, Blake's influence was small, for his works were read by few and were virtually ignored until late in the century, even by those who regarded Blake as a visionary artist. Nonetheless, the barrier between visual and verbal was virtually demolished in the course of the century. New technologies made new possibilities. From the eighteenth century, only the "long ess" (ſ) was lost from the printer's typeset—though it persisted in the handwriting of conservatives nearly to the end of the century (see W. Williams). Dozens of new letterforms were invented for representing English, one being the *dollar mark* or *dollar sign,* a superimposition in print of the letters *U* and *S*. The etymology of the sign was soon forgotten (as etymologies usually are), and the form of the dollar sign with a single vertical stroke arose. The dollar sign, in its variant forms, is of additional interest for inverting the usually linear sequence of English letters—that is, the written form *$10* (with the dollar sign preceding the numerals) is "read" as "ten dollars," just as *£10* is read as "ten pounds." Other new characters were introduced, some of them to be read (as, for instance, the commercial sign for *per* [℔] or apothecaries' symbols for weights—like the sign for *scruple* [℈]—and measures—like the character for *minum* [ℳ]). One of the few of these characters to survive is the *R* with the angled stroke through its right descender (℞)*; in the nineteenth century, it was read as "recipe," though it too soon became opaque and stood as a merely visual sign for "pharmacy" or "medication." Other new characters did not have a reading, though of course they had names. Thus special characters for *section* or *paragraph* could be used as visual cues to textual organization, just as the *asterisk, obelisk, double dagger,* and other characters directed attention from text to marginal references or footnotes. Of these "unread" characters, the *fist* is perhaps the most charming, partly because of its association with job printing, particularly posters concerned with entertainment. All of these characters added to the repertoire of writers and designers of written English. The fact that some have been forgotten can be attributed, in part, to their exclusion from the typewriter keyboard that approached standardization at the end of the century.

Even more consequential for the representation of English in written form was the introduction of lithography. While the War Office in London had made use of lithographic methods to produce maps and other military documents during the Napoleonic Wars, the new method of printing was at first limited to the production of pictorial images, sometimes accompanied by small patches of text. Only at midcentury did lithography begin to displace copperplate engraving, and soon it became the primary method for printing sheet music. From the perspective of English, however, the importance of lithography lay in the potential for printing from hand-drawn letters, allowing innovators to produce, inexpensively, short editions of works with special characters. Among these visionaries was Isaac Pitman (1813–97), and in 1842 he began to publish the *Phonographic Journal* to encourage the use of the system of shorthand he had devised in 1837. Without lithography, he would have been obliged to have types designed for letterpress or to have commissioned an engraver to reproduce his work. With lithography, however, Pitman himself could write in his shorthand system for immediate transfer to printing. The new technology allowed authorial control of the appearance of the printed page in unprecedented ways, and Pitman was thus able to promote his system through a stream of lithographic publications.

The telegraph, too, spawned new expressions of English

TREMONT TEMPLE

GOTTSCHALK!

THE CELEBRATED PIANO VIRTUOSO,

MR. L. M. GOTTSCHALK

Having returned after an exceedingly brilliant and prosperous Concert Tour of over One Hundred Nights in the West, will give in Boston,

TWO GRAND CONCERTS

Tuesday and Thursday, May 5th and 7th,

When he will be assisted by the Distinguished Basso,

Mr. A. C. RYDER,

(Who will on this occasion make his first appearance,) and the Wonderful

BRETTO BROTHERS

MASTER BERNARD, 11 years of age..............**VIOLINIST**
MASTER RICHARD, 7 years of age........**CORNET A PISTON**
THEIR FIRST APPEARANCE IN BOSTON.

CONDUCTOR....................................**S. BEHRENS**

PROGRAMME.—Part I.

1. GRAND FANTASIA—Solo Violin....................................DE BERIOT
   BERNARD BRETTO.
2. OVERTURE—William Tell, arranged for two Pianos.....................GOTTSCHALK
   L. M. GOTTSCHALK and S. BEHRENS.
3. FANTASIA CAPRICE—Cornet a Piston...............................SCHREIBER
   RICHARD BRETTO, 7 years of age.
4. WHO TREADS THE PATH OF DUTY—from the "Magic Flute"..............MOZART
   Mr A. C. RYDER.
5. { A. MARCHE FUNEBRE, in C minor }...............................GOTTSCHALK
   { B. MURMURES EOLIENS }
   L. M. GOTTSCHALK.

PART SECOND.

6. SONG WITHOUT WORDS....................................PROCH
   RICHARD BRETTO.
7. OJOS CREOLLOS....................................GOTTSCHALK
   Performed by the AUTHOR and S. BEHRENS.

   In this overture, which is entirely original, the author has endeavored to convey an idea of the singular rythmical and charming character of the music which exists among the Creoles of the Spanish Antilles. CHOPIN, it is well known, transferred the National Airs of Poland to his Mazurkas and Polonaises and Mr Gottschalk has endeavored to re-produce, in works of an appropriate character, the characteristic traits of the Dances of the West Indies.

8. POSENTI NUMI....................................MOZART
   Mr A. C. RYDER.
9. THE MELANCHOLY....................................PRUME
   BERNARD BRETTO.
10. { A. LE BARDE—Pensée Fugitive............................ }.............GOTTSCHALK
    { B. BURLESQUE ON MARLBOROUGH...................... }
    L. M. GOTTSCHALK.

ADMISSION 50 CENTS.

Seats may be secured to any part of the house without extra charge at Oliver Ditson's Music Store.

DOORS OPEN AT 1-4 PAST 7 O'CLOCK....................TO COMMENCE AT 8 O'CLOCK.

As there are many Editions of Mr. Gottschalk's Works, the public are informed that the only correct Editions are published by HALL & SON, New York, who are the only publishers of Mr. G's Compositions in the United States. Le Bambula, Le Bananier, (caprice.) Le Savant, (ballade.) Ossian de Ballade. Danse Ossianique. Jerusalem, (fantaisie) triomphale.) Souvenier D'Andalouse. La Jota Aragonesa, (Spanish caprice.) Last Hope, (religious meditation.) The Banjo. Marche de Nuit, (midnight march.) Apotheose, (marche solennelle.) Vaste Po tique. Minuet a Seville, (midnight in Seville.) Chant du Soldat. Ricordati, (remember.) Reflets du Passe, (reflects of the past. Chant Gitanesque. Pastorelle Cavaliers, (the knight of the shepherdess.) Caprice on the Cuban Dance. Printemps D'Amdur. (spring of love.) O ma charmante esperange moi, (O. my charmer, spare me.) Basie Moi, (follow me.) Ojos Creollos, (Creole eyes for fairer hands.) Murmures Eoliens. Souvenir de la Havane. Javenae, (youth mazurka.) Moncbega. Griandia. Illusions perdues (lost illusions. La Chutta des feuille, (the fall of the leaves.) Polonia, (grand caprice.) Ardenteo Mazurka. Bervuose, (cradle song.) The Union, (grand paraphrase de concert.) Riponda Mio. Home, Sweet Home.

THE GRAND PIANOS USED BY Mr. Gottschalk ARE FROM THE CELEBRATED MANUFACTORY OF CHICKERING & SONS.

NEW PUBLICATIONS AT HALL & SON'S. "Di Giega Insolita," "Oh, with what Festory,"Waltz sung with distinguished suvess, by Mad'lle Adelina Patti, in London, and Mad'lle Carlotta Patti, in New York, composed by M. Strakosch. GOTTSCHALK'S ILLUSTRATED CONCERT BOOK, an entirely New Edition, containing a full explanation of Mr Gottschalk's Pieces, and how they are to be performed; also, a large number of Illustrations, including Gottschalk, Jenny Lind, Adelina and Carlotta Patti, Kellog, Hinkley, Tereso Carreno, W. B. Pape, W. V. Wallace, Carl Formes, and others, besides Twelve Pages of Music, with the Principal Songs and Duets of the Concert Room. GOOD BYE, MY LOVE—Ballad for Tenor and Soprano Voice, composed by Gottschalk, has just been published by Hall & Son. THE UNION, composed and dedicated to MAJOR-GENERAL McCLELLAN, by L. M. Gottschalk, has just been published by Hall & Son.

F. A. SEARLE, PLAIN AND ORNAMENTAL PRINTER—JOURNAL BUILDING—118 WASHINGTON STREET.

Poster printers made free use of all sorts and sizes of type to produce ornamental sheets designed to be read at various levels of detail. (From an original in the W. L. Clements Library, University of Michigan.)

grammar. Since messages were charged by the word, adroit writers
developed "compressed" forms of English to convey meaning at
the least possible expense. Like poster and newspaper English,
telegraphese (a term first appearing in print in 1885) became "con-
cise and elliptical," as the *OED* glosses it, with the usual anxiety
among conservatives that such abbreviated English would drive
out the full forms. An even more extreme strategy of compression
was expressed in the Anglo-American telegraphic code, allowing
messages to be reduced and hidden in arbitrary words. Using a
dictionary compiled to support the system, the sender could telegraph a string of words that the receiver would decode by reference to the same book. Thus, in the following specimen, *mend* is
expanded in the dictionary to "The matter can be arranged per
your convenience."

Telegram: Mend Tartish Sagatus Abele Narrate Advolation Tinct
    Dracanth Moslings Anes.
Message: The matter can be arranged as per your telegram. [*sic*] It
    can be done safely. You can get some abatement. It will be nec-
    essary to act immediately. Will make the best terms possible.
    May I draw on you for what amount of money is required?
    Must have answer immediately. (Anglo-American Code and
    Cypher Company, iv)

Such systems were, of course, so arcane that they had little direct
influence on English, but the telegraph code was only an extreme
expression of the impulse toward condensation, a linguistic style
motivated in part by the new communications technology and in
part by the idea that English in its full form was wasteful and that
businesslike abbreviations were efficient. Condensation put commercial English at odds with literary expression, and bureaucracies came to favor a terse, abbreviated, and unadorned style of
English.
    Record keeping and communications within large bureaucra-
cies reflected the specialization of the workplace foreseen in the
eighteenth century by Adam Smith. Individual enterprises conducted by sole proprietors gave way to bureaucracies with suppli-

HOW TO CONDUCT WRITING SCHOOLS.

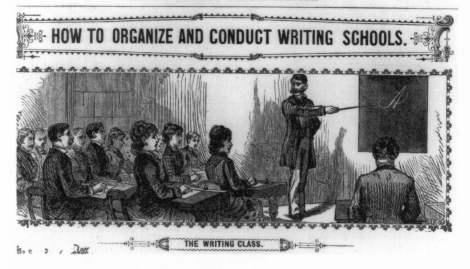

HOW TO ORGANIZE AND CONDUCT WRITING SCHOOLS.

THE WRITING CLASS.

With the rise of bureaucracies, and their insatiable appetite for written records, penmanship was the foundation for a career as a clerk. (From G. Gaskell, 54.)

ers and markets at a distance. For such enterprises to flourish, written documents were essential in keeping track of the flow of goods and services. The evolution of the word *clerk* provides an instructive example for this social transformation. In its earliest English sense, a clerk was a priest or member of a religious order; since this class was among the few possessing the skills of literacy, *clerk* soon was applied more generally to men and women who were literate. By the Renaissance, *clerk* had gained a restricted sense and described those whose work it was to keep written records of governmental proceedings. By the nineteenth century, *clerks,* usually occupying subordinate positions in governmental or commercial bureaucracies, were responsible for a full range of record keeping and correspondence. Greatly increased opportunities for clerks presented themselves as empire and capitalism emerged in the nineteenth century, and with those opportunities came training in handwritten English.

In America, schools of penmanship began to flourish early in the century, and handwriting became a focal subject in common

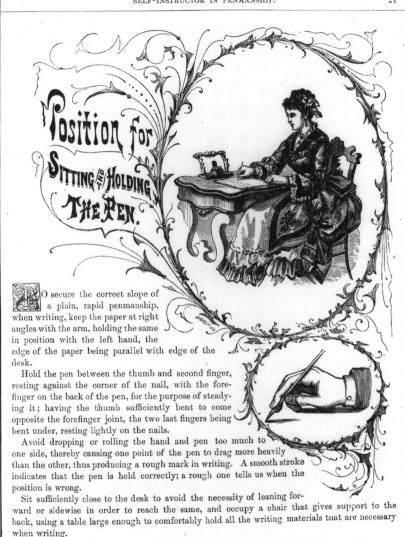

O secure the correct slope of a plain, rapid penmanship, when writing, keep the paper at right angles with the arm, holding the same in position with the left hand, the edge of the paper being parallel with edge of the desk.

Hold the pen between the thumb and second finger, resting against the corner of the nail, with the forefinger on the back of the pen, for the purpose of steadying it; having the thumb sufficiently bent to come opposite the forefinger joint, the two last fingers being bent under, resting lightly on the nails.

Avoid dropping or rolling the hand and pen too much to one side, thereby causing one point of the pen to drag more heavily than the other, thus producing a rough mark in writing. A smooth stroke indicates that the pen is held correctly; a rough one tells us when the position is wrong.

Sit sufficiently close to the desk to avoid the necessity of leaning forward or sidewise in order to reach the same, and occupy a chair that gives support to the back, using a table large enough to comfortably hold all the writing materials that are necessary when writing.

New printing techniques made it possible to integrate type with all kinds of visual imagery. (From T. E. Hill, 21.)

schools. By midcentury, commercial schools and business colleges were established, not only in urban centers but in isolated villages as well (many of them served by itinerant teachers). Representative of the enterprising instructors in such schools was one whose journal is preserved in the Vermont Historical Society: "The Journal of James Guild, Peddler, Tinker, Schoolmaster, Portrait Painter, from 1818 to 1824." His first efforts in Middlebury were profitable.

> Now I was a stranger & not a friend in the place. But I caled myself a writing Master. This was a bold attempt to go into so popular a place as this as a professor of penmanship when I had had only 30 hours instruction, but I thought if I could get a school started, I would run the risk, & in the first place I got me a room, & then went round the Village & told them I was going to teach writing, & if they would send, if they was not satisfied, nothing to pay.
>
> This was new business, & I came here without any recommend or specimen of penmanship, & I hardly knew what a direct ell was, but I told them I was a writer & began my school, & in the first day I had 11 scholars an from that to 20 & now then I was in great business. (Quoted by Nash, 6)

Dozens of success stories like Guild's made a writing career desirable, and attainable, to young persons leaving agriculture for commerce or government. In the first half of the century, nearly four hundred books of model handwriting were published in the United States, and more were available from Britain where (as in printing) conventions were established and exported. In both countries, "it was certainly writing rather than calligraphy that was taught—a plain dull hand, which could (and did) deteriorate when written with speed" (Whalley, 301). The addition of a handwriting examination as part of the battery of civil-service tests in midcentury Britain made penmanship loom even larger in importance. By the end of the century, the triumphalism that was found so satisfying in the notion of English as a "world language" spread to handwriting as well: "The present system of forming and combining letters seems to be perfect. It enables the writer to put his thoughts on paper almost with the rapidity of speech, and it is not probable that it will ever be improved upon" (McCabe 1879, 18).

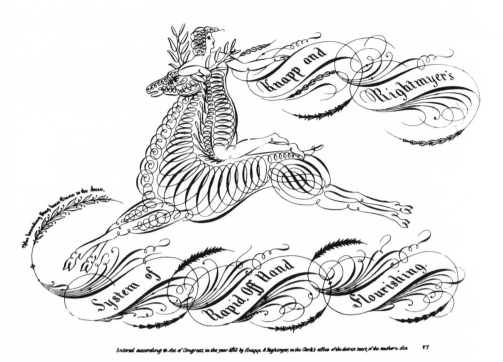

Penmanship was a valuable skill, and writing teachers often created elaborate patterns of flourishes to advertise their talent. This specimen illustrates the text at center left: "The bounding stag bears Diana in the chase." (From Lindstrom, n.p.)

Explosive growth in written English drew more and more speakers to attend to the spelling of English words. Early in the century, conduct books of varying emphasis were published as guides to social behavior for the increasingly urban classes of respectable people eager for instruction. One of these, *The Complete Art of Polite Correspondence,* went through many expansions and refinements throughout the century. Like the eighteenth-century letter-writing guides—the most famous of which was Samuel Richardson's, which gave rise to his immensely popular epistolary novels—this volume gave specimen letters that might be adapted in courtship and marriage. But as the century advanced, more and more subjects were added—for instance, in an edition published in 1857, "From a young Gentleman, Clerk for a Merchant in Philadelphia, to his Father in the Country, soliciting Pocket-

Money." Letter books of this sort described polite behavior, both implicitly and explicitly. Thus the manner of writing, as well as the matter, was given great emphasis.

> It is almost needless to say, that in epistolary, as well as in every other style of composition, the rules of grammar should be strictly observed. As to orthography, it will be sufficient, perhaps, to repeat what has been said on the subject by more than one good writer:— among persons moving in good society, and who may be supposed to have received a tolerable education, although to spell correctly be no merit, to spell incorrectly is a great disgrace. (*Complete Art of Polite Correspondence*, 25)

With spelling enshrined as an evidence of education and gentility, the authority of spelled English increased, especially in the United States, where literacy was diffused through society more rapidly than in Britain.

As a consequence, *spelling pronunciations* (1901) emerged, often reviving ways of saying words that were obsolete or obsolescent. Thus, Walker's *Critical Pronouncing Dictionary* (1791) gave the sole pronunciation of *nephew* as "nev'vu." As a consequence of the spelling, the pronunciation with medial *f* became widely current, both in Britain and North America. A spelling pronunciation emerged for *cucumber* (as the word had been commonly spelled since Coverdale's Bible of 1535).

> The spelling *cowcumber* prevailed in the 17th and beg[inning] of 18th c[entury]; its associated pronunciation was still that recognized by Walker; but [B. H.] Smart['s edition of Walker] 1836 says "no well-taught person, except of the old school, now says *cow-cumber* . . . although any other pronunciation . . . would have been pedantic some thirty years ago." (*OED*)

Other words achieving spelling pronunciations in the nineteenth century can be discerned in an American usage volume published in 1855, *Five Hundred Mistakes*. In this work, Americans are urged to follow the spelling in pronouncing such words as *celery* (rather than as *salary*), *clothes' pins* (rather than as *cloze pins*), *partridge* (rather than *patridge*), *waistcoat* (rather than *weskit*). For some of these, Walker had hoped that the spelling pronunciation was "not

Wooden Wedding.

1875.   1880.

Mr. & Mrs. Henry Clay Daniels,

At Home,

Tuesday evening, July 13, at eight o'clock.

37 Forest Ave.

The invitation is on wooden or imitation cards. For Tin Wedding, paper made in imitation of tin is used. If it is preferred that no gifts be offered the invitation should contain an announcement to that effect.

Crystal Wedding.

1825.   1840.

Mr. and Mrs. Ichabod Crane

request the pleasure of your company at their

Fifteenth Wedding Anniversary,

Wednesday evening, June third. at 8 o'clock.

342 Second Ave.

No gifts received.

The invitation should be on crystallized cards.

As printed invitations replaced handwritten ones, the mechanically reproduced forms imitated the more elaborate styles of penmanship. (From *Treasures*, 199.)

irrecoverable" or the conventional pronunciation "not incurable."
What recalled pronunciations to the spelled forms of words, particularly in the United States, was literacy, particularly writing, as
more and more people became conscious of written conventions.
Spelling pronunciations were particularly common in American
place-names of European origin; among dozens of such names
were *Athens* and *Cairo* (with the stressed vowel of *bay*), *Thames*
(rhymed with *James*), and *Birmingham* (with three stressed vowels).

Whatever served to draw attention to words as spelled gave
increasing authority to written forms of English. Thus, the pronunciation of *often* with a medial *t* was, at the end of the century,
"not recognized in the dictionaries, [but] is now frequent in the
south of England, and is often used in singing" (*OED*, s.v. *often*).
Whole classes of words came to be pronounced according to their
spelled forms; for instance, *l* was restored for many speakers in *fal-
con, fault, Ralph*, and *soldier* in the course of the century.

While education and gentility drew attention to spelling and
granted it an authority it had not previously enjoyed, other developments drew spoken English to the printed page. One such
trend was the explosive growth of shorthand writing. Though systems for transcribing spoken English rapidly had been proposed
as early as 1588, the social conditions that made for burgeoning
documentation in the early nineteenth century spawned proposal
after proposal. During the century, nearly three hundred books
were published on behalf of almost as many shorthand systems,
and even Isaac Pitman, by far the most successful of these inventors, died in 1897 at war with his sons over still more improvements in his notation (see E. Butler; Baker). By far the most popular shorthand methods were phonetic, and skilled transcribers
wrote down the sounds they heard rather than the conventional
written forms of English. Consequently, actual spoken English
came to be written down as heard, only later to be supplied with
conventional spelling, word division, punctuation, and the layout
of the printed page.

At the same time that shorthand was increasingly used by
clerks and journalists, literary fashion swung in the direction of the
vernacular. Wordsworth and Coleridge had celebrated the "real

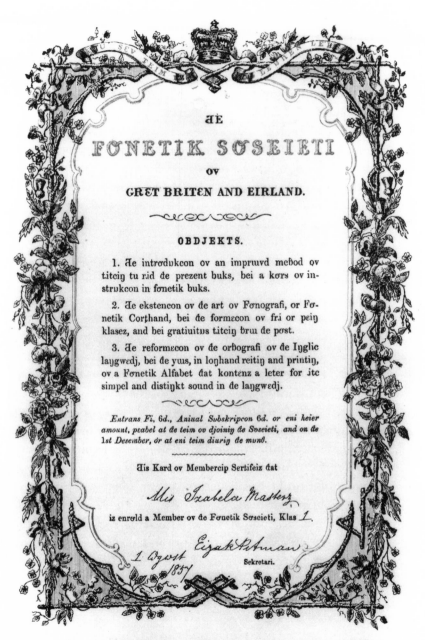

ÐE

FƆNETIK SƆSEIETI

OV

GRET BRITEN AND EIRLAND.

OBDJEKTS.

1. Ðe introdʋkcon ov an imprʋvd meðod ov titcin̩ tu r̩id ðe prezent buks, bei a kɔrs ov instrʋkcon in fɔnetik buks.

2. Ðe ekstencon ov ðe art ov Fɔnografi, or Fɔnetik Cɔrþhand, bei ðe formecon ov fri or pein̩ klasez, and bei gratiuitʋs titcin̩ þrʋ ðe pɔst.

3. Ðe reformecon ov ðe orþografi ov ðe In̩glic lan̩gwedj, bei ðe yʋs, in lon̩hand reitin̩ and printin̩, ov a Fɔnetik Alfabet ðat kontenz a leter for itc simpel and distin̩kt sound in ðe lan̩gwedj.

Entrans Fi, 6d., Aniual Sʋbskripcon 6d. or eni heier amount, peabel at ðe teim ov djoinin̩ ðe Sɔseieti, and on ðe 1st Desember, or at eni teim diurin̩ ðe munþ.

Ðis Kard ov Membercip Sertifeiz ðat

Mis Izabela Masterz

iz enrɔld a Member ov ðe Fɔnetik Sɔseieti, Klas *1*.

Eizak Pitman

Sekretari.

1 Ɔgʋst 1857

PHONETIC SOCIETY CARD OF MEMBERSHIP, 1857

As the need for shorthand transcription increased, new alphabets were created to represent speech sounds. Many of them were designed to promote spelling reform. (From Baker, opposite p. 128.)

language" of ordinary people, though little of it emerged uncleansed in their poetry. Dialect humor, however, became popular, and such writers as Maria Edgeworth, Walter Scott, and their imitators made innovative attempts in serious fiction to render dialogue in "authentic" colloquial styles. The most prominent of vernacular writers, however, was Charles Dickens. His contemporaries recognized him immediately as having a good ear, and the distinctive voices he gave to his characters—Sam Weller or Alfred Jingle in his first popular novel, *Pickwick Papers,* for instance—show an unusual attention to spoken English. At least some of Dickens's skill as a writer of dialogue can be attributed to his training in Thomas Gurney's system of shorthand in 1827 and his employment as a court reporter and journalist from 1828 to 1836. (According to a letter Dickens wrote in 1856, "I left the reputation behind me of being the best and most rapid reporter ever known" [Page, 11].) Shorthand transcription of spoken English helped break down the barrier between the two modes, and written English became more like speech (through literary and journalistic writing) at the same time speech was becoming more like writing (in spelling pronunciations).

Written English became ever more important in the nineteenth century. Documents were composed and kept in unprecedented numbers; popular reading material put written English in the hands of nearly everyone. Commercial interests built upon a foundation of written English, whether in labels for mass-produced goods or through advertising that, by the end of the century, had become ubiquitous. English-speaking society was transformed from a largely oral culture to one awash in documents: certificates for births, marriages, and deaths; titles and deeds of ownership; newspapers, books, and magazines; signs, notices, and posters. English was, by the end of the century, everywhere to be seen.

SOUNDS

DURING THE NINETEENTH CENTURY, the English-speaking population increased more than five times. A share of this increase coincided with an explosive growth in the population of Britain and North America, where improved sanitation and effective medicine together lowered significantly the rate of infant mortality. But a more important social phenomenon than growth in population was the spread of English to new communities, first through migration and then as a second language. London and New York became cosmopolitan cities with unprecedented numbers of immigrants, both from abroad and from the rural hinterlands. Long-established German settlements in Pennsylvania and Spanish-speaking towns in Florida and the American Southwest were transformed by English. India gained an anglophone elite among the long-resident ruling class, which, though small, exercised significant political power and important local influence on language. China was covered with a network of commercial and mission stations where English was regularly used, not only by expatriates but also by Chinese attracted to European culture. By the end of the century, central and southern Africans had imposed upon them the structures of nation-states, and huge populations from Khartoum south to the Cape and on the Atlantic coast from Sierra Leone around the Gulf of Guinea to Cameroon were exposed to English. At the very end of the century, the United States became a colonial power overseas through military conquest in Cuba and the Philippines, spreading English even farther abroad.

Any assessment of the sounds of English speech in the nineteenth century must encompass the astonishing increase in diversity that this geographical and demographic expansion entailed.

Conceptually, the "center" of the language—what counted for schoolbooks and usage manuals—shrank while the "periphery" exploded in size. Most contemporary observers regarded the English of cities as "corrupt" and the speech of foreigners "broken." A handful of writers, located in southern England and in the cities of the eastern United States, took possession of the language and declared that their own preferences were English and those of others merely deviations or mainly corruptions.

The eighteenth century's easy tolerance for ways of speaking turned into harsh rigidity. In 1755, Samuel Johnson had reluctantly acquiesced to the variety of pronunciation: "Every language has its anomalies, which, though inconvenient, and in themselves once unnecessary, must be tolerated among the imperfections of human things" (A-1). His successors persuaded themselves that there was little need for tolerance and large opportunities to eradicate imperfections. In 1791, for instance, John Walker noted that Johnson and Robert Lowth (1710–87), the grammarian whose work continued to be regarded as authoritative well into the nineteenth century, provided the foundation for greater uniformity in pronunciation. In Walker's views, these two authorities had succeeded in arresting change and laying the foundation for correctness.

> While Johnson and Lowth have been insensibly operating on the orthography and construction of our Language, its pronunciation has not been neglected. The importance of a consistent and regular pronunciation was too obvious to be overlooked; and the want of this consistency and regularity has induced several ingenious men to endeavour at a reformation; who, by exhibiting the irregularities of pronunciation, and pointing out its analogies, have reclaimed some words that were not irrecoverably fixed in the wrong sound, and prevented others from being perverted by ignorance or caprice. (iii)

Johnson's reluctant tolerance of "imperfections" gave way to increasing confidence that variety in pronunciation could be reduced to consistency and regularity through instruction and example. Eighteenth-century writers scarcely imagined that people might improve their speech, and their social position, by reading dictionaries and word lists, but nineteenth-century writers presumed such transformations to be possible. Self-improvement volumes appeared in ever larger numbers, culminating in whole dictionaries designed to correct errors in speech (see, for instance, Phyfe). Thus there was an impulse toward consensus among the educated, and would-be educated, but their passion for correctness largely exhausted itself among the vastly increasing population of English speakers. Try as they might, they scarcely affected the ways in which English words were pronounced, and they left as their legacy some scattered lore—which was the best vowel to use in the first syllable of *either* and *neither?*—and an enormous residue of anxiety about how people ought to speak their own language.

Within Britain, there was a widespread belief that rural dialects were fast disappearing, and, consequently, that English was becoming more uniform. The English Dialect Society was founded in 1873 to record local speech forms believed to be on the brink of extinction, an effort in a wider struggle to preserve, or at least document, the more romantic aspects of rural life. So uncritically accepted was the idea that dialects were vanishing that the Society was dissolved in 1896 since it was thought, with the completion of Wright's *English Dialect Dictionary,* to have finished its task. What was missed, of course, was the rise of urban dialects, each as distinctive as the rural speech forms they supplanted. In Britain, city speech was thought to be unworthy of scholarly attention, and the thorough bibliography of dialect studies compiled for the Society in 1877 had no entries whatsoever for the dialects of Birmingham and Liverpool (Skeat and Nodal). In the United States, on the other hand, new dialects were constantly being recognized, not only in the long-established regions along the Atlantic coast but in the new settlements springing up in the central and western regions of the country. When the American Dialect Society was founded in 1889, the contribution of other languages to English in North America was recognized as falling within the purview of investigation, and, though the Society was infused with the same reverence for English-descended rustics that shaped its English counterpart, the cosmopolitan variety of American English was given fuller recognition. In the first volume of the Society's *Dialect*

Notes, for instance, a distinguished scholar thought "the English of the lower classes in New York City and vicinity" worthy of notice, even though "a New Yorker who has four American-born grand-parents is a rarity, and . . . a great majority have not one" (Babbitt, 457–58).

The technology that fostered the spread of written English also abetted the dissemination of spoken English. Railways and steamships made possible the migrations already mentioned, but ease of transportation also immeasurably facilitated travel for tem-porary occasions of business or pleasure. As a result, rural isolation was virtually abolished, and tourism—previously restricted to the wealthy—emerged as an industry. People became accustomed to hearing varieties of English quite unlike their own.

While face-to-face encounters of people speaking different kinds of English increased in numbers, long-distance communica-tion by voice became possible in 1876 through the telephone. In 1877, Edison invented the first practical phonograph, and recorded sound soon became commonplace, bringing music and voice to places distant from their production. In 1896, Marconi was granted a British patent for wireless telegraphy, and in 1901 a wireless message—the letter *s*—crossed the Atlantic from New-foundland to England. In 1898, Valdemar Poulsen patented the *telegraphone,* which preserved sounds on a magnetized wire, and in 1900 the emperor of Austria recorded his voice by this method at the Exposition Universelle in Paris. Not long after, voice messages reached around the world. While broadcasting and international telephony were twentieth-century developments, social structures were put in place in the nineteenth that inaugurated the expecta-tion of an unfamiliar voice from afar speaking English through a machine.

Claims by nineteenth-century imperialists that a homoge-neous anglophone culture was triumphant have obscured the vast increase in the heterogeneity of spoken English. Even among the elite, the attractions of gentility and social ambition did not result in a uniform style of pronunciation. A. J. Ellis, the most assiduous of the nineteenth-century phoneticians, repeatedly declared that "there is no such thing as educated English pronunciation" (pt. 4,

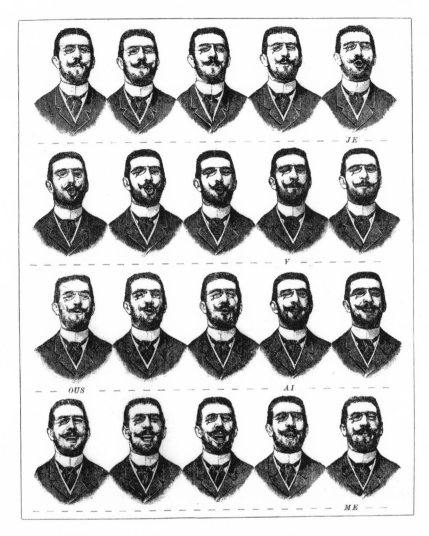

The scientific study of speech sounds flourished in the nineteenth century with minute distinctions connected, often, to excruciatingly small gradations of social class. (From Jespersen 1913, tipped-in illustration.)

1215). As an observer of minute distinctions, Ellis was perhaps inclined to exaggerate the differences among speakers occupying positions of prestige in nineteenth-century London. Nonetheless, he observed that G. B. Airy, the Astronomer Royal and president of the Royal Society, pronounced the site of the observatory in Greenwich as "green witch"; Benjamin Jowett, master of Balliol

College, Oxford, said *education* with the sound in "judge" as its first consonant rather than the "d" prescribed by the elocutionists; a "noble Member of Parliament" employed a "distinctly trilled" *r* at the end of *idea* (pt. 4, 1211–13). Such facts as these suggest that nineteenth-century English speech was as rich in variant pronunciations as the English of any period before or since. Individuals adopted different speaking habits for different occasions, and people differed among themselves. Certain occasions for speaking imposed their own norms. According to Ellis, "the bar has rather hereditary pronunciations, where they are not individual and local. The stage for the higher class of dramas is archaic and artificial. . . . The pulpit is full of local peculiarities" (pt. 4, 1209). Other observers similarly emphasized the variety of English heard in London.

> Now, this pronunciation of cultivated London is not uniform. It is marked with variations due to several causes, one of which is affectation. There are namby-pamby, dawdling speakers, who mince and clip their words, and utter them without distinct articulation; and these speakers, notwithstanding that they are reprehended by those who would preserve a simple, strong, and manly speech, and ridiculed ("Punch" makes fun of them), exert an influence. Indeed, it is impossible for even one man to persist in a peculiarity of speech, if it is not too strangely at variance with the common pronunciation, without exercising a modifying influence upon the speech of those around him. (R. White 1908, 77)

All these distinctions were found among the tiny class of educated Londoners occupying positions of influence in intellectual or political life. How much greater was the variety on the national and international scenes.

Early in the nineteenth century, observers came to believe that English was spoken in its exemplary form by the denizens of men's clubs along London's Pall Mall or by the emerging Brahmin class in Boston. However, many English sounds were not heard in the speech of these urban elites. In Scotland, for instance, the consonant of German *ach* survived from an earlier stage of English among all but the most anglicized classes. Thus most speakers of English in Scotland used a different consonant in *licht, eneuch,*

Rote memorization and choral repetition continued to be staple learning techniques in nineteenth-century schools. With the vowel wheel, illustrated from Wright's *Elements*, students learned explicitly what they knew implicitly: English vowels are distinguished by tongue position on vertical and horizontal dimensions. Tongue-twisters further emphasized the value of careful articulation—for instance, "Theophilus Thistle, the successful thistle sifter, in sifting a sieve full of unsifted thistles, thrust three thousand thistles through the thick of his thumb." (From A. D. Wright, 38.)

lauch, and *dowehter* from that found in the southern English counterparts of these words: *light, enough, laugh,* and *daughter* (J. Murray, 118). In Ireland, the *th* sound in *thin* and *this* was articulated with the tongue behind (instead of below) the upper front teeth. Dialect writers sometimes spelled words containing this sound with a *t* or *d,* even though the Irish English consonants were by no means identical to the southern English *t* and *d* sounds. For instance, *three/tree* and *than/Dan* were sometimes spelled identically (with *t* and *d* respectively) in "colloquial" Irish English as written by outsiders, but the sounds were clearly distinguished in Irish English speech. (Sometimes the Irish English "dental" *t* was spelled *th* as in *poulthry* 'poultry' and *porthering* 'portering'.) In Jamaica, English was influenced by West African languages (either directly or through a Portuguese-based pidgin), and the result was a consonant that can be represented in spelling with *ny* (as in *nyews* 'news' in some varieties of late-twentieth-century English). In words of African origin, this initial *ny* was widely used in Jamaica: *nyam* 'yam', *nyam* 'to eat', *nyami-nyami* 'greedy person'. Under the influence of English, the initial *ny* was sometimes reduced to *y* (as in *yam* or in *yanga* 'a dance' [< *nyanga*]), but other words gained an initial *ny* because of their apparently "African" character (as in *nyong* [< *young*]). Thus, as these few examples show, the array of speech sounds used by monolingual English speakers was larger than the list usually found in the histories of English pronunciation based on upper-crust London models.

The nineteenth century seems also to have produced at least one new consonant that had not previously played a systematic role in the system of English: the glottal stop. Many modern writers assume that this sound, formed by an abrupt interruption in the flow of breath at the back of the oral cavity, is a recent innovation, but it has been in significant use in English at least since the mid–nineteenth century. Phoneticians had noticed the glottal stop, but, since it was not at first perceived to have any distinct social evaluation, it was not discussed in elocution manuals or other books aimed at improving speech.

The first to observe the emergence of glottal stop was Alexander Melville Bell, who remarked, in 1860, that "in the west of Scotland" it accompanied the sound of *t;* by 1867, he had added that it sometimes replaced *t* entirely in *butter* (Andrésen, 12–13). James Murray's minute study of the dialect of the southern counties of Scotland (published in 1873) made no mention of glottal stop, though he included a symbol for it in his table of phonetic characters. (Only because of Murray's skill as recorder and interpreter does this argument from silence have persuasive value; if the glottal stop had been in use in the region he discussed, Murray would have identified it.) A. J. Ellis, however, in 1889, reported five examples from central Scotland: *Saturday, better, water, butter,* and *wanting*. When Otto Jespersen visited Britain in 1887, he noticed the phenomenon in Scotland and the north of England. Up to that time, the only reported examples had been for glottal stop accompanying, or replacing, medial *t*. Jespersen's examples show that the phenomenon had spread to all three voiceless stops, *p, t,* and *k*, in syllable-final position. As Jespersen explained, the stop occurred "immediately before" these three voiceless stops, and the combination made glottal stop virtually "inaudible."

> I have heard it in the following words: in Sheffield *tha't* (very often), *can't, thin'k, po'pe, boo'k;* in Lincoln *i'ts, migh't, cer'tainly, u'p, wha't, bough't, thin'k, si't;* in Glasgow *don't, wan't, o'pen, go't, tha't, brigh'tening, no't;* in Edinburgh in a great many similar words. Sometimes we have the further development that the mouth stop is omitted, as in [wɔ'ər] for *water* (Edinburgh). (pt. 1, 414)

The glottal stop with "the mouth sound" of [p, t], or [k] omitted has become one of the most stigmatized features of British urban speech in the twentieth century.

The social meaning attached to glottal stops was slow to emerge, however. Ellis recorded the view of one of his volunteer field-workers that its use in "get up" was characteristic of "the very vulgar form of Leeds dialect" (pt. 4, 1332). In 1882, A. J. D. D'Orsey complained that the vernacular of London schoolchildren made it difficult for him to distinguish *life, like,* and *light,* perhaps, one might assume in light of subsequent developments, because the final consonants were expressed as glottal stop (quoted by Ellis, pt. 5, 226–27). D'Orsey was not sufficiently skilled as a phonetician to have recognized the change taking place, and Ellis, who certainly was, dismissed his claims, apparently without considering whether the final *k* and *t* in *like* and *light* had been replaced by glottal stop. Writing in 1896, E. H. Babbitt reported glottal stops in *letter, butter,* and *written* as "common, but by no means regular, among the school children" in New York City. Whether this was a parallel development in North America or a matter of British influence is now impossible to say. (It is certain, however, that in New York the most influential form of English from the British Isles, Hiberno-English, did not contribute the glottal stop since the Irish "dental" *t*, with no accompanying glottal stop, appears in the words Babbitt noticed.)

In 1905, Joseph Wright identified another locus of the glottal-stop substitution, in the place of medial *t* before syllabic *l* in *battle, kettle, nettle* (229). This pronunciation he declared to be characteristic of Edinburgh and its hinterlands. Farther afield, Helge Kökeritz studied the dialect of Suffolk in 1926–28; there, he found that the glottal stop was in common use in words like those identified by Bell and Wright in Scotland. The older residents (those born in the 1850s or 1860s) did not use it at all, but in the speech of those born in the last quarter of the century it was "quite common" (93). Kökeritz was uncertain if this use of glottal stops should be called "a class peculiarity," something that subsequent observers would have no difficulty in alleging, but he found that children, who "used the glottal stop rarely in reading aloud, were found to substitute it even for **d** during play-time" (94).

From these sources, it becomes clear that the glottal stop became a noticeable fact of English late in the century, that it was first associated with central Scotland and the northern cities of England, and that it spread rapidly in informal speech to other urban areas, and, eventually, even to isolated rural districts like Suffolk. Associated with lower-class dialects and informal occasions of speaking, the glottal stop has subsequently become part of the consonant system of British English, though in some phonetic environments it remains highly stigmatized (see further Andrésen; J. C. Wells, 260–61). When glottal-stop reinforcement or substitution became common in the nineteenth century in Britain, it did not influence overseas varieties to the same extent as had earlier innovations. While this consonant is found in some, especially eastern, varieties of North American English, it does not appear in the Caribbean (except in Barbados, where glottal stop is used as the final consonant of *about* and *but*), South Africa, Australia, or New Zealand. Even in varieties of English influenced by languages containing glottal stops (e.g., Hausa for Nigerian English, Hawaiian for Hawaiian English), it does not occur. Everywhere that it does occur, however, some of its uses are treated as stigmatized, as exemplary of "rough" speech characteristic of the "vulgar" (despite the fact that high-prestige speakers in Britain often use it between vowels in such words as *reeducate* and in place of final *p*, *t*, and *k* when the next word begins with a consonant: *stop that, got some, clock struck*).

Glottal stop is, apparently, a nineteenth-century innovation in

English. Even if it did occur earlier (and had been overlooked by quite acute phoneticians of the eighteenth century like James Elphinston, Thomas Sheridan, and John Walker), it only began to take on social meaning in the nineteenth century as it spread from northern British cities as a feature of the English of the urban poor. (Its absence from Australian English suggests that it arose after the massive deportations of poor people from the British cities in the first half of the century.) For those who heard it at the end of the century, it was a new sound.

Innovations like glottal stop coexisted with phonological survivals from earlier forms of English that gradually disappeared in the course of the century. Thus the historic pronunciation with *k* in, for instance, *knife, knit,* and *know* was retained by a few older people in Scotland, but Murray opined in 1873 that "the habit of suppressing it in the English taught in school has led the rising generation to drop it also in the vernacular" (122). Even without schooling, however, this initial cluster was disappearing from spoken English, just as *gnat* and *gnaw* had already been reduced to *n* (except for an isolated use of initial *gn* in *gnaw* in northeast Scotland; J. Wright 1905, 462–63).

In the prestige dialect of the London elite, however, there was some tendency in English to produce historic or etymological consonants, a fact that can be surmised from Walker's comments in 1791 on *pneumatick.*

> I have differed from Mr. Sheridan in these words, as I apprehend it is contrary to analogy, and the best usage, to pronounce the initial *p. G* and *k* before *n* are always silent, as in *gnomon, knave,* &c. *B* is not heard in *bdellium,* nor *p* in *psalm, ptisan,* &c. and till some good reasons are offered for pronouncing it in the words in question, I must join with Dr.[William] Kenrick, Mr. [William] Scott, and Mr. [William] Perry [all compilers of pronouncing dictionaries], who have sunk it as I have done.

These remarks illuminate the treatment of initial consonants at the end of the eighteenth century. Initial *kn* and *gn* were no longer pronounced as consonant clusters except by a few Scots; the *k* and *g* were "always silent" in *knife* and *gnaw* among the urban educated elite. As for *pn, ps,* and *pt,* Walker would not have written as he did in this note had not some learned person—or perhaps an unlearned one influenced by the spelling—wished to articulate the initial *p.* English permitted the formation of initial clusters with *kn, gn, pn,* and *ps* from the inventory of available sounds, but most nineteenth-century speakers chose not to use them, though there was not, as Murray would later write, an "organic defect in the English mouth to prevent it" (*OED,* s.v. *Ps-*). Those who did pronounce these consonants were generally understood to be old-fashioned (in the case of *kn* and *gn*) or ostentatiously learned (with *pn, ps,* and *pt*). But the great majority of these "exceptional" initial clusters were pronounced only by those who attempted to "improve" their speech by spelling pronunciations. By the end of the century, writers on usage had no reason to bother with advice about *kn-* or *gn-,* but initial *p-* in these clusters was still worth mentioning: Phyfe, for instance, declared that the initial *ps* in *pseudo-* was "heard," though "seldom," and he gave initial *pt* in *pterodactyl* as a secondary pronunciation. In short, these initial clusters died a slow death. As late as 1908, Murray was still searching to find a "good reason" for initial *p* in *pn-* words: "It is to be desired that it were sounded in English also [as in other European languages], at least in scientific and learned words; since the reduction of *pneo-* to *neo-, pneu-* to *new-,* and *pnyx* to *nix,* is a loss to etymology and intelligibility, and a weakening of the resources of the language" (*OED,* s.v. *Pn-*). Under *Ps-* and *Pt-,* Murray expresses similar etymological longings. Except for the *p* in *psalm* (and its derivatives), a sound lost in Old English times and hence beyond recovery, he hoped that the initial *p* might be restored.

The examples so far given show the complexity of the linguistic scene as reflected in the pronunciation of English in the nineteenth century. Many conflicting forces shaped the varieties of English, and, though it cannot be alleged that any of these forces were new to anglophone culture, the richness of the historical record allows unprecedented insight into the dynamics of change that reshaped English. Some of the oppositions pulling at the shape of English sounds can be briefly summarized: "native" versus "foreign" sounds, archaic versus innovative styles, rural versus

" I believe that a careful mastery of these fifty pages is likely to do more towards the correct use of our language than years of technical grammar." Albert C. Perkins, ten years Principal of Phillips Exeter Academy, and for nine years at the head of Adelphi Academy, Brooklyn.

One Thousand Everyday Donts

By B.A. Hathaway, the author of the now famous " 1001 Questions and Answers."

BAD ENGLISH

How Not To Use It

Price, 30 Cents

A Manual of Misused Expressions occurring daily among all classes, the educated as well as the uneducated, with corrections and the principles of English Grammar involved. Vulgarisms, Slang Phrases, etc., etc., etc., pointed out and corrected.

Hinds and Noble

4 Cooper Institute,   New York City.

Nineteenth-century pedants found a nearly inexhaustible market for usage manuals among the socially anxious. (From Eaton, verso of title page.)

urban dialects, central varieties (i.e., the emergent London "standard") versus peripheral ones (e.g., those of Scotland, Ireland, and the overseas communities), higher versus lower social class. In the course of the century, the conflict among these forces became ever more intense, and the consequences of linguistic differences became ever more severe. All these trends were summed up plausibly, though with characteristic exaggeration, by George Bernard Shaw in 1912 in the preface to his *Pygmalion:* "It is impossible for an Englishman to open his mouth, without making some other

Englishman hate or despise him" (191). Outsiders made the same observation. Thus in 1914, R. E. Zachrisson declared:

> I believe there is no other country in the world where pronunciation plays such an important rôle for social distinctions as in England. The gates of society are inexorably shut to those who cannot utter "the shibboleth of gentility" [i.e., initial *h*]. (429)

If there is one heritage of the nineteenth-century language culture that survives most vigorously, it is the institutionalization of hierarchy among linguistic variants. The nineteenth century is, in short, a century of steadily increasing linguistic intolerance.

Linguistic change takes place at all social levels, but in English-speaking societies only the upper middle class articulates preferences and attempts to manage its direction. For example, in a work scornful of "clerical eloquence," one nineteenth-century American criticized lengthening the vowels in "O Lord," a practice he thought "impossible to a man who feels that he is really addressing his Maker."

> The habit of prolonging a word with a view of increasing its impressiveness, or in any way attempting to evoke solemnity out of sonorousness, is a blunder in all its details. (Gould, 162–63)

Lengthening of vowels in solemn acts of speaking was apparently quite widespread, and another warden of American usage warned against the pronunciation "law'urd" (Soule and Wheeler, 276). That this practice was not restricted to North American preachers is apparent from Murray's observation in the *OED*.

> From a desire to utter the name of God more deliberately than the short vowel naturally allows, the pronunciation is often (gǫd) or even (gǭd), and an affected form (gɒd) is not uncommon. (s.v., *God*)

Pomposity and affectation, among the clergy or any other group, were not new in the nineteenth century. But the ideology that defined them was more clearly articulated than ever before, and that ideology attempted to alter the direction of naturally evolving linguistic change.

What took place linguistically can be traced socially by beginning with three sets of homophones published by William Angus in his *Pronouncing Vocabulary* of 1800: *reason, raisin; Rome, room;* and *satire, satyr.*

Some clue to the relation of *reason* and *raisin* can be discerned from the comment by an English author in 1807: "Reason and raisin are pronounced alike in the age of George the Third, by every person who speaks without affectation" (quoted in the *OED*, s.v. *raisin*). Shakespeare had made puns around the identity of sounds in the two words, but the separation into the two pronunciations found in modern English had already taken place among more speakers than the merely "affected." Dictionaries reported divided usage: Sheridan (in 1780) declared that *raisin* had the vowel of *praise* while Walker (in 1791) listed it with the vowel of *seize.* Walker invoked Shakespeare in defense of his preference.

> This pun evidently shows these words were pronounced exactly alike in Shakespeare's time, and that Mr. Sheridan's pronunciation of this word as if written *rays'n*, is not only contrary to general usage, but, what many would think a greater offence, destructive of the wit of Shakespeare. (s.v. *raisin*)

In his *Dissertations* of 1789, Noah Webster noted that "*Reesin* for *raisin* is very prevalent in two or three principal towns in America," but, he thought, "derivation, analogy, and general custom" do not support that pronunciation. In 1828, he was even more vigorous.

> The word is in some places pronounced corruptly *reezn*. The pronunciation of Sheridan, Perry, and Jameson accords with that which prevails in the Eastern States, which is regular, and which I have followed. (s.v. *raisin*)

It took only half a century for usage to be transformed; the "affected" and non-"Shakespearean" pronunciation of *raisin* became the norm, while the old-fashioned standard was relegated to the status of a form spoken in "some places" where English was "corrupted" and improperly pronounced.

Rome and *room* present a similar instance of an innovation displacing the norm. In 1833, W. H. Savage included the use of *Rome* to rhyme with *broom* in his indictment of corrupt English.

The stage has little authority with regard to pronunciation, and its affectations will be carefully avoided by every person of good taste: burd for beard, aitches for aches, Karto for Cato [the *r* here indicating a lengthening of the previous vowel], rallery for raillery, kwality for quolity (quality), Room for Rome, and very many others are vulgarisms of the theatre, and find disciples only among those whose minds are of the same grade as the historian whom they imitate—they are knights of the unknown tongue. (ix)

The pronunciation of *Rome* as *room* died a rapid death, however. Victoria, the most middle class of English monarchs, recorded in her diary in 1838 (when she was nineteen years old) that

Lord M[elbourne] says *Room* and *Goold,* for *Rome* and *Gold;* I pronounce it in the latter way; asked him if it was right to spell Despatches with an *i* or an *e;* he said he spelt it Despatches, though that was quite modern and came from *Dépêches;* I asked him about how to place *who* and *whom,* which I said puzzled me. (Esher, 2:51).

(Melbourne is representative of the ungrounded etymological thinking of the day; *dispatch* was not derived from French *dépêche,* and the "modern" *des-* spelling is partly owing to Johnson's *Dictionary.* Better information did not entirely put a halt to such advice as Peabody's 1856 recommendation: "*never* spell the word *despatch, dispatch*" [133], and *despatch* remains a less common but prestigious spelling in England to this day. In the first edition of the *OED,* a preference for *dispatch* shows up in "95% of the seventeenth-century examples, 88% of the eighteenth-century ones, 39% of the nineteenth-century ones, and 62% of the twentieth-century ones" [Osselton, 309 n. 4].)

Self-conscious lore about English was influential, at least among people anxious about correctness. Some continued the old pronunciations as Melbourne did—he was born in 1779—but they were regarded as old-fashioned and increasingly as anachronistic. One memoir writer in 1898 recalled:

There was an old Lady Robert Seymour, who lived in Portland Place, and died there in 1855, in her ninety-first year. . . . She carried down to the time of the Crimean War the habits and phraseology of Queen Charlotte's early court. *Goold* of course she said for *gold* and *yaller* for *yellow,* and *laylock* for *lilac.* She laid stress on the second syllable of *balcony.* She called her maid her *ooman;* instead of sleeping in a place she *lay* there, and when she consulted the doctor she spoke of having "used the 'pottecary.'" (Quoted by Phillipps 1984, 140)

As with *raisin,* what began as a dispute over "affectation" in the pronunciation of *Rome* evolved into a new prestige form, shaping the usage of a younger generation but leaving the older one still speaking in the traditional way. All of Lady Seymour's pronunciations, having survived among the nobility from an earlier time, were used unself-consciously and despite the reprobation of the usage writers. (*Ooman* had been declared an "error constantly committed by the ordinary class of people" as early as 1817 [*Errors of Pronunciation,* 23]; gradually disappearing in most varieties of English, this pronunciation survives in the present-day *patois* of Jamaica.)

In 1909, when Henry Bradley edited the entry in the *OED* for *satire,* he alleged that *satire* and *Satyr* "were probably at one time pronounced alike," a statement that suggests by its vagueness that he did not think that time recent. In 1810, however, Stephen Jones offered *sa´-tur* (with the vowel of *hate*) for *satire* without comment, but Savage in 1833 corrected this pronunciation. That the two words remained near homophones later in the century is evidenced by Burgess, who in 1856 included the pair among words to be "carefully distinguished" (34). As late as 1880, Thomas Embley Osmun (who wrote popular usage books under the name Alfred Ayers) reviewed the possibilities for *satire* offered by dictionaries over the prior century and recommended the modern pronunciation. Based on the conflicting testimony of the same dictionaries, however, two American usage writers declared in 1873: "In England sat´er is preferred, in the United States sat´ir" (Soule and Campbell, 80)—perhaps on the assumption that the pronunciation unfamiliar to them must be British and, because of the dictionaries, current. In this case, etymology played a role, since some believed that the literary genre and the mythological figure were related to each other, an erroneous derivation proposed even in antiquity. Walker reported that the pronunciation of the first syllable as *sat* and the second syllable unstressed—that is, the one that makes *satire* and *Satyr* alike—"seems to be that which is most favoured by the learned, because, say they, the first syllable in the Latin *Satyra* is short" (s.v. *satire*). This theory he dismisses, following a consideration of vowel length in Latin-derived English words; he is scornful of those who preen their "learning" and derides

> the affectation of shortening the initial vowel, which this custom has introduced, in order to give our pronunciation a Latin air, [so as to] furnish us with an opportunity of showing our learning by appealing to Latin quantity; which, when applied to English, is so vague and uncertain, as to put us out of all fear of detection if we happen to be wrong.

With arguments like these, the homophones noted by Angus in 1800 were gradually distinguished, each having a particular evaluation—in this case, "affectation" attributed to the "learned."

"Affectation" was commonly blamed as the source of varying pronunciation, but there were other explanations for the differences people noted. Most of them were grounded in moralistic judgments, and there were very few positive labels applied to usages and a great many negative ones. Thomas Preston's work, *A Dictionary of Daily Blunders* (ca. 1880), is not a particularly abusive specimen of the genre it represents; Preston, however, includes such descriptive categories as these: "is an Americanism and should not be used" (of the spelling *theater*), "is a true Cockneyism and should be avoided" (of *and so*), is "erroneously used," is "used by mistake," and is "wrongly used." As the century progressed, books like Preston's presumed a de facto academy of linguistic decision-makers who formed the "rules" of right and wrong. Preston's entry for *wharf* suggests a source of authority.

> The plural of this word is *wharfs,* and not wharves. The latter word was formerly in use, but philologists have decided that the plural of wharf shall be formed like *dwarf,* namely by adding *s* to the singular.

The idea that a band of "philologists" determined spelling and pronunciation was, of course, false, and respectable writers were divided in their spelling, *wharfs* and *wharves.* These opinionated critics needed no appeal to evidence, however. Despite the frequency of *wharves*, Edward S. Gould declared that no respectable English writer would have occasion to write the plural of *wharf*, apparently since respectable writers would not sink to a discussion of naval architecture and would have no occasion to discuss *wharfs*. Gould asserted the decision should be decided by fiat and not left to legislators and journalists, the only people likely to use the word (116–17). He was happy to make it himself in favor of *wharfs*. What arose under these circumstances was a dense accumulation of lore about correctness, so dense, in fact, that the number of corrections grew year by year. As taste makers discerned increasing numbers of shibboleths in English pronunciation, critics censured ever more vigorously.

This oppressive climate for language variety did not, however, put a stop to changes in pronunciation. Among the most interesting of the features to be buffeted by varying opinions during the century was the pronunciation of the final consonant sound in words like *hunting* and *fishing*. As the spelling suggests, this consonant (spelled *ng*, phonetically [ŋ]) had been in systematic use at the time written conventions were established for the language, but from the eighteenth century—and perhaps earlier—there had been a tendency to alternate *n* and ŋ, especially in gerunds and present participles. (Pairs like *kin* and *king, sin* and *sing, thin* and *thing*, had never been confused.) At the beginning of the nineteenth century, William Wordsworth in Britain had rhymed *traveling* and *javelin*, while his near contemporary in the United States, John Trumbull, had paired *fitting* and *Britain*. Commentators had not been especially censorious in favoring one sound over the other, though by the middle of the eighteenth century there was anxiety that some pairs might be confused—for instance, *hearing* and *herein, looking* and *look in* (see Jespersen 1961, 1:355–56).

The situation at the beginning of the nineteenth century is suggested by Walker's observations on the alternation of *n* and ŋ.

> Hitherto we have considered these letters as they are heard under the accent; but when they are unaccented in the participial termination *ing*, they are frequently a cause of embarrassment to speakers

who desire to pronounce correctly. We are told, even by teachers of English, that *ing*, in the word *singing, bringing*, and *swinging*, must be pronounced with the ringing sound, which is heard when the accent is on these letters, in *king, sing*, and *wing*, and not as if written without the *g* as *singin, bringin, swingin*. No one can be a greater advocate than I am for the strictest adherence to orthography, as long as the public pronunciation pays the least attention to it; but when I find letters given up by the Public, with respect to sound, I then consider them as cyphers; and, if my observation does not greatly fail me, I can assert, that our best speakers do not invariably pronounce the participial *ing*, so as to rhyme with *sing, king*, and *wing*. (lxxxviii)

Walker went on to contrive a remedy for what he called *tautophony*, a term he defined in his *Dictionary* as "the successive repetition of the same sound." What he proposed—and doubtless a few followed him in usage while many more copied his proposal in their orthoëpical works—was to use the *-in* termination when the root ended with *-ng*. Thus words like *singin* and *ringin* would achieve greater beauty by not repeating the ŋ sound; for the same reason, roots ending in *-in* would be pronounced with the -ŋ, for instance *sinning, beginning*. The idea of remodeling English to increase euphony was not Walker's invention, though this proposal was his own stillborn idea.

Walker's account of the variability of *-ing* among the best speakers is revealing, and he concluded his observations on these sounds with the recommendation that the ŋ, rather than *n*, be used "wherever the pronunciation has the least degree of precision or solemnity." That the *g* was a silent letter for many is evident enough from naive spellings: *linning* 'linen', *meten* 'meeting', and *Latyng* 'Latin', for instance.

Modern historians of English have occasionally exaggerated the degree to which *n* was used for ŋ in participles and gerunds. Henry Cecil Wyld (1870–1945) alleged that this "substitution . . . was at one time apparently almost universal in every type of English speech."

At the present time [i.e., 1920] this habit obtains in practically all Regional dialects of the South and South Midlands, and among large

"EVIL COMMUNICATIONS," &c.

Lord Reginald. "AIN'T YER GOIN' TO HAVE SOME PUDDIN', MISS RICHARDS? IT'S SO JOLLY!"

The Governess. "THERE AGAIN, REGINALD! 'PUDDIN''—'GOIN''—'AIN'T YER'!!! THAT'S THE WAY JIM BATES AND DOLLY MAPLE SPEAK—AND JIM'S A *STABLE-BOY*, AND DOLLY'S A *LAUNDRY-MAID!*"

Lord Reginald. "AH! BUT THAT'S THE WAY FATHER AND MOTHER SPEAK, *TOO*— AND FATHER'S A *DUKE*, AND MOTHER'S A *DUCHESS!!* SO *THERE!*"

Social distinctions were important to those whose social status was not immediately obvious. Duchesses, laundry maids, and stableboys were often indifferent to correctness. Governesses often were not. (From *Punch*, Sept. 6, 1873, 99.)

sections of speakers of Received Standard English. Apparently in the twenties of the last century a strong reaction set in in favour of the more "correct" pronunciation, as it was considered and what was in reality an innovation based upon the spelling, was so far successful that the [ŋ] pronunciation ("with -*ng*") has now a vogue among the educated at least as wide as the more conservative one with -*n*. (1936, 289)

Wyld was a fierce language snob, but, thanks to a careful transcription of his English published in 1928, we know that he used the -*n* choice only in conversation (e.g., *comin' down*), not in the more formal style evoked by reading a written script (e.g., *in tracing the oral history;* DeWitt, 265–69). In comments describing an Edison recording of W. E. Gladstone, Wyld noted "there is no 'dropping of the *g*' as might have been expected from a man of Mr. Gladstone's generation" (1934, 619). Because he was so publicly proud of speaking a "more conservative" English, Wyld exaggerated the extent of -*n* for -*ng* in the early nineteenth century.

Nonetheless, Wyld was not entirely wrong. As good an observer as Walker had discerned that many excellent speakers were not "invariable," and for some the -*n* must have been regularly used. Among the earliest lists of "mispronounced" words found in pedagogical works is that compiled by Helena Wells Whitford in 1799; she urged the girls in her charge to correct the sentences: "What a cross creature Miss Benson is; I can't help *hatin* her. She is so proud of her *dancin, coss* she is praised for it" (172). The inclusion of this feature in her "register of defects" (156) suggests that -*n* and -ŋ were stylistically variable and subject to improvement. A decade later, Batchelor carefully observed the Bedfordshire dialect and alleged that "it is not easy to sound *ng* in an unaccented syllable." This difficulty did not restrain him from calling those who used *eatin* for *eating* "illiterate" and the pronunciation negligent (105). Without elaborating his correction into a principle, the author of *Errors of Pronunciation* (1817) corrected *pudden* to *pudding.* Savage, in 1833, altered "you dear little darlin" to "darling" (38), though he makes no general indictment of the -*n* pronunciations. By the time Soule and Campbell turned their attention to the matter in 1873, however, the view had become categorical: "Do not pronounce *ing* like *in;* as *eve'nin* for *eve'ning,* *writ'in* for *writ'ing*" (ix). Indeed, the authorities regarded this usage as first among "common errors." In the 1870s, A. J. Ellis was similarly categorical: "educated English pronunciation" always used *ng;* any substitution of *-n* or alternation of *-n* and *-ng* "is provincial or uneducated" (pt. 4, 1164). Yet in 1875, when the young American Richard H. Dana visited the stately homes of England, he remarked, "I notice that the majority of the people I have met so far drop their 'g's' in the present participle. It is 'huntin',' 'ridin',' etc." (25).

Wyld's claim was correct that there had been a "strong reaction" early in the century. Usage writers usually included the question of final *-ing* among the topics discussed, one alleging that the use of *-n* was "extremely common in all parts of the empire" (*Vulgarities,* 39). The author of this volume quoted Walker respectfully on many questions, but he did not have the tolerance of his predecessor and was quite willing to dismiss the *-in* usage as another mark of the speech of "the careless, the thoughtless, and the half educated" (38). Most revealing for the social historian is the presumed audience for these books: the newly rich. The author of *Vulgarities of Speech Corrected* opened his volume with these words:

> Good breeding and gentility are sooner discovered from the style of speaking, and the language employed in conversation, than from any other circumstance. You may dress in the first style of fashion—(that the tailor or the milliner can do for you), and you may, with a little attention, learn to imitate the lounge or swagger of those in high life; but if you have not attended to your manner of speaking, and the selection of your words, the moment you open your lips you will be discovered, like the daw in the fable, that was tricked out in peacock's feathers—to be the mere ape of gentility—assuming airs to which you have no right, and intruding into ranks where you cannot maintain your ground. (3–4)

People who had "by industry or good fortune risen above their original station" (4) yearned for the polish that accompanied hereditary idleness supported by landed wealth. As Wyld would

later explain, the new class was founded on "the wonderful development of industries which followed upon the application of
steam to manufactures, and the invention of new machines for
weaving and spinning." Those who profited from these technologies "passed from a humble station into the ranks of the
squirearchy, and not a few of them into the peerage" (1914, 287),
though, Wyld remarked, it was only the children of these newly
wealthy families who joined fully in the speechways of the historically rich. (Wyld predicted a similar fate for those who, in the
1890s, entered the upper classes "borne upon a stream of South
African gold" [290].) However willing the aristocracy were to
enjoy the money of the social newcomers, their tolerance for diversity did not permit much latitude for deviance in pronunciation.
Hence the writers who devoted themselves to anatomizing "vulgarity" were attempting to enforce the supposed "purity" of a
social dialect threatened with displacement and change. Insofar as
their strictures had an effect, it was to reshape some of the socially
marked features of English pronunciation.

As far as the evidence allows inferences to be drawn—and
spellings with -ing are not a sure guide—the choice of consonants
in polysyllables ending with spelled -ing was stylistically stratified
(ŋ in "solemn" and "precise" speaking; -n in colloquial styles)
and, increasingly through the century, divided along class lines
(ŋ used by the middle classes; -n by the upper and lower ones). In
his study of the regional dialects in England, Joseph Wright found
that -n was "generally" used in rural areas, but there was an important interplay of style and class. According to his findings, "dialect
speakers" in the western Midlands used ŋk "in all present participles and verbal nouns ending in -ing" when they "try to talk 'fine'"
(1905, 224–25). Such "fine" pronunciations were not restricted to
the folk, however; early in the century the commentators had
detected (and scorned) such pronunciations as *anythink, nothink,
lovink,* and *writink* (Whitford, 169; *Errors,* 3; *Vulgarities,* 40). The
treatment of these final syllables was thus clearly stratified socially.
Stylistically, the lower classes attempted to mimic the middle
class—especially in "fine" speaking—though, in the case of *-ink,*
approximately rather than accurately. Eventually, the upper class

came to mimic the middle class too, though Wyld was scornful of the imitation and repeatedly lamented this departure from the "conservative" English of the nineteenth-century aristocracy, especially when the innovations appeared to be impositions of regional dialect or lower-class speech on the "standard." (Wyld's affection for aristocrats—particularly dead ones—was virtually unbounded. Many nineteenth-century writers treated the usage of the privileged elderly with amused condescension, but Wyld approached them with an emotion verging on reverence.)

> "Ed'ard," "husban'," "edjikate," "Injun," "ooman," "masty" (mastiff), "pagin" (pageant), and the like have gone, but [grɪnɪʤ, nɔrɪʤ, ɔfn, lɪtrətʃə, bousən], and many others, survive from the wreckage. These natural and historic forms are growing steadily less, and every "advance" in education sweeps more of them away. It will be interesting to see what fresh pranks the rising generation will play, and with what new refinements they will adorn our language. (1936, 285–86)

The natural evolution of language change was, for Wyld, a dialectic between needless destruction and upstart rebuilding. His own speech habits formed an ineffable ideal.

The cluster of pronunciations expressing the spelled *-ing* illustrates what early-twentieth-century philologists would call *hypercorrection,* a term founded on the notion that speakers who attempt to increase the formality or propriety of their speech may overgeneralize and thus create new variant forms. Thus, the pronunciation represented by *oving* for *oven* allegedly arises from the perception that final *-in* in "better" English is pronounced with the prestige variant *-ing;* hence *oving* is the "correct" form, just as *finding* is the correct way to spell *findin. Nothink* is another product of the same process, with the ŋk resembling the ŋ in its place, though not manner, of articulation. Consequently, *nothink* is the "right" way to say *nuttin.*

Hypercorrection as a linguistic idea is founded on the notion of a standard pronunciation of which the variants are approximations, but such a term misses the fact that variants may be institutionalized and do not arise each time they are used as self-conscious attempts at "improvement." Some speakers in the nineteenth century may have varied stylistically between ŋ and *n* in these words, while others between ŋk and *n*. It is even possible that all three choices may have been used by individuals, varying their styles according to audience and occasion. Such a range of linguistic choices would have been entirely normal, and, though the first to use ŋk may have been striving for a "fine" style, it is not obvious that subsequent usage was connected to a yen for elegance.

Though the nineteenth century lacked the term *hypercorrection,* the idea it incorporates was central to thinking about pronunciation. One midcentury observer in Britain, Parry Gwynne, offered a distinction of two types of error.

> And having remarked on the *lingering* pronunciation [rhyming *singer* with *finger*], it is but fair to notice a defect, the reverse of this, namely, that of omitting the final *g* in such words as *saying, going, shilling,* &c., and pronouncing them "sayin," "goin," "shillin." This is so common an error that it generally escapes notice, but is a greater blemish, where we have a right to look for perfection, than the peculiarities of the provinces in those who reside there. Besides this "sin of omission," there is the "sin of commission," which consists of adding letters where they do not belong: as, *acrost* for *across; attackt* for *attack; heighth* for *height.* (99–100)

Such pronunciations as these were classified as "vulgar genteel" by one writer, the consequence of people attempting "to speak very fine, without a proper knowledge to direct them" (*Vulgarities,* 8).

The "rules" laid down for the pronunciation for final consonants were bewilderingly complex, however, and unpredictable. Thus, pronouncing the final *t* in *currant* and *currants* was vulgar; the correct way to say these words was *curran* and *currans* (*Vulgarities,* 40). For *current* and *currents,* on the other hand, it would be vulgar to drop the final *t*. It was regarded as "right" to omit the *t* in *castle* and *bustle* (*Vulgarities,* 12) but it should be kept in *apostle* (Savage, 46). Similarly, *trait* was regarded as correctly pronounced without a final *t* in Britain (though not in North America) while *bait* was consistently pronounced with it. (*Trait* was viewed as a "recent" borrowing from French and hence requiring a "French" pronunciation. In the sense of "characteristic," *trait* was well established in English by the mid–eighteenth century.)

These forms show the force of analogy and, at the same time, indicate which pronunciations were variable by style and social class. Of course the critics of usage were mainly interested in showing the ignorance of the unlettered, but in these "errors" can be discerned the processes that shaped language variety both socially and stylistically. Since final consonant clusters were so variable in the prestige dialect, it is no wonder that "fine" speaking and writing produced new forms: *fust* 'fuss', *gownd* 'gown', *intermitting* 'intermittent', *nympth* 'nymph', *paragraft* 'paragraph', *regiment* 'regimen', *scholard* 'scholar', *sermont* 'sermon', *sinst* 'since', *triumpth* 'triumph', *urchint* 'urchin', *wonst* 'once' (examples from Pegge, 47–62; Whitford, 166, 177–79; *Errors*, 17; Savage, 55, 77). These and similar shibboleths became staple entries in the usage books, and anxiety about them was raised. To say that such fears were a hindrance to fluency is to understate the case considerably.

Variation in final consonant clusters produced change at other levels of linguistic structure. Final *-st* was routinely simplified to *-s* in words like *fist* and *mist*. The variables shaping this simplification were very much like those still operating in English: a vowel in the following word inhibits simplification (e.g., *mist along the shore*); a following consonant fosters simplification (e.g., *mist by the millpond*). Grammaticality also comes into play; thus, *mist* is more subject to simplification than *missed* since in the latter final *t* (spelled *-ed*) expresses past tense and in the former it does not. Words with final *-st* are likely to retain the *-t* when spoken in isolation and likely to lose it in continuous speech, particularly in informal settings. A rule of this complexity is subject to change, particularly among children and speakers not influenced by spelling or called to occasions of "fine" speaking. When the *t* of *-st* occurs only to express past tense and before vowels, it is natural that the rule be restructured in the usual way that occurs across generational boundaries. Thus the words historically spelled *fist* and *mist* are more and more pronounced as *fiss* and *miss*. A change of this kind becomes especially prominent when it affects other structural rules—in this case, the change puts *fist* and *mist* in the same group with *fuss* and *miss*. The plural and -*s* verbal inflection of these words produces *fusses* and *misses,* and *fist* and *mist* are treated in the same way. By the end of the eighteenth century, this development had already been noted by Walker in London.

> The letter *s* after *st,* from the very difficulty of its pronunciation, is often sounded inarticulately. The inhabitants of London, of the lower order, cut the knot, and pronounce it in a distinct syllable, as if *e* were before it; but this is to be avoided as the greatest blemish in speaking; the last three letters in *posts, fists, mists,* &c. must all be distinctly heard in one syllable, and without permitting the letters to coalesce. For the acquiring of this sound, it will be proper to select nouns that end in *st* or *ste;* to form them into plurals, and pronounce them forcibly and distinctly every day. The same may be observed of the third person of verbs ending in *ste* or *stes,* as *persists, wastes, hastes,* &c. (xviii)

These continued to be socially marked pronunciations, with alternation between *posts* (often pronounced without *t* but with a lengthened *s*) and *postes* (pronounced as two syllables). The appearance of this process in varieties of English outside Britain later in the century (and more recently) is probably a matter of parallel development rather than influence.

Writing at about the same time as Walker, Samuel Pegge also noticed the plural *postes* for *posts,* but he recorded in addition a double plural that he spelled *posteses* (51). In *Errors of Pronunciation* (1817), the writer observed that this characteristic was typical of the lower orders.

> *Post-es, persist-es,* for *Posts, Persists.* These words are frequently so pronounced by the common class of people; as well as many others, having the same termination: as, *resists, insists, &C.* (24)

The anonymous author of *Vulgarities of Speech Corrected* (1826) provided further elaboration.

> In words ending in "st," the natives of London, and of the South of England, always sound an "e" before the "s," so *postes* for "posts"; and not contented with this they sometimes double the "*es,*" as *posteses.* In the same vulgar way we may hear *ghostes,* or *ghosteses* for

"ghosts"; *fistes,* or *fisteses* for "fists"; *mastes* or *masteses* for "masts." I have also heard *persistes* for "persists"; *hastes* for "hast"; *wastes* for "wast"; *wristes* for "wrist[s]"; *chestes* for "chests," &c. (257)

Pegge's posthumous editor, Henry Christmas, provided as a further example: "This is common in Dorset: as wristesses and fistesses: e.g. 'I hit he such a blow with my fistesses, that I most put out both my wristesses'" (51). Following the tendency toward providing an ancient source for modern variety, Christmas offered parallel examples from Gavin Douglas and Shakespeare. These double plurals, however, were likely a more recent creation with their origin in so simple a phonetic detail as the deletion of *t* in final *-st.* This tiny simplification was followed by pluralizing what was regarded as the "proper" singular: thus, *postes* in the singular, *posteses* plural—analogous to *Justice* and *Justices.* Of course these were not conscious decisions made separately by speakers who used the double plurals but the diffusion of a phonetic change that resulted in the application of the universal rule for English plurals, the addition of the *-es* syllable when the root ends in a sibilant. There was no reason to assign this change to "difficulty of pronunciation" (as Walker had done) or to believe that Londoners "always" formed plurals in this way (as the author of *Vulgarities* alleged). But these were naturally evolving linguistic changes that were, for most speakers, arrested or reversed in the course of the century.

As English came to be spoken increasingly outside the British Isles, pronunciations proliferated. For some, this was a matter for melancholy or despair. Thus, the American philologist Maximilian Schele de Vere declared in 1867: "It is unfortunately but too true that English is becoming daily less euphonious. . . ; this deterioration of sounds is progressing at a formidable rate" (54–55). Toward the end of the century, some even feared that English would split into separate languages, sharing only an unphonetic writing system. In 1877, Henry Sweet had predicted that in a century "England, America, and Australia will be speaking mutually unintelligible languages, owing to their independent changes of pronunciation" (196). Harbingers of such developments were already appearing in the vowels, and Sweet reported having heard *take time* pronounced as *tike tarm* (*r* indicating vowel length): "this from speakers who, although not very refined, certainly belonged to the upper middle class" (196). Developments like these, he thought, would cause increasing differences in the geographically and socially separated varieties of pronunciation.

While Sweet's prediction proves to have been premature, he was correct in extrapolating from the eighteenth century to his own day. Southern England and Wales had long been separated in many details of pronunciation from northern England, Scotland, and Ireland, and there was no reason to think the differences would diminish. Beyond Europe, English south and east of Suez was changing in directions different from those in much of the British Isles, and there were even more numerous differences separating Britain from North America. Spheres of influence fostered by empire created, globally, two hemispheres of English: one North American (with Canada drawn firmly within the orbit of the United States), the other incorporating southern England with Australia, New Zealand, South Africa, and India.

Three sound changes that reshaped English in the nineteenth century can be used to illustrate the waves of change that radiated out from the center—that is, from the prestige dialect of southern England. In these examples, the origin of change lies at the center, reaching the periphery of the English-speaking world at different rates determined by history and geography.

Three pronunciations will be discussed in historical sequence: loss of consonantal *r* after vowels and before consonants; vowel changes yielding, for some varieties, a different sound in *gas* and *mask;* shift in the pattern of initial *h* in words like *house* and *herb.* In each of these cases, some evidence can be found for very early instability—often identifiable in the naive spellings of early English writings. The change in English in each of these ways, however, takes its modern shape in the nineteenth century.

Loss of *r* was the earliest of these changes; it affected the prestige variety of southern England, but did not markedly influence English in Scotland or Ireland. Except for a few East Coast cities, it did not reshape the language in North America either, though the other varieties of world English share the preference of London. Differentiation of *gas* and *mask* had a similar, though subsequent, effect, with southern English at the center separating the vowels and the other national varieties of English participating to lesser degrees in differentiating them. Loss of initial *h* is the most recent of the three changes; it does not occur as a stigmatized usage in North America and appears (though less frequently than in Britain) in Australia (as would be expected from the sequence of settlement history). In modern England, *h* loss is a powerful shibboleth in the phonological snobbery of British English—though currently challenged for that dubious honor by glottal stop.

Weakening of *r* from a trilled consonant was first reported in Britain at the end of the sixteenth century, though *r* had already begun to change in the Middle English period, especially before *s* and *sh*. In the seventeenth century, *r* after a vowel first lost its trill (and hence medial and final *r* was differentiated from initial *r*) and then began to vanish (with profound consequences for the southern English vowel system). In its place was left a consonant that appears to have disappeared sometime in the eighteenth century (Jespersen, 1:360), being replaced by a vowel (usually [ə]), causing the lengthening of the prior vowel, or, sometimes, merely being omitted. The result of these changes was to split words into two forms, with and without r, and these were among the characteristics of seventeenth-century folk speech as used by the first permanent English-speaking settlers in North America, among others. In general, the *r*-less member of the pair was less formal than the one retaining the *r*: *burst, bust; curse, cuss; girl, gal; horse, hoss; parcel, passel*. These differentiations were slow to emerge, however, partly because the commonly used word (like *cuss*) could only acquire a distinct meaning once an alternative (like *curse*) had been differentiated from it. Early manuscript town records from colonial New England are full of spellings that reveal this lack of *r* in speech (for instance, *clak* for *clerk, Bostorn* for *Boston;* see Krapp 1960, 2:228–30). What is striking, however, is that the weakening and eventual disappearance of this *r* is not discussed by observers, either in North America or Britain, until the end of the eighteenth century. One likely reason for this indifference to a major sound change is that the innovators in the change were speakers of the prestige dialect, fully satisfied that the letter *r* represented their own speech while the "vulgar" (and consonantal) *r* was a departure from it rather than a survival of earlier usage.

The shift from consonantal to vocalic *r*, though sporadic earlier, gathered force at the end of the eighteenth century. Once again Walker provides the most useful insight into its status, his near contemporaries having been satisfied with the traditional view that "R has uniformly one sound, as in the English word *rear*" (W. Smith, xliii).

> There is a distinction in the sound of this letter, scarcely ever noticed by any of our writers on the subject, which is, in my opinion, of no small importance; and that is, the rough and the smooth *r*. Ben Jonson, in his Grammar [published in 1640], says it sounded firm in the beginning of words, and more liquid in the middle and ends as in *rarer, riper;* and so in the Latin. The rough *r* is formed by jarring the tip of the tongue against the roof of the mouth near the fore teeth; the smooth *r* is a vibration of the lower part of the tongue, near the root, against the inward region of the palate, near the entrance of the throat. This latter r is that which marks the pronunciation of England, and the former that of Ireland. In England, and particularly in London, the *r* in *lard, bard, card, regard,* &c. is pronounced so much in the throat as to be little more than the middle or Italian *a,* lengthened into *laad, baad, caad, regaad;* while in Ireland the *r,* in these words, is pronounced with so strong a jar of the tongue against the forepart of the palate, and accompanied with such an aspiration or strong breathing at the beginning of the letter, as to produce that harshness we call the Irish accent. But if this letter is too forcibly pronounced in Ireland, it is often too feebly sounded in England, and particularly in London, where it is sometimes entirely sunk; and it may, perhaps, be worth of observation, that, provided we avoid a too forcible pronunciation of the *r*, when it ends a word, or is followed by a consonant in the same syllable, we may give as much force as we please to this letter at the beginning of a word, without producing any harshness to the ear: thus *Rome, river, rag* may have the *r* as forcible as in Ireland; but *bar, bard, card, hard,* &c. must have it nearly as soft as in London. (Walker, xc)

Walker thus precisely described the phonetic environment for *r* in southern England: "strong" in initial position (even permissibly trilled); "weak" before a consonant in the same syllable; "soft" or "sunk" in syllable-final position.

Some of the principal authorities on pronunciation at the end of the eighteenth century were Scots, and since Scotland did not participate in the weakening of *r*, it is understandable that they continued to repeat the received wisdom that *r* was "invariable." Their counterparts in the southeast were not quick to supply a social evaluation for the new usage. In 1830, George Jackson gives the unilluminating advice, "learn to pronounce the *r* distinctly" (20), and warns against pronouncing *corn* as "cawn" and *girl* as "gaal" (9, 13). The usually severe Savage provides no general indictment of the pronunciation, though he criticizes *bust* for *burst*. The author of *Vulgarities* inveighs against the courtroom pronunciations "*lu'dd* and *lu'ddship*, or still worse *la'dd* and *la'ddship*" (42) and provides a useful early view of the *r*-less pronunciations.

> [I]t may be remarked in this case that the natives of London leave out the "r" altogether in many words where it ought to be sounded, though but slightly. We thus hear them say *pul* for "pearl"; *wuld* for "world"; *ghell* or *gul* for "girl"; *mal* for "marl"; *cawnt* for "cant"; and *cawd* for "card." (256)

Here the "slight" sound of *r*, the weakened consonant, was put in opposition to a lengthened vowel sound, that of "father" (in *marl*) or of "bawd" (in *card*). These changes, however "vulgar" they might strike a critic's ear, did not materially affect the distinctive sounds of English since the new sounds made the same distinctions in words as did the old ones.

As the *r* sound moved from "soft" to "sunk," however, a new structure of distinctions emerged. Given the perennial anxiety among the elderly that the language will collapse as a consequence of the slipshod pronunciations of the young, it is surprising that these changes did not excite more controversy. With the dissimulation of *r*, a great many separate words came to be pronounced alike (or nearly alike): *arms, alms; farther, father; iron, ion; tuner, tuna*. (The merger of *arse* and *ass* in Britain caused anxiety since *arse* 'buttocks' was taboo in polite society; the solution to this problem was to alter the vowel so the words were pronounced differently, *arse* rhyming with *grass* and *ass* 'donkey' with *lass*.) Since one of the principles of purism is to maintain distinctions at all costs, the fact that these changes were generally ignored by the London elite is especially important. In fact, the changes were not so much ignored as denied by those who made it their business to "regulate" the language. These observers were very much influenced by what Ellis called, rather pedantically, "involuntary interference of orthographical reminiscences with phonetic observations" (pt. 4, 1195). So attached were these observers to the historic spelling of words that the poets of the "Cockney" school (principal among them being John Keats) were routinely roasted for such rhymes as "crosses" and "horses," even though these were full rhymes in the speech of the elite. Even as the change from "weak" to "sunk" *r* spread more widely, the prejudice against rhymes drawn upon it continued with much the same intensity, though significantly the objections arose mainly from those whose speech was shaped outside London. Thus, Thomas Wright Hill (1763–1851), a native of the west Midlands and a schoolmaster in Birmingham, declared in 1821 that the sound of *r* was properly formed when the stream of air was made "to vibrate sensibly." His opinion shows the low esteem with which outsiders viewed the innovative *r* of London.

> Indeed, the *r* of our language, when correctly formed, is among the most pleasant of articulate sounds, and ought more carefully to be preserved for posterity than can be hoped, if the provincialists of the Metropolis and their tasteless imitators be to be tolerated in such rhymes as *fawn* and *morn*, *straw* and *for*, *grass* and *farce*, &c., &c., to the end of the reader's patience. (22)

Resistance to the spreading London fashion was, however, not long sustained in Britain.

As the weakening of noninitial *r* spread through the prestige speech of London, the metropolitan "provincialist" began to regard the *r*-ful varieties of English as deviant. In Northumberland, the trilled *r* had long been formed at the back of the mouth rather than with the tip of the tongue. This pronunciation was soon regarded as an affliction, and as early as 1839 a medical authority had defined *rotacism* (later spelled *rhotacism*) as "a vicious pronunciation of the Greek P, common in the northern parts of England; especially near Newcastle" (Dunglison, 535). Criticisms of *r*-ful speech as a pathology were apparently uncommon, but travelers' tales often included reports of the exotic "burr" of the northeast of England (see *OED*, s.v. *burr*). Resistance by *r*-ful speakers to these criticisms was mostly feeble and ineffectual. In 1873, for instance, James Murray described his Scots English as a norm for *r*-pronouncing.

> Even the initial English *r*, in *road, rung*, is softer and more gliding than the Scotch, which is used with equal sharpness before or after a vowel, as in *rare, roar, rayther, roarer*. In the south of England its subsidence after a vowel into a mere glide renders it impossible to distinguish, in the utterance of some speakers, between *law, lore; lord, laud; gutta, gutter; Emma, hemmer*. (120)

Murray's testimony is of even greater interest since as his eminence and reputation grew in England, he altered his speech toward the southern standard, with the result that he was remembered as having a "'somewhat affected' Scotch enunciation" and "a curious Anglo-Scotch nasal accent" (K. Murray, 109, 298). No wonder that Ellis, less censorious by far than most observers, declared: "The varieties of *r* are the most remarkable in English speech" (pt. 4, 1330n).

Just as the presence of a vowel in the following syllable helped to preserve the *t* in *-st* clusters, so the same phonetic conditioning produced what came to be called "linking" *r*. Linking *r* was heard when weakened *r* occurred at the end of a word and the next word began with a vowel (for instance, "butter and eggs"), a feature that would be noticed only once final *r* had been omitted before a following consonant (for example, "butter churn"). The first of these new *r*s had appeared in the eighteenth century in such constructions as "your aydear is" and "the windore opened" (quoted from Smollett's fiction by Jespersen 1961, 1:372). These pronunciations were allegedly features of uneducated speech, but they probably spread rapidly through all social levels, where weakened *r* was moving toward deletion. In 1779, another Scot, Sylvester Douglas, noted "a very extraordinary use" of this feature among Londoners; "I have been astonished," he wrote, "to hear this barbarous pronunciation in the mouths of some persons of education" (134–35).

Soon linking *r* was established, and intrusive *r* began to appear words like *bananar*. In 1873, Murray concluded his celebration of "Scotch" *r*, quoted above, by noting this recent phonetic practice.

> Hence, when these words are used with a following vowel, a hiatus is avoided by saying draw-*r*-ing, Sarah-*r*-Anne, Maida-*r*-'ill [= Maida Hill], idea-*r* of things, law-*r* of England, phrases which even educated men are not ashamed, or not conscious, of uttering. No such liberties are allowable with the Scotch *r*, which is always truly consonantal. (120)

The insertion of this "unetymological" *r* in such phrases coincided with the movement of "weak" *r* from a consonant to a vowel. Walker had noticed the intrusion of *r* in such words as *window* and *fellow* (producing the forms spelled *winder* and *feller*) and described the pronunciation as "almost too despicable for notice" (lxxiii). The usage writers of the nineteenth century castigated these appended *r*s, and the words listed as containing them were often ones used very frequently (like *Mammarr* 'Mama' and *Paparr* 'Papa') or by educated people (like *Apollorr* 'Apollo'; *Vulgarities,* 255–56). Prejudice against these intrusive *r*s was ingrained early by the London "authorities"—for instance, by Whitford (1799), who reprobated *Mamar,* and by the author of *Errors of Pronunciation* (1817).

> *Idear* for *Idea.* Many people are guilty of this error, when the following word begins with a vowel: as, *I have not the least idea*r *of it.* For the same reason, they sound an *r* at the end of all Christian names ending in *a:* as, *Is Maria*r *out? Is Louisa*r *at home?* Great pains should be taken to avoid this error. (15–16)

In a guide for female servants published in 1825, the author seems to despair of correcting this usage.

> The manner in which certain words are pronounced is also a very evident mark of vulgarity. One of the most remarkable instances

of this kind in England is the sounding of an *r* at the close of words ending in *a* or *o*, as when you say "idea *r*" for "idea," or fello *r*" for "fellow," or windo *r*" for "window," or "yello *r*" for "yellow." This is extremely difficult to be corrected when once it has become a habit; and so regularly does it follow in every word of similar ending, that you may hear persons say "Geneva *r*" for "Geneva," as commonly as children say "mamma *r*" and "papa *r*." (*Duties,* 113)

These writers of the first quarter of the century noted that this intrusive *r* was heard especially from "people who affect to speak well" (*Errors,* 11). As the century progressed, observers were forced to admit that these unhistoric *r*s were not merely used by the vulgar and affected but had extended upward to include "the dialect of good society, in the pronunciation of eminent preachers and University professors" (1886; quoted, with other extracts concerning this feature, by Jespersen 1961, 1:370–72). By the end of the century one authority—a German—even recommended that this *r* be included in instruction in spoken English for foreign learners (as in "put a comma *r* after headmaster").

Pronunciation of noninitial *r* shows a process begun earlier but brought to completion in the nineteenth century. Despite blusterings about the "vulgar" and the Cockney early in the century, the weakening and loss of *r* (and the consequent rise of linking and intrusive *r*) came to completion early and at all social levels influenced by London fashion, just in time for the English of Australia, New Zealand, and South Africa to be drawn within the sphere of the change. In North America, only New England, southern New York, and the coastal South (from Baltimore to New Orleans) took part in the general weakening of noninitial *r*, though even in these districts the loss of *r* was not universal. There is nothing surprising in this parallel development for, despite political differences, the cities were part of a single speech community, increasingly so in the first half of the century, as business and cultural contacts developed between British ports and the seacoast cities of North America.

The question that has been given less attention concerns the opposite side of this change: Why did some regions of the English-speaking community *not* participate? In Britain, the answer seems simple enough; the places retaining historic *r* in some form had systematically resisted the innovations of London English for centuries. That *r* loss did not extend to Ireland, Scotland, or the north of England is not surprising. In the branches of English west and south of Britain on the Atlantic, the regions where *r* loss did not take place included Barbados (but nowhere else in the Caribbean), Newfoundland, the interior North (Ontario, western New York, Ohio), Pennsylvania, and the interior South (western North Carolina, eastern Kentucky and Tennessee).

Explanations offered in the past for these anomalous regions have been generally unsatisfactory, though they may include contributory factors—for instance, schooling with an excessive emphasis on the spelling of English words and consequently support for the retention of *r* as a consonant. Some historians have suggested that the weakening of *r* took place in the coastal cities of North America in response to London fashion (for instance, Van Riper, 13). Still another explanation suggests that the migrations to the interior of eastern North America took place before the change to *r*-less pronunciations was completed in the seaboard cities, but settlement history shows that the migrations took place after the eastern cities had established the *r*-less pattern apparent in rhymes and naive spellings. Further, this explanation does not take account of the fact that there were pockets of *r*-pronouncing within the region of *r* loss—including Plymouth, Massachusetts, the site of the first settlements by English speakers in the early seventeenth century.

The retention of old-fashioned *r*-ful speech in the western reaches of English along the Atlantic basin arose from a cause identical to that operating in Britain. Irish, Scots, and inhabitants of England from the midlands northward all resisted the "tasteless" innovation of London and the example of epigones of London in such cities as Belfast, Liverpool, Boston, New York, and Charleston. This resistance continued unabated through the century, as, for instance, Richard J. Lloyd (from the north of England) maintained. As late as 1895, Lloyd declared that the London pronunciation of *r* was abhorrent to outsiders: "to the four-fifths of

English speakers who use them, the entire dropping of *r* sounds slipshod and emasculate" (53). Charles Remy, an American, regarded *r*-less speech as "grossly inaccurate" and was at a loss to explain why this fashion had been adopted in "the speech of the Harvard or Oxford professor, the farmer of New England, the professional man, the planter, the mountaineer, and the colored man of the South" (419). In his usage book of 1856, Walton Burgess, a New Yorker, had similarly criticized the loss of *r.*

> Be careful to sound distinctly the *r* in such words as *farther, martyr, charter, murder,* &c. Never say, *fah-ther, mah-tyr, chah-ter,* and *muh-der.* On the other hand, avoid *trilling* the *r,* as *mur-er-der, r´r´robber.* It is altogether too tragical for common life. (47)

British writers also tried to stem the drift toward *r*-lessness; as late as 1880, a London "authority" declared:

> Don't drop the sound of *r* where it belongs, as *ahm* for *arm, wahm* for *warm, hoss* for *horse, govahment* for *government.* The omission of *r* in these and similar words—usually when it falls after a vowel—is very common. (*Don't,* 65)

Strictures of these kinds did little to stem the flood of *r*-lessness worldwide, to alter the emergent opinion that the London speech style was the standard for the empire, or to change the idea that the English of Boston, Richmond, and Charleston merited high prestige and deserved imitation by others.

Not everyone rushed to mimic London fashion. Little in the first two centuries of the transatlantic migration of northerners induced a desire to follow London fashions in English. Most North American settlers, in fact, had little direct experience of London speech and less interest in imitating it. Newfoundlanders maintained close contacts with seafarers from Ireland and the *r*-ful areas of the west coast of Britain (see Anderson, 19, for the distribution of *r* in this part of contemporary England). Barbados had become a penal colony for the revolutionaries against the London government in the seventeenth- and eighteenth-centuries (most of whom were Scots and Irish), and the nineteenth-century descendants of these settlers, supported in their speech by further

NINETEENTH-CENTURY ENGLISH

migrants from the *r*-pronouncing areas of southwestern England, simply carried on the pronunciation styles of their ancestors (see Niles). (Descendants of British and African parents were known as "Black Irish," in part because of their retention of *r*-ful speech.) At the time of the American Revolution, Philadelphia was a city dominated by Ulster Irish. (Benjamin Franklin estimated that more than a third of the population of 350,000 was from or descended from English-speakers in the north of Ireland.) New York was not far behind Philadelphia in attracting Scots and Irish at the end of the eighteenth century, and most who left the city for the frontier migrated north and then westward along the Hudson and Mohawk waterways into the areas where consonantal *r* would be maintained into modern times. Similarly, Irish migrants to Charleston soon moved westward through the long-settled plantations of the lowlands to establish smallholder agriculture in the foothills of the Appalachians, taking with them the traditional *r* pronunciation (see Dickson; Leyburn). In all the areas where these migrants settled, the old-fashioned *r*-ful speech was preserved. Of course north Britons and Irish were also represented in the migrations to Australia and South Africa, but they were not the majority, and, most important for English, they did not migrate in family and clan groups (as their kinfolk had to the United States and Canada) but most often as soldiers (with supporting civilian followers) or as convicts sent into exile from the London prisons. Military and penal life did little to support traditional ways of speaking, and despite the social distance between guards and prisoners, London norms eventually prevailed in prestige speech.

Resettlement of former slaves along the Atlantic coast provides an additional insight into the spread of *r* through migration. At the time of the American War of Independence, the British offered freedom to slaves who joined the loyalist cause, and, at the cessation of hostilities, some three thousand men and women were resettled in the Atlantic colonies of Canada. In 1792, some two thousand of them embarked for Sierra Leone, and their colony, established around Freetown, constituted the first anglophone settlement in Africa. The English of these settlers had been formed in the southeastern region of the United States, and surviving documents reveal that *r* was retained in many historic positions; its gradual erosion in spoken English had begun, however. Some spellings show that it had disappeared in speech (for instance, *hon-nah* 'honor' and *yea* 'year'), while its insertion in spelling reveals that the sound did not provide a clue to the written form (for example, *larst* 'last' and *drowr* 'draw'; see C. Jones, 87–90). A generation later, in 1821, an additional eleven thousand former slaves from North America settled in neighboring Liberia. Their English was similarly based in the southeast United States, and they moved to the *r*-less fashion through continual contacts with African-Americans who represented the prestige form of southern coastal American English (see Hancock). Both Sierra Leone and Liberia completed the shift from *r*-ful to *r*-less speech.

This sketch of the history of noninitial *r* in the nineteenth century encapsulates some of the dynamism of sound change characteristic of the period. Despite attempts to manipulate pronunciation through schooling and books of linguistic etiquette, change took place, with the result that *r*-less speech became the norm for London-based varieties and *r*-ful English for the Scottish-, Irish-, and Philadelphia-based varieties—the former influential for much of the empire (though not for Canada), and the latter for the rapidly growing western cities in the United States (like Pittsburgh, Cincinnati, and St. Louis). Of course, the process of *r* loss had begun much earlier, and within the regions there were always minorities holding to the old pronunciations or attempting to advance the new ones. Nonetheless, the prestige pronunciations of the twentieth century emerged from the turmoil of migration and the growth of the English-speaking population in the nineteenth. *R*-loss was one of dozens of potential changes that offered themselves in 1800; it was among the most striking to be codified and stratified in the social beliefs about the sounds of English.

A second transforming nineteenth-century sound change involves the evolution of the vowel sounds in *gas mask*. Four combinations are possible for the vowels in these two words in twentieth-century English: two with the same vowel and two with different vowels. For North Americans and north Britons, this phrase usually contains the same vowel in both words—that of *hat* (phonetically [æ]). For Caribbean speakers, the vowel in both words is that of *father* ([ɑ] or a vowel similar to it). Within Britain among English-descended people, the *father* vowel in both words is regarded as affected. Southern British prestige speech offers a two-vowel model: *gas* with [æ] and *mask* with [ɑ]. Imitators of this prestige variety occasionally confuse the high-status preference and produce *gas* with [ɑ] and *mask* with [æ]. The reversed combination is regarded as comically aberrant, as a confusion induced by a striving after effect and as worthy of contempt. For the great majority of English speakers, therefore, the possibilities are between [æ] in both words or [æ] in *gas* and [ɑ] in *mask*. This modern distinction in southeastern prestige speech in England is almost entirely the result of nineteenth-century sound change, though, as with *r*, earlier evidence can be found for its nascent stages.

For the latter decades of the century, variant pronunciations in these words ranged unpredictably between [*æ*] and various vowels produced with the tongue lowered (centralized or back). Lloyd's 1895 note depicts the situation clearly.

> There remains the doubtful *ă* of *last, after,* &c. Unlike most phonetic difficulties this is not chiefly a question concerning the right sound to be employed, but of the right words in which to employ it. The North favours the short vowel [i.e., [æ]] and the south the long one [i.e., [ɑ]], but I have never met any speaker North or South, who consistently used either the long or the short vowel in *all* the doubtful words. I myself use the long vowel in *path, master, plaster, aunt.* I know many people who oscillate between *păst* and *pāst, demănd* and *demānd,* and so on. The remarkable thing is that they seem to take this departure, so distant both in length and quality, *per saltum;* there are no intermediate shades. The long vowel, therefore, is quite familiar to Northern ears and is always accepted as good educated pronunciation. (53)

Several of these observations offer insight into the situation in England at the end of the century: the phonetic distinction between the two vowels was seen as having no intermediate stage (speakers "jumped" to one or the other); neither vowel was seen as inherently superior, though the [a] was treated by northerners as more likely to be used by southerners (i.e., speakers of the London prestige accent). But most speakers were unpredictably variable in their usage (e.g., either vowel might occur in such words as *past* and *demand*).

This variability was not, however, without social evaluation, for by the end of the century the [a] pronunciations were coming to be regarded as "better" than the [æ] alternatives. Thus, Richard Grant White, an American visitor to Britain, reported in 1880 an increasing use of [a].

> I observed, however, a stronger tendency [than in the speech of "well-educated, well-bred people in the Northern and Eastern States of the Union"] to the full, broad *ah* in some words, and to the English diphthongal *a* (the name of the letter, *aee*) in others. At Westminster Abbey I observed that the officiating canon said "comm*ah*ndment" and "*r*emembr*a*nce," trilling the *r* as well as broadening the *a;* and at King's Chapel, Trinity, Cambridge, where I sat next to the reader, my ear was pleased with his "powe*r* and comm*ah*ndment." I heard the same broad *ah* sound of *a* in transpl*a*nt, p*a*st, c*a*st, *a*sk, and the like from three distinguished authors, one of them a lady, whom I have the pleasure of meeting in London. At the debates among the young men at the Oxford Union, I heard the same broad sound,— gr*ah*nted, cl*ah*ss, p*ah*sture, and so forth. But at St. Paul's, in London, a young deacon who said, "He*ah* beginneth the tenth chapt*ah* of the book of Kings," said, "And then it came to p*ă*ss," and yet worse "p*ă*th," clipping his *a*'s down to the narrow vowel sound of *an*. On the whole, however, the broad sound very greatly prevailed among the university-bred men. (380–81)

For an outsider—White was a puristically inclined American writer on English—the two sounds had acquired distinct social values, the [a] sound in the "doubtful" words having acquired a prestige value and the [æ] sound being regarded as either "provincial" or "worse" than the [a].

At the beginning of the nineteenth century, the distribution of these vowels was quite different. The [a]—later to become the prestige vowel—was recognized by Walker in only a few English words. For Walker, the [a] sound was rarely found in English anywhere.

[B]y some [phoneticians] it is styled the middle sound of *a*, as between the *a* in *pale,* and that in *wall:* it answers nearly to the Italian *a* in *Toscano, Romana,* &c. or to the final *a* in the naturalized Greek words, *papa* and *mamma;* and in *baa;* the word adopted in almost all languages to express the cry of sheep. We seldom find the long sound of this letter in our language, except in monosyllables ending with *r,* as *far, tar, mar,* &c. and in the word *father.* There are certain words from the Latin, Italian, and Spanish languages, such as *lumbago, bravado, tornado, camisado, farrago,* &c. which are sometimes heard with this sound of *a;* but except in *bravo,* heard chiefly at the Theatres, the English sound of *a* is preferable in all these words. (xxxvi)

This sound Walker called the "open" sound of *a*, but he also identified a "long" counterpart of the same vowel quality. The choice of this long sound (phonetic [æ:]) was conditioned in monosyllables by the nature of the following consonant.

The long sound of the middle or Italian *a* is always found before *r* in monosyllables, as *car, far, mar,* &c., before the liquids *lm;* whether the latter only be pronounced, as in *psalm,* or both, as in *psalmist;* sometimes before *lf,* and *lve,* as *calf, half, halve, salve,* &c.; and, lastly, before the sharp aspirated dental *th* in *bath, path, lath,* &c. and in the word *father;* this sound of the *a* was formerly more than at present found before the nasal liquid *n,* especially when succeeded by *c, t,* or *d,* as *dance, glance, lance, France, chance, prance, grant, plant, slant, slander,* &c.

The hissing consonant *s* was likewise a sign of this sound of the *a,* whether doubled, as in *glass, grass, lass,* &c. or accompanied by *t,* as in *last, fast, vast,* &c.; but this pronunciation of a seems to have been for some years advancing to the short sound of this letter, as heard in *hand, land, grand,* &c. and pronouncing the *a* in *after, answer, basket, plant, mast,* &c. as long as in *half, calf,* &c. borders very closely on vulgarity. (xxxvi)

The complexity of this "rule" for the prestige pronunciation of these words is a good indication of the instability of choice at the very beginning of the century.

Modern writers on the history of the sounds of these words have acknowledged this complexity. Jespersen noted that "in some instances it is very difficult to explain . . . the final result" of the sound shift (1963, pt. 1:310), and both Wyld and Wells assert that "the details and timing of the changes involved are not altogether clear" (J. Wells, 232; see Wyld 1936, 204). Compounding the difficulty is that writers on pronunciation copied from one another (thus obscuring the change in progress) and that comparisons with other languages were often highly approximate. ("Italian *a*" is a typically unhelpful parallel; Giuseppe Baretti, who published an English grammar for Italian learners in 1771, says nothing of English [æ] and conflates the [æ] of *actor* with the [a] of *father* [see Barisone, 78, 80].) Nonetheless, the late-eighteenth-century writers on English pronunciation provide the best evidence for the situation that presented itself to speakers in the decade of the 1790s and in the first years of the new century.

Walker's observations quoted above provide a useful point of departure. To begin with, he declared that the sound in question was "seldom" found in English. In this, he repeated the views of Robert Nares, who compiled a word list in 1784 that he believed to contain "all the words in which this sound of *a* occurs," a grouping of just over one hundred that he thought "inconsiderable" (3–7). Like Walker after him, Nares identified the phonetic environments especially conducive of the use of *a*: *-f* (e.g., *staff*), *-lC* (e.g., *calm, half,* and *salve*), and *-s* (e.g., *glass, cask, mast*). Walker, however, adds *-r* as an especially favorable context for the selection of *a;* by adding this environment to those listed by Nares he was supplying the missing link between eighteenth- and nineteenth-century pronunciations, the fact that the vocalization or loss of *r* had the effect of lengthening the previous vowel. It is important to note, however, that the word lists provided by Nares and Walker do not correspond to the distribution of [æ] and [a] in any twentieth-century dialect of English.

In addition, Walker recognized that a sound change was afoot and that progress toward [a] had been "advancing" for some years. That a change was taking place was reported by other writers of the 1790s. Thus William Smith—having extended the [a] to many more words than Nares or Walker—recognized in 1795 that a change was occurring.

In almost all the words which are the subject of the seven foregoing notes, the pronunciation of Messrs. Sheridan and Walker is daily gaining ground; from its being adopted by the best actress, which this, or perhaps any age ever produced; as also by some of our first-rate speakers in both Houses of Parliament (8)

While helpful as evidence that a change was in progress, Smith's observation is somewhat confused by the fact that Sheridan had not identified the [a] words and Walker had used the symbol for the sound sparingly. Consequently "the pronunciation of Messrs. Sheridan and Walker" was divergent, and it is not obvious just what sound was "gaining ground." The influence that Smith construes as a cause was probably an effect; the "best actress," Sarah Kemble Siddons (1755–1831), and the members of Parliament were articulating an emergent prestige norm whose exact qualities remain elusive. Such usage Smith attributed to "all the natives of London" (7), though he intended by that expression the elite rather than the mass of the citizenry. Whatever the sound was, it met with his approval since he called those who used it "good" and "accurate speakers" (7–8).

Other observers also noted the emergent social meaning attached to the *a* words, though not as enthusiastically as Smith had. Stephen Jones, writing in 1798, criticized Sheridan for having failed to distinguish the *a* of *half, calf, psalm, ah,* and *father* from that of *hat, camp,* and *man.*

> Mr. Walker's more correct ear led him to admit this fourth sound of *a* (which, indeed, ranks *second* in his scheme); but seems to have employed it with too much timidity: I hope it will not be found that I have been too prodigal in the use of it. It occurs in this dictionary in such words as *la⁴st, pa⁴st, a⁴sk,* &c.; and I must venture to express my humble opinion, that giving to those and similar words the flat dead sound of *a* in *la¹ck, la¹tch, pa¹n, a¹nd,* &c. is encouraging a mincing modern affectation and departing from the genuine euphronical p[r]onunciation of our language. (vi)

The revulsion Jones expressed for the "flat dead sound of *a*" was echoed in 1809 by Batchelor.

> It has been before noted, that the vowels of *task* and *order* are perceptibly longer than the similar ones in *pan* and *top;* yet, in these

instances two opposite errors should be guarded against: they should neither be produced with the tedious provincial drawl, nor according to what Mr. Jones calls "a mincing, modern affectation," by which *lass, palm, past, dance,* &c. are passed over as hastily as *pan, mat, lack,* and *fan.*

It will be observed, that the long sound of these letters occurs, mostly, before double consonants, and particularly before *l* and *r;* as, in *balm* and *born.* (18–19)

If all these observers were evaluating the same pronunciations, there were now three possibilities for words of this class: (1) a "traditional" pronunciation in which most of the words in question had the same vowel; (2) a "mincing" innovation (Jones), one perhaps bordering "very closely on vulgarity" (Walker); (3) a sound typifying "a tedious provincial drawl" (Batchelor).

In their dictionary of 1821, George Fulton and George Knight mirror the advance of the sound change. For them, the words spelled with *r* and *lC* following *a* now have the vowel of *ha*—for instance, *bar, farce, calm,* and *calf.* This same sound is "contracted" to the vowel of *ass* in a variety of phonetic environments—for instance, *staff, pass, bath,* and *dance* (x). While the class of words with *a* became much larger as successive lexicographers turned their attention to it, the distinction was still one based on length—"prolonged" and "contracted" in the terminology of Fulton and Knight.

The question still remains, however, of just what was the quality of this short-long pair. The answer suggested by many historians is confirmed by an unnoticed experiment designed by Robert Willis (1800–1876), an English scientist famous throughout the century for his engineering talents. In 1828–29, Willis presented two lectures to the Cambridge Philosophical Society subsequently published as "On the Vowel Sounds, and on Reed Organ-Pipes." In treating English vowels, Willis measured the pitches he thought best corresponded to the long vowels of his own speech. (He was a Londoner, born to privilege and educated privately until he matriculated at Cambridge in 1822.) His results show that the "short" and "long" variants of *a* were diverging in quality. Measured as distance between the vibrating reed and the end of the resonating pipe of Willis's apparatus, the distinction that had emerged between [æ] and [æ:] was clearly shown. While these findings were criticized (for instance by Henry N. Day) for confusing pitch with vowel quality, they do show the relative positions of the vowels. Both [æ] and [æ:] were distinct from [ɑ:] (particularly with following [r]), but *paw* remains distinct from *naught*. The modern vowel system had emerged, though with different realizations of the vowels from those of present-day British or American English (see Catford 161, Edwards).

In 1836, B. H. Smart revised Walker's *Dictionary* and offered the following view of the question:

> ă This sound, which is properly deemed the second sound of the letter *a*, differs in quality as well as in quantity both from ā or a^1 and a^3:—it is much nearer to the latter than the former.—indeed so near, that in theory they are considered identical; but it is not, practically, so broad as a^3. The word *fat* in a Londoner's mouth has even a narrower sound than *fat* (a coxcomb) has in a Parisian's. Perhaps in no language other than our own is there that complete shutting in or stoppage of a sound at the next instant from its utterance, which is characteristic of this and the following five sounds. At the same time, it must be confessed that when *f, s,* or *n* follow the letter, we are apt, even in London, to give a slight prolongation to the vowel, which would in other cases be quite rustic; as in *graft, glass,* or *plant;* which slight prolongation was universally accompanied by a decidedly broader sound, such as might be signified by *gra³ft, gla³ss, pla³nt.* Among speakers of the old school, this is yet the mode of sounding *a* in such situations; but metropolitan usage among educated people has for a long time inclined to change a practice which the orthography of the words manifestly does not warrant. (v)

According to Smart, the "traditional" usage of the 1790s had become obsolescent by the 1830s. It consisted of the [æ] vowel in nearly all of the words, but the innovations had begun to displace that usage. The pronunciation that so offended Walker and Jones was the "shortening" of this [æ] as a consequence of "mincing"; thus, *lass, palm, past,* and *dance* were pronounced "nearly as hastily" as *pan, mat, lack,* and *fan.* A primary distinction, then, was established between "short" and "long" vowels in these words, so that by the time Smart turned his attention to the "slight prolongation" of the vowel, traditional usage had come to be associated with the "tedious provincial drawl" criticized by Batchelor. What made the situation so unstable was that the words "properly" used with the short or long variant of [æ] could not be predicted.

The orthoëpists, finding it difficult to deal with unstable variant usages, tended to squabble over notation systems rather than to assess the linguistic situation. Yet the variety of usage in the first decades of the nineteenth century was anticipated by Jones in a preface dated 1798.

> Let it be asked, for instance, if a difference of sound be not required in the two words pa⁴ssable and pa¹ssible? yet Mr. Walker makes none; or in the words fa¹t, fa⁴ther; ba¹rren, ba⁴rter; ca¹rrot, ca⁴rman? yet all are marked alike by Mr. Sheridan. If the decision be against me, I have egregiously erred, and shall bow to correction. If otherwise, I shall take credit for no small portion of courage, that could lead me, in a point of such importance, to try a fall with so able a rhetorician as Mr. Walker. I beg, however, to be allowed to repeat, that though I have in very many instances used this sound, I have not done it licentiously or indiscriminately; but have restrained myself in every instance wherein a shadow of doubt as to its propriety presented itself to my mind. I consider it as a legitimate English sound; and believe its unmerited degradation and disuse to be of very recent date. To prevent, however, any misconception of my meaning in the use of this sound, be it observed that my 4th *a*, though it is more open than the *a* in *hat*, stops considerably short of the broad protracted pronunciation so commonly heard among the vulgar, who say, *fáäther, cáälf, háälf*, &c. (ix)

What so complicated the situation at the very end of the eighteenth century was the process of "correction" in conflict with the principle of description. But Jones and his contemporaries began to guide the curious in their attempt to steer a way between the "mincing" of the *a* vowel made too "flat" and "short" and the "broad protracted pronunciation" of the vulgar and the provincial.

All the muddled commentary of the period makes clear that an audible sound change was in progress with the greatest change taking place among the London elite, who were variously influential in the outlying districts (just as they had been with the earlier process of the vocalization of *r*). Not only was length an issue in the *a* words, so too was vowel quality. In fact the [æ] and [æ:] variants were undergoing realignment in the direction of other vowels, though this change did little to affect the English of Ireland or Scotland or of the interior of North America (except in a few isolated examples where *ant* and *aunt* might be distinguished in dialects otherwise typified by the traditional [æ] in the other affected words). Among the London elite, however, the *a* words tended to split in two directions, leaving behind a residue of forms where [æ]was maintained. Thus, Walker assigned [æ] to *ample, sample, example,* and *trample,* but Jones, almost immediately, recognized that *ample* and *trample* had the [æ] vowel while *sample* and *example* had acquired a different vowel, the ancestor of modern RP [*a*]. Walker had recorded the [æ] sound in *mask,* but Jones used the "new" [*a*] and thus provided the first differentiation that is the basis for the modern shibboleth *gas mask.* In *plant* and *rant,* Jones identified both as having [æ], but by the time Murray turned his attention to these words in the *OED,* they had been differentiated, the former with [*a*] and the latter with [æ].

The new distribution of the *a* words split the class: some words remaining the same, some vowels moving forward and up in the mouth, others down and back. (In these sound changes, the nineteenth century recapitulated a process that had earlier taken place in Middle English.) Linguistic conservatives often wished to preserve earlier pronunciations, and thus the author of *Vulgarities* inveighed against any departure from "traditional" [æ] "in such words as *chawnce* 'chance'; *dawnce* for 'dance'; *pawst* for 'past'; *bawsket* for 'basket': *awfter* for 'after'; *awnser* for 'answer'; *plawnt* for 'plant'; *mawst* for 'mast'; *grawss* for 'grass'; *cawn't* or *can't* for 'cannot' &c" (256–57). Savage poured out scorn on the use of [*a*] in words that "properly" should have kept [æ].

> [W]hat if a *Fribble* [an "effeminate dandy" in Savage's gloss] should say to us, I put the pl*ant* with the *glas* into the *bas-ket* which was *gr-anted* me and carried it as a *samp-le* to the *cas-tle.*—We ask of every man if it would not disgust him to sickness? (xxvi–xxvii)

(Savage's correction of "razor strop" to "strap" is another evidence of his preference for [æ] [75].) The same complaint about the "new" sound of *a* underlies Percival Leigh's derision, in 1840, of "cockneys" who pronounced "caun't" and "shaun't" for *can't* and *shan't* (25). The momentum of linguistic change, in southern England at least, was so forceful that the point of these complaints is nearly lost on modern readers from that part of the anglophone world. Throughout the century, critics attempted to preserve the traditional [æ] pronunciations against the "vulgar" innovations. Thus George Jackson in 1830 urged the vowel sound of *hat* in *gather* and *have* (instead of *gether* and *hev*). Savage reprobated the pronunciation of *catch* as *ketch*. "Duncan" in 1877 wanted an [æ] in *haunt* and *gauntlet* (rather than what he spelled *hawnt* and *gawnt-let* [56]). But the shift from [æ] proved irresistible among those hewing to the London fashion. Jackson, Savage, and the others would have been dismayed to discover that by 1880 the advice had turned in favor of the pronunciation they had ridiculed: "Don't pronounce *calm* and *palm* as if they rhymed with *ham*. Give the *a* the broad sound, as in *father*" (*Don't*, 65).

The sound change begun in earlier centuries was thus elaborated in a typically nineteenth-century way into a series of shibboleths. With so erratic a pattern of usage, the elite could stigmatize outsiders in unprecedented detail. Oliver Wendell Holmes, the Boston "autocrat," poked fun in 1858 at English used to "reach immense conclusions, touching our lives, our fortunes, and our sacred honor." One such "insignificant" piece of evidence came from "telling a person who has been trying to please you that he has given you pretty good 'sahtisfahction'" (109). Holmes was a humorist, finding amusement both in the affectation and in the judgment of usage, but he and his educated readers obviously believed that *satisfaction* should have kept its traditional [æ] and not acquired the "new-fangled" [*a*]. Richard Grant White, Holmes's near contemporary, who was not a humorist but a linguistic snob, wrote rather more seriously about the matter.

> It may here be pertinently remarked that the pronunciation of *a* in such words as *glass, last, father,* and *pastor* is a test of high culture. The

tendency among uncultivated persons is to give *a* either the thick, throaty sound of *aw* which I have endeavored to describe, or, oftenest, to give it the thin flat sound which it has in "an," "at," and "anatomy." Next to that tone of voice which, it would seem, not to be acquired by any striving in adult years, and which indicates breeding rather than education, the full, free, unconscious utterance of the broad *ah* sound of *a* is the surest indication in the speech of social culture which began at the cradle. (1872, 62)

White's judgment about the "social culture" of one's "breeding" would not have surprised Savage and his contemporaries. However they would have been astonished to learn that neither the "thin flat sound" nor the "thick" pronunciation, but instead another sound, one that they had worked so hard to eradicate, had become the index of prestige.

The full range of variants produced by the change affecting *a* words was described by the highly censorious but acute author of *Vulgarities* as early as 1826.

The letter "a," for example, when pronounced short, has properly a sound intermediate between "e" in "fell," and "a" in "fall," but a Scotsman endeavouring to speak English almost uniformly mistakes it for the first and pronounces "bad"—*"bed,"* "tax"—*"tex,"* "lamb"—*"lemb,"* "black"—*"bleck,"* "hand"—*"hend,"* "back"—*"beck,"* "fat"—*"fet,"* "cattle"—*"kettle."* This is miserable and disgusting affectation, but it does not stop at the words where the "a" is properly short, but is foolishly carried into words where the "a" should sound broad, as in "far," or "water," and the affecting Scotsman will accordingly pronounce "command"—*"commend,"* "demand"—*"demend,"* &c. This broad sound of "a" is also given to words where it should be short, as "wax"—*"wawx,"* "waft"—*"wawft,"* "canal"—*"canawl,"* "lamb"—*"lawmb,"* "dam"—*"dawm,"* "many"—*"mawnny,"* "any"—*"awny."* The last two are very common affectations. (224–25)

What makes these observations especially interesting is that the "Scotsman endeavouring to speak English" had quite a good ear for the restructuring of the [æ] words then taking place in southern England, recognizing which variants had moved up and forward and which down and back in the articulation space. In 1874, "foreigners" told A. J. Ellis that he made "no distinction between *man* and *men*," and he concluded that the difference among (.a, ah, æ) is "very difficult, and few ears are to be trusted" (pt. 4, 1147).

A factor contributing to the spread of [*a*] in southeastern England was the vast increase in the number of loanwords that entered English in the nineteenth century. Walker had noted that borrowings from Latin, Italian, and Spanish were likely to have the [*a*] pronunciation, giving as examples *lumbago, bravado, tornado, camisado,* and *farrago*. Some of these had been long established with English pronunciations, but the growing tendency in the nineteenth century was to give "continental" vowels to perceived loanwords. One of the words mentioned by Walker, *bravo*, had existed in English since the sixteenth century but had been commonly pronounced "brave-o." The modern pronunciation with [*a*] displaced this tradition in the nineteenth century. Even Walker did not recommend the [*a*] in all the words he listed; thus, *lumbago*, though "often pronounced with the Italian sound of *a*," was correct in his view with a more "English" sound, that is [æ]. Savage and the other writers of the 1820s did their best to regulate the pronunciation of loanwords; thus, Savage recommended *blancmange* with [*a*] (instead of *blue-monge*). Smart, in 1836, recommended [æ] in *giraffe*, but that pronunciation was displaced in Britain by the [*a*] "properly" used in a borrowing, even a long-established one. Whether such words became (or remained) "English" depended on a great variety of factors, among them frequency and breadth of use. By the end of the century (as recorded in the *OED*), a set of related words might have various vowels. *Canto* 'subdivision of a poem' and *canticle* 'hymn' kept their "English" [æ], but *cantata* and *cantabile* were pronounced with the "continental" [*a*]. The social meaning attached to these variants was clear: use of [æ] in "foreign" words was old-fashioned or aristocratic; use of [*a*] was either "correct" or "hypercorrect" depending on the preferences of a tiny elite. Mocking this snobbery, W. S. Gilbert, in 1884, put the following rhyme words in the mouth of a female character given to self-congratulation over her "correct" manners: *bravado, tornado, gambado, mikado. Mikado* and *bravado* were both well established with [*a*] (though in earlier centuries, the stressed syllable of *bravado* had the vowel of *cave*). By the 1880s *tornado* and *gambado* did not "properly" contain the [*a*] vowel. The joke lies in her excess of "correctness" in the use of the continental vowel in all four, and such excess by overuse of [*a*] extended well into the twentieth century. For the nineteenth century, however, the use of these vowels remained extremely unstable. Writing in 1874, A. J. Ellis was at a loss to predict the outcome of the change. "In a performance of *King John*," he wrote, "I heard Mrs. Charles Kean speak of '(kææf) skin,' with great emphasis, and Mr. Alfred Wigan immediately repeated it as '(kaaf) skin,' with equal distinctness" (pt. 4, 1148). By 1890, stratification of usage by social class seems to have emerged. In that year, speaking at Edison Studios, London, Florence Nightingale pronounced the word *Balaclava* with [*a*] in its first and third syllables; on the same occasion, Kenneth Lanfrey, a bugler who had accompanied the Light Brigade, pronounced the word with [æ] in both (see Vincent).

With usage so widely varying, dictionary makers hoped to ascertain a "compromise" or "intermediate" vowel. The most prominent exponent of this solution was the American lexicographer Joseph Emerson Worcester. He proposed a symbol that bridged the distance between *æ* and *a*.

> The *fifth* sound of *a*, marked thus ã́, is an *intermediate* sound of this letter, between its short sound, as in *fat, man,* and its Italian sound, as in *far, father:*—this sound being somewhat shorter than the Italian sound of *a*. With respect to the class of words which, in this Dictionary, have this mark, there is much diversity among orthoepists. Most of these words are marked by Nares, Jones, and Perry with the Italian sound of *a*, as in *far, father;* but Walker, Jameson, Smart, Reid, and Craig mark them, or most of them, with the short sound, as *a* in *făt, măn;* Fulton and Knight mark them as being intermediate between the short and the Italian sound; and Smart, though he gives to *a* in most of these words the short mark, says, in relation to it, "that when *a* is followed by *f, s,* or *n,* there is, in many words, a disposition to broadness in the vowel, not quite in unison with the mode of indication, as may be perceived in an unaffected pronunciation of *grass, graft, command*. This broadness is a decided vulgarism, when it identifies the sound with *ä*. The exact sound lies between the one indicated and the vulgar corruption. (xiii)

The proposed "intermediate" sound became a regular feature of nineteenth-century pronunciation schemes, particularly when Noah Webster's successors adopted it in their popular dictionaries of the later part of the century.

Acute contemporary observers derided the intermediate sound as a fiction, however. William Dwight Whitney, in his 1874 sketch of his own usage, declared "in my natural utterance I have absolutely no knowledge of anything intermediate between *far* and *fat*" (207). Reviewing Richard Grant White's *Words and Their Uses,* he pointed out the linguistic situation in southern New England.

> We happen to be of the number of those fortunate or praiseworthy people to whom the open "Italian" sound of *a* is natural in such words as *glass, last, pastor;* but we are unable to take to ourselves so much credit therefor as Mr. White is eager to give us. We heartily wish this mode of utterance were indeed a sign of high culture from the cradle up, or that people could be persuaded to regard it as such; for we detest the flattened utterance *păss,* as part of the phonetic degradation of English; but we fear that the difference depends on locality rather than culture; and, moreover, that in another generation or two, he who says aught but *păss* will be laughed at as a provincial. (1871, 307)

Whitney's irony was an attempt to explode the idea that the difference between the two vowels was evidence of "degradation" or "a sign of high culture." He was quite straightforward, however, in his inability to predict which of the two would prevail "in another generation or two."

In the early twentieth century, philologists continued to debate whether or not there was an "intermediate" vowel between [*a*] and [æ]. Louise Pound declared that "this compromise vowel is somewhat academic, or artificial" (1915, 387), and George Philip Krapp declared that Worcester's compromise vowel "was an invention of theory [rather] than . . . an established custom in practice" (1960, 2:75). Such artifice, however, allowed the dictionaries to stake out a neutral position between the two sides of the usage dispute. When Whitney had turned his hand to lexicography in *The Century Dictionary,* he stated frankly that the "interme-diate" sound "should be regarded rather as pointing out the vary-ing utterance here described than as imperatively prescribing any shade of it" (1889–91, 1:x). Murray was similarly willing to allow artifice to displace description; in the *OED,* he declared: "The vowel in p*a*ss, comm*a*nd, variously identified by different speakers with *a* in m*a*n, and *a* in f*a*ther, is symbolized by the avowedly ambiguous *a*" (l:xxxiv; see further Penzl; Bronstein; MacMahon, 100–101).

The variation in the [æ] and [*a*] words took on great social significance, particularly in America, where democratic impulses in education attempted to foist the "prestige" pronunciation on children whether they wanted it or not. Writing in the early twen-tieth century, Krapp reflected on the prior era of language instruction.

> The result [of attempts to promote good English] has been to give the [a:] extraordinary dictionary and academic prestige in the face of a strongly opposing popular usage. The reasons for this are several: first, that standard British speech and some forms of New England speech have [*a:*] in the words in question; second, that New England has exerted, and to some extent continues to exert, a strong influence upon formal instruction and upon notions of cultivation and refinement throughout the country; and third, that the pronunciation [æ] is often prolonged, or drawled, and nasalized in a way that makes it seem not merely American, but provincially American. To steer between the Scylla of provincialism, [æ:], and the Charybdis of affec-tion and snobbishness, [*a:*], many conscientious speakers in America cultivate [a:]. The writer has tested this sound on many different groups of speakers from various sections of the country, and has never found one who used the sound who did not do so with a certain degree of self-consciousness. If the cult of this sound continues long enough, it may in time come to be a natural and established sound in the language. In the meantime, it seems a pity that so much effort and so much time in instruction should be given to changing a natural habit of speech which is inherently just as good as the one by which the purist would supplant it. Especially in public school instruction it would seem to be wiser to spend time on more important matters in speech than the difference between [hæf] and [ha:f]. (1919, 64)

As with other attempts to manage linguistic change, the futile attempt to intervene in a sound shift did not ultimately affect unself-conscious pronunciation. In Canada, *drama* still keeps its historic [æ] in broadcast speech. American *sass* retains [æ] while its cognate *saucy* is pronounced with a "new sound" resulting from the nineteenth-century change. Hunters in the United States will shoot *partridge* (with [a]) but describe themselves as having been on a *pat hunt* (with [æ]). Australia maintains a length contrast between [æ] and [æ]: (though it is a minor contrast), thus maintaining two centuries later the opposition whose beginning point was in the 1790s (see Hammarström, 7–9). Such residual pronunciations are not surprising in a sound change so recent as this one.

Once the change had commenced, no amount of "authority" was effective in altering its overall direction in the anglophone world, and the ideology it encapsulated was, if not persuasive, at least a cause for anxiety. Writing from the Merton chair of English language at Oxford in 1934, H. C. Wyld expressed his surprise that [a] was "rare" in provincial speech and declared with Olympian confidence that [æ:] "is neither as sonorous nor as beautiful" as *ă* (607). This preposterous statement would have astonished the observers of the 1820–40s who had worked so hard to maintain [æ] against the inroads of the "vulgar" [a]. Throughout the century, however, the evaluation of the two sounds was often confused. In 1915, C. H. Grandgent of Harvard deduced the situation in New England from the early decades of the previous century.

> [W]e may infer that "ah" first prevailed in vulgar speech, and that "făst" as late as 1840, retained a flavor of bygone preciosity. To-day, on the contrary, in the consciousness of most Americans, "fahst" implies a striving after old-world elegance, while "făst" is characteristic of up-to-date democracy. (14)

Grandgent also noticed the "curious" fact that some teachers in the [æ] areas inculcated [a], while the reverse was true in the [a] territory.

(From the viewpoint of linguistic historiography, the scant treatment of [æ] and [a] reflects the view that English had achieved its modern form some centuries ago. An excellent and thorough history of English, published in 1987, says simply of the sounds in *laugh, dance,* and *car:* "This new [æ:] developed into [ɑ:] in the course of the 19th century" [Lass, 131]. Wyld was compelled by the evidence to place the change in a "comparatively recent" era, not much earlier than the end of the eighteenth century (1936, 204–5). Even the intriguing idea that women led the change to [ɑ] has not received attention; A. J. Ellis, in 1874, associated the use of [ɑ] with "ladies, and especially those who do not like broad sounds" [pt. 4,1148]. In part, this neglect is a consequence of the view that "educated" and "refined" speech is conservative, though it is abundantly clear in this case that the new prestige norm in RP was a recent innovation that took place in spite of the best efforts of the regulators to discourage it.)

A third sound change that took on significant social meaning in the nineteenth century involved the use of *h.* Of the three sound changes considered here, it is the most recent and influences England but not Ireland, Scotland, Canada, or the United States. Australia, New Zealand, and (to a lesser extent) South Africa also participate in the change; in the Caribbean, it appears sporadically (with examples reported from the Bahamas but not from Barbados, Tobago but not Trinidad [Winer, 16]). On the basis of this present-day geographical distribution alone, it is reasonable to locate this change in the nineteenth century.

Murray's account in the *OED* provides an introduction to the history.

> In recent times, the correct treatment of initial *h* in speech has come to be regarded as a kind of shibboleth of social position; this has resulted in the cultivation of the educated usage in many quarters where it is not native. But even in educated pronunciation, there are cases in which *h* is usually mute, e.g. at the beginning of a syllable after certain consonant groups, as in ex*h*aust, ex*h*ortation, and in such suffixes as *-ham, -hope,* in *Chatham, Clapham, Durham, Greenhope, Stanhope, Tudhope, -herd* in *shepherd,* as well in the pronouns *he, his, him, her,* when unemphatic and as it were enclitically combined with the preceding word, as in "I met-him on-*h*is horse." In the corresponding neuter pronoun *it,* originally *hit,* in which the unemphatic use predominates, the *h* was long ago dropped in writing as well as speech. (But in Scotch the emphatic form is still *hit.*) (*OED,* s.v. *H*)

That *h* was variable in earlier forms of English is apparent from spelling and early commentary. Thus, John Palsgrave in 1530 had observed that *h* was not pronounced in *honest, honour, habundance,* and *habitation,* among other words. Nonetheless, the dropping of *h* did not become a conscious shibboleth in Britain until the very end of the eighteenth century (see Wyld 1936, 296). In North America, for the most part, the historic usage generally prevailed, with spelled *h* pronounced in most words excepting *heir, heirloom, herb,* and a few others.

Walker listed only fifteen words where initial *h* was "properly" omitted (including *heir* and *herb*). Significantly, Samuel Pegge's description of London "vulgarisms" does not mention *h*. (Pegge had died in 1800 and his work was published posthumously.) As early as 1799, however, Helena Wells Whitford had noticed that the "young females" she taught in her London school were given to saying *eart* 'heart', *ardened* 'hardened', and *abit* 'habit'; perhaps her acute sense of nuances of pronunciation was a result of her American birth (the family emigrated to Britain in 1774 when Helena was fourteen, her parents displeased by the revolutionary inclinations of their South Carolina neighbors).

Fictional illustrations of socially significant *h* appear in Laetitia Matilda Hawkins's four-volume novel, *The Countess and Gertrude* (1811). According to T. L. Kington Oliphant, these usages anticipate a flood of despicable usage.

> We now find tricks played with the letter *h;* the evil habit was just coming in, which has now overspread the whole land South of Yorkshire; a lady's-maid talks of a *himperial* (imperial), iii.96; a rustic talks of a *ot* loaf, iv.232; these are early instances of the vilest of all our corruptions in speech. (2:202)

Hawkins (1760–1835) certainly did not invent these usages; Fielding and Smollett had anticipated her in using them in fiction (though sparingly), but she was clearly alert to two aspects of *h* about which an elaborate lore developed in the nineteenth century—*h* loss (in words where it had historically been pronounced) and *h* insertion where no such sound was represented in spelling.

In 1809, Batchelor reported as an example from "the Cockney dialect . . . *Give my orse some hoats*" (29). The usage writers soon added this feature to their repertoire of mistakes. In 1817, *Errors of Pronunciation* warned against *art* for *heart* and *harm* for *arm*. Jackson, by 1830, was mainly concerned with *h* insertion (in, for instance, *howdacious* 'audacious', *hinkstand* 'inkstand', and *hoile* 'oil'), but he recommended that the *h* be omitted in *hospital, hour, herb, heir, honour, hostler, humour,* and *humble,* words earlier noted by Walker as lacking *h* in prestige speech. The author of *Vulgarities* (1826) had a much more extensive list that included both *h* loss and *h* insertion (258–61). It was, he claimed, a selection from a longer catalog, too long for publication in his book (though sufficient demand would encourage him to publish it separately). By 1836, Smart declared that the process of this change arises from "perverseness." Successive writers extended the description and intensified the abuse.

The author of *Vulgarities* declared that "these mistakes are by no means confined to London, but may be met with in every part of England" (257). But the omission of *h* was balanced by a severe view of those who pronounced their *h*s too vigorously. Savage, in fact, provided a defense of the stigmatized feature in his recognition that Londoners did not confuse *heartless* and *artless,* even when the former lacked its initial *h*.

> If the Metropolitans drop a sound so inimical to that softness which constitutes a peculiar beauty in speech, they are justified in so doing upon all the principles of good taste: they reject a harshness to adopt an excellence. A native of London would make no difference in the sound, were he to say "she is artless," or "she is heartless," fully persuaded that the context and spirit of the discourse would exhibit the sense without the possibility of perversion or the chance of misunderstanding.
>
> But the Provincials, accustomed to a harsh determination of the voice[,] regard this nonaspiration as the most unvenial of sins. Habituated to the halloo of the chase, to speak against the roaring of the wind, to call from hill to hill, to vociferate in the forests, they acquire a peculiarity of intonation by which they are instantly recognised; and, if they obtain an easiness of guttural enunciation, they must admit that the pre-eminence thus exclusively possessed is not unaccompanied with disadvantage, for like Midas who, when he had

obtained the favour of the God, was compelled to turn every thing
into gold, so the rustics attach their rough breathing indiscriminately
to every letter capable of receiving it. We thus hear of H-India, h-
orthography, h-ell-wide, h-ebony, h-instinct, h-oxen, lacerating at the
same time their own larynx and afflicting the more delicate tympana
of their metropolitan auditors by a cacophonous pseudology as
ridiculous as it is falsely imagined to be proper. (xxxvi–xxxvii)

This argument from climate and from the practice of yelling sup-
posedly fostered by outdoor life was taken quite seriously as an
explanation for sound change. More interesting, however, is Savage's implied approval of *h* loss in London as a "natural" consequence of "softness" and "good taste." Such an explanation suggests that he regarded *h* loss as a characteristic of polite society as
well as of ladies' maids and rustics. *H* insertion, on the other hand,
he regarded as "cacophonous pseudology."

Savage's palliation of the emerging deletion of *h-* has another
side in his recognition that Londoners do not confuse *artless* and
heartless. Of course he suggests that the "context and spirit of the
discourse" would obviate any ambiguity. Writing in 1842, another
critic of usage notes both *h* loss and *h* insertion as "that most cockney of errors." He recognized that the sound change was systematic and therefore the affected words not likely to be confused.

> It is a very difficult question to determine whence this vice arose. It
> could not come of ignorance of orthography; because the obstinacy
> with which the offender goes wrong in every possible case, seems to
> imply a positive knowledge of the rule so steadily broken, without
> which the doctrine of chances must sometimes tell and lead him
> right. Nor are we aware of any dialectic difference among our Saxon
> ancestors, of which our friends, the cockneys, are the inheritors. Be
> this, however, as it may, there is not a more certain sign for exclusive-
> ness to seize upon; and there is not a footman in all St. James's who
> would give entrance to the man who should ask, "Hi say, his your mas-
> ter in the ous?"—no, not even though the fellow himself knew no bet-
> ter than to reply, "No, e hisn't, e's gone to Ighgate." (Morgan, 217)

("Positive knowledge of the rule" is still adduced to minimize
the importance of this sound change; in present-day London,

Harry Hawkins Had His Hen in an old Hat-box, lined with Hay and Hair.

The great shibboleth to emerge in nineteenth-century British English was the loss of historic initial *h* and the insertion of epenthetic *h* in words beginning with vowels. Pamphlets aimed at self-improvement and ridicule by comedians kept the feature uppermost in the anxieties of the ambitious. (Eccles, frontispiece. Reprinted by permission from the copy in the British Library; for a similar illustration, see Mugglestone 1995, 134.)

J. C. Wells reports, "a London school teacher tells me he has only to look sternly at any child who drops an /h/, and that child will say the word again, this time correctly" [1:254].) The "exclusiveness" of *h* use had been fully established by the 1830s, and vituperation about the norm was often expressed in moral terms. At the same time, efforts were made to assist the afflicted in mastering the use of *h*—for instance *Poor Letter H: Its Use and Abuse* (by "the Hon. Henry H.," 2d ed. London, 1854) and *Henry Hawkin's H Book: Shewing How He Learned to Aspirate his H's* (by Ellen Ann Shove Eccles, London, 1857). These works were often droll, however, produced for the amusement of the (mostly) secure rather than the improvement of the (mostly) deficient.

The fact that *h* shift (and *h* anxiety) were localized in south-eastern England invited further humor, some of it international. Thus "Duncan" in 1877 told an anecdote to illustrate the fact that North Americans did not participate in the process: "'Do you drink hale in your country?' an English cockney asked of an American. 'No,' the latter replied: 'we drink thunder and lightning!'" (43). Perhaps less amusing was Kington Oliphant's story of "a servant who had dropped into a large fortune."

> [He] asked his master how he was to pass muster in future as a gentleman. The answer was, "Dress in black and hold your tongue." (2:226 n. 2)

By the end of the century, the doctrine of *h* as the "shibboleth of social position" (in Murray's words) had achieved its full flowering. Kington Oliphant seems not to have been too severe in reporting the social consequences of this shift.

> As I have made a few strictures upon American vagaries, I ought, in common fairness, to acknowledge that no American fault comes up to the revolting habit, spread over too many English shires, of dropping or wrongly inserting the letter *h*. Those whom we call "self-made men" are much given to this hideous barbarism; their hopes of Parliamentary renown are too often nipped in the bud by the speaker's unlucky tendency to "throw himself upon the 'Ouse." An untaught peasant will often speak better English than a man worth half a million. Many a needy scholar might turn an honest penny by offering himself as an instructor of the vulgar rich in the pronunciation of the fatal letter. (2:226)

An American visitor to the House of Lords in 1880 found that not all "hopes of Parliamentary renown" had been dashed and that *h* loss and insertion were both to be heard there. He galled his English audience by pointing out that some members of the nobility confused '*igh* and *high*, while "persons of the greatest pretensions to literary culture said '*ivery*' or '*hivery*' for '*every*,'although some of them had diplomas from Oxford or Cambridge" (Fonblanque, 331).

Fiction writers and the humor magazine *Punch* made full use of the possibilities of *h* loss or *h* insertion to represent "nonstandard usage." Charles Dickens was the most popular author in making fictional characters distinctive through the use of the vernacular. In 1836, in *Pickwick Papers,* the first of his works to achieve great popularity, Dickens created two Cockney characters, Sam Weller and his father. Their language might easily have been constructed solely on the basis of Pegge's characterization of 1800, and it is full of traits that exercised the usage writers. In a typical specimen, Sam is represented as a thorough Cockney.

> This here money he's anxious to put someveres vere he knows it'll be safe, and I'm wery anxious too, for if he keeps it, he'll go a lendin' it to somebody, or inwestin' property in horses, or droppin' his pocketbook down a airy, or makin' an Egyptian mummy of his-self in some vay or another. (860–61)

Unexpectedly, *h* does not figure as a shibboleth in this passage, though Savage had already denounced *hairy* 'sunken courtyard giving access to the basement of a dwelling' (< *area*) as an impropriety of London English (9), and *orses* had also been mentioned by Batchelor as Cockney usage.

Though anticipated by Laetitia Hawkins, other writers were slow to adopt *h* as a social marker in fictional speech. Among the first to achieve great popularity for it was R. S. Surtees, whose serial stories of John Jorrocks, a Cockney grocer turned fox hunter, were collected as a volume in 1838 and reached a wide audience. Surtees was, however, at first quite tentative in representing *h*, and in the early Jorrocks tales he provided glosses for "'are (hare)" and "'ams (hams)," though none for "'osses" and "'ounds" (1968, 13, 51). Surtees became celebrated as a humorist with a good ear for English; both Dickens and Thackeray admired and imitated his rendering of social nuance in dialogue. As a northerner, Surtees was well placed to observe sound changes evolving in the south. Though increasingly regarded as a "coarse" writer, Surtees used all the socially salient features discussed in this chapter and more to decorate the speech of his richly varied sportsmen (see Welcome).

Percival Leigh's *Comic English Grammar* reveals that the use of *h* (whether inserted or omitted) had become a stock figure of linguistic fun by 1840. Savage's attribution of strongly aspirated *h* to rural hallooing was forgotten, and Leigh attributed the distribution of the sound to phonetic "ease"—initial *h* omitted when the prior word ended in a consonant and pronounced when following a vowel. *H* was also likely to be strongly aspirated, he thought, when it occurred in "the expression of excited feeling."

> You *h*ignorant *h*upstart! you *h*illiterate 'og! 'ow dare you to *h*offer such a *h*insult to my *h*understanding?—You are a *h*object of contempt, you *h*are, and a *h*insolent *w*agobond! your mother was nothing but a *h*apple-woman, and your father was an 'uckster! (43)

By the end of the century, the subject merited an entire volume, *The Aspirate,* by Geoffrey Hill (author of *The English Dioceses*). Hill mixed humorous anecdote with ill-informed speculation about *h* in languages other than English, declaring with apparent solemnity that persons who did not agree in their use of *h* should not marry each other (13). He noted that *h* was often "abused" by strivers and parvenus.

> In English an "h" is often put on by those among the uneducated who wish to talk correctly. . . . It is not as a rule the very poor who introduce h's, but the small shopkeeper and the villager who reads at home in the evening instead of going to the public house. They are slightly better educated than many of those with whom they associate, and naturally wish to make their superiority evident; for some reason they adopt this plan of doing so. We have been told that there lives or was living a short time ago at Grasmere a village schoolmaster who, as coming from the Midlands, or, as Northerners would say, from the South, would drop his h's. The people of Grasmere do not naturally drop theirs; but in their opinion the English of the schoolmaster was model English, and therefore they would drop them if they wished to show themselves off in their best light—if, for example, they spoke to tourists. (43–44)

As for the other sound changes discussed in this chapter, evidences can be found in spellings that suggest prior variability, but the nineteenth century codified the social meanings associated with the use of *h*, and unnoticed variation coalesced into an artifact of regional and class distinction.

In treating *h*, nineteenth-century historians were inclined to project present prejudice into past practice. Thus A. C. Champneys, in 1893, recognized that consciousness about *h* had begun to form "in the latter part of the last century," but he put the origin of the change at a much earlier date. "The most terrible example is at the end of the Apostles' Creed, in the East Midland dialect of English (about 1250), namely, 'life with-*h*utin *h*end'" (360). Of course there is no evidence that this insertion of *h* was regarded as "terrible" in the thirteenth century, but Champneys was so formed by the views of his own day that he misconstrued the historical evidence to see these *h*s as insertions and thus gave the most "vulgar" of English sounds its own horrible history.

Not all nineteenth-century descriptions of *h* were so suffused by aesthetic outrage and moral displeasure. The rise of scientific language-study made it possible for scholars to take a more dispassionate view of such blemishes, and some recognized that the sound changes identified in antiquity could be discerned in contemporary speech. Early in the century, Erasmus Rask and Jacob Grimm had explained the prehistoric split of consonants, accounting for the correspondence of such Germanic and Latin-Romance words as *fatherly* and *paternal, thrice* and *triple, hundred* and *century, twosome* and *duet, kin* and *genus.* The social origins of such a change, however, remained elusive, and scholars wondered how a speech community could come—either gradually or suddenly—to such distinct pairs. With the evolution of philology as an examination subject in midcentury, "boys and girls in their teens are sometimes required not merely to state, but to *explain* the Law in question" (Douse, 1). So widespread was the fascination with the operation of "sound laws" in antiquity that some scholars looked to language variety of their own day to see how change took place.

In 1876, Thomas Le Marchant Douse undertook to show analogies between the Germanic "consonant shift" and the distribution of *h* in the speech of England. Douse's abstract schema for sound change was based on two particular principles: a "dissimilating sentiment" (by which sounds are lost) and a process of "cross compensation" (by which they are restored, though in a different arrangement). These principles come into operation, Douse explained, as a consequence of the "principle of least effort": "human nature" inclines speakers to simplify their exertions in speech (and elsewhere). Social class was for Douse the most inviting explanation for speech change; "the standard and literary dialect of a language" is slow to change since literate speakers "resist a too rapid debilitation" (37). Illiterate and nonstandard speakers are unable to "resist" the debilitating principle and thus introduce changes that may trickle upward to affect the standard dialect. Such had been the case, he thought, when the Germanic and Romance languages had begun to evolve differing consonants from a common parent language. First laxity unsettled the inherited system; then, among a portion of the population, arose "an uneasy sensation, a dim consciousness, that something is defective or amiss in their own phonetic machinery" (45). For Douse, sound change could be explained simply on the basis of the idea that the upper classes were more fastidious and less inclined to reduce their efforts; the lower classes were careless and given to "debilitation." Such could be seen in southern British *h*.

> A favourite example of Cross Compensation is furnished by the de-aspiration and the compensatory aspiration of the thorough-bred Cockney, and others. . . . People who at one moment talk about the '*air* of the '*ead* almost invariably terrify us the next moment with the truly Gorgonian *h*air of the *h*atmosphere: such vagaries form an inexhaustible mine of bad jokes for our comic journals. (38)

The main hope for resistance to the "debilitation" expressed by these speakers was, he thought, "the rapid march of education."

Douse's primitive sociology and mechanistic approach to sound change did not differ markedly from many explanations that followed his. Viewed from North America, however, his claims seemed particularly dubious. Reviewing his book, Whitney questioned Douse's claim that historic *h* was everywhere dropped (or "dissimilated") and unhistoric *h* systematically inserted before initial vowels (or "cross-compensated"). Whitney further doubted that the acute class consciousness attached to *h* in modern English could have had any parallel in antiquity; "to assume that anything like this should have been the case in a primitive community is little short of absurd," he wrote acerbically (1877b, 76), though he had admitted elsewhere that he had himself formerly drawn the same analogy between *h* and the prehistoric consonant shift (1877a, 26).

Another American, Charles Astor Bristed, shared Whitney's doubts that *h* loss and insertion were as systematically employed as the English writers were wont to claim.

> The result of my own experience and observation I sum up thus: In London, no man above the rank of a servant or a small tradesman says *a hass* or *a hangel*. Thackeray and Trollope may be quoted against this assertion. But I do not put implicit faith in novelists as philological authorities. . . . (129)

Whitney was even able to quote Douse against himself by citing the observation that *h* was stylistically variable, that insecure speakers were given to "a frantic sprinkling of *h*'s in the wrong places" when addressing those of higher social class (Douse 47; Whitney 1877b, 76). Such stylistic variation had no place in Douse's theory of sound change. Both Bristed and Whitney urged that the distribution of *h* be studied with less moralizing and more attention. In Whitney's words, "it is a great pity that he [Douse] or some other Londoner does not take them up for a really penetrating scientific investigation" (76). Even Ellis, rightly revered by the Americans for his dispassionate inspection of minute detail, had not provided a satisfactory account of the matter (see Bristed, 128–30).

During the nineteenth century, new shibboleths emerged— represented by the sound of *r* in *girl*, the choice of vowel in *glass*, and the pronunciation of words like *herbal*. All of these involved existing sounds of English but also a change in their incidence and distribution. Language change had long aroused the anxiety of purists, but the nineteenth-century purists were stimulated to unprecedented heights of venom and scorn. Old aristocrats might speak as they pleased, but the middle classes, in both Britain and North America, were torn by new strictures and bewildering rules for correctness. Urban English was a threat to gentility and grace;

rural English seemed merely quaint or uncouth. Thought by some to be on the verge of splitting into unintelligible tongues, English as a whole had never been so richly various in its pronunciation, and never before had variety aroused such intense passion among those who feared that the English-speaking community would shortly be torn apart in a modern-day collapse of the Tower of Babel.

WORDS

WRITING EARLY IN OUR CENTURY, James Redding Ware recognized the vast change that had recently taken place in the English word-stock.

> "Passing English" ripples from countless sources, forming a river of new language which has its tide and its ebb, while its current brings down new ideas and carries away those that have dribbled out of fashion. (v)

In elaborating this image, he drew on the long-traditional metaphor of language as a spring issuing pure waters that might be "defiled" by inaccuracy and impropriety. He was doing no more than repeating the received wisdom of his day, and he was right in recognizing the nineteenth century as an era of new English. Innovations flooded the English vocabulary with new words as more and more people talked about more and different things.

Delimiting just which words are in English (and when and how they got there) is a difficult task, and even the best-documented words in English can rarely be traced much beyond the written record into oral use. Antedating earliest citations in the *OED* and the other historical dictionaries of English has occupied lexically minded readers since the publication of its first installment in 1884. But however incomplete the record of the English vocabulary, broad trends can be discerned with little difficulty. In general, the more frequent the word, the longer it has existed in English. Thus about 75 percent of the twenty thousand most frequent words in the modern language were already in use by 1450. Expanding our view to the next sixty thousand words provides a quite different picture; more than half of these were introduced after 1700. Some sense of the ebb and flow of the English vocabulary can be obtained from the *Chronological English Dictionary* (Finkenstaedt and Leisi): from 1730 to 1739, 577 new words were introduced to English; from 1830 to 1839, 2,521. The great difference between these two decades, a century apart, suggests in broad strokes how important lexical creativity was to the nineteenth century. A grumbly puristic essay in the *Daily Telegraph* in 1896 deplored the author's own "age of windy and pretentious gabble—when the number of persons who can, and will, chatter 'about and about' the various arts is quite in unprecedented disproportion to the number of those who are content to study these various arts in patience and, above all, in silence" (Ware, s.v. *about and about*).

Some glimpse of the method by which new words could be created can be gained through the evolution of the "arts" about which people were "chattering 'about and about.'" Scientific vocabulary was a particularly rich domain for the lexical imagination. Early in the century, medical doctors were especially active in naming inflammations of various organs: *tonsillitis* (1801), *hysteritis* (1803), *gastritis* (1806), *mastitis* (1842), *prostatitis* (1844), *colitis* (1860), *appendicitis* (1886). By the end of the century, it was even possible for professors of medicine to use *itis* as an independent form with the general meaning of "affliction." With the development of *anesthetics* (1846)—and *anesthetists* (1882) to *anesthetize* (1848) patients—surgeons entered a new round of word creation to describe the process of removing diseased parts from the body: *hysterectomy* (1886), *gastroectomy* (1886), *colostomy* (1888), *prostatectomy* (1890), *appendectomy* (1895), *tonsillectomy* (1899). So it was that *-itis* and *-tomy* became productive suffixes in English, restricted almost entirely to scientific vocabulary but nonetheless in widespread use. As surgeons became adept at cosmetic and restorative procedures, the suffix *-plasty* also achieved popularity. *Plastic surgery* itself was a loan translation from the work of a German physician and entered English in 1839. And whatever could be improved by surgery was given a grandly Grecian name: *rhinoplasty* (1823) for the nose, *cheiloplasty* (1842) for the lips, *heteroplasty* (1855) for tissue, *morioplasty* (1888) for missing body parts in general, and dozens of other such words. (Invention of the slang term *sawbones* [1837, "surgeon"] was a futile gesture of resistance against the lexical onslaught.)

As physicians gained respectability by developing an arcane and learned vocabulary, so other scientists invented a discipline by means, virtually, of words alone. Early in the century, Europeans became fascinated with racial classification through the measurement of skulls, and this pseudoscience was known as *craniognomy* (1813), *phrenology* (1815; a borrowing from both French and German), and *craniometry* (1861). Key regions of the skull were given Greek names—for instance, *basion* (1878), *nasion* (1878), and *pterion* (1878), and from these points it was possible to derive a *cephalic index* (1866). Skulls were thick or *brachycephalous* (1853), thin or *dolichocephalous* (1836); a line drawn downward from the forehead allowed classification of faces into *opisthognathous* ("retreating teeth" in Huxley's words, 1877), *prognathous* (jut-jawed, 1836), and *orthognathous* (straight-jawed, 1853). "The European is orthognathous," wrote the anthropologist E. B. Tylor *(OED),* a facial type he associated with high culture, intelligence, and beauty.

The trend in word creation represented by these examples revived the inkhorn controversy of the sixteenth century and raised two objections. The first was to the obscurantism of the new words: however transparent to the learned, they bewildered those unacquainted with Latin and Greek. For all their admiration of the classics, many midcentury observers doubted that the new English words from these sources were a boon.

> In no way is our language more wronged than by the weak readiness
> with which many of those who, having neither a hearty love nor a
> ready mastery of it, or lacking both, fly to the Latin tongue or to the

Greek for help in the naming of a new thought or thing, or the partial concealment of an old one, calling, for instance, nakedness
nudity, and a bathing-tub a lavatory. By doing so they help to deface
the characteristic traits of our mother tongue, and to mar and stunt
its kindly growth. (R. White, 1872, 22)

Blunt and commonplace words from the Germanic portion of the
word-stock were, in this view, almost always to be preferred to the
polysyllabic and arcane vocables from the classical languages.

A second objection arose from the classicism that was never far
below the surface of nineteenth-century linguistic commentary.
The suffixes *-itis* and *-tomy* were both derived from Greek; hence
they should only be attached to words of Greek origin. *Bronchitis*
(1808) and *laparotomy* (1878) thus were both well formed. *Vagini-
tis* (1846) and *ovariectomy* (1889) were monstrous because their
roots are from Latin and their suffixes from Greek. Such "mistakes" in the creation of new words were visible only to those who,
schooled in Greek and Latin, arrogated to themselves a privileged
authority to opine about English. Consequently there arose a law
of *etymological harmony,* mandating that new combinations should
be of like origin.

> The strict rule for the construction of a compound word is that
> all parts must be from the same language, i.e., all Greek, or all Latin,
> or all English. Thus, since *bi* is a Latin prefix, and *gamy* a Greek root,
> *bi-gamy* is a mongrel word, or, which is the Greek for "mongrel," a
> hybrid. The word should be, strictly, *di-gamy.* (Abbott and Seeley, 22)

That English usage did not conform to such regulation obliged the
regulators to admit that "this rule is often violated": "custom, and
custom only, can determine where to draw the line." (There was
even, at midcentury, an effort to distinguish *bigamy* and *digamy* for,
respectively, the simultaneously and successively twice married.)
"Custom" in medical vocabulary limited creations to the classical
languages, whether or not they were "hybridized," and encouraged
the use of such labels as *tympanic membrane* (1860) in place of long-
established English *ear drum* (1645). In the usual way, etymological
harmony dissolved into English practice: in 1879, dog lovers saw no
incongruity in designating their mania as *canophilia,* and in 1889,

George Bernard Shaw could describe, derisively, an excessive fondness for the music of Richard Wagner as *Wagneritis*.

Attention to word origins, however, produced what modern linguists call the *etymological fallacy,* the belief that the true meanings of words lie in their roots. From it arose such absurd allegations as the view that *dilapidated* could only be used properly for decayed stone structures (since the word incorporates the Latin *lapis* 'stone') or that *decimated* properly means the destruction of a tenth part of something (since it comes ultimately from Latin *decem* 'ten'). That this view was not limited to parlor etymology is illustrated by a nineteenth-century courtroom lawyer in a trial involving a railroad passenger injured in a derailment.

> "Doctor, to what do you attribute this condition of the plaintiff which you describe?"
>
> "Hysteria, sir; he is hysterical."
>
> That waked me up. I said: "Doctor, did I understand—I was not paying proper attention—to what did you attribute this nervous condition of my client?"
>
> "Hysteria, sir."
>
> I subsided, and the examination went on until it came my turn to cross-examine.
>
> "Do I understand, I said, "that you think this condition of my client wholly hysterical?"
>
> "Yes, sir; undoubtedly."
>
> "And therefore won't last long?"
>
> "No, sir; not likely to."
>
> "Well," said I, "Doctor, let us see; is not the disease called hysteria and its effects hysterics; and isn't it true that hysteria, hysterics, hysterical, all come from the Greek word ὑστέρα?"
>
> "It may be."
>
> "Don't say it may, Doctor; isn't it? Isn't an exact translation of the Greek word ὑστέρα, the English word 'womb'?"
>
> "You are right, sir."
>
> "Well, Doctor, this morning when you examined this young man here," pointing to my client, "did you find that he had a womb? I was not aware of it before, but I will have him examined over again and see if I can find it. That is all, Doctor; you may step down." (B. Butler, 1016–17)

That such etymological cross-examination could be taken seriously may seem preposterous, yet this argument not only won the case but the transcript continued to be reprinted in a manual of cross-examination republished through much of the twentieth century (Wellman). Such was the status of Greek among Anglo-American intellectuals that to ascertain etymology was to claim truth.

Greek was a major source of new terms in the nineteenth century; 70 percent of the Greek-derived words in the eighty-thousand-word core vocabulary appeared after 1800. Ralph Waldo Emerson reported to his American readers after a visit in 1848 that "Oxford is a Greek factory, as Wilton mills weave carpet, and Sheffield grinds steel" (156). He further repeated the nineteenth-century idea that a knowledge of Greek was virtually equivalent to education itself.

> Access to the Greek minds lifts [the Englishman's] standard of taste. He has enough to think of, and, unless of an impulsive nature, is indisposed from writing or speaking, by the fullness of his mind, and the new severity of his taste. The great silent crowd of thorough-bred Grecians always known to be around him, the English writer cannot ignore. They prune his orations, and point his pen. Hence, the style and tone of English journalism. The men have learned accuracy and comprehension, logic, and pace, or speed of working. They have bottom, endurance, wind. When born with good constitutions they make those eupeptic studying-mills, the cast iron men, the *dura ilia,* whose powers of performance compare with ours as the steam-hammer with the music box. (158)

Emerson recognized, however, that Oxford had been "perverted" from its ancient origins, that it did not offer access to the talented poor nor admit the public to lectures supported by endowments requiring that "all men thereunto to have concourse." The ancient universities did not afford a democratic vista, and, as Greek factories, they mainly produced persons prejudiced against their own language.

In fact, the teaching of Greek at the universities had little to do with the influx of Greek-derived vocabulary into nineteenth-century English. Most terms of rhetoric and grammar, a major domain

for influence from classical Greek, had already been borrowed
during the Renaissance, and only a handful of the new words arose
from theology. Most of these did not reach general currency, and
an excess of them was trying to the patience of even the Oxbridge
Grecians. (Ernest Weekly provided, without a precise reference,
the following specimen: "A gulf divides the exaltations of the mys-
tics from the tachypraxia of the microsplanchnic hyperthyroidics
or the ideo-affective dissociations of the schizothymes" [87].) Most
of the innovations from Greek were provided by scientists, who
were not necessarily adept at Greek but who easily learned the
emergent rules in English for forming new terms from classical
elements.

Many nineteenth-century scientific words ultimately from
Greek were borrowed into English from continental scientific discourse, first from French and later from German, though nation-
alistic pride among commentators on usage often obscured these
intermediate stages of borrowing. Until the end of the eighteenth
century, most words with *-meter* in English were formed from Greek
roots (e.g., *anemometer, chronometer*) but the principle of etymological harmony was soon weakened in the nineteenth. Thus *gasometer*
'reservoir for illuminating gas' (1808), *galvanometer* (1802), and
alcoholometer (1859) show that *-meter* could be attached to technical
words whatever their origin, including the names of scientists.
(Luigi Galvani, the eighteenth-century Italian, is the eponymous
source of *galvanometer;* Alessandro Volta, his nineteenth-century
compatriot, is the source of *voltmeter* [1882].) Science in the
period was preoccupied with measuring, and vocabulary was created on the most imaginative principles to describe the instruments of measurement. The end of the eighteenth century produced *pedometer* and *odometer* for recording distance; the
nineteenth offered *viameter* (1831), *cyclometer* (1880), and *distanceometer* (1883). A few purists attempted to introduce the
spelling *hodometer* (1848) for *odometer* on the grounds that it was
more "accurately" Greek, but by that time *-(o)meter* had become
entirely English, allowing such derisive terms for measuring popular opinion as *foolometer* (1837) and *democratometer* (1859).

A similar pattern can be traced in uses of *-graph,* another productive suffix used imaginatively in nineteenth-century science. In 1796, for instance, Alois Senefelder of Munich invented a printing process he called, in German, *Lithographie;* introduced into Britain, it was first called *polyautography* (1806) but soon renamed *lithography* (1822) and its products *lithographs* (1822). Similarly, photography was invented in Paris in 1826 and the process called by its inventor *héliographie.* Addressing the Royal Society on March 4, 1839, John Herschel introduced the terms *photography, photographic,* and *photograph,* beating by just two months the introduction of the corresponding French terms in the publications of the Academy of Sciences in Paris. Edison's *phonograph* (1877) was first called by that term in both Britain and the United States, but Britain came to favor *gramophone,* a term coined there and patented in 1887. (The suggestion that a "more correct" spelling would be *grammophone* did not take hold, "correct" here meaning closer to the Greek root.) Inventions flooded the landscape, and new terms were invented for them: *heliograph* 'instrument for measuring sunlight' (1853), *seismograph* (1858), and *hygrograph* (1864). Such words were often separately coined by various inventors, few of them having any profound knowledge of Greek. The resulting compounds were, for the most part, firmly English, and so were their pronunciations. Murray's nostalgic comment on *hygro-* reveals the cultural climate in which they were created and used: "ʋ in Gr[eek] is short, and the etymological pronunciation would be (hig-); but the tendency to take *y* as long *i,* has in this, as in other cases, prevailed against the etymology." Etymology did little to preserve the principle of harmony either, and roots of many origins appeared with *-graph* just as they had with the words formed with *-meter*—for instance, *hurrygraph* 'quick sketch' (1851) and *jellygraph* 'process for reproducing writing on paper' (1900).

The names of newly discovered or freshly classified natural objects, particularly minerals and fossils, gave great productivity to the suffix *-ite.* Murray described it as having produced "a vast number of modern names in which *-ite* is added to an element expressing colour, structure, physical characters or affinities, or to the name of a locality, discoverer, mineralogist, distinguished scientist, or other person whom the discoverer may have desired to commemorate" (*OED*, s.v. *-ite*). These include *graphite* (1796), *leadhillite* (1832), *albite* (1837), *calcite* (1849), and *darwinite* (1861), among many others. The process of word creation had the effect of schematizing the vocabulary acceptable to scientists, and older forms were driven out of use by the terms that replaced them. Thus the "scientific" name for *black lead* (or *plumbago*) became *graphite* (1796), and *chlorite* the name for *talc* (1794).

Ordinary usage tended to preserve the traditional names; thus, pencils contained *lead* rather than *graphite* and the cosmetic powder remained *talc,* not *chlorite.* Nineteenth-century science, however, tended to push traditional names into a background of derided ignorance and superstition, preferring instead the "systematics" borrowed, both verbally and intellectually, mostly from Germany and France. System led to new rules for word formation, particularly in chemistry, where *-ic* and *-ous* produced such adjective pairs as *mercuric* (1828) and *mercurous* (1865), *phosphoric* (1800) and *phosphorous* (1815). Likewise, *-ide* and *-ine,* for instance, could be appended to nouns to form new chemical names for elements in chemical compounds. Lavoisier had coined the term *oxygen* (borrowed into English from French in 1790) and derived from it *oxide* (such as *ferrous oxide* [1873]). Early in the century, chemists distinguished *chlorine* from *chloride, fluorine* from *fluoride, iodine* from *iodide,* and *bromine* from *bromide.* These principles of word formation made it possible to generate related sets of new words on rational principles and to generate them in vast numbers. The full flowering of word creation is apparent in the following extract from a standard work on chemistry from 1877. "Two dioxybenzoic acids are obtained by fusing the two disulphobenzoic acids with potassium hydroxide" (*OED*, s.v. *dioxy-*). The principal words here are all of nineteenth-century creation: *potassium* (1807), *benzoic* (1819), *hydroxide* (1851).

For purists, these new words were not an obvious ornament to the language. To them, the core vocabulary was essentially literary and the study of that core an antiquarian pursuit. Thus there was some uncertainty about the status of these new words, doubts expressed at midcentury by Richard Chenevix Trench.

The most mischievous shape which this error [of overinclusiveness] assumes, consists in the drafting into the Dictionary a whole army of purely technical words; such as, indeed, are not for the most part, except by an abuse of language, words at all, but signs; having been deliberately invented as the nomenclature, and, so to speak, the algebraic notation of some special art or science, and having never passed the threshold of this, nor mingled with the general family of words. It is not unfrequently a barren ostentation which induces the bringing in of these, that so there may be grounds for boasting of an immense addition made to the vocabulary. Such additions are very cheaply made. Nothing is easier than to turn to modern treatises on chemistry or electricity, or on some other of the sciences which hardly or not at all existed half a century ago, or which, if they had existed, have yet been in later times wholly new-named—as botany, for example. (1860, 57–58)

This "army of purely technical words" was, however, pressing hard to expand the vocabulary of English. What had been created was a set of new principles of word formation governing such forms as *disulphobenzoic* with prefixes, suffixes, novel roots, and innovative forms for "inflecting" words to express the chemistry of compounds. Trench was, however, correct in identifying the "algebraic" quality of these newly created words; all the following were formed during the century: *sulphobenzamate, sulphobenzamide, sulphobenzide, sulphobenzol.* Additionally each new noun had its own adjectival form, making chemical discourse increasingly forbidding to the uninitiated and despicable to the impassioned purist. Trench was right in thinking that "algebraic notation" made possible innovations in English words that would have been unthinkable before. One wag even used the algebra to create what he alleged to be the "longest" English word: *æqueosalinocalinosetaceoalumnosocuprovitriolic* (Moore, 149n). It purported to describe, in adjectival form, the properties of spa water in Bristol in southwestern England.

Scientific word fervor did not afflict everyone. The most traditionally minded were content with the hoary and unscientific word *brimstone* rather than the more modern-seeming (though long-established) *sulphur.* Americans tended to favor the unetymologi-

With the rise of modern science, new vocabulary replaced ancient folk terminology. (From *Treasures*, 263.)

cal spelling *sulfur*, and the rule of harmony was violated in *sulphobenzol* with its combination of Latin and German (*benzene* < *Benzin*). Inventors, however, caught the fever for classical-sounding words, and among the new products of the century were the *Eccaleobio* 'incubator for hatching eggs' (1839), *Carborundum* (1892), and *Herbicide* (1894). For the classically fixated, these verbal inventions were anathema. No wonder Trench and others were content to ignore these developments altogether, urging that they be excluded from dictionaries and dismissed by the literati.

Even so, nineteenth-century scientific words began to penetrate the core vocabulary, particularly when the products of chemistry, for instance, became part of everyday life. The following are only exemplary: *phosphate* (1795), *iodine* (1814), *chloroform* (1834), *bromide* (1836), *aniline* (1850), *saccharin* (1880). At the end of the eighteenth century, scientists were viewed as eccentrics (as, for instance, in William Blake's prose work, "An Island in the Moon" [ca. 1785]); in the nineteenth, they were perceived as the source of new products and processes valuable in everyday life (as *aniline* dyestuffs transformed cloth making or *chloroform* the practice of surgery). Scientific words entered into the center of educated discourse, and enterprising manufacturers chose names evocative of science for new products like *margarine* (1836), *linoleum* (1864), *gasoline* (1869), *butterine* (1874), *vaseline* (1874), *cosmolene* (1876), *petrol* (1892), *plasticine* (1897), and *aspirin* (1899).

By the end of the eighteenth century, science had witnessed a conflict between the *methodists* and the *systematicists* over whether classifications should be natural or artificial. As revealed in the English vocabulary, the systematicists won the battle, and the artifices for creating new English words were employed on an international scale. Thus the element *manganese* (1783) was systematized, and from it developed the words *manganite* (1827), *manganic* (1828), *manganate* (1828), and *manganous* (1842). Such words achieved sufficient popularity to make new-naming on scientific principles a fashion. From the United States came the *telegram* (1852); from Canada, *kerosene* (1854); from Australia, the *banksia* bush (1788 < Joseph Banks); from South Africa, *kimberlite* (1887 <Kimberley); from New Zealand *dunite* (1868 < Dun Mountain). All of these were created on recently formulated principles of word building.

By midcentury, many people used these "scientific" words regularly. A book devoted to the husbandry of sheep, for instance, contained both the traditional and the new terms in its list of medications: *Epsom Salts (Sulphate* [1790] *of Magnesia), Hartshorn (Ammonia* [1799]), *Ethiop's Mineral (Black Sulphuret* [1790] *of Mercury), Sugar of Lead (Acetate* [1827] *of Lead), Lunar Caustic (Nitrate* [1794] *of Silver), Aqua fortis (Nitric* [1794] *acid), Verdigris (Acetate* [1827] *of Copper)* (Randall, 384–92). Old terms and new are listed in no particular order of preference in this glossary, but it is arranged with cross-reference so shepherds can find a term whether they look for it under the old or the new name. Similarly, a work devoted to *domestic science* (1870) suggests remedies for poisoning from chemicals "often kept in the house for cooking or medical purposes" (Beecher and Stowe, 303); these include such newly named elements as *phosphorous* (1794), *iodide* (1822) *of potassium* (1807), *strychnia* (1826), and *saleratus* (1837). The emergence of *dietetics* (1799) and other forms of scientific cooking produced a similar array of new terms formed from "classical" elements: *chlorophyll* (1819), *protein* (1844), *calorie* (1866), and *carbohydrate* (1869).

New words with a scientific flavor were not greeted with universal enthusiasm. Writing in 1829, an anonymous author (signing himself "A. C. C.") ranged widely among the "corruptions of the English language."

> But I have dilated so long on the corruptions of the English language, occasioned by the introduction of French, that I have scarcely time or room to animadvert at sufficient length on another and almost equally prevalent method, of debasing the sterling metal of our noble tongue, adopted by scientific writers. These gentlemen are remarkable for using a certain kind of jargon, neither Latin nor English, but a compound of both, which would prove as completely unintelligible to an ancient Roman, if resuscitated for the purpose, as it is to a modern Englishman, unacquainted with the tongues of old . . . . [W]e call that science which treats of the knowledge of animals, *zoology,* instead of *animal science,* or a similar intelligible compound; the knowledge of *water-power* we term *hydrodynamics;* a *heat-measurer* or *heat-meter,* a *thermometer,* &c. But perhaps all this gibberish, though absurd and ridiculous enough, is not so bad as the practice of introducing German terms of art into mineralogy. (122)

These "German terms of art" included such innovations as *gneiss* (1757), *feldspar* (1772), *floetz* (1811), *loess* (1833), *fahlband* (1880), and *schlieren* (1898). And these only from the relatively restricted field of mineralogy.

A. C. C. urged the use of transparent compounds constructed from English elements, an idea increasingly popular in the course of the century, though rather among literati than among scientists. *Heat-measurer* was no threat to *thermometer* (which had, in any case, been generally used in English since the early seventeenth century). William Barnes, the Dorset poet and schoolmaster, was an indefatigable proponent of such words as *birdlearned* rather than *ornithological,* and in 1869 he stated the principle upon which such words should be favored.

English has become a more mongrel speech by the needless inbringing of words from Latin, Greek, and French, instead of words which
might have been found in its older form, or in the speech of landfolk
over all England, or might have been formed from its own roots and
stems, as wanting words have been formed in German and other
purer tongues. (101)

Wary of the old word-fabricator, the editors of the *OED* seldom
quoted Barnes except from his dialect poetry, and though both
inbringing and *landfolk* are listed, Barnes is not mentioned in those
entries. He does appear occasionally when he revived older
forms—for instance, *longsome* (for *lengthy*), *offgoing* (for *departure*),
and *suchness* (for *quiddity*). While Barnes's campaign for his own
words was generally unsuccessful, nineteenth-century English did
invent or revive compounds formulated on the principles he
espoused: *selfhelp* 'self-reliance' (1831), *outcome* 'result' (1832),
thisness 'hæcceity' (1837), *output* 'production' (1858), *up-to-date*
'abreast of the times' (1868).

Like most linguistic innovators, Barnes and his fellow "Saxon-
ists" emphasized a trend already under way in English. Early in the
century, *auto-* and *self-* offered essentially synonymous prefixes for
the creation of new words. Only a few new words were created
using *auto-*, however—among them *autobiography* (1809), and *automatic* (applied to machinery in 1802). Most of them were either
derivatives of words already in existence—for instance, *autocracy*
(1655) yielded *autocrat* (1803), *autocratic* (1813), and *autocratically*
(1860)—or applied in limited technical contexts—for example,
autophony 'self-examination of one's voice' (1862) or *autolaryn-
goscopy* 'self-examination of one's larynx' (1870). *Self-* compounds,
according to Henry Bradley's account in the *OED*, had achieved a
particular vogue in the seventeenth century, particularly in philosophical and theological writings, but the nineteenth century
revived the practice of forming words with *self-*, using the prefix
with "unlimited application." Some of these were in competition
with their *auto-* counterparts—for instance, *self-acting* (1824) with
automatic, *self-fertilization* (1877) with *autogamy* (1880), and, of persons, *self-reliance* (1827) with *autonomy* (1803). What made these
words created with *self-* "unlimited" was that the prefix could be

attached to virtually any word class: *self-abandonment* (1818), *self-awareness* (1880), *self-directed* (1808), *self-effacement* (1866), *self-loathing* (1899), *self-sacrificial* (1855). For those who debated the propriety of new English words, these new formations with *self-* counted as ones properly belonging to the language since most of them were made "from its own roots and stems."

While the inventors, scientists, and medicine men were introducing polysyllables into English, others continued the practice of abbreviation. Purists had long objected to this practice as destructive of etymology, and in 1710, Jonathan Swift had decried the use of *mob* (< *mobile vulgus* 'the fickle crowd') and *phiz* (< *physiognomy* 'face'). Such complaints had, of course, little influence on usage. Thus, when the rage for cycling swept across Britain and North America, shortening was almost immediate. In 1868 *bicycle*, both the thing and the word, was imported from France; almost immediately, two shortened forms competed with each other, *cycle* (1870) and *bike* (1882 but probably used earlier). Attempts to introduce *dicycle* (1870) as "a more regularly formed word"—that is, according to the doctrine of etymological harmony—or to revive *velocipede* (1818 for the two-wheeled vehicle propelled by running rather than peddling) were unsuccessful, and both *cycle* and *bike* continued as the principal variants of *bicycle* along with short-lived colloquialisms like *bone-shaker* (1874), *kangaroo* (1884), and *spider* (1874).

Shortening by various methods continued to be a regular feature of nineteenth-century word creation. Clipping could pare away at polysyllables to leave a single syllable behind: *cab* (1829 < *cabriolet*), *pants* (1840 < *pantaloons*), *pub* (1859 < *public house*), *circs* (1883 < *circumstances*), *fan* (1889 < *fanatic*); *van* (1829 < *caravan*), *bus* (1832 < *omnibus*); *flu* (1839 < *influenza*), *tec* (1879 < *detective*). These shortened forms could, in turn, be lengthened to express additional meanings, for instance, *cabby* 'cab driver' (1870). Another kind of shortening, back formation, produced verbs from nouns and adjectives: *absorb* (1882 < *absorption*), *book-keep* (1886 < *book-keeping*), *burgle* (1889 < *burglar, burglary*), *legislate* (1805 < *legislator, legislation*), *sculpt* (1864 < *sculptor*), *stage-manage* (1879 < *stage-manager*), *ush* (1824 < *usher*).

"Blending" parts of words together was made famous by Lewis Carroll, who in 1872 devised *chortle* as a blend of *chuckle* and *snort*. Such creations he called "portmanteau words," drawing on the idea of a piece of luggage containing interior compartments. Blends of this kind were not his invention, however, and many nineteenth-century innovators created new words by that system: *squattocracy* (1843 < *squatter* + *aristocracy*, Australia), *chattermag* 'chatterbox' (coined by William Barnes from *chattering* + *magpie*, 1844), *Michigander* (1848 < *Michigan* + *gander*, first documented in a speech by Abraham Lincoln), *squarson* (1876 < *squire* + *parson*), *slanguage* (1885 < *slang* + *language*), *insinuendo* (1885 < *insinuation* + *innuendo*), *beerage* (1891 < *beer* + *peerage*), *brunch* (1896 < *breakfast* + *lunch*), *smog* (1905 < *smoke* + *fog*). For the most part, these blends were, at least initially, intentionally facetious (see Pound 1914).

The most extreme process by which words can be condensed produces *initialisms* (1899) in which the names of the initial letters of words in a phrase are pronounced separately—for example, *OK* (1839). Though extremely common in twentieth-century English, acronyms—where the string of initial letters is pronounced as a word—were rare in the nineteenth. *Dora* (1917 < *Defence of the Realm Act*) is usually taken to be the first acronym, but it was anticipated by *Peruvian*, a derisive name for Jews coined in South Africa at the very end of the century (1897 < *PRU* < Polish and Russian Union). Since this domain of lexical history is sparsely documented, there may have been acronyms not yet recognized as such—for instance, *colinderies* or *colinda* (1886 < *Colonial and Indian Exhibition*; Ware), the latter written on souvenir caps from the exhibition. In a few cases, single letters could be used to form derived words—for instance, *Xtian* and *Xtianity* (< *Christian*), which had been earlier coined as written abbreviations and may have been pronounced (as, for example, *Eksmas* [*Xmas* < *Christmas*]).

Initialisms were not new in the nineteenth century, of course, but they constituted a rich device for the creation of new expressions. Some are still current: *R. I. P.* 'rest in peace' (< *Requiescat in pace*, 1816) and *R. S. V. P.* 'reply' (< *respondez-vous s'il vous plait*, 1845). Many were ephemeral and soon forgotten; the following specimen, from the *Boston Morning Post,* June 12, 1838, shows a typical effusion of this kind of wit.

> *Melancholy*—We understand that J. Eliot Brown, Es., Secretary of the Boston Young Men's Society for Meliorating the Condition of the Indians, F. A. H. (fell at Hoboken, N. J.) on Saturday last at 4 o'clock P. M. in a duel W. O. O. F. C. (with one of our first citizens.) What measures will be taken by the Society in consequence of this heart rending event R. T. B. S. (remains to be seen.) (Quoted by A. Read, 5)

This spate of creation produced few enduring inventions—*N. G.* (< *no go*) or *G. C.* (< *gin cocktail*) did not last long—with the notable exception of *O. K.* (< *oll korrect* < *all correct*). Dickens caught the fashion too, and in 1838, in *Oliver Twist,* he had one of the characters declare: "It's all U. P. there"; *U. P.* was simply a faddish way of saying *up,* and the fad was not enduring. Nonetheless, initialisms proliferated through the century and on both sides of the Atlantic: *G. A. R.* (1867 < Grand Army of the Republic 'Union Veterans of the Civil War') *G. O. M.* (1882 < Grand Old Man 'W. E. Gladstone']); *G. O. P.* (1887 < Grand Old Party 'Republican Party', 1879 < 'Democratic Party').

One impulse in the creation of initialisms was their widespread use in fraternal organizations. Ware went so far as to call the conventional abbreviations on invitations and calling cards *masonics* (s.v. *T. W. B. F.*), an indication of their semisecret and ritualistic use in such organizations. Samuel Fallows, in 1883, compiled a fat volume containing the abbreviations used by "secret and benevolent societies." Masonic letterheads, he noted, usually contained the letters *I. T. N. O. T. G. A. O. T. U.* (< In the Name of the Grand Architect of the Universe) and among the charities of the Masons was the *F. B. W. & D. B.* (< Fund of Benevolence for Widows and Distressed Brothers). Similarly, the Orangemen toasted *T. G. M. O. K. W.* (< The Glorious Memory of King William) and viewed reverently the *M. W. S. G. L. U. S.* (< Most Worshipful Supreme Grand Lodge of the United States). The secretive quality of these abbreviations cleansed the taboo from some expressions, allowing them to be used without affront—for instance, *P. D. Q.* (< pretty damn quick, 1875).

Abbreviation making is one of the more conscious methods of word creation, and so is deriving words from proper names. The nineteenth century was particularly adept at using suffixes to create words from names—for instance, *Dickensesque* (1856), *Dickensy* (1859), *Dickensian* (1881), *Dickensiana* (1886), *Dickensite* (1888), *Dickensish* (1890). Sects and schools of thought (many carefully delineated by Blunt in 1874) were particularly prone to these labels. Commentators on the ideas of Robert Owen, for example, produced *Owenite* (1829), *Owenism* (1830), *Owenize* (1833). Since many words from names were spontaneously created and ephemeral, Murray coined the term *nonce word* (1884) to categorize them. Yet as part of the process of word creation, they contributed richly to nineteenth-century vocabulary. Murray was right, however, in recognizing that they were often reinvented, and after the tide of Owenism had ebbed, *Owenist* (1870) and *Owenian* (1880) were created afresh as synonyms of *Owenite*. Then, as now, it was difficult to estimate which new terms would endure. In the last months of 1880, for instance, the word *boycott* (< Charles C. Boycott) flashed onto the scene. Almost immediately the new word assumed a variety of forms and functions: *boycotting* (1880), *boycottee* (1880), *boycottism* (1881), *boycotter* (1881), *boycotted* (1882). Such was the popularity of this innovation that analogous forms were created—for example, *Endacotted* 'illegally arrested' (< from the name of an otherwise forgotten London constable, Endacott, 1887 [Ware]). Though *boycott* was a recent nonce word, Murray provided a detailed treatment of it and its derivatives when he issued, in 1887, the portion of the *OED* including it. Dozens and dozens of names became words in the course of the century: *macadam* 'paving material' (1826), *hansom* 'type of carriage' (1847), *bloomer* 'loosely fitted women's trousers or undergarments' (1851), *gladstone* 'cheap French wine' (1864), 'traveling bag' (1882), *watt* 'measure of electricity' (1882), *sideburns* 'style of facial whiskers' (< Burnside, 1887), *zeppelin* 'dirigible' (1900). A linguistic term was even devised to categorize them—*eponym* (1846).

For some observers, these new words were an ornament to English. Pride in the "achievement" of the English vocabulary was expressed in a historical work published in 1922 by Thomas Stenhouse; the full, and revealing, title of his narrative was *Lives Enshrined in Language; or, The Sociological Aspect of Words: A Much Enlarged Edition, being an Account of some Proper Names which have become Common Parts of Speech, or Terms of Grammar, expressing and perpetuating the memory of National and Racial Characteristics or Individual Peculiarities and Experiences.* In it, he treats the rise of eponyms as memorials to their creators.

> Dolly Vardens, Blumers, Burberries, Cardigans, and Chesterfield . . . have a secure footing; there is no doubt as to spencers and jaegers and tam o'shanters; may Benjamins and Glengarries be admitted with Tussores and Shantungs? (7)

Perhaps in these particular estimates, Stenhouse's crystal ball may have been a little clouded, but his pride in the past is more revealing of the desire to celebrate word creation than his success as a prophet.

Stenhouse's delight in these new names from the commercial world was not typical of nineteenth-century puristic thought. Throughout the era, innovations were usually viewed with anxiety or hostility. An anonymous writer from 1804 caught, much better than Stenhouse, the spirit of the age.

> Another circumstance, just hinted at, which is peculiarly humiliating, and which, I should hope, a little recollection of the manly spirit of our ancestors would yet cause us to resent, is, that all these endeavours to expel the natives ["native" English words], and to place foreigners in their room, is not the work of scholars and critics, but of persons who have never, in any nation, been ranked among the ablest linguists. We are not beat out of our language by Royal Academies and Royal Societies, by armies of Lexicographers, and hordes of Philologists, but by a combination of Milliners and of Mantua-makers, of Perfumers and of Hair-dressers, of Cabinet-makers and Upholsterers, of Taylors, and of Cooks, the fabricators of pantaloons, and the architects of pastry, by the Authors of stews, and Compilers of soups. It is from them we are humbly to receive the language in which we must dress our wives and our daughters, and furnish our houses and our wardrobes, our dinners and our desserts. It is they who are rendering Dr. Johnson's Dictionary obsolete, that they may supply its place by a Polyglot of pies and puddings, of pickles and flummeries. ("The Projector," 818)

Haberdashers had supplied most of the new words Stenhouse had celebrated in the passage previously quoted, but most of them are Anglo-American names—for example, *glengarry* (1845 < Glengarry valley in Scotland), *bloomer* (1851 < Amelia Bloomer), *cardigan* (1868 < the earl of Cardigan). Such names-into-words from native sources were less enraging to Stenhouse's predecessor than words borrowed from other languages.

Nearly all the categories mentioned by the anonymous "Projector" were abundantly supplied with words from abroad, particularly from French: cookery (*au gratin* [1806], *à la carte* [1826], *menu* [1837], *creme caramel* [1845], *éclair* [1861], *napoleon* [1896]); furniture (*chaise longue* [1800], *suite* 'set of matching furniture' [1805], *chiffonier* [1806], *vitrine* [1880]); fashion (*chignon* [1783], *couturier* [1818], *coiffeur* [1847], *sachet* 'kind of dry perfume' [1855], *camisole* [1866]). Far from attempting to keep out these foreign words, purists turned their attention to sustaining their "foreign" pronunciations. Thus in 1833, W. H. Savage warned against such anglicizings as *blue-monge* for *blancmange*, *shampillyons* for *champignons*, and *likerish* for *liquorice*. Despite the *chic* (1856) implied by French in high society, the English element in the vocabulary remained predominant. In a list of materials for dressing a widow in mourning, for example, an etiquette book of 1881 suggested the following: *Albert* or *rainproof crape*, *balbriggan* (1859), *barathea* (1862), *cambric*, *cashmere* (1822), *kid*, *lawn*, *lisse* (1852), *muslin*, *paramatta* (1834), *silk*, *tarlatan*, and *tulle* (1868) (*Manners*, 99). Only those words supplied with dates are of nineteenth-century origin; these reflect, as do their earlier counterparts, an empire of fabrics whose names are derived from the places in Australia, Ireland, France, and India where the materials were first produced.

In *Ivanhoe*, Walter Scott drew attention to the distinction between French-derived and English names for animals and their flesh. When served as meat, *deer* became *venison*, *pig pork*, and *cow beef*. For Scott, these lexical distinctions supported his nineteenth-century interpretation of medieval life—the English in the fields and forests and the Normans in their manors and castles. The same tacit contrast informed the naming of food in his own day, and the English upper classes acquired a sudden taste for sauces,

many of them derived from French and the earliest ones introduced by refugees from revolutionary France: *béchamel* (1796),
roux (1813), *soubise* (1822), *ravigote* (1830), *velouté* (1830), *mayon-
naise* (1841), *hollandaise* (1841), *remoulade* (1845), *lyonnaise*
(1846). Even a sauce with German origins was known in England
as *sauce à l'Allemande* (1827); those of native origin were few—for
instance, *tartar* (1855) and *worcestershire* (1863).

Food fads reached even families living modestly in rural
America, and people with pretensions to gentility caught the taste
for French *cuisine* (1786). A *Domestic Cyclopædia* noted in 1882
that "the descriptive terms used in that cookery are now so commonly introduced into culinary and other treatises that a vocabulary of them can hardly fail to prove practically useful" (Goodholme, s.v. *French cookery*). The list consists almost entirely of
nineteenth-century borrowings—for example, *baba* (1827),
beignet (1835), *brioche* (1826), *crouton* (1806), *éclair* (1861), *gateau*
(1845), *quenelle* (1845), *saute* (1813), *timbale* (1824), *vol-au-vent*
(1828). In North America, where imported cooking styles were
more common than in Britain, new terms came from other languages—for instance, *cole slaw* (Dutch, 1794), *hamburger* (German, 1889), *blintz* (Yiddish, 1903), *salami* (Italian, 1852), *tortilla*
(American Spanish, 1831). The extension of empire to India
brought to Europe a cuisine that also became well known: *chutney*
(1813), *papadom* (1820), *vindaloo* (1888). Nonetheless, French
provided the greatest number of new words for culinary practices
and products through the century, even when the new dish was
invented in the anglophone world (as, for instance, *salmi of prairie-
hen* [Goodholme, s.v. *grouse*]).

Knowledge of new words was part of fashion, and high society
could make cruel use of the culinary vocabulary to distinguish the
ignorant from the worldly-wise. An account of good manners, written by an anonymous "Member of the Aristocracy," provided illuminating evidence for the prestige of French food names.

> "Would you like to look at the *menu*?" observes a gentleman to a
> lady whom he has taken down to dinner, handing it to her, as he
> speaks, after having rapidly glanced at it himself.

"Thank you," returns the lady, taking it from him. "What is 'Idem à la Béchamelle'?" referring to some dish that is new to her, and a lady, whether married or single, never need to blush at displaying her ignorance where an *entrée* or made dish is concerned. A man does not think less of a woman for being unversed in the mysteries of French cooking; if he has any knowledge of the to her unknown dish, he is pleased to impart it; if the dish is a stranger to him he is equally willing to discuss it, and to speculate as to its nature. (*Society Small Talk*, 48–49)

Such reassurances that ignorance would be treated kindly barely mask the importance of knowing the latest culinary fads—particularly for those who would read a conduct manual of this kind in hopes of shining, or at least averting disgrace, in society.

Cultivation in the finer things of life—as perceived by the upper classes—introduced new words in the arts. In music, Italian provided a rich vocabulary of borrowed terms. International popularity of Italian opera and growth in amateur musicianship both fueled this trend in vocabulary. Dozens of borrowed terms for the tempo and manner of performance came into use: *accelerando* (1842), *decrescendo* (1806), *leggiero* (1880), and *scherzo* (1852), for instance. Some evidence for the importance of foreign borrowings can be seen in the names of stops for the piece of musical furniture, the reed organ, developed and popularized during the century. It was called by various names: *harmonium* (1840), *parlor organ* (1847), *melodeon* (1847), *melodium* (1847), and *eolina* (1847). Many of the "voices" of this instrument were distinctly foreign-sounding (if not actual borrowings): *clarabella* (1840), *clarionet* (1880), *trumpet harmonique* (1876), *salicional* (1843), *suabe* (1855). Even more impressive (though these terms have not been precisely dated) were stops labeled *Vox Florante, Vox Angelicus, Vox Celeste, Vox Humana, Vox Jubilante* (see Gellerman, 97–99). Other newly invented instruments also were given exotic names: *saxophone* (1852), *melophone* (1859, a kind of *accordion* [1885]), *xylophone* (1866). Only at the end of the century did someone even bother to record the homely name for bellows-driven reed instruments: *squeeze box* (Ware).

The visual arts, too, required new terms with which to assert connoisseurship, and French or Italian was the usual source of them. These included "schools" of art—for instance, *impressionist* (1876) and *luminarist* (1888)—but also techniques of making art: *grisaille* (1848), *alla prima* (1849), *haut relief* (1850), *graffiti* (1851), *buon fresco* (1874), *cire perdu* (1876), *paillette* (1878), *trompe l'oeil* (1889). At least a portion of the motive for these borrowings was their overtone of cosmopolitan sophistication. Even the most common of earth hues, red ochre, acquired in the course of the century novel synonyms ranging from *kokowai* (borrowed from Maori, 1836) to *terre rosa* (a painter's color marketed by the mail-order house Sears and Roebuck in 1897). With the rise of china painting as a popular craft, new color names were required; suggestions in a home reference work of 1883 included such novelties as *mauve* (1859), *turquoise* (1859), and *chamois* (1872). The best paints, this North American book advised, were "those of Lacroix of Paris" (*Treasures*, 390), and French paints were better if known by their French names.

The flood of borrowed words was to some purists a catastrophe, turning the gallimaufry (as one observer, in 1579, had termed the mixture of Latin, French, and English current in his day) into an overcooked stew made from words of diverse origin. A contrary opinion presented the language as an evidence of anglophone cosmopolitan superiority.

> The English-speaking people of the nineteenth century, whether they live at home in the British Isles, emigrate to America, Australia, New Zealand, or the Cape, or are the descendants of Englishmen, Scotchmen, and Irishmen who have emigrated a hundred or two hundred years ago, are continually making additions to their admirable mother tongue. The English language is endowed with a higher vitality than any other now spoken upon the globe, and begs, borrows, steals, and assimilates words wherever it can find them without any other rule of accretion than that the new word shall either express a new idea or render an old one more tersely and completely than before. (C. Mackay 399)

This view, expressed here by Charles Mackay, presumes a more rational process of vocabulary development than the record can support. English speakers around the globe seldom plucked foreign flowers to ornament the language or selected terms to hone the edge of intellect. Most borrowings were near or exact synonyms of existing English words; thus *menu* (1837) provided the cachet of French elegance to the native *bill of fare*, and *café noir* (1841) was no more than *black coffee* (1796). An *English horn* (1838) was the same instrument whether called by that name or by *corno inglese* (1856), as some music critics wished to do. An *aquarium* (1847) was, after all, nothing more than a jumped-up *tub of fishes* (pre-1800).

Mackay wanted to use the evidence of words to demonstrate that English had a "higher vitality" than any other language, and many of his successors have been content to allow the copious vocabulary to serve as an evidence of excellence in English. Less *jingoistic* (1878) interpretations of borrowings are to be sought in two places. One is the unparalleled enterprise of nineteenth-century lexicographers. Whitney's *Century Dictionary* (1889–91) contained nearly half a million definitions. When Mackay wrote, in the 1860s, the most popular large dictionary in Britain was John Ogilvie's *Imperial* (1850), a two-volume work based upon Noah Webster's. Ogilvie alleged on his title page that his dictionary had the virtue of "comprising all words purely English," but a single column (chosen at random) contains *boiobi* 'a green snake, found in America', *boitiäpo* 'a Brazilian serpent', and *bolbocerous* 'a genus of Coleopterous insects'. None of these words found their way into the *OED,* and even biologists might have questioned whether they were "purely English." The sheer bulk of such large dictionaries, however, was taken as unquestioned evidence of the "vitality" of the language.

A second explanation for the size of the English word-stock lies in the global dispersal of speakers of the language. More than any other linguistic community then or earlier, anglophones in the nineteenth century explored the remotest parts of the globe and encountered new things described in languages new to them. Exploration of the high Arctic, for instance, had brought English-speakers into contact with Inuit peoples from the seventeenth century forward. (*Inuit* as a word entered English in 1765, though the term *Eskimo* [1584] was more commonly used in the nineteenth century.) From the perspective of the *OED*, the following borrowings had become English by 1900: *aglu* 'a breathing hole in the ice made by a seal' (1835), *angekok* 'shaman' (1767), *igloo* 'snow house' (1662), *kamik* 'seal-skin boot' (1891), *kayak* 'canoe covered with seal-skin' (1662), *komatik* 'dog-sled' (1824), *muckluck* 'high seal-skin boot' (1868), *muktuk* 'whale skin eaten as food' (1835), *nunatak* 'peak of rock appearing above ice' (1877), *parka* 'long, hooded coat' (1780), *piblokto* 'sickness affecting dogs' (1898), *tupik* 'hut or tent of skins' (1864), *ulu* 'crescent-shaped skinning knife' (1864), *umiak* 'large boat' (1769). Of these, *igloo, kayak,* and *parka* achieved widespread currency. A more comprehensive inspection of writings about the Arctic—as provided, for instance, by Tabbert—shows that dozens more such words were used in "English" contexts, yet their existence is not so much evidence for "vitality" as for the curiosity of visitors and settlers in the far north. They do not support the idea that anglophones sought "new ideas" (as Mackay had claimed); they attest to an appetite for enlarging English by embracing the otherness of newly encountered cultures.

Like most languages, English acquires new words and elaborates new senses of existing words by use of the materials already available. With the explosive growth of *railroads* (1773), first drawn by horses and subsequently by *locomotives* (1829), new terminology comprising mostly native elements flowed into the lexicon. *Railway* (1776) was, at first, the common term in Britain and in North America, but in the United States *railroad* became the more usual word, while British usage kept the word *railway*. These two words rapidly entered a process of word formation with prefixes and suffixes including *Anti-Railwayist* (1881), *berailroaded* (1852), *prerailroad* (1860), *railroader* (1881), *railroadiana* 'matters pertaining to a railroad' (1838), *railroadish* (1855), *railroadship* 'connection by a railroad' (1883), *railwayize* 'furnish with a railway' (1873), *railwayless* 'lacking a railway' (1860). From the initial noun, *railroad* acquired verbal uses—"Nearly every country except China has been railroaded" (1894)—and a metaphorical extension meaning "to rush": "The way men are railroaded to the gallows" (1898).

Nominal modification allowed innumerable combinations like *railroad carriage* (1839) and *railway signal* (1838). As William A. Craigie noted in the *OED*, "the great development of railways in the 19th c., leading to an extensive use of the word in various connexions, has given rise to many attributive collocations of a more or less permanent character, while the number of those which may be formed at will is infinite" (s.v. *railway*). (In a private letter to Craigie, Murray severely criticized the inclusion of such "attributive use of these words" in the *OED;* such combinations as *railway director* [1837] were, he thought, "a grammatical, not a lexicographic matter" [quoted by Burchfield, 17]).

Combinations like *railway director* took on an independent vitality. "A plant conspicuous at railway stations in India" acquired two names—the *railroad-creeper* (1891) and the *railway-creeper* (1895). A *railway novel* (1871) was a piece of light fiction suitable for reading on a journey, and a *railway rug* (1883) was a *lap robe* (1866) used in chilly railway carriages. By the end of the century, there was even an affliction called *railway-spine* 'produced by concussion in a railway accident' (1878).

Other words were added to English at midcentury through the revival of native materials such as adverb-forming prefix *a-*. Words like *aflame* and *astir* were old in English, but Robert Browning determined to revivify this method of making new words, particularly by converting verbs normally expressed in his day with *-ing*. Among his creations were *astrain* 'straining' and *atingle* (both 1856) as well as *ahunt* (1875) and *aspread* (1879). Elizabeth Browning added to the pattern *atremble* (1856) and *athrob* (1857). Other literary figures chimed in: *asway* (William Morris, 1858), *asmear* (Charles Dickens, 1861), *asquirm* (William Dean Howells, 1866), *aswing* (Edward Dowden, 1876), and *awreck* (Joaquin Miller, 1878). Some of these were imitated by others; thus *aspout* (1870), *aquiver* (1883), and *awhirl* (1883) appeared in magazines and newspapers whose writers had caught the fashion. Similarly, the suffix *-(e)ry* 'the practice of doing' conveyed the idea expressed by the word stem; old in English were words like *archery* and *bigotry*. On this pattern, the nineteenth century produced *basketry* (1851), *dentistry* (1838), and *snobbery* (1843). Though not one of the most productive processes of word creation, these two methods of making new words paved the way for *photographers* (1847) to be *atremble* over "the *wizardry* [1583] of *Kodakery* [< Kodak, 1893]" when that slogan appeared in advertising at the end of the century.

Even the oldest elements of the English vocabulary could be revived and reshaped. The prefix *be-* in Old English had the meaning "near" or "around" in words like *below* 'near low' or *become* 'come about'. These prefixes, however, had become so firmly fused to the words they formed that they were no longer considered as separable elements. Later *be-* acquired an extension of this meaning, glossed by Murray as "covered with" as in *becloud* 'cover with clouds' (1598) or *bejeweled* (1557). Nineteenth-century innovators made this *be-* a living prefix. Thomas Carlyle was particularly fanciful in such creations: "Open scoundrels rode . . . bediademed, becoronetted, bemitred" (1837). Partly as a result of Carlyle's stylistic verve, others joined the trend. In Murray's words, "in modern use (e.g. with Carlyle) the force of the *be-* is often merely rhetorical, expressing depreciation, ridicule, or raillery, on the part of the speaker toward the appendage or ornamentation in question" (s.v. *be-*). Many of these new words might be glossed as "overrun with or afflicted by": *bedaughtered* dowagers (1830), *bepilgrimed* shrine (1857), *berailroaded* landscape (1852), *betaxed* people (1884). Innovations of this kind do not "express a new idea or render an old one more tersely and completely than before" (as Mackay had explained the motive for innovation). In fact, they lengthen the corresponding words to no obvious purpose—*behatted* (1812) and *begabled* (1860) are synonyms of *hatted* (1552) and *gabled* (1849). What they accomplish is to provide stylistic nuance and novelty, both aspects of innovation insufficiently appreciated in most treatments of English words.

Another prefix to explode in popularity was *non-*. Though long established in English, particularly in the technical vocabulary of the law in words like *nonjuring* (1691) or *nonsuit* (1380), *non-* underwent "very extensive development" in the nineteenth century (as Murray explained in the *OED*). Thus a Manchester newspaper could write in 1884 of "non-acquaintance with the English tongue," and at about the same time, at the height of the temperance movement, a law journal offered the category of *non-abstainer* (1882). The fashion for prefixing with *non-* extended to a great variety of grammatical forms: *non-beer-drinking* (1866), *non-contentiously* (1885), *non-agricultural* (1848), *non-factory household work* (1835), *non-umbrellaed spectators* (1864), *non-worker* (1851), among many others. By this method, almost any concept or quality could be turned to its opposite, and semantic distinctions or verbal nuance could be highlighted (for instance, the long established term *immoral* [1660] was elaborated by being set in contrast to *amoral* [1882], *nonmoral* [1866], and *unmoral* [1841]). The dynamism of word creation was harnessed by the emerging social sciences, in particular, in forming new technical vocabulary though the use of *non-*.

Dictionaries, with their separately entered "words" and neatly divided senses, give a misleading impression about precision in the use of language. Vocabulary is constantly in flux. Both *sincerity* and *sincereness,* for instance, had been available since the early sixteenth century, with *sincerity* by far the more common of the two. The use of *sincereness* by Robert Browning (1844) and by Matthew Arnold (1879) was not to draw a distinction between that word and *sincerity* but a result of spontaneous creativity in word formation, recorded in the *OED* because of the literary reputation of these two writers, while the use of *sincereness* by others was probably ignored as merely a mistake. Similarly, *citizenship* (1611) had no need of the nineteenth-century synonyms *citizenry* (1819) or *citizenhood* (1871), though once these new words came into use it was possible to distinguish "the citizenship of the students" from, say, "the citizenry of the school." It is by no means clear that everyone who utters them makes a distinction between *admonishment* and *admonition,* for instance, or between *conciseness* and *concision.* They may be different, of course, or be made different. In many contexts, *abolishment* and *abolition* are synonyms, but only the latter came to be used in the United States for opposition first to the slave trade and then to the institution of slavery itself. That distinction having been made, it was possible to derive from it new words—for instance, *abolitional* (1846), *abolitionary* (1859), *abolitiondom* (1857), *abolitioner* (1855), *abolitionize* (1854)—and new combinations: *abolition party* (1852) and *Abolition Society* (1790). One opposed to slavery favored *abolition* not *abolishment* and was an *abolitionist* not an *abolisher.*

Each act of speaking (or writing) creates new senses for the words used. For the most part, these senses will be indistinguishable from their predecessors expressed by the same word, but the imperceptible process of "drift" causes a shift away from old meanings to new ones. Sometimes this drift expands the range of meaning; this process H. W. Fowler—a nineteenth-century purist writing in the twentieth century—called "slipshod extension." Like many of his classically educated contemporaries, Fowler objected when words drifted beyond their denotation in their source language. Thus, *dilemma* for him could only be a choice between two things, not among several; even worse was the further "extension" in which a *dilemma* meant a state of confusion or uncertainty. When Emerson wrote of "the dilemma of a swimmer among drowning men" (*OED,* s.v. *dilemma*), he was guilty of "slipshod extension." Pleading for preservation of the etymology, Fowler urged that if a *dilemma* could not be limited to two things, at least it should involve a "definite number." "A person who has taken a taxi & finds on alighting that he has left his money at home is in a difficulty; he is not in a dilemma, but he will very likely say afterwards that he found himself in one" (Fowler, 541). The drift from a choice between two options to a muddle among many vaguely defined ones is one direction of meaning shift.

Many meaning shifts move words in imperceptible ways. Before mechanical propulsion, all *sailing* ships were driven by wind passing across the sails; in the nineteenth century, a ship might *sail* by wind or by steam power. *Steaming* (1831) out of port was normal for a *steamship* (1819), but the same vessel might equally *sail* from the harbor even though there were no *sails* aboard. No purist seems to have objected to the "slipshod" extension of *sail* in such usages or described the new application as "loose" (as Murray had done in his definition of the unetymological uses of *dilemma* in the *OED*). The fact that ships continued to *sail* was natural enough, a meaning extension not noticed even by vigilant word-watchers.

Sail applied to *steamships* and broadened its scope. A meaning shift that narrowed the application of a word is illustrated by *commode*. When introduced from France in 1786, *commode* described an elaborate piece of furniture with drawers and compartments, often used in drawing rooms and bedrooms. By 1851, the *commode* was increasingly used in reference to "a small article of furniture enclosing a chamber utensil" (*OED*), the *utensil* (1699 in this sense) being a *chamber-pot* (1570, a term sparsely documented by the *OED*). With the miracles wrought by plumbers in the nineteenth century, the *commode* was narrowed in application to the vitreous china bowl, a device also known as a *water-closet* (1842 in the modern sense) or a *stool* (a *stool* had described a piece of furniture containing the *chamber utensil* since medieval times). The modern meaning of *commode* 'water closet' emerged from the process of specialization from the large and decorative piece of furniture, then to the modest cabinet containing the chamber pot, and then to the porcelain fixture with attached plumbing. It did not take place through sudden innovation by some imaginative user of English but through the drift of application natural among the anonymous many in a changing language community.

Euphemizing (1857) English was a process of substituting prettier words for ones with nasty associations; an opposite process produced *dysphemisms* (1884). *Commode* was a way of getting around mentioning *pot* or *vessel,* both euphemisms for the container universally found in nineteenth-century bedrooms. Another shortening, according to the *OED,* was used in the "crockery trade": *chamber.* Dysphemisms included *mingo, piss-pot,* and *thunder mug* (listed with others by Farmer and Henley, s.v. *It*). A racy American joke book published in 1888 makes humor out of the contrast of rural dysphemism and urban euphemism.

> The newly wedded country gent was registering at the Grand Pacific. The urbane clerk suggested the bridal chamber. Groom did not seem to take. The clerk again repeats his question, "Don't you want a bridal chamber?" Countryman—Wall, you might send one up for her, I guess, but I can piss out of the window. (*The Stag Party,* 89)

Victorian prudery and yearning for euphemism has doubtless been exaggerated, but the desire for nicer words for indelicate subjects produced such synonyms as *night article* (1922 but probably in earlier use), *jerry* (1859), and *po* (1880). The last of these renders *pot* as a French word and conceals the vessel in the decent disguise of a foreign tongue.

Euphemism and dysphemism also played a role in the most enduring of the nineteenth-century innovations in English, the naming of places in the world. Settlements hacked out of the rough North American wilderness were given names like *Eden, Paradise,* and *Climax;* others indistinguishable from the first in topography or fertility were called *Hell, Hog Eye,* or *Peculiar.* The process is shown in an Idaho town first called *Rattlesnake* (after the *Rattlesnake Creek*); when the Union Pacific Railroad arrived, a tent camp was raised for the track workers and called *Tuttville* after one J. A. Tutwiler, a stagecoach driver and entrepreneur; as a village grew up around the *depot* (1832), it acquired the more elegant name of *Mountain Home* (see Boone, 263). With the bigotry typical of the century, Idaho namers applied the terms *Jap Creek, Chink Gulch,* and *Nigger Creek.* But they also designated places as *Belleview, Fairylawn,* and *Blossom.*

Naming and renaming was a primary activity that affected words in the nineteenth century. The names of military heroes and political leaders were applied liberally to settlements around the world: *Monrovia* in Liberia (< James Monroe, U.S. president), *Nelson* in Canada and New Zealand, *Washington* in nearly every U.S. state, *Macquarie* and *Cook* in Australia. Of these, the most widely applied was *Victoria* for the monarch whose name ornaments capital cities in Australia, Hong Kong, and Canada, *Lake Victoria* in central Africa, and the immense *Victoria Falls* in southern Africa. There are *Victoria*s on every continent except South America, including geographical features in the Arctic and in Antarctica. In 1850, a newly discovered asteroid was, inevitably, named *Victoria* too.

As people thought about their personal geography, new names and new senses flourished. *Uptown* (1802), *downtown* (1836), and *crosstown* (1886) formed the points of the compass for many residents of U.S. towns and cities. Building plots in the United States were laid out in *blocks* (1823 < *blocks of lots* [1815]), and this way of thinking about the townscape also spread to Australia (1833). Shopping districts were organized on rational plans, often based simply on a grid of streets designated by numbers (e.g., *Fifth Avenue*). By midcentury residents of Melbourne were in the habit of *doing the block* or promenading with the expectation of buying something in a *store* (a U.S. usage borrowed by Australians and used instead of the usual British expression *shop*). Such walks took *shoppers* (1860) along what Mayhew's Londoners called the *main drag* (1851; 1:218) or what Americans were likely to call a *business street* (1881). People in the anglophone world might live as *roomers* (1871) in a *rooming house* (1893) or in a *bunkhouse* (1876) or in a *shack* (1878) or a *maisonette* (1793) or a *semi-detached* house (1859) or an *apartment house* (1874)—all of them new names for housing. Some of them might have a *door bell* (1815) at the entrance and contain such novelties as a *recreation room* (1854), a *foyer* (1859), a *half bath* (1875), or a *linen closet* (1880). Illumination in sumptuous public places or mansions might be by means of a *gaselier* (1849, a blend of *gas* and *chandelier*) or some more humble method of supplying *gaslight* (1808); *electric light* (1843) was not generally available until the end of the century. *Underwear* (1879), though mostly submerged in *unmentionableness* (1870) included novelties of all kinds: *knickers* (1881 < *knickerbockers* [1809]) and *jock straps* (1886, < *jock* 'penis'), for instance. As the world was transformed, so with it was the vocabulary.

Personal names changed too. People eager to assimilate to anglophone culture changed their names to something that sounded more "English" than what they had received at birth. *Josef* and *José* became *Joseph; Maria* and *Mashenka* became *Mary*—if not in the first generation, then in the second or third. Surnames like *McGillicuddy* or *McGeoghegan* were often reduced to *Mack; Schoen* and *Schneider* to *Shane* and *Snyder; Alberti* and *Canadeo* to *Albert* and *Kennedy.* Renaming oneself, or choosing names for one's children, became a cultural embrace between people and English words. When the children of the nineteenth century became political leaders a generation later, some of them bore a richly multicultural palimpsest of names: John George Diefenbaker in Canada, William Vacanarat Shadrach Tubman in Liberia, Hastings Kamuzu Banda in Malawi, and Solomon West Ridgeway Dias Bandaranaike in Sri Lanka.

The nineteenth century also reshaped the landscape of English, not so much by naming or by euphemism or by creation or borrowing of new words as by the shifting relations among existing ones. In a modern thesaurus under the heading "people who are friends" (McArthur, 91) are found *friend, friendship, acquaintance, acquaintanceship, pal, chum, mate,* and *buddy.* None of these terms is exotic, and the list might easily be extended to include many other modern words—including names for women friends—and further nuance in the definitions and distinctions provided for them.

Two of these words were not available at the very beginning of the nineteenth century; *aquaintanceship* was first recorded in 1803, and *buddy* did not appear in the sense of "friend, companion" until 1850. *Pal, mate,* and *chum* already existed in English well before 1800 and, with *buddy,* can now be used as forms of address restricted, according to the modern British thesaurus, only by the fact that *pal* and *buddy* are likely to be American and *mate* "especially British, especially working class." In the nineteenth century, these words were used in the same form and in the same way as terms of address. Not until the end of the century, however, did *pal* lose its association with the British criminal subculture—it meant an accomplice in crime—and in 1841 a writer was at pains to explain *pal* as describing women who consorted with criminals. One of the specimen sentences in the modern thesaurus—"They've been pals for years"—would not have had the same meaning a hundred years before that work was compiled. Similarly, *chum* was primarily used of criminals and convicts; a *new chum* in Australia was a recently arrived convict and, later in the century, a term for any new immigrant. By extension, *chum* also meant "schoolfellow" or "fellow student," and it did not acquire its generalized meaning of "good friend" until modern times. *Mate* (and *matey*) arose among sailors, and the maritime association was certainly stronger through the nineteenth century than it is today.

Nineteenth-century English was abundantly supplied with terms of address, of course, but *mate, pal, chum,* and *buddy* occupied a relatively minor place among them, even at the end of the century. Terms of affectionate and informal friendship were frequently coined or borrowed: *amigo* (United States, 1837), *alanna* (Ireland,

1841), *birdeen* (Ireland, 1896), *boyo* (Ireland, 1870), *bub* (United States, 1839), *cobber* (Australia and New Zealand, 1895), *cocker* (England, 1888), *doddie* (Scotland, ca. 1890), *fella* (England, 1864), *kiddo* (United States, 1896), *guy* 'man, fellow' (England, 1847), *maat* (South Africa, 1900), *pard* (United States, 1872), *side-kicker* (United States, 1903), *tootsie* (United States, 1895). More formal terms accumulated from other languages in the colonial outposts of English: *burra sahi* (India, 1807), *inkosi* (South Africa, 1827), *mem-sahib* (India, 1857), *morena* (South Africa, 1835), *oubaas* (South Africa, 1824), *sahib* (India, 1696), *taubada* (New Guinea, 1891), *tuan* (Malaya, 1779). Abusive labels were probably more frequent than the familiar or respectful ones; among the nineteenth-century innovations were *bludger* (Australia, 1900), *bounder* (England, 1889), *faggot* (used as a derisive term for a woman, 1840), *omadhaun* (Ireland, 1818), *partan* (Scotland, 1896), *pounce* (England, 1861), *rube* (United States, 1804), *scunge* (Scotland, 1824), *sod* (England, 1855). These terms—a selection from a huge and badly documented number—could be bitterly offensive or cheerfully affectionate. Each word was shaped by the context of use and by the available alternatives. As each emerged or faded from the scene, its departure or arrival affected all the others.

Even the most stable of the words in the domain of friendship was subject to semantic evolution. In his influential thesaurus of 1816, George Crabb laid out the difference between *friendship* and *love*.

> *Love* subsists between members of the same family; it springs out of their natural relationship, and is kept alive by their close intercourse and constant interchange of kindnesses; *friendship* excludes the idea of any tender and natural relationship; nor is it, like *love*, to be found in children, but is confined to maturer years; it is formed by time, by circumstances, by congruity of character, and sympathy of sentiment. *Love* always operates with ardour; *friendship* is remarkable for firmness and constancy. *Love* is peculiar to no station; it is to be found equally among the high and the low, the learned and the unlearned; *friendship* is of nobler growth; it finds admittance only into minds of loftier make; it cannot be felt by men of an ordinary stamp. (380)

This exercise in definition has little in common with the parallel treatment of the two words in a modern thesaurus. The modern author of such a work, of course, attempts to describe the words as they are used by the community and would make no distinctions of this kind if they were not supported by usage. Yet Crabb was a thoughtful lexicographer, and his account offers some hint that even so stable-seeming a word as *friendship* may have shifted its semantic ground as the world changed through the course of nineteenth-century English.

In the preface to his *Dictionary* of 1755, Samuel Johnson had written "that words are the daughters of earth, and that things are the sons of heaven." In many respects, the nineteenth century attempted to reverse these equations. As "things" lost their fixity and certainty—a loss occasioned in part by the Higher Criticism of the Bible, which highlighted the human rather than the divine aspects of Scripture—"words" became a new source of racial memory and authority. Unprecedented efforts were made to recall words long dead, if not for use at least to be enshrined in dictionaries. Noah Webster and his successors made strenuous efforts to market an English dictionary for every home library, and it was sometimes observed that households with one book owned the Bible and those with two the Bible and the dictionary. In both Britain and North America, the study of words became a school subject, and textbooks to serve the young flourished. Trench's *On the Study of Words*, for instance, was published for school use, and his American editor, Thomas D. Suplée, recommended that pupils "be compelled to commit the outlines and exercises to memory, place them on the blackboard, and then, assuming the rôle of lecturer, proceed to expand the leading ideas" (8). A. L. Mayhew, an Oxford word enthusiast, performed the same pedagogical transformation of Trench's work for British schools.

Hobbyists, variously equipped for the work, became "word hunters," a metaphor from field sports made explicit in Abram Smythe Palmer's *Word-Hunter's Note-Book* (1876).

> That in every case I have been successful in running down my quarry would be too much to expect. The most enthusiastic lover of the

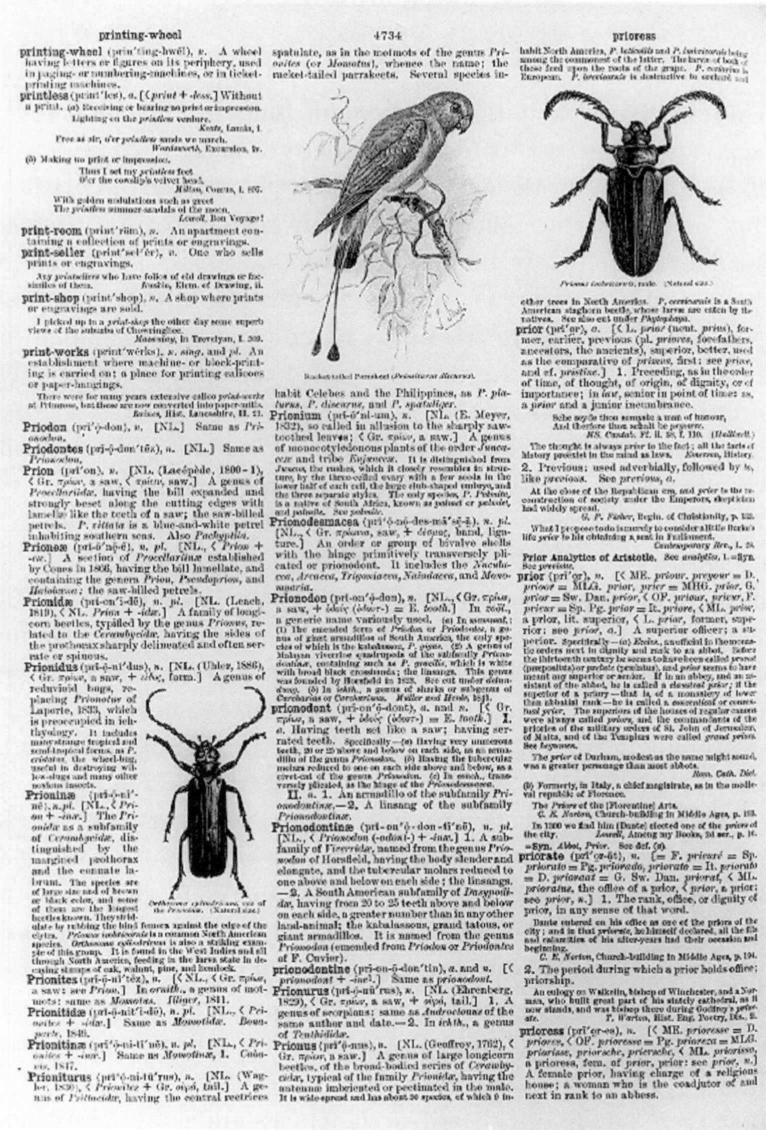

printing-wheel 4734 prioress

printing-wheel (prin'ting-hwēl), *n.* A wheel having letters or figures on its periphery, used in paging- or numbering-machines, or in ticket-printing machines.

printless (print'les), *a.* [< *print* + *-less.*] Without a print. (*a*) Receiving or bearing no print or impression.

> Lighting on the *printless* verdure.
> *Keats*, Lamia, i.

> Free as air, o'er *printless* sands we march.
> *Wordsworth*, Excursion, iv.

(*b*) Making no print or impression.

> Thus I set my *printless* feet
> O'er the cowslip's velvet head.
> *Milton*, Comus, l. 897.

> With golden undulations such as greet
> The *printless* summer-sandals of the moon.
> *Lowell*, Bon Voyage!

print-room (print'röm), *n.* An apartment containing a collection of prints or engravings.

print-seller (print'sel'ėr), *n.* One who sells prints or engravings.

> Any *printsellers* who have folios of old drawings or facsimiles of them. *Ruskin*, Elem. of Drawing, ii.

print-shop (print'shop), *n.* A shop where prints or engravings are sold.

> I picked up in a *print-shop* the other day some superb views of the suburbs of Chowringhee.
> *Macaulay*, in Trevelyan, I. 339.

print-works (print'wėrks), *n. sing.* and *pl.* An establishment where machine- or block-printing is carried on; a place for printing calicoes or paper-hangings.

> There were for many years extensive calico *print-works* at Primrose, but these are now converted into paper-mills.
> *Baines*, Hist. Lancashire, II. 21.

Priodon (prī'ǭ-don), *n.* [NL.] Same as *Prionodon.*

Priodontes (prī-ǭ-don'tēz), *n.* [NL.] Same as *Prionodon.*

Prion (prī'on), *n.* [NL. (Lacépède, 1800–1), < Gr. πρίων, a saw, < πρίειν, saw.] A genus of *Procellariidæ*, having the bill expanded and strongly beset along the cutting edges with lamellæ like the teeth of a saw; the saw-billed petrels. *P. vittata* is a blue-and-white petrel inhabiting southern seas. Also *Pachyptila.*

Prioneæ (prī-ō'nǭ-ē), *n. pl.* [NL., < *Prion* + *-eæ.*] A section of *Procellariinæ* established by Coues in 1866, having the bill lamellate, and containing the genera *Prion*, *Pseudoprion*, and *Halobæna*; the saw-billed petrels.

Prionidæ (prī-on'i-dē), *n. pl.* [NL. (Leach, 1819), < NL. *Prion* + *-idæ.*] A family of longicorn beetles, typified by the genus *Prionus*, related to the *Cerambycidæ*, having the sides of the prothorax sharply delineated and often serrate or spinous.

Prionidus (prī-ǭ-nī'dus), *n.* [NL. (Uhler, 1886), < Gr. πρίων, a saw, + εἶδος, form.] A genus of reduviid bugs, replacing *Prionotus* of Laporte, 1833, which is preoccupied in ichthyology. It includes many strange tropical and semi-tropical forms, as *P. cristatus*, the wheel-bug, useful in destroying willow-slugs and many other noxious insects.

Orthosoma cylindricum, one of the *Prioninæ*. (Natural size.)

Prioninæ (prī-ǭ-nī'nē), *n. pl.* [NL., < *Prion* + *-inæ.*] The *Prionidæ* as a subfamily of *Cerambycidæ*, distinguished by the margined prothorax and the connate labrum. The species are of large size and of brown or black color, and some of them are the largest beetles known. They stridulate by rubbing the hind femora against the edge of the elytra. *Prionus imbricornis* is a common North American species. *Orthosoma cylindricum* is also a striking example of this group. It is found in the West Indies and all through North America, feeding in the larva state in decaying stumps of oak, walnut, pine, and hemlock.

Prionites (prī-ǭ-nī'tēz), *n.* [< NL., < Gr. πρίων, a saw: see *Prion.*] In *ornith.*, a genus of motmots: same as *Momotus.* *Illiger*, 1811.

Prionitidæ (prī-ǭ-nit'i-dē), *n. pl.* [NL., < *Prionites* + *-idæ.*] Same as *Momotidæ.* *Bonaparte*, 1849.

Prionitinæ (prī'ǭ-ni-tī'nē), *n. pl.* [NL., < *Prionites* + *-inæ.*] Same as *Momotinæ*, 1. *Cabanis*, 1847.

Prioniturus (prī'ǭ-ni-tū'rus), *n.* [NL. (Wagler, 1830), < *Prionites* + Gr. οὐρά, tail.] A genus of *Psittacidæ*, having the central rectrices spatulate, as in the motmots of the genus *Prionites* (or *Momotus*), whence the name; the racket-tailed parrakeets. Several species inhabit Celebes and the Philippines, as *P. platurus*, *P. discurus*, and *P. spatuliger.*

Racket-tailed Parrakeet (*Prioniturus discurus*).

Prionium (prī-ō'ni-um), *n.* [NL. (E. Meyer, 1832), so called in allusion to the sharply saw-toothed leaves; < Gr. πρίων, a saw.] A genus of monocotyledonous plants of the order *Junceaceæ* and tribe *Eujunceæ.* It is distinguished from *Juncus*, the rushes, which it closely resembles in structure, by the three-celled ovary with a few seeds in the lower half of each cell, the large club-shaped embryo, and the three separate styles. The only species, *P. Palmita*, is a native of South Africa, known as *palmiet* or *palmiet*, and *palmite.* See *palmite.*

Prionodesmacea (prī'ǭ-nǭ-des-mā'sē-ä), *n. pl.* [NL., < Gr. πρίων, saw, + δεσμός, band, ligature.] An order or group of bivalve shells with the hinge primitively transversely plicated or prionodont. It includes the *Nuculacea*, *Arcacea*, *Trigoniacea*, *Naiadacea*, and *Mesomyaria.*

Prionodon (prī-on'ǭ-don), *n.* [NL., < Gr. πρίων, a saw, + ὀδούς (ὀδοντ-) = E. *tooth.*] In *zoöl.*, a generic name variously used. (*a*) In *mammal.*: (1) The emended form of *Priodon* or *Priodontes*, a genus of giant armadillos of South America, the only species of which is the kabalassou, *P. gigas.* (2) A genus of Malayan viverrine quadrupeds of the subfamily *Prionodontinæ*, containing such as *P. gracilis*, which is white with broad black crossbands; the linsangs. This genus was founded by Horsfield in 1823. See cut under *delundung.* (*b*) In *ichth.*, a genus of sharks or subgenus of *Carcharias* or *Carcharinus.* *Müller and Henle*, 1841.

prionodont (prī-on'ǭ-dont), *a.* and *n.* [< Gr. πρίων, a saw, + ὀδούς (ὀδοντ-) = E. *tooth.*] **I.** *a.* Having teeth set like a saw; having serrated teeth. Specifically—(*a*) Having very numerous teeth, 20 or 25 above and below on each side, as an armadillo of the genus *Prionodon.* (*b*) Having the tubercular molars reduced to one on each side above and below, as a civet-cat of the genus *Prionodon.* (*c*) In *conch.*, transversely plicated, as the hinge of the *Prionodesmacea.*

II. *n.* 1. An armadillo of the subfamily *Prionodontinæ.*—2. A linsang of the subfamily *Prionodontinæ.*

Prionodontinæ (prī-on'ǭ-don-tī'nē), *n. pl.* [NL., < *Prionodon* (*-odont-*) + *-inæ.*] 1. A subfamily of *Viverridæ*, named from the genus *Prionodon* of Horsfield, having the body slender and elongate, and the tubercular molars reduced to one above and below on each side; the linsangs. —2. A South American subfamily of *Dasypodidæ*, having from 20 to 25 teeth above and below on each side, a greater number than in any other land-animal; the kabalassous, grand tatous, or giant armadillos. It is named from the genus *Prionodon* (emended from *Priodon* or *Priodontes* of F. Cuvier).

prionodontine (prī-on-ǭ-don'tin), *a.* and *n.* [< *prionodont* + *-ine*¹.] Same as *prionodont.*

Prionurus (prī-ǭ-nū'rus), *n.* [NL. (Ehrenberg, 1829), < Gr. πρίων, a saw, + οὐρά, tail.] 1. A genus of scorpions: same as *Androctonus* of the same author and date.—2. In *ichth.*, a genus of *Teuthididæ.*

Prionus (prī'ǭ-nus), *n.* [NL. (Geoffroy, 1762), < Gr. πρίων, a saw.] A genus of large longicorn beetles, of the broad-bodied series of *Cerambycidæ*, typical of the family *Prionidæ*, having the antennæ imbricated or pectinated in the male. It is wide-spread and has about 30 species, of which 9 inhabit North America, *P. laticollis* and *P. imbricornis* being among the commonest of the latter. The larvæ of both of these feed upon the roots of the grape. *P. coriarius* is European. *P. laticollis* is destructive to orchard and other trees in North America. *P. cervicornis* is a South American staghorn beetle, whose larvæ are eaten by the natives. See also cut under *Phytophaga.*

Prionus imbricornis, male. (Natural size.)

prior (prī'or), *a.* [< L. *prior* (neut. *prius*), former, earlier, previous (pl. *priores*, forefathers, ancestors, the ancients), superior, better, used as the comparative of *primus*, first: see *prime*, and cf. *pristine.*] 1. Preceding, as in the order of time, of thought, of origin, of dignity, or of importance; in *law*, senior in point of time: as, a *prior* and a junior incumbrance.

> Sche seyde thou semyste a man of honour,
> And therfore thou schalt be *pryowre.*
> *MS. Cantab.* Ff. ii. 38, f. 110. (*Halliwell.*)

> The thought is always *prior* to the fact; all the facts of history preexist in the mind as laws. *Emerson*, History.

2. Previous; used adverbially, followed by *to*, like *previous.* See *previous*, *a.*

> At the close of the Republican era, and *prior* to the reconstruction of society under the Emperors, skepticism had widely spread.
> *G. P. Fisher*, Begin. of Christianity, p. 132.

> What I propose to do is merely to consider a little Burke's life *prior* to his obtaining a seat in Parliament.
> *Contemporary Rev.*, L. 28.

Prior Analytics of Aristotle. See *analytic*, 1.=**Syn.** See *previous.*

prior (prī'or), *n.* [< ME. *priour*, *preyour* = D. *prioor* = MLG. *prior*, *prier* = MHG. *prior*, G. *prior* = Sw. Dan. *prior*, < OF. *priour*, *prieur*, F. *prieur* = Sp. Pg. *prior* = It. *priore*, < ML. *prior*, a prior, lit. superior, < L. *prior*, former, superior: see *prior*, *a.*] A superior officer; a superior. Specifically—(*a*) *Eccles.*, an official in the monastic orders next in dignity and rank to an abbot. Before the thirteenth century he seems to have been called *provost* (*præpositus*) or *prelate* (*prælatus*), and *prior* seems to have meant any superior or senior. If in an abbey, and an assistant of the abbot, he is called a *claustral prior*; if the superior of a priory—that is, of a monastery of lower than abbatial rank—he is called a *conventical* or *conventual prior.* The superiors of the houses of regular canons were always called *priors*, and the commandants of the priories of the military orders of St. John of Jerusalem, of Malta, and of the Templars were called *grand priors.* See *hospitaller.*

> The *prior* of Durham, modest as the name might sound, was a greater personage than most abbots.
> *Rom. Cath. Dict.*

(*b*) Formerly, in Italy, a chief magistrate, as in the medieval republic of Florence.

> The *Priors* of the [Florentine] Arts.
> *C. E. Norton*, Church-building in Middle Ages, p. 193.

> In 1300 we find him [Dante] elected one of the *priors* of the city. *Lowell*, Among my Books, 2d ser., p. 16.

=**Syn.** *Abbot*, *Prior.* See def. (*a*).

priorate (prī'or-āt), *n.* [= F. *prieuré* = Sp. *priorato* = Pg. *priorado*, *priorato* = It. *priorato* = D. *prioraat* = G. Sw. Dan. *priorat*, < ML. *prioratus*, the office of a prior, < *prior*, a prior: see *prior*, *n.*] 1. The rank, office, or dignity of prior, in any sense of that word.

> Dante entered on his office as one of the priors of the city; and in that *priorate*, he himself declared, all the ills and calamities of his after-years had their occasion and beginning.
> *C. E. Norton*, Church-building in Middle Ages, p. 194.

2. The period during which a prior holds office; priorship.

> An eulogy on Walkelin, bishop of Winchester, and a Norman, who built great part of his stately cathedral, as it now stands, and was bishop there during Godfrey's *priorate.* *T. Warton*, Hist. Eng. Poetry, Diss., ii.

prioress (prī'or-es), *n.* [< ME. *prioresse* = D. *priores*, < OF. *prioresse* = Pg. *prioreza* = MLG. *priorisse*, *priorsche*, *priersche*, < ML. *priorissa*, a prioress, fem. of *prior*, prior: see *prior*, *n.*] A female prior, having charge of a religious house; a woman who is the coadjutor of and next in rank to an abbess.

Among the great achievements of book design was *The Century Dictionary* (1889–91), an encyclopedic lexicon with handsome layout, 8,000 pictorial illustrations, and precisely identified quotations illustrating usage. Though the *Oxford English Dictionary* earned enduring fame, *The Century* was promptly published and almost immediately profitable. Editing was supervised by William Dwight Whitney; design and execution were overseen by Theodore Low De Vinne for the Century Company, New York. Sixty years later, Carl Purington Rollins, printer to Yale University, offered this judgment: "In this matter of presswork alone the *Century Dictionary* outranks any other dictionary of its time, and I believe that for compactness, legibility, convenience of arrangement of definitions it is the most successful of our dictionaries" (quoted by Blumenthal, 31).

chase must be prepared for some blank days. This I may say, however, that if I have not dogged every word which I have started through all its doublings till it has taken cover at last in "Noah's ark," I have at least never desisted from the pursuit, nor rested content till I have run it to earth in a Sanskrit root; and that, in the eyes of a philologist, is pretty much the same as winning its brush. (viii)

Words that might have become extinct in earlier centuries—or at least hidden from use in muniment rooms or in unread books— were given new life in the nineteenth century, if not in peoples' mouths, at least in their dictionaries.

SLANG

THOUGH ITS FIRST USES IN reference to language appear in the mid–eighteenth century, *slang* in the modern sense is very much a nineteenth-century word. Francis Grose's *Classical Dictionary of the Vulgar Tongue* (1785) was the first major compilation of such English, one much enlarged and elaborated in a series of nineteenth-century glossaries eventually culminating in the massive dictionary by J. S. Farmer and W. E. Henley, *Slang and Its Analogues* (1890–1904). Grose defines *slang* merely as "cant language," connecting the word to *cant* 'the language of vagabonds, beggars, and criminals'. Canting dictionaries had appeared in the mid–sixteenth century, ostensibly as guides for the unwary, who might use them to thwart criminals with designs upon their purses or persons, and the sales pitch to make the glossaries appear useful to their purchasers continued into the nineteenth century. A "safeguard against the cheats, swindlers, and pickpockets" was compiled by William Perry in 1818, though he shortly left lexicography and went into the service of a brewer, according to John Badcock, who used Perry's *London Guide* as the foundation for his own compilation, *Slang: A Dictionary* (1823). Badcock claimed that his work offered "examples, proofs, and monitory precepts, useful and proper for novices, flats, and yokels," but these collections were seldom applied in such practical ways but appealed to that portion of the book-buying public fascinated by the doings of bucks, swells, Corinthians, and demireps. (Badcock defines *Corinthian* as "a man highly togged" and elaborates: "We would confine the word to nobility and gentry of education, who join heartily in the sports of turf or the ring, the latter particularly; but well-dressed prigs assume the envied name, or seedy sordid knaves, who have no souls for these things.")

By the end of the century, collections of slang had departed from light-hearted and salacious glossaries like Badcock's and, in addition to a few slight collections, moved through John Camden Hotten's *Slang Dictionary* (1859, much enlarged in 1874) to Farmer and Henley's multivolume work, with its solemn apparatus of the citation dictionary whose definitions are elaborated by precisely identified and dated quotations to show the development of words and senses. (Farmer's printer, Thomas Poulter, refused to print the second volume, and Farmer sued him for breach of contract. Poulter countersued on the grounds of "indecencies" and won a judgment of £114, forcing Farmer to seek—and fortunately find—another printer for the further volumes.) Documentation of one of the most vigorous areas of nineteenth-century linguistic innovation thus moved from the light-hearted to the solemn and scholarly. To begin with, attention to *slang* continued the long-established fascination of English-speakers with "low" and "racy" language used by exuberant *slangsters* (1830) and *slangwhangers* (1807; the *OED* supplies quotations from Washington Irving and Thomas Chandler Haliburton). In the course of the century, *slang* extended its range from *cant* to vivid, ephemeral, and informal English of all sorts.

The century brought also with it a flowering of interest in vernacular English. Among the first nineteenth-century contributors to slang lexicography was Hewson Clarke, in his anonymously published *Lexicon Balatronicum: A Dictionary of Buckish Slang, University Wit, and Pickpocket Eloquence* (1811). While giving full credit to Grose as an innovator in his *Classical Dictionary*, Clarke noted that his predecessor had not anticipated the recent explosion of racy language in high society; Grose was "not aware, at the time of its compilation, that our young men of fashion would at no very distant period be as distinguished for the vulgarity of their jargon as the inhabitants of Newgate" (iii).

Writers on slang had long emphasized the secret nature of the language, mistaking, certainly, the likelihood that the honest people would remain undisturbed by conversations conducted in it. In this tradition of concealment, however detached from actual experience, Clarke suggested that his book would have practical value.

> We need not descant on the dangerous impressions that are made on the female mind, by the remarks that fall incidentally from the lips of the brothers or servants of a family; and we have before observed, that improper topics can with our assistance be discussed, even before the ladies, without raising a blush on the cheek of modesty. It is impossible that a female should understand the meaning of *twiddle diddles*, or rise from the table at the mention of *Buckinger's boot*. (vii)

That women would be both innocent and ignorant seems to have been the assumption of the day, though it is hard to imagine that the topic of conversation would be very successfully concealed by the use of slang of this kind. Some flavor of Clarke's philological method can be discerned in his treatment of the two exemplary phrases that he thought "a female" could not possibly understand. *Twiddle diddles* he glossed simply as "testicles" without further elaboration, but *Buckinger's boot* required an anecdote. The entry for *Buckinger's boot* begins simply enough with "the monosyllable," a euphemism that Farmer and Henley tracked to a source written in 1714. *Monosyllable*, in turn, is defined as "a woman's commodity": *commodity*—the commercial metaphor was obvious to the contemporary user of this slang—as "the private parts of a modest woman, and the public parts of a prostitute." While the medical term *testicles* was an adequate gloss for *twiddle diddles*, no such synonym served for *Buckinger's boot*. But Clarke's entry offers more: "Matthew Buckinger was born without hands and legs; notwithstanding which he drew coats of arms very neatly, and could write the Lord's Prayer within the compass of a shilling; he was married to a tall handsome woman, and traversed the country, shewing himself for money." In all this circumlocution, *Buckinger's boot* is never directly defined, helping, ostensibly, to preserve the blush on the cheek of modesty while arousing a salacious glint in the eye of the *buck* (defined by Clarke as "a gay debauchee").

Fashionable young men were increasingly attracted to the jargon of the "inhabitants of Newgate," who were, in the first decades of the century, regarded as the originators of slang. Memoirs of

A COMPLETE CUTTER...(warranted steel.)

. . . .

PUBLISHED BY D. LONGWORTH, NEW-YORK.

Youth culture expressed itself in the Regency dandy during the time of the Prince Regent (1811–20). Elaborate clothing and outrageous English were part of *dandymania*. Beaux, bucks, demireps, and green girls presided over a society of frivolous pastimes and low-life adventures. (From Evans, frontispiece; see Laudermilk and Hamlin.)

criminals had sometimes been accompanied with glossaries supplied, often, by prison chaplains, but the convict James Hardy Vaux wrote his own *Vocabulary of the Flash Language* in 1812 and later appended it to his *Memoirs* of 1819. Words still current today and listed by Vaux include *bang up* 'a person, whose dress or equipage is in the first style of perfection is declared *bang up to the mark*' (McLachlan, 226); *cleaned out* 'said of a gambler who has lost his last stake at play' (232), a usage later picked up, in *Oliver Twist,* by Dickens; *do the trick* 'to accomplish one's purpose' (236; Vaux's glossary provides the first instance of this subsequently popular usage). Of course Vaux's *Vocabulary* is also filled with expressions no longer common (if they ever were), for instance *Knapping a Jacob from a Danna-Drag*.

> This is a curious species of robbery, or rather borrowing without leave, for the purpose of robbery; it signifies taking away the short ladder from a nightman's cart, while the men are gone into a house, the privy of which they are employed emptying, in order to effect an ascent to a one-pair-of-stairs window, to scale a garden wall, &c., after which the ladder, of course, is left to rejoin its master as it can (249).

Transported for a seven-year term to New South Wales for stealing a handkerchief, Vaux compiled his dictionary while laboring in a penal colony in Australia. Through his *Memoirs* he gained an undeserved reputation as an adventurous rogue, so much so that in 1866 Dickens declined to publish an account of his life in *All the Year Round:* "The mere details of such a rascal's proceedings, whether recorded by himself or set down by the Reverend Ordinary, are not wholesome for a large audience, and are scarcely justifiable (I think) as claiming to be a piece of literature" (quoted in McLachlan, xxx). Of course, a large audience, then as now, was enthusiastic about tales of crime and eager to inform itself about the language of roguery.

Scattered evidence suggests that criminal slang was in international use in the English-speaking world. In Scotland, Vaux's near contemporary David Haggart dictated his life story while awaiting execution on July 18, 1821. Haggart was surrounded by the usual crowd of lawyers and chaplains (who testified to the devotion of his "religious exercises"), but his companions also included the linguistically curious and a scientist-lawyer eager to record "craniological information" (see 159–72). Describing his apprenticeship as a pickpocket, Haggart used the slang of urban criminals in London even though he had never traveled outside Scotland.

> Picking the suck is sometimes a kittle job. If the coat is buttoned, it must be opened by slipping past. Then bring the lil down between the flap of the coat and the body, keeping your spare arm across your

man's breast, and so slip it to a comrade; then abuse the fellow for jostling you. When we foregathered with Barney, he shewed us the dumbie stuffed with cambric-paper, and he quized his brother for having given us so much trouble about luke. But when Barney and I got by ourselves he shewed me the blunt, which consisted of L.100 in ten pound notes, and L.101 in twenty-shilling notes, making in all L.201. I was never happier in my life than when I fingered all this money. (17)

The glossary appended duly lists the respectable equivalents for these technical terms: *blunt* 'money, bit', *dumbie* 'pocket-book, lil', *lil* 'pocket-book, dumbie', *luke* 'nothing', *suck* 'breast-pocket'. There is little surprise that language of this kind turns up throughout the British Isles and in North America; as Haggart's life amply demonstrates, travel toward opportunity—especially fairs and race courses—and away from incarceration was a regular feature of criminal life.

The nineteenth century continued the long-established curiosity about criminal biography. In 1879, for instance, *Macmillan's Magazine* published a carefully glossed "Autobiography of a Thief in Thieves' Language" prepared for print by J. W. Horsley, the chaplain at Clerkenwall Prison in London. His essay gave the eager public an idea of the working habits of thieves and their use of slang.

> One day I went to Croyden and touched for a red toy (gold watch) and red tackle (gold chain) with a large locket. So I took the rattler [train] home at once. When I got into Shoreditch I met one or two of the mob, who said, "Hallo, been out to-day? Did you touch?" So I said, "Usher" (yes). So I took them in and we all got canon [drunk]. When I went to the fence he bested (cheated) me because I was drunk, and only gave me 8*l.* 10*s.* for the lot. So the next day I went to him and asked him if he was not going to grease my duke (put money into my hand). So he said, "No." Then he said, "I will give you another half-a-quid;" and said, "Do anybody, but mind they don't do you." (502)

Slang of this character was, by the last quarter of the century, almost immediately collected and interpreted by linguistic observers. (So, for instance, *usher* in this passage was subject to conflicting interpretations—whether it was connected to Yiddish *user* 'it is so' or to the colloquial pronunciation of *Yes, Sir.*)

Sometimes linguistically curious prisoners recorded the language they heard from other convicts. Thus, Michael Davitt added to the graffiti in Newgate Prison: "M. D. expects ten years for the crime of being an Irish Nationalist and the victim of an informer's perjury" (Davitt, 149). His account of his imprisonment (from 1870 to 1877) included linguistic notes, among them a letter he declared to be an exact reproduction of the holograph.

> Deere Jim
>   i was in quod, doin 14 days when i heerd you was lagged i blakked Polly S——'s peepers who called me names she was fuddled and hit me fust, when i kolered her nut and giv her a fine slugging and her mug was all over blud the spiteful thing bit me she did, and funked fight, when we were both taken by the Kopper, and the beek only giv me 14 days, and her got 21 for hitten me fust and been fuddled, cheer up Jim i am sorry wot you are lagged, and i wont pal with nobody wile your in quod. good by Jim from your tru luv Sally. (151)

What is particularly characteristic of the era is Davitt's interest in linguistic matters and his recognition that including information about slang would increase the appeal of his book.

While *slang* wages linguistic warfare against respectability, its documentation partakes of the same impulse toward "scientific" treatment found elsewhere in nineteenth-century language studies. Its extension of application from the usage of criminals to the language of honest people suggests a fascination with the colloquial that coexisted with efforts through schooling to regulate and standardize English for the masses and consequently to ensure that English would be constrained by the genteel. Under the bootheel of linguistic respectability, *slang* extended its meaning to language "not approved" by the censorious. Thus the *OED* records such phrases as *lawyer's slang* (1802–12) and *scientific slang* (1834) as exemplary of "the special vocabulary or phraseology of a particular calling or profession" (*slang*, sb. 2, sense 1.b). A yet further extension of this usage forms the basis of a sally by Fred Vincy in George Eliot's *Middlemarch.*

"Excuse me, Mamma [says Rosamond to her mother]—I wish you would not say, 'the pick of them.'"

"Why, what else are they?"

"I mean, Mamma, it is a rather vulgar expression."

"Very likely, my dear; I never was a good speaker. What should I say?"

"The best of them."

"Why, that seems just as plain and common. If I had had time to think, I should have said, 'the most superior young men.' But with your education, you must know."

"What must Rosy know, Mother?" said Mr. Fred, who had slid in unobserved through the half-open door while the ladies were bending over their work, and now going up to the fire stood with his back towards it, warming the soles of his slippers.

"Whether it's right to say 'superior young men,'" said Mrs. Vincy, ringing the bell.

"Oh, there are so many superior teas and sugars now. Superior is getting to be shopkeepers' slang."

"Are you beginning to dislike slang, then?" said Rosamond with mild gravity.

"Only the wrong sort. All choice of words is slang. It marks a class."

"There is correct English; that is not slang."

"I beg your pardon, correct English is the slang of prigs who write history and essays. And the strongest slang of all is the slang of poets."

"You will say anything, Fred, to gain your point." (Eliot 1964, 99)

Fred's definition of *slang* as "all choice of words" stretched usage beyond what was possible for most nineteenth-century writers and speakers, but Eliot used her character to display the extension of meaning by which *slang* moved away from the register of criminals toward that of respectable people.

Hotten's *Slang Dictionary* asserts an expansive view of slang not unlike that held by Eliot's fictional Fred.

There is scarcely a condition or calling in life that does not possess its own peculiar Slang. The professions, legal and medical, have each familiar and unauthorized terms for peculiar circumstances and things, and it is quite certain that the clerical calling, or "the cloth"—in itself a Slang term given at a time when the laity were more distinguished by their gay dress from the clergy than they are now— is not entirely free from this peculiarity. Every workshop, warehouse, factory, and mill throughout the country has its Slang, and so have the public schools and the Universities of Oxford and Cambridge. Sea Slang constitutes the principal charm of a sailor's "yarn"; and our soldiers have in turn their peculiar nicknames and terms for things and subjects, proper and improper. A writer in *Household Words* (No. 183) has gone so far as to remark, that a person "shall not read one single parliamentary debate, as reported in a first-class newspaper without meeting scores of Slang words"; and "that from Mr. Speaker in his chair, to the Cabinet Ministers whispering behind it—from mover to seconder, from true blue Protectionist to extremist Radical—Mr Barry's New House echoes and re-echoes with Slang." (Hotten, 42)

Such observations—those quoted by Hotten had been published in 1853 by George A. Sala, a painter and journalist—reveal an essential ambivalence about *slang*. Slang is to be deplored for its risqué and informal character, yet it is alleged to manifest the vitality and vigor of linguistic creativity. Slang thus emerges from a narrow and despised corner of English into the very center of respectable society. Though aspiring to an ideal fixity of a classical tongue, commentators were prepared on the evidence of slang to declare English to be superior to all other languages because of its "vigorous" innovations. Sala urged that a slang dictionary be compiled, ostensibly so the fastidious would know what words were "authorized," but his fascination with the vast array of synonyms for drink and money (among other domains) suggests that he was enthralled with the richness of slang rather than beguiled by the austere simplicity of an idealized English.

The richest domain for creativity in slang in the English-speaking community involves sexual practices, and the Victorians were no less likely than earlier English-speakers to create new words for the "unmentionable." Farmer and Henley's dictionary is a particularly rich source for a domain excluded from the *OED*, the *Century*, and other respectable dictionaries. The compilers devote nine densely packed, double-column pages to synonyms for "the female *pudendum*" (s.v. *monosyllable*) including "analogues" in French, German, Spanish, Portuguese, and Dutch. Nearly the same space is devoted to "the *penis*" (s.v. *cream-stick* and *prick*), but perhaps the most interesting array of terms is found under *greens*, "*to have, get, or give one's greens, verb phr.* (venery). To enjoy, procure, or confer the sexual favour. Said indifferently of both sexes." This lengthy list includes "conventionalisms" (which cannot be regarded as *slang* in the usual way, including "to have carnal knowledge of") and more than a column of expressions alleged to be used by women (including expressions not likely to have been in very widespread use like "to take Nebuchadnezzar out to grass"). The fact that fewer than a dozen synonyms for menstruation are listed (s.v. *flag*) may well result from Farmer and Henley's ignorance of women's usage rather than from a paucity of words and phrases for this aspect of sexual biology. Sexual terms then in common usage (and recorded in such Victorian works of pornography as *My Secret Life* [completed in 1860 but not published until 1966]) included many terms now obsolete but once familiar—for instance, *gamahuche* 'cunnilingus or fellatio' (1865), *godemiche* 'dildo' (1879), *olisbos* 'dildo' (1887), *tribady* 'lesbianism' (1819), and *Uranian love* 'homosexual love' (1893). The full range of nineteenth-century sexual slang is, for the most part, lost as a result of the conviction that "decency and voluptuousness in its fullest acceptance cannot exist together" (*My Secret Life,* 7). Even the lexicographers and pornographers do not supply the complete record, though such language was codified in nineteenth-century English as never before.

Only by chance do documents containing the slang of sexual encounters survive. One of these, an American joke book titled *The Stag Party,* was published in 1888 with no indication of place of publication, doubtless because the compiler and printer feared prosecution. It contains a wealth of bawdy stories like the following.

> A gentleman wanting some cundums called at a drug store, but finding none but young lady clerks was about to go elsewhere. The young lady manager stopped him and insisted so firmly on knowing what he wanted that he at last stated his wish. Turning to one of the

girls, she said: "Nettie, some cundums for this gentleman." Nettie asked him to step to the rear of the store, where in an enclosed room there was a bed, when throwing herself upon it she pulled up her clothes and asked him to shove it in. He was astonished, but thought it was good enough for him, so he pulled out his dodger and shoved it in very gently. She grabbed him by the but and crammed the whole tool into her, then threw him off, and jumping up walked out in the store, and turning to another clerk said: "Cundums, size 6½.["] (70)

Dodger may have had a fleeting existence—it appeared in print only in this and a nearly contemporary joke book, as far as is known—or it may have been in widespread use. The documentary record makes it impossible to tell. But public respectability is unlikely to have greatly discouraged private raconteurs, and slang of this kind certainly flourished.

Many historians have expatiated on Victorian prudery, a sense of the word *Victorian* developed in the twentieth century. Cleansing language of indelicacies was no specialty of the era, of course, though Thomas Bowdler's expurgation of Shakespeare in 1818 (resulting in the word *bowdlerize* [1836]) or Noah Webster's similar treatment of the Bible in 1833 are infamous examples of lexical dirty-mindedness (see Perrin). Many of the examples of this tendency in spoken English are found in the travel books written by unfriendly British travelers to the United States, particularly Frances Trollope, Frederick Marryat, and Charles Dickens. They reported an American inclination to offer synonyms for words thought to be in some way crude; nearly all the examples of this tendency draw on existing English words: *bosom* for *breast, limb* for *leg, rooster* for *cock, seat* for *bottom.* Cleaning up the language was a transatlantic affair, however, and from the end of the eighteenth century there had been a running joke in Britain to find "delicate" synonyms for *trousers: inexpressibles* (1793), *indescribables* (1794), *etceteras* (1794), *unmentionables* (1823), *ineffables* (1823), *indispensables* (1828), *innominables* (1834–43), *nether garments* (1835), *inexplicables* (1836–37), *netherlings* (1852). Intensifiers for use in mixed company provided another territory for euphemism; among the various substitutes developed in the course of the century were *all-fired* (< *hell-fired*, 1837), *bally* (< *bloody*, 1847), *dashed*

(< *damned*, 1887), *goldarn* (< *God damn*, 1832), *participled* (< *damned*—"a participled Tory"—1887), *Sam Hill* (< *hell*, 1839), *something* (< *damned*—"It's the somethingest robbery I ever saw in my life—1859), *tormented* (< *damned*—"not a tormented cent"—1867).

While both Britons and Americans were increasingly disturbed by the vulgarity they associated with bodily functions, their interest in vernacular and colloquial language became more and more pronounced during the century, and not only among the writers and consulters of slang dictionaries. Most important of these developments for slang in the early part of the century was the emergence of organized sports, some legal (like horse racing) and some forbidden (like prizefighting). These pursuits naturally interbred with the slang of urban amusements. Thus Badcock noted that *swells* drawn to one attraction were likely to find themselves involved in another.

> Most of the amateurs in one species of sport evince a certain taste for one other species, at least, some for all; and it is not uncommon to find the same gentleman alternately in the Cock-Pit, at the Chase, in the Ring, or on the Turf, now fighting a cross-bred canine, now baiting the badger; occasionally, he frequents the haunts of the Bon-ton, and during the sprees of Town-life he must see much of those *Varieties* which alone render this life supportable. (xiii–xiv)

During the Regency, the literary underpinnings of sport were established, both in newspapers—particularly the *Sporting Magazine* (1792–1836; see Cone)—and in works of reference giving historical depth to, for instance, the brutal and bloody entertainments of *milling* or *pugilism* (both terms that became popular for bare-fisted prize fights). Among the best known of these books was *Boxiana; or, Sketches of Ancient and Modern Pugilism, from the Days of the Renowned Broughton and Slack to the Championship of Crib* (eventually expanded to five volumes), mainly the work of Pierce Egan and illustrated with handsome portraits engraved by George Smeeton. These volumes are filled with slang in celebratory essays on present and past fighters, including round-by-round descriptions of the principal matches (see also Liebling).

Two aspects of nineteenth-century sporting life transformed

THE SECOND CONTENT BETWEEN CRIB & MOLINEUX, SEPT 28 1811.

Published by Geo. Smeeton, Dec.r 17, 1812.

Prizefighting was one of the popular blood sports of the early nineteenth century, and journalists built around it an elaborate array of synonyms that brought low-life slang into general currency. The bout above was described by Pierce Egan as both "ferocious and sanguinary. FIFTY-FIVE minutes of unprecedented *milling*" (1812, 408). (Reproduced by permission from the copy at the Beinecke Rare Book and Manuscript Library, Yale University.)

local dialect into national and respectable usage, the commercialization of sport and the cult of athleticism. Some local games, many of them relatively free from rules (like shin kicking or hurling stones at chickens), became national pastimes with governing boards and regularly scheduled matches. More or less modern forms of games, and the names to describe them, were organized and consolidated in the course of the century: *croquet* (introduced from Ireland in 1852), *rugby football* (1864), *lawn-tennis* (1874), *basketball* (1892), and *soccer* (1889, < *socker* < Association football). The terminology of sport emerged from local practices into slang and eventually to widespread use. While Rugby School arrogated to itself the origin of "Rugby" (cloaking the origins of the game in a kind of mythic aura akin to that invented for American baseball), many British national sports did have their beginnings in school and university competitions. A specimen of terminology of a game that did not gain national prominence is found in the etymologically attentive *Winchester Word-Book* (Wrench 1891), a description of the special vocabulary associated with Winchester School.

> In early College football there seem to have been three methods of scoring, a *goal*, a *gowner*, a *schitt*, worth respectively 3, 2, and 1. The last behind stood between two gowns which made a goal. The ball passing over his head or between his legs scored 3, over the gowns 2, over the rest of "worms" 1. When the whole of "worms" was made to count equally, every goal was a schitt. (s.v. *schitt*)

Such sports terminology from slang was partly traced by the *OED*, especially for games attracting the attention of the educated. While undertaking his magnificent slang dictionary, John S. Farmer turned his hand to *The Public School Word-Book* (1900), giving some treatment to the language of games. Most sport did not involve women, mainly because of the Victorian belief that women possessed a finite supply of "vitality" while male strength could be "re-created" through athleticism (see Holt), though the introduction of *rational dress* in 1883 made it sartorially possible for women to cycle or play tennis.

As games gained national prominence, so there evolved a style of journalism designed to attribute spice and variety to what were generally tedious and unvaryingly repetitious events. To create a sense of excitement, writers plumbed the shallow depths of everyday metaphor to lend vigor to English, and they created a stock of verbal clichés that became the hallmark of sports commentary. Thus, a comic novel about British undergraduate life contained the following description of the hapless hero's first attempt at boxing:

> Mr. Smalls doubtless gave a very correct *résumé* of the proceeding (for, as we have before said, he was thoroughly conversant with the sporting slang of *Tintinnabulum's Life* [a fictional magazine]), when he told Verdant, that his claret had been repeatedly tapped, his bread-basket walked into, his day-lights darkened, his ivories rattled,

his nozzle barked, his whisker-bed napped heavily, his kissing-trap countered, his ribs roasted, his nut spanked, and his whole person put in chancery, stung, bruised, fibbed, propped, fiddled, slogged, and otherwise ill-treated. (E. Bradley, 105–6)

The daily quest for novelty in the emergent popular press contributed both slang and stock imagery to the language at large.

While games were an important source of slang, the predominant area for linguistic creativity continued to lie in urban amusements. At the beginning of the century, one of leaders of the fashionable was Beau Brummell (George Bryan Brummell, 1778–1840), who encouraged *dandymania,* a tendency toward extravagant dress among both men and women (*dandyzette* is the feminine form given by Badcock). The great vogue for *dandyism* was from 1816 to 1819, though the term *dandy* 'an elegant dresser' was in earlier use along the Scottish border. As Badcock notes in his entry for *dandy,* fancy clothing was accompanied by language similarly flaunting convention.

Dandy—an invention of 1810, and applied to persons whose extravagant dress called forth the sneers of the vulgar; they were mostly young men who had this designation, and they were charged with wearing stays—a mistake easily fallen into, their wide web-belts having that appearance. Men of fashion all became dandy soon after: having imported a great deal of French manner in their gait, lispings, wrinkled foreheads, killing king's English, wearing immense plaited pantaloons, the coat cut away, small waistcoat, with cravat and chitterlings [frilled shirt fronts] immense: Hat small; hair frizzled and protruding. If one fell down, he could not rise again without assistance. Yet they assumed to be a little *au militaire,* and some wore mustachios. Lord Petersham was at the head of this sect of mannerists.

"Killing king's English" meant, of course, the use of slang, some drawn from sports and those urban pastimes "which alone render this life supportable," and some from extravagant linguistic creativity known as *Regency flash* or *flash lingo;* as Badcock declared, "the acquisition of *flash* puts many a man *fly* to what is going on, adversely or otherwise."

Flash lingo was well known and not only to the tiny group of people able to dress the dandy and roister through London. A "comic sketch" by W. T. Moncrieff, first performed at the Royal Coburg Theatre, October 9, 1820, offered a dialogue between the proprietor of a debtor's prison and the father of one of the inmates. The son's clever servant, Plan, has explained to the father that the institution he is visiting is one of the Inns of Court where the son is studying the law. Plan's plan is to free the son on his father's surety by bribing the jailer.

Old Scapegrace. But, to come to business—I'm a plain country gentleman—never was in London before, don't know much about
your Town customs.

Bearward. No, you seem to be rather green; you don't appear to be
quite fly.

Old Scapegrace. Green—fly—what does he mean by that? I don't
look like a green fly, I'm sure;—some of their law terms, I suppose; he's at his Greek. To go on, Sir; it appears to me, that the
close confinement of your College don't agree with my Son.

Bearward. There's very few it does agree with, my Pidgeon; its very
necessary though, notwithstanding.

Old Scapegrace. Pidgeon—more Greek—the fact is he wants to go
out.

Bearward. He's not particular in that respect, my rum Duke.

Old Scapegrace. Rum duke—more Greek.

Bearward. You've only to post the poney—sport the flimseys—
down with the blunt—bleed freely, and the things done. Are
you up—are you awake?

Old Scapegrace. Poney—flimseys—blunt—up and awake—a great
deal more Greek. What does it all mean? *(to Plan.)*

Plan. The fees, Sir, the fees. (Moncrieff, 20)

The sketch ends happily when the son, released on his unsuspect-
ing father's payment, promptly returns married to a heiress, sets

himself free, and gains his father's blessing. Such performances demonstrate at least a passive awareness of fashionable slang among an audience larger than those who habitually used it.

In 1821 appeared the immensely popular work by Pierce Egan, *Life in London: or, The Day and Night Scenes of Jerry Hawthorn, Esq., and His Elegant Friend Corinthian Tom, Accompanied by Bob Logic, the Oxonian, in Their Rambles and Sprees through the Metropolis.* Illustrated with Hogarthian prints by Richard and George Cruikshank, *Tom and Jerry* spawned sequels, imitators, and enlargements. Dramatized versions, among them one by W. T. Moncrieff that ran for two years, made slang even more popular, and the more elaborate editions of Egan's book contained tipped-in sheets of music to allow amateur performers to play and sing the songs composed for the characters. (Lavishly produced books of this type continued to be offered to up-market book-buyers, for instance: *Dens and Sinks of London Laid Open: A Pocket Companion for the Uninitiated, to which is added a modern flash dictionary containing all the cant words, slang terms, and flash phrases now in vogue* [1848]—embellished with "humorous illustrations" by George Cruikshank.) A brief specimen shows how important slang is in Egan's popular work.

> This group . . . displays a complete picture of what is termed "LOW LIFE" in the Metropolis; drunkenness, beggary, lewdness, and carelessness, being its prominent features. It is, however, quite *new* to thousands in London. TOM AND JERRY have just dropped in, by way of a *finish* to the evening, in their route towards home, and quite *prime* for a *lark* [1811]. Knowing the use of their *morleys,* fear is out of the question; and *coffee* or a *turn-up* is equally indifferent to them. Upon the entrance of these *Swells* [1810], a general *stare* is the result: the *Cyprians* are throwing off their *leering ogles* towards them, in the hopes of procuring a *Call:* and if the latter are caught in any ways inclined to *roosting* from being *swipy,* the young *buzzmen* will make them pay dearly for the few *winks* they may enjoy. (Egan 1821, 181)

Even this lively text shows the impending shadow of Victorian wowserism that would soon settle upon Anglo-American life, and the censorious opening sentence anticipates the more serious social criticism found in Henry Mayhew's *London Labour and the London Poor* (1851).

Mayhew's work shows another side of nineteenth-century linguistic curiosity, the recognition that "low life" was not all boisterous fun with criminals merrily celebrating their crimes in alehouses and wayward sons returning to the safety of the drawing room from the pleasures of the stews. Like other social reformers of midcentury, Mayhew agonized over the misery, squalor, poverty, and disease that afflicted so many of London's huge population of poor. All of those whose stories are told in *London Labour and the London Poor* are treated with respect, and each is recorded in an individual voice, some using the specialized jargon of their trades (e.g., ratters and sewer scavengers). Many of Mayhew's sketches are presented in a colloquial style whose usages include instances of the enlarged definition of *slang*. Two specimens will give a flavor of this rich text and the slang it contains, the first an account of a pair of amputees who contrived to beg by presenting themselves as disabled seamen.

> I was to dress like him in a sailor's jacket and trousers and a straw 'at, and stand o' one side of a picture of a shipwreck, vile he stood on the 'tother. And I consented, and he learned me some sailors' patter, and at the end of the week he got me the togs, and then I went out with him. We did only middlin the first day, but after a bit the coppers tumbled in like winkin'. It was so affectin' to see two mariners without ne'er an arm between them, and we had crowds round us. At the end of the week we shared two pound and seven shillings, which was more nor a pound than my mate ever did by his self. He always said it was pilin' the hagony to have two without ne'er an arm. My mate used to say to me, "'Enry, if your stumps had only been a trifle shorter, we might ha' made a fortun by this time; but you waggle them, you see, and that frightens the old ladies." (4:428)

A second specimen recounts the story of an Irish farmer who had become a costermonger in London.

> But the sore times came, and the taties was afflicted, and the wife and me—I have no childer—hadn't a bite nor a sup, but wather to live on, and an igg or two. I filt the famine a-comin'. I saw people a-feedin' on the wild green things, and as I had not such a bad take, I got Mr. —— (he was the head master's agent) to give me 28s. for possession in quietness, and I sould some poulthry I had—their iggs was a blessin'

to keep the life in us—I sould them in Limerick for 3*s.* and 3*d.*—the poor things—four of them. The furnithur' I sould to the nabors, for somehow about 6*s.* Its the thruth I'm ay-tellin' of you, sir, and there's 2*s.* owin' of it still, and will be a perpitual loss. The wife and me walked to Dublin, though we had betther have gone by the "long say" [*sic* for *way*, i.e., across the Atlantic], but I didn't understand it thin, and we got to Liverpool. Then sorrow's the taste of worruk could I git, beyant oncte 3*s.* for two days harrud porthering, that broke my back half in two. I was tould I'd do betther in London, and so, glory be to God! I have—perhaps I have. (1:105–6)

Voices like these speak from an unregretted past, but their language evinces the texture and slanginess of colloquial English of the century.

Mayhew's close attention to humble people brought to light a kind of slang formed on a new principle. In recording the conversation of a London beggar, Mayhew discovered a deliberate invention in language to keep ahead of the high livers who found their amusements in low life.

The cadgers' talk is quite different now to what it was in the days of Billy [William IV, reigned 1830–37]. You see the flats got awake to it, so in course we had to alter the patter. The new style of cadger's cant is nothing like the thieves' cant, and is done all on the rhyming principle. This way's the caper. Suppose I want to ask a pal to come and have a *glass* of *rum* and smoke a *pipe* of *tobacco,* and have a game at cards with some *blokes* at *home* with me, I should say, if there were any flats present, "Splodger, will you have a Jack-surp*ass* of finger-and-*thumb,* and blow your yard of *tripe* of nosey me *knacker,* and have a touch of the *broads* with me and other heaps of *coke* at my *drum.*" (1:418)

This passage presents the first reliable evidence of the emergence of rhyming slang. The beggar here quoted regarded the linguistic game as new—Mayhew's first volume was published in 1851, and Hotten, commenting on it in 1859, thought the new method of creating slang was only twelve or fifteen years old. Though commentators have been tempted to give it an earlier origin, rhyming slang seems to have been invented in the 1840s (see Barltrop and Wolveridge, 32; also W. Matthews, Franklyn; Wheeler and Broadhead).

The "rhyming principle" illustrated in Mayhew's account

reveals something about pronunciation in urban London: *backer* (< *tobacco*) and *nacker, cards* and *broads, home* and *drum.* The principle entails rhyming a phrase with two elements with the single word to be "concealed." Thus, in the passage quoted by Mayhew, *Jack Surpass* stands for *glass, finger and thumb* for *rum, yard of tripe* for *pipe,* and *nosey* (or *noser*) *me* (< *my*) *knacker* for *backer.* In the 1859 slang dictionary by the anonymous Ducange Anglicus such rhyming slang is exemplified in detail: *artful dodger* and *lodger, German flutes* and *boots, flounder and dab* and *cab, linen draper* and *paper, Charley Lancaster* and *handkercher* 'handkerchief', *oats and chaff* and *footpath, gooseberry puddin'* and *woman.* All these he attributes to "thieves," and his example for *nose* (s.v. *I suppose*) suggests the origins of rhyming slang in cant: "I gave him a blow with this neddy on the I suppose" is glossed as "I gave him a blow on the nose with this life-preserver" (= *blackjack* [1867], *cosh* [1869]). In the fully developed form of rhyming slang, the element of the phrase that does not rhyme substitutes for the concealed word. Thus "playing old gooseberry with anything" is founded on the rhyme *gooseberry puddin'* and *woman;* it means to treat the thing as a woman would do—in Anglicus's explanation, "spoiling, upsetting it." Subsequent developments show how rhyming slang introduced lexical innovations. *Barnet Fair,* a north London festival celebrated since medieval times, was the rhyme for *hair,* but by extension it also was used for *head* as in the phrase "she hit him on the Barnet." A contemporary reviewer celebrated the publication of *The Vulgar Tongue* by noting its appeal to women.

> Our fair readers who wish to captivate our bold sex may here find the prettiest phrases, and our country cousins who would perfect themselves in "the flash words principally used in London," as now and then made public through the medium of those very interesting police-reports, cannot do better than "nab the chance," and buy this "leary" little book. (Review of Anglicus's *Vulgar Tongue,* 17)

Leary here means "flash, artful, sly," and Mayhew's beggar would not have been pleased to know that such compilations could help flats "get awake" to slang innovations.

Another principle of concealment produced *back-slang* (1860) in which the spelling of words is reversed to produce the slang term: for instance, *rouf-yenep* (< *four pence* [1852]). Some of these expressions suggest the use of this method of word formation among criminals: *neves* (or *nevis*) appeared in *nevis stretch* (seven-year prison term, 1901), *slop* (< *police*, 1859). Mayhew wrote a particularly discerning chapter on costermonger's habits of "the words spelt backward, or rather pronounced rudely backward" (1:23). He recognized that even illiterates were proficient in the technique by interviewing a fourteen-year-old boy and posing hard questions.

> To test his ability, I asked him the coster's word for "hippopotamus"; he answered, with tolerable readiness, "musatoppop." I then asked him for the like rendering of "equestrian" (one of Astley's bills having caught my eye). He replied, but not quite so readily, "nirtseque." The last test to which I subjected him was "good-naturedly"; and though I induced him to repeat the word twice, I could not, on any of the three renderings, distinguish any precise sound beyond an indistinct gabbling, concluded emphatically with "doog"—"good" being a word with which all these traders are familiar. It must be remembered, that the words I demanded were remote from the young costermonger's vocabulary, if not from his understanding. (1:24)

While not as influential a source for later English as rhyming slang, back-spelling has produced a few enduring words, such as *yob* 'hooligan' (1859).

Though Mayhew is the most famous of the nineteenth-century chroniclers of the underside of urban life, he was not the only writer to portray the language of the poor. In 1868, James Dabney McCabe published *The Secrets of the Great City: A Work Descriptive of the Vices, the Mysteries, Miseries and Crimes of New York City*. Like many such works, it purported to counsel readers to "a total avoidance of the vicinity of sin" (16) while nudging them toward the neighborhood of virtue. A few specimens of "the thief language" (358–59) suggest that some terms were in use on both sides of the Atlantic (like *bene* 'good, first rate' and *bingo mort* 'a drunken woman'), some of which had been recorded in the earliest canting dictionaries in Britain three centuries before. Popular curiosity about the racier side of the city was satisfied in the United States, as it had been earlier in Britain, by the appearance of newspapers devoted to "scandal." The best known of these serials was the *National Police Gazette* (1845–1906), which enriched English with slang terms in its coverage of the lurid side of criminal and the competitive aspect of sporting life. George Matsell, "proprietor" of the *Gazette*, even published a glossary to assist readers with the inside dope about both crime and sport. He was as eager as any other journalist to bring to light the mysteries of the criminal culture, and in 1859 he published *Vocabulum; or, The Rogue's Lexicon*. Like other writers of the day, Matsell provided a dense (and fictitious) example and then glossed it.

> "The coves had screwed the gig of the jug, when Jack flashed the darkey into it and found it planted full of coppers. 'Bingavast!' was the word; someone has cackled." "The thieves had opened the door of a bank with false keys, and when they looked in with the aid of a dark lantern, they found the place filled with officers. One of the thieves cried out: 'Be off! some one has cackled.'" (s.v. *darkey*)

Matsell recognized that crime and sports treated together constituted a formula for journalistic popularity, and his work shows the linguistic continuity of English slang in the United States. Slang of American coinage became increasingly abundant, and some words in subsequent widespread use were first put in print by Matsell: *beef* 'to complain' (1866), *cop* 'police officer' (1859), and *graft* 'illegal payment' (1865). American games, whether imported or locally invented, gave rise to slang that became widespread and generalized: *hit a homer* 'succeed' (from baseball [1868]), *stymie* 'obstruct' (from golf [1902]), *tout* 'to canvass votes' (from horse racing [1881]).

With the gradual expansion of the scope of *slang*, humorous lexical innovations were increasingly considered as falling within the scope of the term. A celebratory review of Hotten's *Slang Dictionary*, by Charles Nordhoff, offered the following approving account of new expressions in politics:

> Mr. Hotten has some amusing paragraphs about *slang*, which he separates entirely from thieves' jargon. Slang is low English; and the

English are perhaps the most slangy of civilized nations—though they accuse us Americans of being their masters in this art of indirect expression. If we speak of our President as "Uncle Abe," they call their Queen "little Vic," their Prime Minister "Pam," the leader of the Opposition "Dizzy"; and every grade of society in England, if we may believe Mr. Hotten, has its own peculiar slang. In English politics, for instance, a *plumper* [1785] is a single vote at an election—not a *split-ticket* [1842]; and electors who have occupied a house, no matter how small, and boiled a pot in it, thus qualifying themselves for voting, are termed *pot-wallopers* [1701]. A *quiet walk over* [1838] is re-election without opposition and much cost. A *caucus* [1763] meeting refers to the private assembling of politicians before an election, when candidates are chosen and measures of action agreed upon. This term originated in America. A *job* [1667] in political phraseology, is a government office or contract obtained by secret influence or favoritism. Only the other day the London *Times* spoke of "the patriotic member of Parliament *potted out* [*drunk*, 1622] in a dusty little lodging somewhere about Bury Street." The term *quockerwodger* [1860], although referring to a wooden toy figure which jerks its limbs about when pulled by a string, has been supplemented with a political meaning: a pseudo-politician, one whose strings of action are pulled by somebody else, is now often termed a *quockerwodger*. (604–5)

Nordhoff's sense of the antiquity of political slang was ill informed—he had no better dictionary than Hotten's to consult—but he was right in thinking that nineteenth-century politics was full of the racy, informal language that the expanded definition of *slang* encompassed. Thus the Americans produced such parties and factions as the *Know-Nothings* (1854), *Locofocos* (1837), *Mugwumps* (1884), *Quids* (1805), *Readjusters* (1879), and *Silk-Stockings* (1812). While British slang was not as splendidly imaginative as these American examples, British politicians wallowed in slang of their own. Opponents of the *Whigs* (a name accepted for one of the major parties before 1750) were particularly vituperative, and in the first half of the century produced the following derivative forms: *Whiggess, Whiggify, Whiggification, Whiggissimi, Whiggize, Whiggological, Whiglet, Whigling, Whigship, Whigamore, Whiggery, Whigging, Whiggish, Whiggishly, Whiggism, Whiggy, Anti-whiggosity, Philo-whig* (all defined and illustrated by Philipson, 86–92).

Nineteenth-century Britain was increasingly urban, but in North America, frontier and rural life was the preoccupation (or the plight) of the majority. For many, this existence was nasty, brutish, and short, and much of the resulting slang was characterized by mordant humor. Various combinations with *dead* illustrate this tendency—for instance, *dead beat* 'sponger' (1863) and *dead broke* (1841). Other American slang usages have entered respectable English internationally: *rip-roaring* (1834), *quick on the trigger* (1808), *make the fur fly* (1834), and *roughneck* (1836). In addition, American reverence for learning (though few had personal access to it) produced slang terms created out of classical (or classical-seeming) materials. Many of these have since fallen out of use: *absquatulate* (1830), *bodaciously* (1832), *catawampously* (1834), *conbobberation* (1845), *exflunct* (1831), *obflisticate* (1833), *snollygaster* (1862), *sockdolager* (1830), and *spondulicks* (1856), for example, appeared in national periodicals, usually in humorous contexts. Metaphor, the usual source for slang, provided *prairie schooner* 'wagon with a large canvas cover' (1841), *rotgut* 'cheap whiskey' (1831), and *slush fund* 'illicit political moneys' (1874; < *slush* 'scraps of animal fat for rendering clandestinely sold by butchers and cooks'). Terms for alcoholic drinks were a particular American specialty in slang: *chain-lightning* (1837), *coffin varnish* (1817), *ding bat* (1838), *eye-opener* (1817), *firewater* (1817), *nose paint* (1881), *tanglefoot* (1859), *sheep dip* (1865), *snake medicine* (1865), among many others. Gambling also presented a rich domain for the American imagination in slang: *bunko* (1875), *card sharp* (1884), *craps* (1843 < French *crebs* in New Oreans < metropolitan French < British English *crabs* 'hazard' [1768]), *full house* (1887), *keno* (1814 < French *quine*), *monte* (1841), *poker* (1838), *skin game* (1868), *working the telegraph* (1859), and many others (see T. Clark).

Americans delighted in slang, particularly when the expressions involved extravagant metaphors. Another joke from *The Stag Party* depends almost entirely on slangy colloquialisms for its humor.

> A young man with a breath like a glue factory and a nose like an auction flag, stepped up to the Michigan Central ticket office, and

roughly elbowed a would-be purchaser of a pasteboard pass to Kalamazoo.

"Well, hold on, don't shove that way!" expostulated the traveler.
"I've got as much right here as you have."

"O, you go to Jerico [*sic*], you wall eyed snuff-dipper," replied the
aggressive youth.

"Why! What in—well, I'm danged if you ain't the freshest bloke
that every crawled out of a corn crib. Do you blow off at sixty pounds,
or run your gauge up to one hundred and forty?"

"I'll blow off enough for you, you variegated sneak-thief. I'm on
the—"

The man *en route* for Kalamazoo suddenly took his fist out of the
place where the young man's teeth had formerly been located,
kicked in a couple of his ribs, and was just preparing to add a few
more architectural ornaments to his head piece, when an officious
policeman collared him and got him to walk up to the other end of
the platform.

"I was told," explained the young man when seated in the drug
store, "that I hadn't got cheek enough to get along in a big city, and
was rather too retiring and bashful like. So I kinder tried to cultivate
it and give it a little exercise. That's what caused most of the trouble."
(43)

Cheek 'insolence, effrontery, or audacity' (as elegantly glossed by
Lighter, 1:386) was a word created in the nineteenth century and
used on both sides of the Atlantic, as in this anecdote, by city
dwellers to deride the *uppity* (1880) ways of recently arrived *yokels*
(1812), *rubes* (1896), and *hillbillies* (1900). Mayhew's street folk in
London and Americans on the frontier talked about *cheek* and
practiced the behavior associated with it. Exchanging insults was a
product of social instability in which people struggled for the
upper hand—one nineteenth-century author even invented the
term *upperhandism* for the practice. In African-American usage, it
produced *slipping in the dozens* (an expression not attested until
1915 but certainly in earlier use.) In Australia *chiacking* (1855), in
Britain *ballyragging* (1820), in northern Ireland *barracking* were
terms for verbal abuse, sometimes for playful amusement, sometimes with deadly consequences.

During the great renaissance of slang in the nineteenth century, Canadians were only marginal participants, at least as far as can be determined from the written record. Documentation has been very much shaped by the fact that those who contributed to written history were inclined to stress respectability and loyalty to Britain, both political and linguistic. Thus, censorious observers, whether migrants or visitors, attributed unwanted and informal linguistic innovation to the long-established French or recently arrived American part of the population. Writers based in, or filtered through, the publishing houses of Toronto and Montreal were more likely to deplore slang than to assert it as a sign of colonial vitality, and doubtless many Canadian slang creations were unrecorded and were never compiled into lexicons (like *hootchino* 'home-brewed whisky' [1898], a "villainous decoction" according to one visitor to the Yukon [see Avis]). In 1857, A. Constable Geikie was alarmed about the prospect of "our noble mother tongue" falling under U.S. influence. Slang words troubling to Geikie included *bug* 'insect', *chisel* 'cheat'—both historically British—and *make tracks* 'run away' (1835–40). Even a spelling like *plow* (instead of *plough*) could be treated as "a savage and heretical disregard of everything in the shape of orthodox precedent," though Joseph Addison—usually regarded as exemplary of a "pure" English style—had used *plow* without censure.

Such comments should not be taken to imply a lack of innovation in Canadian slang, only that recent immigrants from England and native purists were likely to deplore it or (worse from the perspective of the historian) to ignore it. The same creative impulse for multiplying words (for money and sexual recreation, for instance) resulted in a rich vocabulary for diarrhea in the badly nourished provinces—for instance, *the skithers* (brought from the slang of northern England and Scotland), *back door trots, blueberry run, flying axehandles, green apple quick-step, run outs and walk ins,* and *short-taken* (not all are attested in nineteenth-century Canadian English, but all of them are likely to have been in oral use then; see Pratt). Having adopted decimal currency in 1858, Canadians had no use for their rich inheritance of terms for British coinage, and *cent* for a hundredth part of a *dollar* was the official name in Canada, though anti–United States Canadians made efforts to substitute *copper* and *penny* on the grounds that they were authorized by British use and *cent* was a vile American slang term. Festive gatherings of one kind and another gained informal names, some borrowed (like *potlach* [1883]), some imported and modified in sense (like *bee* and *frolic*), and some formed from existing English elements (like *oyster social* for a feast with oysters as the main course; see Avis; Story, Kirwin, and Widdowson). Some of the terminology in the rich set of historical dictionaries for Canadian English came from learned naming, but much of it arose from the informal creativity with which ordinary folk encountered the new land and its peoples.

Conventional language histories allege that among North Americans, citizens of the United States were especially creative inventors (and users) of slang. British writers willingly ceded the prize for slang innovations, partly because of their native tradition of favoring the restrained and genteel in language. American writers accepted their own myth that they were a "young nation" and embraced the idea that slang, the province of youthful creativity in language, was their own best contribution to English. Among the most exuberant proponents of *slang* as the vital element in English was Walt Whitman.

> Slang, profoundly considered, is the lawless germinal element, below all words and sentences, and behind all poetry, and proves a certain freedom and perennial rankness and protestantism in speech. As the United States inherit by far their most precious possession—the language they talk and write—from the Old World, under and out of its feudal institutes, I will allow myself to borrow a simile even of those forms farthest removed from American Democracy. Considering Language then as some mighty potentate, into the majestic audience-hall of the monarch ever enters a personage like one of Shakespeare's clowns, and takes possession there, and plays a part even in the stateliest ceremonies. Such is Slang, or indirection, an attempt of common humanity to escape from bald literalism, and express itself illimitably, which in the highest walks produces poets and poems, and doubtless in pre-historic times gave the start to, and perfected, the whole immense tangle of the old mythologies. For, curious as it may appear, it is strictly the same impulse-source, the

same thing. Slang, too, is the wholesome fermentation or eructation of those processes eternally active in language by which the froth and specks are thrown up, mostly to pass away; though occasionally to settle and permanently crystallize. (54–55)

Yet Americans were not the only emerging anglophone community to embrace "protestantism in speech." If some Americans were ambivalent about the balance between propriety and popularity in their language, Australians were even less inhibited, combining as they did their own history as a penal colony peopled by citizens at war with British social conventions with the mythology of "opening" a new nation on unexplored ground.

Slang found an ideal setting in the community of prisoners that formed the majority of Australians early in the century. Most convicts had been sentenced to transportation from the criminal subculture of British cities, especially London. Though not all were London-born, most had spent time there, and many were professionals in the highly stratified world of crime. These origins were reflected in their English; as one of the naval officers in charge of prisoners in the *First Fleet* (1788) observed,

> A leading distinction, which marked the convicts on their outset in the colony, was an use of what is called the *flash* or *kiddy* language. In some of our early courts of justice, an interpreter was frequently necessary to translate the deposition of the witness, and the defense of the prisoner. This language has many dialects. The sly dexterity of the pickpocket; the brutal ferocity of the footpad; the more elevated career of the highwayman; and the deadly purpose of the midnight ruffian, is each strictly appropriate in the terms which distinguish and characterize it. (Watkin Trench, 1793; quoted by Langker, 3)

Naturally enough, solidarity among the prisoners led to continuing use of underworld cant with its verbal humor: *nubbing cheat* 'gallows', *school* 'company of gamblers', *star the glaze* 'cutting or removing glass from a showcase or shop window in order to pilfer the goods behind it'. Innovation occurred when technical terms from *flash lingo* acquired new senses as a result of new surroundings; *swag* 'booty, stolen goods' eventually became the name for a tramp's bedroll or bundle (1841). From that source, *swag* yielded *swagman* (1869) and *swagwoman* (1894), as well as such related forms as *swag carrier* (1881), *swagless* (1885), and *to swag* 'travel as an itinerant worker' (1859). This process of sense extension was, in Australia, a primary source of new slang meanings. Unlike the North American and African extensions of the anglophone community, Australia was virtually without settler groups speaking languages other than English from which borrowings might be derived. Continued migration from Britain, however, exported newly fashionable linguistic practices including rhyming slang: *jimmies* (1845 in New Zealand; < *Jimmy Grants* 'immigrants'), *rubby* (1897; < *rubbity* < *rubbity-dub* 'pub'), *oscar* (1905; < *Oscar Asche* 'cash'), *on me Pat Malone* 'alone' (1908).

Given the social origins of early settlers, it is no surprise that words carrying a strong sense of opprobrium elsewhere, like *bastard* and *bugger*, acquired friendly and even affectionate senses. Diminutives with *-ie* or *-y* were used to create slang terms, often expressive of affection: *bushie* 'yokel' (1887), *schoolie* 'schoolteacher' (1889), *slushy* 'cook's assistant' (1880). Australian slang made hearty use of metaphor: *concertina* 'side of mutton ribs' (1897), *jeweller's shop* 'rich deposit of gold or opals' (1853), *windmill magistrate* 'illiterate judge' (1869; < use of an *X* as a signature). Slang creations drawing on Aboriginal languages of Australia were uncommon, but a few did rise to sustained currency (for instance, *to go bung* 'die, break down' [1882]). A few borrowings, though not all slang in the narrow sense, achieved international currency, for instance, *boomerang* (1790) (also known as a *throwstick* [1847]). Figurative comparisons achieved wide currency through several generations—for example, "poor as a bandicoot" (a marsupial regarded as usually lean and hungry) and "so bare you could flog a flea across it" (said of desolate, barren landscape). What struck visitors about the role of slang in Australian English, however, was that it was used by educated and uneducated alike, and usages were likely to punctuate solemn and ceremonious talk on occasions at which the use of slang might be avoided elsewhere (see Ramson).

English settlement in southern Africa took place in a very different linguistic context. Though dating only from the beginning of the century, waves of anglophone migration created a social mix in which slang could flourish. The first migration resulted in small communities in the "English cities" of Cape Town, Grahamstown, and Port Elizabeth, and in 1822 the governor declared English the official language (in order to thwart the long-established Dutch settlers in the cities) and attempted to attract ministers and teachers to provide (among other things) linguistic uplift. The second wave of migrants arrived in 1848 in Natal and was, at least by reputation, the refuge of impecunious English aristocrats and military officers on half-pay reserve. Slang from Natal was seen as "genteel" (and the English of their descendants is labeled "respectable South African English" by present-day historians). Mineral discoveries in the 1870s brought a third, and more socially diverse (and international) congeries of settlers hoping to acquire instant wealth in the gold and diamond fields of the Witwatersrand (promptly abbreviated to *Wits,* usually with the initial "v" indicative of its Afrikaans origin). Linguistic curiosity was, as elsewhere, well represented among the immigrants, most enduringly by Charles Pettman, whose account of South African English appeared in print in 1913. His *Africanderisms* reflects very clearly, however, the state of the language in the late nineteenth century: "This Glossary was begun on the day of the author's landing in Cape Town in October, 1876, when he jotted down in his notebook a few of the strange words that then fell upon his ear" (v).

Given his profession as a member of the Anglican clergy, it is not surprising that Pettman did not provide insight into the racier slang of mining camps, military encampments, or establishments he viewed as immoral (for example, *donder* 'bastard, blighter' [1872] and *gentoo* 'prostitute' [not attested until 1934 but from the name of a ship arriving in South Africa in 1846]; see Silva). Further, it is difficult to estimate just how common some of his slang listings might have been, but he certainly was prepared to jot down (or copy from books) terms that struck him as out of the ordinary. Even with these limits, however, Pettman offered a view into the diversity of South African slang creation. Much of it consisted of borrowings from Afrikaans (like *commando,* later in international use, which Pettman declares to be "now used with a considerable degree of laxity"). Not educated in philology, Pettman was inclined to overestimate Dutch/Afrikaans influence; thus, he associated both the verb and noun *scoff* 'eat voraciously, food' [1855 in Natal] with Dutch *schofttijd* 'breakfast', and certainly *scoff* in both uses was common in South Africa (and elsewhere). The complexity of the etymology, and of the social circumstances that produced it, can be discerned in the fact that the first printed citation found in the *OED* occurs in another of those London lexicons of the underworld, *A Swell's Night Guide* (1846), just prior to the first South African use, thus suggesting at least a parallel influence from cant.

Despite Pettman's tendency to overstate them, borrowing from the Afrikaans language provided many slang innovations, for instance *baas* 'mister, sir', which extended in meaning to "employer," just as the American adaptation of the same word had earlier produced *boss* from Hudson River Dutch in colonial America (first attested in America in 1649). English words and word elements were used in most slang terms: *canteen*, glossed by Pettman as "a low-class drinking place" (attested in South Africa in 1852 but in prior garrison use); *good-for* 'I.O.U., promissory note' (1879). Mining produced locally specialized terminology to supplement words and phrases already in use elsewhere: *blue ground* (also the *blue*) 'diamond-bearing matrix in the Kimberley region' (1886), *peg off* 'define the perimeter of a mining claim', *slimes* 'the fine grey matter which under the old gold-winning process used to run away from the battery as waste, but which now under the new processes yields a good percentage of gold' (Pettman's definition; this term for spoils was, however, in prior British use). A few slang words were reintroduced to English by other European settlers in South Africa—for instance, *goniva* 'an illicitly acquired diamond' (< Yiddish < Hebrew *genavah* 'a stolen thing') derives from Jewish migrants to Johannesburg, though the root had already entered English (and had been used by Dickens). Indian laborers and British soldiers brought usages from the Indian Ocean basin into use in South Africa, though most of these had become slang elsewhere. Slang increasingly acquired an international flavor, and at least a few gold miners might have pursued their explorations in

California, Canada, Australia, and South Africa (all of which were sites of nineteenth-century gold rushes).

The word *schlenter* illustrates the complexity of locating the origins of slang words. In Australia and New Zealand, it means "a trick" and in South Africa "something counterfeit" (especially a counterfeit diamond). The earliest printed example comes from the south island of New Zealand, but its likely Dutch origin led the editor of the *OED Supplement* to suggest: "The history of this word is obscure; the Austral. and N. Z. forms are possibly borrowed from S. Afr. English, but by what route is not clear." Probably the exact direction of influence can never be known, but such accidents of the printed record illustrate how fluid the English of the nineteenth century had become. Perhaps more than any other group, those who used slang most frequently were also the most mobile: fortune-seekers, adventurers, and settlers who spread the diversity of English slang around the world.

Among the most productive realms of slang were the countries of south Asia under British rule—India, Ceylon, Burma, and the states of the Malay Peninsula. Unlike the other areas swept by the anglophone diaspora, these countries were populous, and contact between colonial and native peoples was intimate. Service in the East India Company (and subsequently when India became part of the British Empire) required fluency in local languages of British civilian officials. Military personnel were likely to speak indigenous languages as well, particularly if assigned to police duties or put in command of *sepoys* 'native soldiers, disciplined and dressed in the European style'. In such a setting, slang inevitably emerged, and it too was documented in fine nineteenth-century style by Henry Yule and A. C. Burnell.

Appearing in 1886, Yule and Burnell's dictionary was titled *Hobson-Jobson: A Glossary of Anglo-Indian Colloquial Words and Phrases*. Mainly Yule's work, the collection was intended to represent linguistically the reduction of the inscrutable East to what the British soldier could grasp and articulate. Thus, *hobson-jobson* is glossed as "a native festal excitement" and explained in a way deeply revealing of the colonial mind.

This phrase may be taken as typical of one of the most highly assimi-
lated class of Anglo-Indian *argot*. . . . It is peculiar to the British soldier and his surroundings, with whom it probably originated, and
with whom it is by no means obsolete, as we once supposed. . . . It is
in fact an Anglo-Saxon version of the wailings of the Mahommedans
as they beat their breasts in the procession of the *Moharram*—"Yā
Hasan! Yā Hasain!" (Yule and Burnell, 419)

Not mainly a slang dictionary, *Hobson-Jobson* presented a key to the
highly mixed language of the raj. This "camp language" (as Yule
called it) might contain sentences like: "The old *buckshee* is an
awful *bahadur*, but he keeps a first-rate *bobachee*." Unintelligible
except to insiders—this sentence Yule translated as "The old pay-
master is an awful swaggerer, but he keeps a first-rate cook" (Yule,
128)—many of the words and phrases were the natural result of
language mixture arising in a bilingual setting.

Yule included slang among his entries, and his treatment of it
is typical of the late nineteenth century—the attempt to use etymology to reveal layers of the past, just as paleontologists had written history by interpreting successive layers of fossils in sedimen-
tary beds. In a revealing sentence, Yule pursued this notion,
carefully distinguishing *vernacular* from *vulgar* and *profane* in an
effort to reveal a complex linguistic past in the ordinary language
of everyday.

Even phrases of a different character—slang, indeed, but slang generally supposed to be vernacular as well as vulgar—*e.g.* "that is the
cheese"; or supposed to be vernacular and profane—*e.g.* "I don't care
a *dam*"—are, in reality, however vulgar they may be, neither vernacular nor profane, but phrases turning upon innocent Hindustani vocables. (Yule, 122–23)

In his treatment of *cheese*, Yule was anticipated by Hotten, who had
defined its slang meaning as describing "anything good, first-rate
in quality, genuine, pleasant, or advantageous" and traced it to
chīz in "Hindostanee and Persian." Its arrival in Britain, Hotten
thought, was facilitated by Gypsies. Yule agreed with Hotten's etymology but suspected that Anglo-Indians (i.e., British residents in

India) were those who had carried it home from Asia. James Murray, a correspondent and supporter of Yule, endorsed the putative source of slang *cheese* in the *OED* (though reviewers criticized him for doing so). For *dam,* Yule wrote an extensive essay on ancient and modern Asian coinage in which the origins and value of the *dām* were speculatively considered.

> And this [he concluded] leads to the suggestion that a like expression, often heard from coarse talkers in England as well as in India, originated in the latter country, and that whatever profanity there may be in the animus, there is none in the etymology; when such an one blurts out "I don't care a *dām!*" *i.e.* in other words, "I don't care a brass farthing." (Yule and Burnell, 293–94)

Perhaps sensitized by the cool reception of the etymology for *cheese,* Murray acknowledged Yule's "conjecture" and declared it "ingenious, but [it] has no basis in fact" (*OED*). What is important for an understanding of the intellectual background of slang collecting is that "deep" etymology had become a respectable enterprise, however unworthy or distasteful the terms.

As nineteenth-century usages flirted at the edge of respectability, the word *slang* itself came more and more to incorporate the informal vocabulary of educated and respectable people. College and university slang was well documented, partly because graduates were more inclined to lexicography than were criminals or frontier folk. One such work was published in 1824: *Gradus ad Cantabrigiam; or, New University Guide to the Academical Customs and Colloquial or Cant Terms peculiar to the University of Cambridge.* It was the precursor of many others, both in Britain and the United States, documenting the special vocabulary of teachers and students. The most comprehensive of these early word books appeared in 1851 in Cambridge, Massachusetts. Having persuaded himself of the value of gleaning "a few grains of philological lore from the hitherto unrecognized corners of the fields of college life" (v), Benjamin Homer Hall published a much enlarged edition of his work in 1855 with identified quotations and historical depth. Greatest attention was paid to Harvard and Yale Colleges, but more than thirty American institutions of higher education were listed in an index. Accounts of the English universities provided Hall with still more terms, and he was able to demonstrate that *sophomore,* impugned by a contemporary in Britain as an "American barbarism," was actually in ancient use at Cambridge and thence transported to Harvard and Yale before the American Revolution. The etymology of the word was, in short, respectable.

Most of Hall's collection consisted of words illuminating sober history and the curriculum, but slang also appears—for example, *lem* was in use at Williams College for a privy, while the same structure was known at Harvard as a *minor.* (Latinity at Cambridge produced *obeum,* a convenience at King's based on the fictional etymology that it had been erected by O[scar] B[rowning] [see Farmer].) Games and other pastimes are also represented in Hall's dictionary—for instance, *fives* 'a kind of play with a ball against the side of a building' and *shin* 'to tease or hector a person by kicking his shins'. Later collegians recorded usages that derived from English universities and remained current in the United States—like *rusticate* 'expel' and *wooden spoon* (given to the most popular member of the junior class at Yale < the recognition given the lowest-ranking person to pass examinations at Cambridge; see Bagg, 42–49).

By the end of the century, philological lore from college life had been thoroughly explored, and informal usage was increasingly documented. So, for instance, three fraternities at Cornell University thought fit to enshrine their slang as an appendix to their yearbook, discriminating *full* 'comfortably intoxicated' from *corned* 'salubriously intoxicated' (Reeves, Ballard, and Parke). A student at the University of Michigan was urged by his professor to develop a typology of local usage including such categories as hyperbole ("wouldn't that cook you?" 'an expression of extreme surprise'), abbreviation (*fem. sem.* 'female seminary'), and other word-forming strategies (e.g., *all-gone-up-ness* 'a feeling of total exhaustion'; see Gore).

Recording such usages for posterity, and providing them with a pedigree from antiquity, was a special concern to philologists, increasingly so during the second half of the century. What is striking about these collections is their elevation of slang, or at least of the study of it, to respectability. Thus Hotten quotes (with approval) the philologist R. G. Latham's assertion that "the thieves of London are the conservators of Anglo-Saxonisms" (24), high praise in an era when "Anglo-Saxon" words were thought to be of greater value than Latin-Romance borrowings.

By the end of the century, *slang* had expanded its range of meaning to include all the informal and nonce vocabulary of the anglophone empire, and in 1897, Albert Barrère and Charles G. Leland offered to the public two volumes of *A Dictionary of Slang, Jargon & Cant, Embracing English, American, and Anglo-Indian Slang, Pidgin English, Gypsies' Jargon, and Other Irregular Phraseology* (a limited edition for subscribers only had appeared in 1889–90). This was the culmination of a century of attention to the racier portion of the English vocabulary and much influenced by the standards of lexicography set by Murray for the *Oxford English Dictionary*. Barrère and Leland claimed for their work the philological depth that had come to be the standard for English lexicography generally.

> The present is the first Slang Dictionary ever written which has had the benefit of contributors who thoroughly understand Celtic dialects, Dutch, German, and French slang, and who were thus enabled to establish their relations with English cant, and one of these gentlemen is equally at home in Pidgin-English, Gypsy, and Shelta or tinker's slang, which by-the-bye is one of the three principal slangs of the kingdom and is here made known for the first time in a work of this kind; this being also the first Slang Dictionary to which the rich and racy slang of the fifth continent—the mighty Australian commonwealth of the future—has been contributed by one long resident in the country and familiar with its life and literature [= D. B. W. Sladen]. (Barrère in Barrère and Leland, vii).

The "gentleman" acquainted with Pidgin-English, Gypsy, and Shelta was Leland, an American best known to the public as a humorist (as author of *Hans Breitmann's Ballads*) but, as a restless traveler, also known as an authority on these languages usually ignored by those whose attention was constrained by high literary culture. Leland was brusquely dismissive of such persons: "Any-

thing like a distinct history of the development of English slang
has hitherto been impossible, owing to the ignorance of most of
those who have put themselves forward as its analysts and lexicographers" (Leland in Barrère and Leland, xvii).

Much had changed in the treatment of slang during the century. The early glossarists regarded it mainly as ephemeral and
owing mostly to the unrestrained linguistic imagination of what
Victorians had come to call the "dangerous classes." But under the
influence of the new philology that view broadened and deepened
so that slang was at the center rather than at the periphery. Its history, Leland wrote, was the story of the "transition of languages
into new forms" (Leland in Barrère and Leland, xix). The eminent British anthropologist E. B. Tylor had declared in 1874 that
"every serious student of English must take it up and treat it seriously" (513), and, in 1893, Brander Matthews opined that the
threat to English came not from "alleged corruptions" and "doubtful locutions" but rather from the purists who "seek to check the
development of idioms and limit the liberty which enables our
speech freely to provide for its own needs as these are revealed by
time" (1893a, 311). Responding to critics of his view, Matthews
acknowledged that his recognition of slang was based on a fully
democratic view of English.

> What I desired to say, and what I thought I had said, was that the *exclu-
> sive* control of language ought not to be in the hands of a *single* class,
> even though that class were composed wholly of "our most compe-
> tent scholars." (1893b, 108)

Others, though willing to accept the vitality of slang for the health
of the language, were eager to endow the learned classes with the
privilege of regulating the language and to demand that they distinguish good from bad.

> But another side of this moral is that one must make sure that what is
> rejected *is* slang, and not the protoplasm of legitimate and classic
> English. Protoplastic germs look uncommonly alike. ("Slang," 426)

Distinctions between slang and other kinds of words and phrases
were increasingly blurry. Writing for undergraduate students in

1901, James Bradstreet Greenough and George Lyman Kittredge recognized the current wisdom that language is based on convention.

> Even bad grammar is essentially just as good as good grammar; it becomes bad merely because it is associated with persons that we dislike or look down on. (72)

But they were unable to leave the matter as one of disliking and liking, the elite and the others. They concluded that slang was unhealthy: "Finally, the unchecked and habitual use of slang (even polite slang) is deleterious to the mind" (73).

While others were inclined to see *slang* in terms of metaphors drawn from uncleanliness and disease—"protoplastic germs" is just one example of this rhetorical move—John S. Farmer saw his inquiry through a metaphor based on exploration and empire.

> Authorities differ between themselves, and often with themselves when asked to set down in plain scientific terms the marks which distinguish the vagrant words of slang from correct and orthodox English. Nor is the difficulty removed or lessened by an analysis of the genesis, or the application of this vast and motley crowd of heterodox words: of a verity the borderland between slang and the "Queen's English" is an ill-defined territory, the limits of which have never been clearly mapped out. It is, therefore, not without hesitation, that I have ventured to explore this "Dark Continent" of the World of Words. If I cast a ray of light where before was darkness, or reduce to some sort of order where much was confusion—well and good: if, on the other hand, my steps at times chance to falter, others will, in such a case, be able to profit by my experience as I have by that of my predecessors. (Farmer in Farmer and Henley, 1:vi)

At the beginning of the century, Badcock had exclaimed of *slang:* "What a host of enemies will not this one little word engender?" (iv). By the end of the century, *slang* was an emergent territory of discovery and its cartography a testament to linguistic erudition.

GRAMMAR.

Attitudes toward grammar during the century hardened into ideology. Using standard forms of the language was a requirement for gentility (and much else), and there arose a new class of zealous pedants who assumed the task of regulating the language. According to one of them, Henry H. Breen, Esq. F.S.A, "the most striking characteristic of English literature in the nineteenth century, is the loose and ungrammatical diction that disfigures every species of prose composition" (3). A writer in the influential *Blackwood's Magazine* opined: "with the exception of Wordsworth, there is not one celebrated author of this day who has written two pages consecutively without some flagrant impropriety in the grammar." The American pedant who quoted this view, William Mathews, LL.D., "Author of *Getting on in the World; or, Hints on Success in Life,*" added to it: "the statement, we believe, is undercharged" (324).

Not all the pedants inquired too deeply into the cause of the bad state of English. It was possible for some of them to console themselves about "flagrant impropriety" by reflecting on the superiority of the language and the fierce independence of the English speakers using it.

> The prose of the leading English authors . . . exhibits more slovenliness and looseness of diction, than is found in any other literature. That this is due in part to the very character of the language itself, there can be no doubt. Its simplicity of structure and its copiousness both tend to prevent its being used with accuracy and care; and it is

so hospitable to alien words that it needs more powerful securities against revolution than other languages of less heterogeneous composition. But the chief cause must be found in the character of the English-speaking race. There is in our very blood a certain lawlessness, which makes us intolerant of syntactical rules, and restless under pedagogical restraints. (Mathews, 327)

Thus the pedants disputed, some arguing that bad grammar was a sign of bad character, both individual and national; a few others, like Mathews, declaring that it arose from vitality and vigor. For pedants on both sides of this dispute, English was a "moral barometer" (Mathews, 60).

So rich is the array of grammatical criticism in the nineteenth century, it is possible to overlook the ways in which English grammar changed the means of expression. Outrage or resignation as expressed by the pedants was often ill informed—though the accumulation of dictionaries and grammars gave increased foundation to comments about the language—but changes were indeed afoot leading to new ways of using English. New grammatical processes arose; old ones fell into disuse. The mixture of belief about correctness and behavior in using the language illuminates a complex cultural and linguistic era.

Prolonged worry about grammatical nuance was ostensibly not the custom of the literary elite. Of even the most highly educated, a thorough knowledge of the classical languages was no longer expected, and the comprehensive knowledge of grammar entailed in the study of Latin and Greek withered into a handful of unconnected ideas about propriety in English. Writing a biography of Leslie Stephen for publication in 1906, Frederic William Maitland captured the ideas of one of the most prominent Victorian writers. Not only had Stephen edited the *Cornhill Magazine* from 1871 to 1882—and attracted to its pages such eminences as Robert Browning, Thomas Hardy, and Henry James—he was the presiding editor of the vast *Dictionary of National Biography,* one of the monuments of nineteenth-century English scholarship. Stephen's public claim was that he did not want to trouble himself with grammar; privately, he seems to have cared a great deal about it.

Stephen never "bothered" about style, and was inclined to think that any "bothering" about style was a sign of weakness. He had his likes and dislikes. Thus "personality" for "person" would drive him wild. Such was his disgust for a French word in an English sentence, that I am proud of having caught him using *éloge* in his old age. He told me that he had tried hard to keep out of the Dictionary [of National Biography] such phrases as "he was given an appointment," "he was awarded the prize"; and he pointed with pride to the "Do not ring unless an answer be required," that was visible upon his front door; but I doubt he had thought profoundly of the subjunctive. (265)

To think "profoundly" about the subjunctive would be pedantic; to post one in a prominent place was to display an ornament.

Stephen's dislikes were merely quirks and quibbles. *Personality* had been coined by Coleridge and was coming into increasing use as psychologists set about categorizing mental types. (Stephen's daughter, Virginia Woolf, would use it in 1919 in the sense of "eminent person.") French words had been sprinkled in English sentences since medieval times, though the revival of "Saxonism" at midcentury had once again brought them into question among the linguistically self-conscious. From the days of Edmund Spenser forward, English writers had formed the passive voice without expressing the active subject; "even so fastidious writer as Macaulay uses the new construction with *promise, offer, deny, allow, forbid, refuse*" (Jespersen 1961, 3:310). In making a show of the subjunctive, Stephen was able to associate himself with what was imagined to be an archaic and passing nuance of English grammar. (Historians of the language in Stephen's day believed the subjunctive to be in rapid decline: Hodgson [1882] declared it was "dying out in the language" [107]; Henry Bradley [1904] thought that "perhaps in another generation the subjunctive forms will have ceased to exist except in the single instance of *were*" [53]. As the subjunctive continues to thrive in the twentieth century, these anxieties have proved groundless. See Nichols.)

Despite his ostentatious indifference to grammar, Stephen could be invoked as an authority in a transatlantic linguistic dispute. Writing in 1893, Fitzedward Hall listed specimens of American usage that in his view showed a decline in English used in the

United States. Though Hall was American-born and American-
educated, he was celebrated in Britain for his views on English,
and when he criticized an American author for writing a schoolbook "besprinkled with locutions which go far to realize finished
debasement" of the language, there were English readers ready to
nod agreement. Not quite so despairing was Ralph Olmsted
Williams, another American but one less afflicted with the colonial
cringe. The matter in question was whether one should say *born in*
some town or city or *born at* the town or city. Hall viewed *born in
Boston* as an Americanism and "indefensible"; Williams thought
that Stephen's *Dictionary of National Biography* "may be regarded as
a very trustworthy reflection of educated British usage" (75). The
practice in this work of many hands was that people were *born in*
London but *born at* Sheffield or Salisbury or Penzance. Occasionally other cities were given the treatment with *in:* Edinburgh, Glasgow, Aberdeen, Dublin. Williams attempted to distinguish large
cities (requiring *in*) from smaller ones (requiring *at*). The distinction in practice was by no means so simple. The prepositions did
not divide Americans from Britons, nor did population or prominence figure importantly in the choice of one preposition or the
other. Individuals were unpredictable. William Mitchell Ramsay,
the celebrated archeologist, was inconsistent in the same work
with the same birthplace. "Was Christ born at Bethlehem?" he
asked in one paragraph (1898; quoted by the *OED*, s.v. *Pauline*);
"Was Christ born in Bethlehem?" he demanded in another
(quoted s.v. *guerrilla*).

Minor idioms and constructions took on enormous social
meaning. A British journalist took Americans to task for their
inability to ape the manners of London.

> Even the hated and despised Anglo-maniac himself, who drops his
> R's, and drawls his A's, and imitates the chappies and otherwise
> affects the clipped English of Pall Mall and Piccadilly, can always be
> detected for a born Yankee in certain minor idioms and construc-
> tions. I know an American who has lived for twenty years in England,
> who is more English than the inhabitants of the Ward of Cornhill,
> and who blushes up to his eyes if you remind him of the fact that, as
> fate would have it, he was born in [*sic*] Boston. But to this day he con-

sistently says "all the time" for "always"; and instead of "perhaps" he invariably uses "maybe." (Allen, 375)

When this indictment appeared in 1888, the *OED* had not yet revealed that *maybe* 'perhaps' was thoroughly British and had been used by Swift and Thackeray. Nor was *all the time* 'always' used only by Americans; in 1849 E. E. Napier had described his *Excursions* in southern Africa and reported the words of a Scottish doctor describing a boar hunt: "As you may readily fancy, I was *all the time* in a most confounded stew, lest the tender, pulpy branches should give way, and leave me to the tender mercy of Miss Piggy" (2:248; emphasis added).

"Modernization" of old texts provides useful clues to linguistic change. Matthew Gregory Lewis, famous as the author of the gothic novel *The Monk,* kept a journal of two voyages, in 1815–16 and 1817, to his family plantation in Jamaica. On the return from the second of these, he died at sea, but two editions of the *Journal* were subsequently published, one in 1834, the second in 1845. In revising the archaic language of the first edition, an unknown purifier removed some of Lewis's comments on interracial sex and even changed the grammar to suit Victorian fashion. Thus, Lewis wrote of a dolphin brought on shipboard: "we eat him" (41); the reviser altered this verb to "we ate him" (19).

Such changes in the prestigious use of the English strong verbs can be traced in James White's *The English Verb* (1761). For White, as for Lewis, the normal past tense of *eat* was *eat* (to rhyme with *bet*). White also reported that the present tense of *read* had the long vowel and the past tense the short vowel as found in all varieties of modern English. But *spread* and *sweat* contained the same long vowel as *read,* both forming past tense and past participles in the same way with the short vowel of *read* (31–32). In 1833, W. H. Savage declared that "Dr. Johnson was one of the last who retained *heerd*" for the past tense of *hear* (xi–xii), though in North America and elsewhere *heerd* persisted well into the nineteenth century. (By the twentieth century, linguistic geographers were able to locate only two instances of *heerd* in New England. See Atwood, 16.) Such past tenses and past participles were not regulated by system but by custom. Savage anticipated the future when he recommended *climbed* for *clomb* (10), *burst* for *bust* (10), *rose* for *rizz* (21). However he was not so prescient when he recommended *thrashed* for *threshed* (31), and he failed to stamp out *lit* and *lept* for *lighted* (22) and *leaped* (43). Despite the general tendency of innovative verbs to form their past tenses and past participles with *-ed*, new strong verbs also appeared in the course of the century—including *snuck* (< *sneak*, 1887) and *dove* (< *dive*, 1855).

A second kind of grammatical instability in past tenses and past participles concerned the pronunciation of the verb forms containing *-ed*. (This variation continues in a few modern English words—for instance, *hallowed* with three syllables in the Lord's Prayer but two syllables otherwise.) Pronunciation of the *-ed* as a separate syllable was much more frequent in the nineteenth century, particularly when speakers or readers wished to achieve a tone of archaic solemnity.

> In the Scriptures, words ending in *ed*, whether verbs or participles, seem to have been, as a general rule, pronounced distinctly, so that the termination *ed* formed a separate syllable. We still find this pronunciation among our peasantry; and the parish clerks of country churches, perhaps without an exception, continue to give full force to the final syllable of verbs and participles ending in *ed*. It is amongst these that we must trace the tenacity of custom, and judge of that which has been from that which is. (Harrison, 323)

In less formal styles—and even with the reading of the Scriptures in cultivated urban settings—the *-ed*, except with roots ending in *-t* or *-d*, was reduced to *-d* or *-t* (depending upon whether the previous sound was voiced or voiceless). Syllable reduction, according to an observer at midcentury, was especially likely following liquids and *z* or *v* (Harrison, 324)—for instance, *lulled, furred, buzzed,* and *lived*. Harmony in voicing between the final sound of the verb stem and the choice of *-t* and *-d* was regarded as important: "we can say *spurn'd*, and *kill'd*, and *climb'd*, and *prov'd*, and *remov'd*, and *graz'd;* but we instinctively shrink from *spurnt*, and *kilt*, and *climbt*, and *provt*, and *removt*, and *grazt*" (325). Yet the extension of this principle was also a source of anxiety: "Are we doomed to admit into the English language such terms as *quackt, stackt, awakt, nakt, digt, fixt,* &c?" (326). The answer was, of course, affirmative with the exception of *naked* (with two syllables) and *awake* and *dig* (with their strong forms).

According to the grammarians, English formed the simple tenses of regular verbs in two patterns: *I love/I loved* and *I do/did love.* At the end of the eighteenth century, some of them began to criticize the second of these two possibilities as redundant (see Sundby, Björge, and Haugland, 379), but both methods continued to be listed in the verb paradigm in grammars well into the new century—Cobbett, in 1818, noted that English allows "I *do execute* my work." Doubtless the grammar books lagged behind usage, and in practice unemphatic *do* to express the simple tenses was restricted to special contexts: legal ("I do solemnly swear"), religious ("till death us do part"), and poetic ("Thoughts that do often lie too deep for tears"). Unemphatic *do* did continue, but in literary contexts it was usually a conscious archaism (as in William Morris's "Their heavy-laden hearts did sore confound" [1867]) or an expression of rustic dialect (as in Mary Augusta Ward's "they do say as Jim Hurd's in it" [1894]). With the exception of these special uses, unemphatic *do* nearly disappeared from "polite" English, though it continued to be used in districts uninfluenced by metropolitan fashion (see *OED;* Visser 3.1:1507–10; Ihalainen).

A second revision in Lewis's *Journal* provides additional insight into the changing structure of the verb phrase. Describing his visit in 1816, Lewis had written about his early-morning errands.

> This was a day of perpetual occupation. I rose at six o'clock, and went down to the Bay to settle some business; on my return I visited the hospital while breakfast was getting ready. . . . (24)

The editor preparing the 1845 edition altered these words to "while breakfast was being got ready" (68). An American contemporary of Lewis's would probably have written *gotten ready,* a form of the past participle that was becoming obsolete and dialectal in the prestige dialect of southern England. (Despite writing for a U.S. audience in the *Dictionary of American English,* Craigie reminded the world that *gotten* was "not limited to ignorant writers and speakers" in America. He did not mention that it had been used fifty-four times in the Authorized Version of the Bible.) Far more controversial, however, was the change from *was getting ready* to *was being got ready*.

The authoritative discussion of this structure was provided by Fitzedward Hall, who, in 1873, devoted a lengthy chapter of his *Modern English* to what he called the "English imperfects passive." That this verb phrase was new he then had no doubt, and he drew attention to the revision just quoted from Lewis's *Journal* (325n). By Hall's day, the innovation had attracted attention in Britain, and he began his chapter by quoting an anonymous letter published in 1866.

> All really well educated in the English tongue lament the many innovations introduced into our language from America; and I doubt if more than one of these novelties deserve acceptation. That one is, substituting a compound participle for an active verb used in a neuter signification; for instance, 'The house is *being built*,' instead of 'The house *is building*.' (quoted by F. Hall 1873, 321)

Correctly pointing out that not all innovations in British English came from America, Hall noted that the approving tone of this author was not typical of other usage writers; "*are being*," the *North American Review* had observed in 1837, "is an outrage upon English" (45:504; quoted by F. Hall, 1873, 322). The earliest examples then known to Hall were by two of the youthful poets who would shape nineteenth-century literature: "a fellow whose uttermost upper grinder *is being torn out* by the roots by a mutton-fisted barber" (Robert Southey, 1795) and "While my hand *was being drest* by Mr. Young, I spoke for the first time" (Samuel Taylor Coleridge, 1797). In the *OED*, Murray drew upon Hall's collection and offered the letter from Southey as the first example known to him (s.v. *be*). In 1893, Hall was able to add further examples beginning with one in 1667 (in a note reprinted by Williams, 63), and the *OED* itself contains one from Defoe's *Journal of the Plague Year* (1722, s.v. *pass*).

The "imperfects passive" was founded upon verb phrases of the type "the house is building." In the mid–eighteenth century, this structure had drawn the ire of Samuel Johnson.

There is another manner of using the active participle, which gives it a passive signification; as, The grammar is now printing, *grammatica jam nunc chartis imprimitur.* The brass is forging, *æra excuduntur.* This is, in my opinion, a vitious expression, probably corrupted from a phrase more pure, but now somewhat obsolete: *The book is a printing, The brass is a forging; a* being properly *at,* and *printing and forging* verbal nouns signifying action, according to the analogy of this language. (1755, b4)

Much as he might find them vicious and corrupt, Johnson despaired of reverting to a state of English "more pure" than that of his own day. His immediate successors as grammatical critics found "the house is *a building*" either obsolete or "improper" (Sundby, Björge, and Haugland, 378–79)

For nineteenth-century purists, structures patterned along the lines of "is being built" were the corrupt forms improperly founded on the correct and elegant "is building." In 1850, Matthew Harrison observed that "the phrase 'is *being built,*' and others of a similar kind, have been for a few years back, gradually insinuating themselves into our language; still they are not English" (339). For J. W. Gibbs *is building* was "the free and natural expression" (Hall 1873, 337), *is being built* "formal and pedantic." Other critics were even less judicious, and phrases of the type of *is being built* were declared to be "uncouth English," "not English," a "corruption of language," and "a monstrosity, . . . illogical, confusing, inaccurate, unidiomatic" (Hall 1873, 338–39; Visser 3.2:2016). Henry Alford, in 1864, was resigned to it: "the inaccuracy has crept into the language, and is now found everywhere, in speech and in writing" (1888, 121). Such ferocity and distaste had no effect on the development of the language, of course, and the *OED* is replete with examples of the emergent structure: "the western annexe is being rapidly completed" (*Times,* 1862, s.v. *annex*); "A campaign is being carried on in Paris" (*Pall Mall Budget,* 1887, s.v. *campaign*). By the end of the twentieth century, this dispute has been so far forgotten that Anne Telscombe, who ably "completed" Jane Austen's *Sanditon* and attempted to be faithful to the language of the unfinished manuscript, used structures that would have been entirely unfamiliar to Austen—for instance, "your fate is being mourned throughout Sanditon" (317). Of course it would not have been likely that Telscombe would employ the alternative natural to Austen: "your fate is now mourned throughout Sanditon." Similarly, twentieth-century Bible translators abandoned these structures in the Authorized Version in favor of modern usage: "when it *was in building*" becomes "while it *was being built*" (1 Kings 6:7); "those that are ready to be slain" is rendered as "those who *are being taken away* to death" or "those *being hurried away* to their death" (Prov. 24:11).

Reviewing the history of this construction in 1928, G. H. McKnight found it "so thoroughly established and so familiar that it is not easy to conceive of the feeling of an earlier time when it grated on the nerves of the purist like a neologism" (510). That "earlier time" was not far in the past. In 1883, *Harper's Weekly* offered its American readership a humorous conversation between an "old gentleman" and a "young lady."

> Old Gentl.—Are there any houses *building* in your village?
> Young Lady—No Sir, there is a new house *being built* for Mr. Smith, but it is the carpenters who *are building.*
> Old Gentl.—True, I sit corrected. *To be building* is certainly a different thing from *to be being built.* And how long *has* Mr. Smith's house *been being built?*
> Young Lady—(looks puzzled for a moment, and then answers rather abruptly) Nearly a year.
> Old Gentl.—How much longer do you think it *will be being built?*
> Young Lady—(explosively) Don't know.
> Old Gentl.—I should think Mr. Smith would be annoyed by its *being so long being built,* for the house he now occupies being old, he must leave it, and the new one *being only being built,* instead of *being built* as he expected, he cannot.
> Here the gentleman perceived that the lady had disappeared. (Quoted by Visser 3.2:2429)

For modern readers, the humor is elusive and the grammatical point obscure, mainly because the new structure is so widely used as to be unremarkable.

The development of *is being built* and similar locutions needs to be considered in the context of the progressive (that is, the *-ing* forms of verbs). According to one authority, writing in 1940, "I would estimate that our day uses five to ten times as many progressive forms as did 1600, and ten to twenty times as many as 1500, or—more rashly, perhaps—that the use has approximately doubled in each successive century throughout Modern English" (quoted by Visser 3.2:1997). In the nineteenth century, the increase in the use of the progressive was even more dramatic; personal letters show a tripling of the structure between 1800 and 1880 (Arnaud, 84). With the increasing frequency of the progressive generally, it is no wonder that resistance to *is being* rapidly disappeared, and *is being* with a following adjective or noun came into full flower. ("This *is being wicked*" and "This *is being candid*" appear first at the very end of the eighteenth century [Visser 3.2:1956].) Such structures are very rare in Jane Austen—consider "There *was* no *being displeased* with such an encouragement" (*Emma,* 1816)— but occur frequently in the late twentieth-century completion of *Sanditon* by Anne Telscombe—"Sir Edward *was being* very *eloquent*" and "her sister *was being* a shade *premature.*"

In part, this change took place through the flattening of the distinctions among past participles, adjectives, and nominal modifiers. For Austen, *displeased* was a past participle whose verbal force was somewhat mitigated by the use of *with* rather than *by,* the preposition that would usually signal the agentive: "such encouragement was not displeasing" is the active counterpart of "there was no being displeased *with/by* such encouragement." Similarly, Austen could write, "She was now, on being settled at home, at leisure" (*Pride and Prejudice,* 1813) and "He was rich, and being turned on shore, fully intended . . ." (*Persuasion,* 1818). In these examples, "settled at home" had lost some of its verbal force and paralleled "in residence," just as "turned on shore" was the naval synonym of "on half pay." The clearest test for the collapse of distinction between participle and adjective, however, is in the use of *very* in place of *very much.* According to Craigie, "the correctness of this usage, which has been prevalent from the middle of the 17th cent[ury], depends upon the extent in which the participle has acquired a purely adjectival sense" (*OED,* s.v. *very* 2c).

The drift of participles toward adjectives was, as Craigie recognized, well established before the beginning of the century: *very advanced period of life* (1628, *OED*, s.v. *advanced*); *very illuminated individuals* (1661, *OED*, s.v. *illuminated*); *very composed* (1744, *OED*, s.v. *stickle*); *very attached* (1779, *OED*, s.v. *persecute*); *looked very pleased* (1794, *OED*, s.v. *very*); *very celebrated* (1799, *OED*, s.v. *puff*). This process of participles becoming adjectives continued to accelerate during the nineteenth century: *very distinguished attainments* (1824, *OED*, s.v. *persecute*); *very altered* (1837, *OED*, s.v. *deteriorate*); *very coloured spectacles* (1877, *OED*, s.v. *agent provocateur*). Some critics decried these innovations as "Americanisms," a term freely applied in Britain to almost any doubtful or despised usage; their history was, however, ably laid out by Fitzedward Hall (1873, 54–55). Their increased use tended to blur earlier distinctions founded on grammar: "she was pleased" (adjective < participle) and "she was cheerful" became structurally parallel, as did "he was very frail" (adjective), "he was very human" (noun), and "he was very celebrated" (adjective < participle).

Linguistic coalescence of grammatically distinct forms had further consequences as English developed in the nineteenth century. The adjectives and nouns following *is being* seemed, according to Jespersen, to denote "some characteristic mental or moral quality, and very often a transitory condition or behaviour is meant in contrast to the person's habitual or real character" (4.226). The vast expansion of the *is being* construction thus allowed the difference between dynamic and stative adjectives to be expressed conveniently—for instance, "you *are being* very *hard*" (Thackeray, 1861; Visser 3.2:1956) in opposition to "you are very hard" and "I *am getting old*" (Mary Augusta Ward, 1894; Visser 3.2:1955) in contrast to "I am old." Another effect was to make stative adjectives gradable in a way that had not previously been easily possible—for instance, in "Men are ambitious of . . . being grandiloquent" (*OED*, s.v. *grandiloquent*) and "The yawner . . . is not being intentionally rude" (*OED*, s.v. *yawner*).

This same linguistic evolution produced *is getting* + past participle, a structure regarded by one historian as having "arisen by the end of the nineteenth century" (Visser 3.2:2430). In fact, the combination was rather older: "The Greeks were getting / Just finished" (1764; *OED*, s.v. *fratch*); "By Jove, I am getting hedged" (1863; *OED*, s.v. *hedge*); "All the girls about here are getting snapped up quick" (1889; *OED*, s.v. *snap*); "The rebels are getting tired of war" (1896; *OED*, s.v. *sowing*). *Is getting* followed by an adjective had long been established, and the increasing popularity of past participles with the same phrase contributed to smooth out the differences between them. By the end of the century, Henry James—fastidiously attentive to the shades of grammatical parallelism—could conjoin them: "without fearing that one's taste is getting vitiated [past participle], . . . one's judgment is getting superficial and unjust [adjectives]" (*English Writers*, 36).

All of these developments arose from the greatly increased use of verb phrases containing forms of *be* and *have* as auxiliaries. Otto Jespersen, who never met a linguistic change he failed to celebrate, summed up the development in these words:

> through the enormous extension in the course of the Modern English period of the use of the expanded tenses the language has been enriched with means of expression that allow nice logical distinctions and at the same time in many cases have emotional value. In comparison with the uncompounded verbal tenses these forms with *be* + participle serve to actualize and vivify. (4:213)

While the potential for these expanded tenses had long existed in English, only in the nineteenth century did they begin to be exploited for the "nice logical distinctions" and "emotional value" recognized by Jespersen. In using them, according to a careful student of the matter, "Jane Austen is clearly an innovator" (Phillipps 1970, 112). Even so, her use of alternatives was not always clearly motivated by nuance: "I am dying to shew you my hat" and "I die to see him" (both from *Northanger Abbey*); "It is raining furiously" and "Oh! it rains again"; "Whitworth goes in their Train as Lord Lieutenant" and "Tom Chute is going to settle in Norfolk" (all four from her letters). However, Austen wrote "it rained almost all the way there" (letter) and never "it was raining" (as did, for instance, Hardy, *Tess*), and Hardy could make a distinction she never attempted in "she once was crying" and "now she cried aloud" (both from *Far from the Madding Crowd*).

So simple a development as preferring "it is raining" to "it rains" did not escape observation. At the end of the eighteenth century, Hester Piozzi had noted a general tendency for a participle (like *feeling*) to "encroach" the territory of a noun (like *sensibility*):

> 'tis the age for verbal nouns to increase their consequence, and from mere participles—so called, as every one knows, because they participated of both natures—are going forward to become substantives completely, and signify *things* as well as *actions;* taking up their plural numbers of course, and ranking with the nouns as if originally of their family. (1:234)

Piozzi's prediction came true in the nineteenth century, and, though there were sporadic earlier examples, English acquired such "plural numbers" as *rainfalls* (*OED*, s.v. *honey*), *snowings* (*OED*, s.v. *snowing*), and *thunderings and lightnings* (*OED*, s.v. *lulled*). In the following generation, another critic of English noticed the same thing: "Since the era of Dr. Johnson, there has been a growing tendency to make substantives the principal ministers and envoys of thought, to the exclusion of verbs, participles, and gerunds" ("Anglicus," 458).

These shrewd insights pointed to a tendency that developed rapidly in the nineteenth century: the use of a few general verbs like *give, have,* and *take* with nouns instead of verbs alone. Some of these expressions were long established: "[They] clapped with their hands and gave a shout" (vs. *shouted;* 1576, *OED,* s.v. *give*); "he gave a glance" (vs. *glanced;* 1605, *OED,* s.v. *glance*); "And did you step in, to take a look at the grand picture? (vs. *to look;* 1761, *OED,* s.v. *daub*). With the nineteenth century, however, the number and frequency of these expressions increased: "Come and have a swim" (undated nineteenth-century nursery rhyme; *OED,* s.v. *yellow-belly*); "I will have a look into this letter" (1821; *OED,* s.v. *slovenlike*); "It has a look like the bridge of a lute" (1832; *OED,* s.v. *bridge*); "What if I . . . take a look round?" (1864; *OED,* s.v. *show*); "Mrs. Pattison took me a drive in her little pony carriage" (1870; *OED,* s.v. *pony*); "We had a drive of ten miles" (1897; *OED,* s.v. *Pict*). Austen uses such expressions regularly—"Both gentlemen had a glance at Fanny" (*Mansfield Park*)—and increasingly *had a glance* and *glanced* acquired a semantic distinction, as had *gave a shout* and *shouted*, as did "She had hardly ever given a thought to her financial position" (1882; *OED*, s.v. *financial*) from "She had hardly thought about her financial position." Some of these distinctions were "nicely logical," though some were merely synonyms. In either case, the expressions with *give, have,* and *take* display the nineteenth-century fondness for nouns.

These choices were open to social as well as semantic distinction. From Middle English forward, it had been possible to say both *take leave* and *leave, make a confession* and *confess, make a choice* and *choose.* By the end of the nineteenth century, however, some of these choices had been made subject to the excruciating social-class discrimination that suffused the English-speaking world. In Somerset Maugham's *Of Human Bondage* (1915), Tom Perkins returns from a distinguished career to assume the headmastership of his old school. The teachers are fearful of his leadership, not least because he is the son of a bankrupt linen-draper. At the end of his first conversation with his staff he says cheerfully, "I want to go round and *have a look* at the shop." The retiring headmaster is hard of hearing, and his wife repeats the words for his benefit: "He wants to go round and *look* at his father's old shop" (quoted with discussion by Olsson, 13). Maugham's narrative voice concludes: "Only Tom Perkins was unconscious of the humiliation which the whole party felt." *Have a look* represented a violation of tradition; *look* asserted it. Using nouns instead of available verbs, at least sometimes, was socially threatening. Using nouns was a sign of the modern.

Nouns could be invented (like *kodak* [1888]) or borrowed (like *kohlrabi* [1801]) but most emerged by processes based on the internal resources of the language, particularly through derivational morphology in which words are reshaped by grammar. Often the use of suffixes converted parts of speech toward new nouns: americanize (1816) > *americanization* (1860); industrialize (1882) > *industrialization* (1906); socialize (1828) > *socialization* (1884). Other suffixes also allowed the creation of new nouns from verbs—for instance, "Why should there be a distinction between a *flogger* and a *flogee*? (*OED*, s.v. *flogee*; emphasis added).

New nouns could also be created by adding suffixes to old ones: *sermonette* (1814), *cigarette* (1842), *wagonette* (1858), *leatherette* (1880). Though the process was disquieting to grammarians who revered inflected languages like Latin, nouns were increasingly formed from verbs without any change in the form of the word— for example, "she had better have her cry out at once and have done with it" (Austen, *Sense and Sensibility*). Phrasal verbs acquired nominal counterparts in increasing abundance after 1800: *throw-back* (1856), *hold-up* (1878), *hand-out* (1882), *rake-off* (1888), among many other examples.

What was even more striking, however, was the elaboration of nouns through compounding. Of course compounding was not new in English, but the nineteenth century made it a principal method of forming new words. Thus *ice cream* (1744) and *ice water* (1722) already existed, but a huge number of new compounds was created on this pattern: *ice age* (1873), *ice ax* (1820), *ice bag* (1883), *ice boat* (1819), *ice box* (1846), *ice floe* (1819), *ice man* (1851), *ice pack* (1853), *ice pick* (1877), *ice skate* (1897), *ice storm* (1876). Both the first and second elements of the compound could become productive: *carpet bag* (1836), *clothes bag* (1879), *ditty bag* (1860), *hand bag* (1867), *mail bag* (1812), *nose bag* (1796), *shopping bag* (1886). Linguistic historians have pointed out what must have been apparent to many at the time: "the meaning of the group cannot be discovered by its analysis; it is intelligible only to those who are acquainted with its meaning" (Kruisinga 2.3:148). With the flowering of these compounds, an aspect of grammar was elaborated as never before, the semantic relations "hidden" in compounds. Thus a *carpet bag* is made from carpeting; a *hand bag* is carried in the hand; a *nose bag* is shaped to fit the nose (of horses); a *shopping bag* contains items purchased in stores.

Nineteenth-century grammarians had little to say about these compounds. Writing in 1795, Lindley Murray merely mentioned their existence.

> Various nouns placed before other nouns assume the nature of adjectives; as, sea fish, wine vessel, corn field, meadow ground, &c. (49)

The "nature of adjectives" was not an idea he bothered to explain, and the two definitions he offered for *adjective*—expresses a "quality" and admits degrees of comparison—were not at all helpful in explaining how *sea* in *sea fish* partook of this "nature." Subsequent grammarians were no more illuminating, partly because their idea of grammar was founded on inflectional languages, and partly because the flowering of these compounds was so recent. Early in this century, Jespersen observed: "It is noteworthy that most of the quotations showing the gradual approach [of "first word" nouns] to adjectivity have been found in nineteenth century authors" (2:325). Of course he recognized that the Elizabethan era had also been productive in such phrases, and he took their absence in the intervening two centuries to be a result of "the prevailing classicism."

Whether the eighteenth century had fewer such compounds is open to question, but by 1800 there were many compounds that were unexceptionably English, though the modern principles for distinguishing them had yet to be sorted out. For instance, should the writing fluid be called *Indian ink* (1665) or was it permissible to write the compound *India ink* (1884)? In the eighteenth century, a *Turkey merchant* could be a sailing ship, a trader with the Ottoman Empire, or a poultry seller. But a *Turkish merchant* could also describe the English entrepreneur. The nineteenth century began to distinguish such synonyms as new compounds were created. One of Jane Austen's flightier characters uses both *dinner table* and *dining table* in the same monologue (*Mansfield Park*, 220); it is not obvious that these were ever sharply distinguished except as markers of social class. On the other hand, *battlefield* (1818; *OED*, s.v. *untombed*) shifted the semantic territory of the traditional *field of battle*, giving the latter a more ceremonial flavor. *Point of view* was joined by *viewpoint* (1856), itself likely influenced by the creation of *standpoint* (1829).

Further distinctions were made between compounds and phrases. In *glass house*, Matthew Harrison pointed out, two equal stresses signaled a phrase: a *gláss hóuse* is a house made of glass. Stress on the first element only was a sign of a compound that, in his view, needed a hyphen when it appeared in writing: a *gláss-*

house is a house for the manufacture of glass (155). Applying this principle more generally, Harrison provided a lengthy list of compounds that *might* arise.

> Then (to work out the principle) we may *hope* to see the máster buílders, the shíp-builders, the lord chancellors, the schóol-masters, the prime minister, the hígh-church-men, and the lów-church-men, mén-singers, and wómen-singers with sílver-toned voices; together with the ópera-dancers, and the hórse-guards, and the fóot-guards, the ców-keepers, the cóal-porters, the líghter-men, the cópper-smiths, the tín-men, the músical-instrument manufacturers, ladies in silk gowns, and wáter-men in cork jackets, and waiters with córk-screws and wíne-coolers, even the anti-stay-and-corset-young-women-killing society, all in a quíck-sailing vessel, going to see the snów mán, made by the mílk-man of Máry-le-bone, and then proceeding to view the "yárd-long-tailed" monkey, and the elephant possessing the strength of a twénty-horse power stéam-engine, now exhibiting in Bíshop-gate-street-without, a sight never-to-be-forgotten. (156–57)

Having worked out the principle, Harrison could then criticize Gibbon for having written *a bull's hide* instead of the more correct *bull-hide*. In his fanciful list of phrases and compounds, he identified a grammatical development that flourished in the nineteenth century.

Purists who greeted innovations with anxiety or disgust eventually awoke to the explosive growth of these new compounds. Writing in 1867, Edward S. Gould scorned *standpoint* as a stellar instance of "solemn philological blundering."

> "Stand-point" does not mean point of view for two good reasons, one of which suffices; namely, it does not mean anything. It is not an English word. (34–35)

Further elaboration of this blunt attack was provided by Richard Grant White, who used *standpoint* to launch a general assault on compounds.

> Granting for a moment that *stand-point* may be accepted as meaning standing point, and that when we say, from our stand-point, we intend to say from the point at which we stand, what we really mean is, from our *point of view,* and we should say so. Periphrasis is to be

avoided when it is complicated or burdensome, but never at the cost of correctness and periphrasis is sometimes not only stronger, because clearer, than a single word, but more elegant. *Stand-point,* whatever the channel of its coming into use, is of the sort to which the vulgar words *wash-tub, shoe-horn, brew-house, cook-stove,* and *go-cart* belong, the first four of which are merely slovenly and uncouth abbreviations of *washing-tub, shoeing-horn, brewing-house,* and *cooking-stove,* the last being a nursery word, a counterpart to which would be *rock-horse,* instead of *rocking-horse.* Compounds of this kind are properly formed by the union of a substantive or participle, used adjectively, with a substantive; and their meaning may be exactly expressed by reversing the position of the elements of the compound, and connecting them by one of the prepositions *of, to,* and *for.* Thus *death-bed,* bed of death; *stumbling-block,* block of stumbling; *turning-point,* point of turning; *play-ground,* ground for play; *dew-point,* point of dew; *steam-boat,* boat for or of steam *(bateau de vapeur); starvation-point,* point of starvation; *horse-trough,* trough for horses; *rain-bow,* bow of rain; *bread-knife,* knife for bread; *house-top,* top of house; *dancing-girl,* girl for dancing; and *standing-point,* point for or of standing; and so forth. But by no contrivance can we explain *stand-point* as the point of, or to, or for, stand. (1872, 232–33)

This analysis is, of course, mostly nonsense, but it does reflect an emergent notion that compounds with participles were better than ones with nouns. Thus *dining table* ought, on this principle, to be preferred to *dinner table.* But to suggest that compounds like *go-cart* and *shoe-horn* were "abbreviations" was to mistake history; the *OED* provides a quotation with *go-cart* from 1689, and *shoeing horn* dates only to 1855 while *shoe-horn* is first cited in 1589. The blast from White about *standpoint* stimulated his epigones, and objections to it on "logical" grounds—that is, one cannot stand on a point, as one critic put it—survived into the twentieth century. Osmun, in 1881, warned readers about *standpoint:* "This is a word to which many students of English seriously object, and among them are the editors of some of our daily papers, who do not allow it to appear in their columns" (Ayres 1911, 261).

Compounds identified by Murray and his successors in the *OED* give some flavor of this kind of lexical invention. Some thirty were attested for the first time in quotations from 1850, including

such familiar phrases as *bed-rock, foot-hill, lamp-shade,* and *rifle-range.*
What is of special interest for nineteenth-century English is that
these compounds could be themselves used as "first words" in further compounds—for instance, from the group of 1850, *part-song
book* (1850), *water-color drawings* (1862; *OED,* s.v. *scumble*), and *tea-
rose silk* (1900).

Stringing nouns together was not altogether new in English.
In 1719, for instance, it was possible to write *quill-driving Prigs*
(*OED,* s.v. *quill-driver*), and in 1781 one could discuss *Hand-in-
Hand insurance plates* (*OED,* s.v. *insurance*). What happened in the
nineteenth century, as Harrison had observed, was that this
method of expanding noun phrases became more and more common. When *rail-ways* were first mentioned in a parliamentary act in
1776, the phrase was regarded as a combination of two nouns
(*OED,* s.v. *railway*). In 1805 more nouns could be added: *Surrey Iron
Rail-Way* (*OED,* s.v. *track*). Before long, whole phrases could be
inserted in "first word" position—for instance, *Sunday-go-to-meetin'
clothes* (1846; *OED,* s.v. *Sunday*) and *gold-moth-haunted beds of pickerel-
flower* (1867; *OED,* s.v. *pickerel-weed*). Legal and commercial English
were particularly inclined to these strings—for example, *Bastardy
Laws Amendment Act* (1872; *OED,* s.v. *affiliation*) and *G. W. R. Railway Time Table* (1891; *OED,* s.v. *convey*). (That *G. W. R.*—Great Western Railway—had become an unanalyzed abbreviation is clear
from the use of both *R.* and *railway* in this example.)

Language historians have evaluated these strings in several
ways. Henry Bradley, the first to be named to assist Murray as a
coeditor of the *OED,* declared: "The development of the attributive construction has greatly increased the flexibility and compactness of the language" (66). John Earl regarded the use of nouns as
"first words" as "the palmary example of the great import of collo-
cation in our language" (540), and he cited without censure such
a "string of substantives" as *The Bath Church Sunday School Association.* Jespersen viewed these strings as "supplementing the want in
English of an adequate manner of forming adjectives from substantives" (2:327–28). While recognizing the futility of correcting
these structures, some purists attempted to call attention to them.

> The noun construction is a construction that is well-nigh univer-
> sally employed, and yet, in strictness, it is commonly—perhaps invari-
> ably—ungrammatical. Wordy it certainly always is. By noun construc-
> tion I would designate that construction that expresses action, doing,
> without employing a verb in any form soever. (Ayres 1911, 184)

Osmun wanted to replace nominalizations like *preservation* with
participles or infinitives. For him, "the preservation of the strong"
would be much improved if expressed as "preserving the strong"
or "to preserve the strong." Such constructions mean that "both
grammar and rhetoric" would be improved (Ayres 1911), and
these alternatives would thwart the accumulation of strings of
nouns. In this, as in many other recommendations, Osmun was
without influence—except, perhaps, on his successors in the business of regulating usage.

Authors who exploited linguistic nuance for literary ends
sensed the emergence of noun strings as representative of "modern" English. In *Barchester Towers*, Trollope signaled the "progressive" views of an innovating Bishop by having him establish a
"Bishop's Barchester Young Men's Sabbath Evening Lecture-
Room" (chap. 10). In the view of the traditional clergy celebrated
in the novel, nothing good could come of a place so compacted
with nouns. Titles of legislation and newspaper headlines were
especially fertile for expansion in the "first word" position—for
instance, "The Marriage with a Deceased Wife's Sister Bill" (from
the *Times* of the 1870s; Poutsma, 2.1:20). Even those who scorned
newspaper English—for example, Richard Grant White—did not
notice these emerging structures, and twentieth-century observers
tended to identify the very end of the century as the time when
there began "an enormous increase in the application of these
expanded nominal constructions" (Straumann, 108). Once these
strings had been thoroughly established, novelists could exploit
them for ironic purposes—"a great deal of the public-spirited,
British Empire, tariff-reforms, governing-class spirit" (Woolf, *Mrs.
Dalloway*, 67). Boosters of modernity even identified noun strings
as a consequence of the fast pace of twentieth-century life; "the
tempo of modern life, pulsing in the columns of the newspapers,

has produced a stenographic speech rivaling that of Tacitus"
(Teall, 62).

"Stenographic" English was by no means a twentieth-century
invention, and modern authors were not the first to persuade
themselves that haste produced a need to condense the language.
One of the earliest of the usage books launched an attack in 1826
on "mercantile pedantry" that specialized in abbreviation.

> [I]nstead of assenting to an opinion by a plain "yes," or "I agree with
> you in that," the mercantile pedant's favourite expression will be "I
> say *Ditto* to that." Again, instead of observing that a young lady resem-
> bles her mother, he will say "She is the very *ditto* of her mother."—
> This word *"ditto"* ought to be under an *embargo,* and ought never to
> be *exported* out of the ledger and the invoice, or at least it ought not
> to be *imported* into good society. The words *"per"* and *"via,"* for "by"
> and "by way of," are other instances of the mercantile pedantic. For
> example—"He intends to go *per* the mail, and return *per* the stage":
> "They go *per* the packet *viâ* Calais, and return *per* the *steamer viâ*
> Brighton." A pedant of this class instead of "on the contrary," will say
> *"Per contra;"* or instead of "several," will think *"sundries"* more ele-
> gant,—these terms are so in his books, but ought never to be heard
> in his conversation, if he is desirous of speaking elegantly. What
> would be thought in genteel society, of a person who would say *"Per
> advice this day received, viâ* Dantzic from Petersburg, I am informed
> that war is *ordered* by the Emperor;" or *"I am advised this day, per the Dol-
> phin,* that our affairs in India are far from prosperous." Some mer-
> cantile pedants still more vulgarly, will talk indiscriminately of an act
> of Parliament, or a blood-horse, or a celebrated beauty, or an old
> woman, as *"a pretty piece of goods."* With those persons, also, every
> thing and every circumstance is vulgarly termed *"a concern,"* as if it
> were connected with the transactions of their "firm;" or involved *"a
> good* or *a bad spec,"* which is the vulgar contraction for the word "spec-
> ulation." (*Vulgarities,* 143–45)

As early as 1678, Edward Phillips (in his *New World of Words*) had
noted that *ditto* was "a word used much in Merchants Accompts,
and relation of foreign news," (*OED*), and the other expressions
Vulgarities criticized were mostly long established. The most recent
was *spec,* according to the *OED* originally American but certainly in

widespread use in Britain early in the century. All of them were justified by their users as consequent upon the urgency of commercial life.

The author of *Vulgarities* did not object to mercantile English in general, only its importation into "good society." Certainly the expressions he mentioned were routinely used in business transactions, and a sample of model letters—from the *National Encyclopedia of Business and Social Forms* (1879)—shows how abbreviations were used with a highly ornamented, though conventional, grammar: "Agreeably to your esteemed order of the first inst., we have now the pleasure to enclose invoice of goods amounting to $1500, subject to five per cent, discount for prompt cash" (McCabe, 247). Here, the condensed style is represented by the omission of *an* before *invoice* and the loose attachment of the concluding phrase to the rest of the sentence; the elaboration lies in such expressions—also loosely attached to what follows—of the opening words: "Agreeably to your esteemed order of the first inst.," that is, the first of the same month as the reply. Similar elaboration of grammar is found in another model letter, this one from a "sugar refiner applying for a situation": "Being out of employment at present, and hearing you required a sober, steady, active, and pushing man to superintend your business up-stairs, I write to inform you that for years I was head up-stairs man at Messrs. Newhall and Co's" (250). *Head up-stairs man* is just the sort of phrase that nineteenth-century business English produced in abundance.

Increasingly, British pedants blamed Americans for linguistic innovations, usually without discerning too particularly the source of the unwanted expressions. Expanded noun phrases were by no means exclusively American, but it was possible to give an "American" flavor to English prose by using them in abundance.

> For the use of slang we have always shown a growing partiality; but its prevalence of late years is mainly owing to that quintessence of Rebellion and Radicalism; that amalgamation of Socialism and Slavery; that galaxy of Stars and Stripes; our encroaching, annexing, inter-meddling, repudiating friend; our outlandish, off-handish, whole-hoggish, go-a-headish brother, Jonathan Yankee. (Breen, 69)

What is especially "American" here is not so much the vocabulary as the grammar with its piled-up modifiers reflecting exactly the exuberance in English that the author wished to condemn.

Elaboration of noun phrases was not just "modern" or "American"; it was also "scientific." From the founding of the Royal Society in the seventeenth century, British scientists had been eager to keep the relation of words and things fully explicit. In the nineteenth century, the remarkable developments in steam and electric power renewed interest in the empirical, rather than the speculative, sciences. The "tendency to make substantives the principal ministers and envoys of thought" was nowhere more apparent than in scientific English.

> The theory of magnets and of the phænomena of paramagnetic and diamagnetic bodies *is expressed* with reference to the "lines of inductive magnetic action"; and elementary proofs of the tendency of paramagnetic bodies toward places of stronger magnetic action, and diamagnetic bodies toward places of weaker action, *are given*.

In this typical sentence—from James Clerk Maxwell's *Theory of Heat* (1883, 368)—everything is expressed in elaborated noun phrases. The main verbs, here italicized, are drawn from a limited set, mostly ones articulating the approach or the findings of the inquiry: *assume, calculate, conceive, demonstrate, discuss, express, give* (results), *show,* and similar words. Prepositions structure the noun phrases; in the sentence just quoted, *of* appears eight times, and *toward* twice.

Nineteenth-century scientific English established the impersonal style as the medium of professional science. Franklin's account of his electrical investigations in the 1740s shows a transition from the focus on the experimenter to attention to the experiment.

> This kite is to be raised when a thunder gust appears to be coming on, and the person who holds the string must stand within a door, or window, or under some cover, so that the silk ribbon may not be wet; and care must be taken that the twine does not touch the frame of the door or window. (107)

Here "the person who holds the string" is prominent, though the use of the passive voice submerges other agency: *is to be raised, care must be taken*. Subsequent science made "the person who holds the string" grammatically invisible.

> Returning to the phenomena in question, the first thought that arises in the mind is, that the electricity circulates with something like *inertia or momentum* in the wire, and that thus a long wire produces effects at the instant that the current is stopped, which a short wire cannot produce. (Faraday, 330)

Science here takes place among thoughts arising "in the mind," not by a scientist standing in a door or window sheltered from the rain. "Returning to the phenomena in question" is the business of this thinker, not the activity that produces the thoughts. English logical connectives came to structure the expression of the thoughts; in the following example, each sentence begins with an adverbial showing how the ideas are connected to one another.

> *For instance* if a metal ring is spun about a diameter, the number of lines of induction from the earth's field which pass through it will change continuously, so that currents will flow in it. *Furthermore*, energy will be consumed by these currents so that work must be expended to keep the ring in rotation. *Again* the wheels and axles of two cars in motion on the same line of rails, together with the rails themselves, may be regarded as forming a closed circuit of continually changing dimensions in the earth's magnetic field. *Thus* there will be currents flowing in the circuit, and there will be electromagnetic forces tending to retard or accelerate the motions of the cars. (Jeans, 454; emphasis added)

No "person" is here visible; the "logical" adverbials are provided by the impersonal, grammatically invisible scientist.

The impersonal style gave new emphasis to what twentieth-century linguists would call the "discourse margin," that is the portion of the discourse devoted to managing and explaining the relationship of propositions as words like *furthermore* and *thus* do in the example just quoted. Some strategies on the discourse margin emerged from the conventions of mathematical proofs, and the imperative forms of *assume, grant, let,* and others often were employed as sentence openers.

> *Let* the body expand (or contract) without communication of heat until it reaches the standard temperature, the value of which, on the thermodynamic scale, is T. Then *let* the body be kept at the standard temperature and brought to the standard pressure, and *let* H be the number of units of heat given out during this process. (Maxwell 1883, 163)

Sometimes the discourse margin comes even closer to the propositional logic of mathematics.

> For *let ACGM,* Fig. 20, represent a flat plate of glass or any other substance which will not suffer the electric fluid to pass through it, seen edgeways; and *let BbdD,* and *EefF,* or *Bd* and *Ef,* as I shall call them for shortness, be two plates of conducting matter of the same size, placed in contact with the glass opposite to each other; and *let Bd* be positively electrified. (Cavendish, 57; emphasis added)

In this example, "as I shall call them for shortness" comes at the discourse margin, as does the initial *for let.* While this opener had occurred in Shakespeare's *Othello,* it had come to be a sign of scientific discourse. Though in its full form—"for let *you* [represent] a flat plate of glass"—the opener acknowledges the scientist and the audience, it had by the nineteenth century become a stock formula, one akin to another feature of the discourse margin, the equilateral triangle formed by three dots that was intended to be read as "therefore."

The grammar of science was not exclusively noun phrases, colorless verbs, and logical connectives. In the early part of the century especially, participles also played a role, particularly on the discourse margin.

> On *introducing* a fine platina wire at *x,* and *employing* the electro-magnet at D, no visible effects occurred as long as contact *was continued;* but on *breaking* contact at G or E, the fine wire was instantly ignited and fused. (Faraday, 331; emphasis added)

All of these italicized participles have "the experimenter" and the subject, though that person is never explicitly represented in the grammar. These verbal forms without explicit subjects had long existed in English. (Chaucer had appended "to speke generally" to a sentence without naming the speaker [Visser 2.2:1145].) Admired nineteenth-century writers did the same, often in the discourse margin: "Speaking of daughters, I have seen Miss Dombey" (Dickens). Mental-process verbs were commonly used in this way: *allowing, granting, including, supposing,* and others. But these were not the only participles that appeared in the writing of meticulous and revered authors: "wanting to be alone with his family, the presence of a stranger . . . must have been irksome" (Austen, *Mansfield Park,* 194).

The first of the pedants to regard these participles as faults was Goold Brown, who had stunned the world of usage authorities by his vast treatise *The Grammar of English Grammars* in 1851. Brown declared that the subjects of these participial forms needed to be clearly expressed.

> Participles, in general, however construed, should have a clear reference to the proper subject of the being, action, or passion. The following sentence is therefore faulty: "By *establishing* good laws, our *peace* is secured. (620)

A sentence like this one he regarded as "utterly unintelligible," "a downright solecism—a positive absurdity" (620–21). Brown's method was to amass thousands of instances of the flaws he detected, and he provided copious examples of the structure that would shortly be called the "dangling" or "separated" participle (627). The hostility of the pedants had little effect, particularly on scientific English, where the grammatical invisibility of the experimenter was valued as a sign of impersonal truth.

Impersonality also expressed itself in the formation of possessives. As nominal modifiers became more and more common, English presented grammatical synonyms: "shore birds" and "birds of the shore." Similarly, the genitive relationship could be expressed in two ways: "a cat's fur" and "the fur of a cat." These alternatives had long been available, of course, and were stylistically, if not semantically, distinct (see Altenberg). With personal names, however, these structures were not synonyms, and there was a sense of awkwardness or impossibility in such combinations as "the eyes of Samantha." Such structures did occasionally occur: "It was a trouble to him to think of this face of Florence" (Dickens; quoted by Jespersen, 3:22), but the "normal" expression was "Florence's face." During the century, the alternatives became less vividly distinct, and it was possible to title a volume *Plays of Shakespeare* as opposed to the more "natural" *Shakespeare's Plays*. In discussing this restriction, Murray in the *OED* explained that the genitive should be inflected unless it was "difficult or awkward." The instance of such a difficult case was offered in "The widow of a man who had been killed at a level crossing" (1895; *OED*, s.v. *of*, sense 49). But the impersonal style of science was increasingly exempt from such a rule.

> *The theory of Faraday* with respect to the induction of currents in closed circuits takes the following form. (Maxwell 1910–11, 368; emphasis added)

The choice between these alternatives is conditioned by a variety of factors. Animate nouns (particularly personal names) were less likely to appear after the *of*, so *the theory of Faraday* depersonalizes "Faraday" in comparison to *Faraday's theory*. The grammatical status of the two nouns also influences the choice: *the doctor's arrival* and *the arrival of the doctor* are both possible when *doctor* is the subject of *arrive;* when doctor is the object, the choice with *of* is more likely—*the certification of the doctor by the examiners*. Still another influence is the number of modifiers attached to the head noun, and the longest noun phrase usually comes second: *the widow of a man who had been killed at a level crossing* versus *a man who had been killed at a level crossing's widow*.

Conflict among these principles caused consternation among the pedants. Brown considered what might be done with a structure like "The duke of Bridgewater's canal." *Duke* and *canal* seemed to him in this example to be "intimately" joined, and one possibility was to encase the entire phrase in hyphens: "*The Duke-of-Bridgewater's* canal."

> With deference to [Lindley] Murray and others, *"The King of Great Britain's prerogative,"* is but an untoward way of saying, *"The prerogative*

of the British King"; and, *"The Lord mayor of London's authority,"* may quite as well be written, *"The authority of London's Lord Mayor."* (Brown 1851, 489)

Even though the use of the *of* structure with a personal name violated a principle, its use in these examples seemed to Brown to be "quite as agreeable" as the use of the inflected genitive, *-'s*.

What was at stake here arose from a larger development in the history of English, the millennium-long disappearance of inflections to express grammatical relationships. Inflected genitives vanished into uninflected nouns: *St. John's*, Newfoundland, is older both historically and linguistically than *St. John*, New Brunswick. Group genitives were replaced by the possessive with *of:* "the wife of a clergyman of the Church of England" (Thackeray; quoted by Jespersen 7:317). The flight from inflection became a squabble over the placement of the apostrophe, a visual rather than a verbal sign of a grammatical relationship about to wither away. (One tribute to the nineteenth-century pedants is the prominence of instruction about the apostrophe in schoolbooks.) English grammar became more linear with position more important than inflection. Thus *Eve's Daughters* turned into *daughters of Eve* in the nineteenth century.

This natural development of age-old tendencies led to a conflict between grammatical and thematic development of sentences. "Thematic" development meant the placement of important words in important places, regardless of their grammatical propriety. "Grammatical" development meant the relationships of government and concord. The pedants were engaged in a struggle to keep grammar paramount against the forces of thematic arrangement. As modern grammarians have recognized, "communicative factors" play an increasingly important role, and not only in the choice between inflected genitive and *of* (Quirk et al., 1282). In general, the word mentioned last has thematic prominence (e.g., a man who had been killed at a level crossing's *widow*), while the head of the *of* genitive has grammatical prominence (e.g., the *widow* of a man who had been killed at a level crossing).

Grammar and theme were often at odds, and the pedants

squabbled over such issues as whether "The wages of sin *is* death" (as the Authorized Version proclaimed) was better or worse than "The wages of sin *are* death" (e.g., Brown 1851, 552). Some of them declared in favor of *are* since *wages,* the grammatical subject, is plural; others favored the use of *is* since, in Brown's words, *sin* was the "proper subject," that is, the theme. Similar disputes arose over "Two and two makes four," the proponents of *makes* viewing "two and two" as a singular proposition treated thematically, while those who favored *make* used grammatical principles to argue that the sentence had a compound subject and consequently required a plural verb. Arguing in favor of the former, Brown wrote: "Any phrase or sentence which is made the subject of a finite verb, must be taken in the sense of *one thing*" (549). But this principle presented its own difficulties. One grammarian used this idea to defend "The King and Queen appearing in public *was* the cause of my going." In that case, the noun phrase is treated as a whole and thematic. But the proponents of *were* regarded this sentence as "a palpable solecism" since grammar required a plural verb with a compound subject (Brown, 549).

To explain the anomalies presented by such sentences, Osmun coined the term *attraction* (Ayres 1881, 58), and Jespersen developed it into a general principle.

> Very frequently in speech, and not infrequently in literature, the number of the verb is determined by that part of the subject which is nearest to the verb, even if a stricter sense of grammar would make the verb agree with the main part of the subject. This kind of attraction naturally occurs the more easily, the greater the distance is between the nominative and the verb. (2:179)

Jespersen's citations show that this principle was old in English, but he also offered many nineteenth-century examples—for instance, "the *fore-part of his thighs,* where the folds of his mantle permitted them to be seen, *were also* covered" (Scott, *Ivanhoe*). Here the thematic focus on *thighs* overrides the grammatical subject *fore-part* to select the plural verb *were,* a choice not noticed by the author nor by most readers because of the distance between the verb and both subject and theme. Prescriptive grammarians of the nineteenth century termed this process an "error of proximity" and found copious examples to illustrate it—for instance, "the *danger* of seditions and insurrections *have* [has] been talked of" (1807; Hodgson, 150). These "errors" were found in the most revered stylists—for instance, Matthew Arnold: "Culture points out that the harmonious *perfection* of generations of Puritans and Non-conformists *have* [has] been, in consequence, sacrificed" (from *Culture and Anarchy;* quoted by Hodgson, 152). Since their notions of grammar allowed no place for "thematic" agreement, the pedants blamed such usage on "inadvertence" (if they were generous) or "ignorance" (if they were not).

In general, the nineteenth century saw an increasing role for thematic organization, and writers often allowed thematic considerations to outweigh grammatical concord. In doing so, they were partly encouraged by rhetoricians who attempted to subordinate grammar to theme.

> Grammar differs from composition, as a knowledge of the rules of building differs from architecture. Grammar is based on material laws and on custom: composition on insight and taste. Grammar is largely mechanical; composition, organic. The one shapes sentences according to external rule; the other, according to feeling and sentiment. Grammar teaches us to speak and write accurately; composition, clearly, impressively, efficiently. Grammar is a means; composition, the end. (J. Angus, 367)

Of course there is no endorsement of error in this view, but the most perspicacious of the pedants allowed for the fact that grammar and thematic organization might sometimes be in conflict, and one did not inevitably take precedence over the other.

One of the powerful tools by which theme could dominate grammar lay in the use of the passive voice, since it allows for the active subject and the object to be interchanged to suit thematic development. Though twentieth-century pedants have sometimes inveighed against the passive on the grounds that it is "clumsy" or "weak," most of their nineteenth-century predecessors said little or nothing about it. Writing in 1898, Henry Sweet stated a reservation that would not have occurred to most of his successors.

[W]e still hesitate over and try to evade such passive constructions as *she was given a watch | he was granted an audience* because we still feel that *she* and *he* are in the dative, not the accusative relation. (1958, 2:118)

Such historical memory was only available to a language historian, and passives of this type, though rare before 1500, had come into increasing prominence and use. Through the nineteenth century, there was "a considerable increase in the incidence of the indirect passive" (Visser 3.2:2147), and examples were to be found abundantly in the "best" writers: "he had been bid more for his wool than anybody" (Austen, *Emma,* 27); "as she was given to understand by his words" (Austen, *Northanger Abbey,* 208).

As a more verbal style with its depth of subordination was displaced by one developed in a more linear way through noun phrases, the pedants found something else about which to complain.

> There is a style unknown to any system of rhetoric, ancient or modern. It is peculiar to the nineteenth century, and may, not inappropriately, be called the *railway* style. It is alike remarkable for the rapidity of its transitions from thought to thought, and for the length of theme the writer may go over without drawing breath. It has no time for colons or semicolons, and bestows but a passing notice on the commas. As to full stops, it admits of only one, and that it calls a *terminus.* Stops were well enough in the steady, stately, stage-coach phraseology of the Johnsons, but they are unsuited to our days of electricity and steam. (Breen, 141)

Balanced and coordinated sentences built around infinitives and participles gave way to a noun phrases coming one after another like railway carriages. Though the style here subject to complaint was not entirely new in the nineteenth century, it was certainly facilitated by an increased use of the passive. In the exemplary passage to illustrate the railway style, Breen fabricated a long sentence consisting of clauses linked to a previous clause with *who* and *which;* this sentence can only be manufactured by the use of the passive to couple the ideas to each other. With the increased popularity of this style, the passive was employed with verbs where it was already established, and it was created for verbs with which it had never been used before. These included *cause* and *pay,* and, according to Visser, "it is especially with the verbs *allow, give, show, teach* and *tell* that the usage must be considered as having become firmly established" (3.2: 2147). Nearly all of these appear in the impersonal style so favored by professional writers, from scientists to journalists.

Prepositional verbs were introduced in even greater numbers: "If the phenomena *are reasoned upon* . . ." (1812; Humphrey Davy, *Chemical Philosophy*); "These facts will *be* further *weighed upon* as we proceed" (1817; H. T. Colebrooke, *Algebra*); "This is a fallacy to be most carefully *guarded against* in dealing with all Biblical questions" (1883; A. Roberts, *Old Testament Revision*). (All these examples are cited from Visser 3.2: 2129–30.) In these clauses, the implicit subject of these passive verbs is the intellect involved in *reasoning, weighing,* and *guarding.* Of course most of these verbs were used freely in personal constructions as well, but their introduction allowed the impersonal style to flourish.

As passives became more and more common, alternatives to the long-standing forms of *be* developed to express it. As early as 1652, according to the *OED*, *got acquainted* appeared, side by side with *was acquainted.* In many of these, *get* in the sense of *become* operated to distinguish the *be* from *get* forms. Thus, *get married* (1864; *OED*, s.v. *antimonarchal*) and *was married* could be synonyms—"They were/got married last week"—but could also express different shades of meaning: "They were married for a lifetime" and "They got married for a life-time." For many nineteenth-century writers, the passive with *get* was innovative. Austen wrote, "when I first heard she was going to be married" (*Emma*, 79); Telscombe failed to mimic her model when she composed the sentence, "Arthur to be getting married!" (*Sanditon*, 174). In general, the *get* forms were more colloquial than formal, more dialectal than standard. Defining *strummel* in 1812, Vaux illustrated the use of *get* in place of *have:* "To *get* your strummel faked in twig, is to have your hair dressed in style" (McLachlan, s.v., *strummel;* emphasis added). Twain's narrator writes of "the night Huck Finn was killed," but Huck himself says "since the night I got killed" (680,

665). As the century came to an end, the semantic and stylistic distinctions between the two forms blurred: "The projecting fibres . . . get laid along the yarn" (1884; *OED*, s.v. *starry*). Dozens of passives with *get* are first attested in the nineteenth century: *get paid* (1839; *OED*, s.v., *periodical*); *got engaged* (1859; *OED*, s.v., *tent*); *gets done* (1871; *OED*, s.v. *sonnet*). Some of them were employed for stylistic nuance; others simply arose side by side with the *be* forms because the passive had become so much more common.

The two features just discussed—attraction and the increased use of the passive—asserted thematic organization above grammatical principle. This same clash led to arguments about the *split infinitive*. Though that term is not attested until 1897, the structure had been singled out for censure half a century earlier. When Edmund Burke—a stylist revered by nineteenth-century critics—had written "to far exceed" and "to effectively stifle," the pedants said, he was wrong. *To* in this construction must be followed immediately by the verbs *exceed* and *stifle*.

The earliest complaint about split infinitives came in 1834 in the *New-England Magazine* by a writer identifying himself only by the initial "P."

> The practice of separating the prefix of the infinitive mode from the verb, by the insertion of an adverb, is not unfrequent among uneducated persons; as, "To fully understand it," instead of "to understand it fully," or, "fully to understand it." This fault is not often found in print, except in some newspapers, where the editors have not had the advantage of a good education. I am not conscious, that any rule has been heretofore given in relation to this point: no treatise on grammar or rhetoric, within my knowledge, alludes to it. The practice, however, of not separating the particle from its verb, is so general and uniform among good authors, and the exceptions to it are so rare, that the rule which I am about to propose will, I believe, prove to be as accurate as most rules, and may be found beneficial to inexperienced writers. It is this:—*The particle*, TO, which comes before the verb in the infinitive mode, must not be separated from it by the intervention of an adverb, or any other word or phrase; but the adverb should immediately precede the particle, or immediately follow the verb. (469)

P. had found two examples of this construction in Byron and speculated that "there are, perhaps, others." In Britain, the offensive construction was detected in 1840 in Richard Taylor's edition of the great nineteenth-century work of crank etymology, John Horne Tooke's *Diversions of Purley*. "Some writers of the present day," Taylor wrote, "have a disagreeable affectation of putting an adverb between *to* and the infinitive" (Tooke, xxx). Taylor appended to this observation a series of examples from Wycliff and noted parallel examples in other medieval Germanic languages, but he did not cite any from "writers of the present day." By an act of independent discovery, Henry Alford in 1864 also identified the newfound error.

> But, surely, this is a practice entirely unknown to English speakers and writers. It seems to me that we ever regard the *to* of the infinitive as inseparable from its verb. (1888, 133)

That the "separation" was common in English was soon pointed out by Fitzedward Hall, who noted, with his usual keen sense of the pedants' disparity between precept and practice, that Osmun's edition of John Donne contained five examples (1882, 18).

Goold Brown, in 1851, had not discovered the problem of "separation." By 1868, Samuel U. Berrian published an enlarged edition of Brown's *Grammar*, and by that time the issue had sprung to awareness. Berrian viewed the matter with a tolerance not characteristic of his mentor.

> Of the infinitive verb and its preposition *to*, some grammarians say, that they must never be separated by an adverb. It is true, that the adverb is, in general, more elegantly placed before the preposition than after it; but, possibly, the latter position of it may sometimes contribute to perspicuity, which is more essential than elegance. (661)

"The right to place an adverb sometimes between *to* and its verb should," Berrian concluded, "be conceded to the poets."

From these modest beginnings, the doctrine of the split infinitive moved into the domain of public linguistic lore. When British diplomats were negotiating the Alabama claims and other

disputes with the United States in 1871, they were vexed by con-
stant instructions from London enabled by the undersea cable,
and some of them wished to be free of the niggling points raised
by the Foreign Office.

> The Home Government kept putting in their oar, and once—for
> which much may by literary persons be forgiven them—they
> telegraphed that, in the treaty, they would *not* endure adverbs between
> "to" (the sign of the infinitive) and the verb. The purity of the English
> language they nobly and courageously defended. (Lang, 2:13)

This passage was quoted by Thomas R. Lounsbury in 1908 as
exemplifying a preposterous example of a grammatical fetish.
Tennyson had not split infinitives, he observed; Browning, on the
other hand, was "curiously addicted" (261).

> Thus the usage, little heeded, gained ground steadily. By the middle
> of the nineteenth century it had become common. Then the cham-
> pions of purity of speech suddenly woke up to the gravity of the situ-
> ation. Following the time-honored fashion of locking the stable door
> after the horse has been stolen, they started a systematic crusade
> against the practice. It has been kept up with little interruption from
> that day to this. At no period, indeed, has the attack upon the usage
> been so virulent as during the past dozen years; and at no period has
> its futility been so apparent. The purists had been aroused from their
> torpor too late, if, indeed, their awakening at any time would have
> made any difference in the result. (263–64)

The power of editors and school teachers has been exercised
against splitting *to* from the verb that follows it, but with only small
success except in the most fastidiously scrutinized English. To the
extent that this campaign has been successful, "grammar" has
partly triumphed over theme, since thematic organization calls for
putting the modifying adverb closest to the verb to which it per-
tains. More recent observers have noted that the structure has
been "gradually gaining ground" since the fourteenth century and
"is more characteristic of our most prominent authors than of the
minor writers" (Curme, 461); "the one thing we know for certain
about the frequency of the split infinitive is that it noticeably
increased in the 19th century" (Gilman, 868).

In other ways, theme asserted its claims in nineteenth-century usage. Controversy about the placement of *only* had erupted in the eighteenth century and continued to exercise pedants in the nineteenth. Louth's example sentence came in for much discussion: "I only spoke three words." Brown found the controversy "hypercritical" (635), but, as elaborated by others, readers were invited to believe that *only* attached to words nearest to it and that "logic" required the distinction be made between "Only I spoke three words" and "I spoke three words only." In fact, the placement of *only* (and similar words) rarely creates genuine ambiguity, though the pedants were adroit at fabricating plausibly ambiguous examples. Once again this issue arises mainly in writing, since the rhythm of speech would make it quite clear which of the two interpretations of "I only spoke three words" was intended. Since there was no "grammar" regulating the placement of adverbs, proponents of theme were more successful in asserting the claims of adjacency than they had been in treating the split infinitive. In the fragmentary way of such disputes, however, the controversy raged mainly around *only*, though the placement of *even* often raises similar issues.

A similar conflict drove the competition of "two first" and "first two." Jane Austen had habitually written "two first dances," but Telscombe was naturally drawn to "first two dances" in her completion of *Sanditon*. The issue here had long divided English. Historically, "two first" was the traditional usage, but in the sixteenth century "first two" emerged side by side with it. Bradley explained the matter in the *OED* (s.v., *first*, 2e).

> This [i.e., "first two"] is now the universal form in the case of high numbers; but for numbers up to 3 or 4 many writers use it only when the number specified is viewed as a collective unity contrasted with the second or some succeeding 2, 3, or 4 in the series.

The matter was hardly so simple. Supervising the work of subeditors, Bradley allowed "two first quots." (s.v., *effeminate*) and "first two quots." (s.v. *genius*). "Putting the numeral last," Jespersen explained, connected it with the noun that followed (2:361). Arguing for "two first" at midcentury, Osmun admitted that the two structures were synonymous; for him, the question was "which of the two is the more precise and correct?" (1888, 106). "Hardly any good English expression gets so much wrath expended on it as this," he concluded (108). Reviewing the matter in 1908, Lounsbury left the issue of correctness open to further study but argued that the preferences of the best writers should be encouraged, whatever the logical arguments adduced in favor of one or the other of the usages (124–34). While "two first" still occasionally appears (Gilman, 448), the adjacency of the numeral to the following noun has carried the day as position has come to be more and more forceful as a principle of English structure.

By no means all of the grammatical changes that took place in the nineteenth century occasioned an expenditure of wrath. With verbs like *come, go, become,* and *grow*—technically defined as "mutative intransitives"—a shift was taking place. At the beginning of the nineteenth century, these could be used with either forms of *be* or of *have.* Jane Austen's usage was conservative, but like most of her contemporaries she found uses for both. "She *had* gone home" and "she *is* gone home" (*Emma,* 108 and 211). "I *am* grown wretchedly thin" (*Northanger Abbey,* 14) and "she *had* just grown intimate" (*Mansfield Park,* 450). "He *was* become perfectly reconciled" (*Emma,* 401) and "his penance *had* become severe" (*Persuasion,* 242; emphasis added). Comparing American and London English early in the century, John Pickering thought that *to have arrived* was American and *to be arrived* was British. In a careful study of British comedies and private letters (supposed to be the least self-conscious kinds of English), Rydén and Brorström found that, in the eighteenth century, forms of *have* and *be* appeared with *arrive* in a ratio of 108 *be* to 15 *have.* In their nineteenth-century sample, the ratio had changed to 37 *be* to 167 *have* (44–46). With mutative intransitives generally, the change in preference from *be* to *have* took place "in the early decades of the nineteenth century" (198). For the most part, the pedants gave this change little notice. Goold Brown, for instance, recognized that "our ancient writers . . . very frequently employed" *have;* "with a very few exceptions, present usage is clearly in favour of the auxiliary *have* in preference to *be*" (1851, 370—a view repeated by Berrian in his enlargement of Brown's *Grammar* in 1868 [388]).

During the nineteenth century, young people studied grammar assiduously—doubtless more intensively than any time before or since. Since grammar as a school subject had long been in place, there was little need to justify the time spent studying it. Goold Brown, for instance, in his short *Institutes* of 1850 pointed out that one could easily command the language without grammatical study; "but he who is desirous either of relishing the beauties of literary composition, or of expressing his sentiments with propriety and ease, must make the principles of language his study" (iii). This rationale was simply an expansion of Lindley Murray's claim, expressed on his title page, that the work was of value "for assisting the more advanced students to write with perspicuity and accuracy." Other authors of textbooks added the notion that grammatical study was akin to logic, and hence the study of English would lead to increased mental discipline and acuity. A few others emphasized the psychological processes involved in using English, and rote learning of definitions gave way, at least in progressive schools, to a reliance on the pupil's tacit knowledge of the language and to inductive methods of discerning it (see Michael, 367–68). By the end of the century, and with the vastly improved reputation of scientific inquiry, the study of grammar was urged on the grounds that it "is as much a *real* study as botany or chemistry" (Daniel, iii). With the unprecedented emphasis on gentility, grammar was viewed as a prerequisite to polite behavior, and etiquette books urged particular forms of English, often in excruciating detail. These works promised to "enable any person of common intelligence, by study and perseverance in practice, to avoid most of the gross errors which mar the speech of many people" (Duncan, 5).

Only rarely was the value of grammatical study questioned, and most schoolchildren were given no choice in the matter of memorizing definitions and rules. A notable exception was William Cobbett's *Grammar of the English Language* (1818), itself an unremarkable recital of the usual categories and definitions but founded on radical principles.

" And, when its yellow luster smiled   Each mother held aloft ber child
O'er mountains yet untrod,   To bless the bow of God.
See pages 54, 55, 56, and 57   Clark's First Lessons.

With increased literacy and mass schooling, the study of English grammar was seen as valuable for its own sake—intellectual discipline—as well as for its presumed consequences—correct and fluent expression. The girl at the right points to the grammatical category while the boy at the left shows its use in an actual sentence, a stanza from Thomas Campbell's "To the Rainbow" (1819). (From S. Clark, 54.)

A journalist and gadfly, Cobbett (1763–1835) was suspicious of nearly all institutions, including schools. During the first of his two residences in the United States, he published *Porcupine's Gazette,* in which he described himself as "an author who appears particularly chosen as a conqueror of the democrats, jacobins, and French faction in America" (December 4, 1797). On his return to England he began the *Political Register,* and in volume after volume he challenged prevailing assumptions. In 1807, he assailed instruction in Latin and Greek.

> Learning, truly so called, consists in the possession of knowledge and in the capacity of communicating that knowledge to others; and, as far as my observation will enable me to speak, what are called the

learned languages, operate as a bar to the acquirement of real learning. (11:36)

He challenged the "*learned* gentlemen of the two universities" to
debate this point, but they did not deign to respond. In the same
year, he pointed out that Napoleon had conquered Europe without knowing Latin or Greek. He recalled that the London papers
had derided an intercepted letter of Napoleon for its bad spelling.

> This letter was the subject of a good deal of merriment, which lasted
> for several days, and would, probably, have lasted much longer, had
> not the attention of the learned and the witty been called off by the
> news of the battle of Austerlitz, which served, too, as a sort of practi-
> cal illustration of the inutility of Latin and Greek in the performance
> of great actions in the world. (12:750–51)

Praising Napoleon in 1807 was hardly likely to cultivate the good
opinion of most English readers.

In 1811, Cobbett returned to the same theme, this time
denouncing the relevance of the Roman Empire to a debate about
freedom of the press. Allusions to antiquity, he wrote, are especially foolish in such a discussion since there were no presses in
Greece or Rome; citations of ancient authors merely "arise from
the vanity of appearing to know more than the people at large."

> With men, who have been at great schools, there is, too often, some-
> thing of the school-boy sticking to them through life. Having had
> their education under *word-mongers*, they are extremely fortunate if
> they ever get completely rid of the love of dealing in the same ware
> themselves. Having, for so many years, been accustomed to look
> upon the knowledge of *words* in outlandish languages as the highest
> of all human qualifications, it is no wonder that they continue to
> interlard all their writings with references to the history of the coun-
> try where those languages flourished, such references affording
> them an excuse for indulging in a display of their school-boy knowl-
> edge. (19:450)

Given his contempt for mere words and his hostility to *word-mon-
gers*, it is remarkable that Cobbett determined to write a grammar.
The motive was expressed in the subtitle added to the edition of

1826: "intended for the use of schools and of young persons in general; but more especially for the use of soldiers, sailors, apprentices, and plough-boys."

Having made himself both unpopular and impoverished in England, Cobbett returned to the United States, where he wrote his grammar for publication in December 1818. Before the end of January, it had sold more than 10,000 copies, and the subsequent English editions totaled more than 100,000 before the time of his death. The *Grammar* consists of a series of letters to his son James, then fourteen years old; it shows clear evidences of Cobbett's feat of memorizing Lindley Murray's grammar in his own youth. "Grammar," Cobbett alleged is "the gate of entrance" to "knowledge connected with books" (17). Real learning, as he had already declared in the *Register*, consisted in practical knowledge, and to his son he especially urged knowledge of the "rights and liberties" of England. He commended an appreciation of historical examples of rulers being toppled by "the just vengeance of the People":

> when you come to read the history of these struggles in the cause of freedom, you will find that tyranny has no enemy so formidable as the pen. And, while you will see with exultation the long-imprisoned, the heavily fined, the banished WILLIAM PRYNNE, returning to liberty, borne by the people from Southampton to London, over a road strewed with flowers; then accusing, bringing to trial, and to the block, the tyrants from whose hands he and his country had unjustly and cruelly suffered; while your heart and the heart of every young man in the kingdom will bound with joy at the spectacle, you ought all to bear in mind that, without a knowledge of *Grammar*, Mr. PRYNNE could never have performed any of those acts by which his name has been preserved, and which [that] have caused his memory to be held in honor. (Cobbett, 18; Osmun's brackets)

The heady prospect of such an example was intended to inspire James Cobbett; it also was intended to arouse the soldiers, sailors, apprentices, and plowboys of England.

Cobbett was audacious in using Prynne as an instance of the enabling power of grammar. Far from the plowboys expected to profit from Cobbett's *Grammar*, Prynne (1600–1669) had been a graduate of Oxford and a member of the English Bar (Lincoln's

Inn, 1628). An ardent Puritan and controversialist, he was thoroughly grounded in the learned languages despised in the *Political Register* and was imprisoned for a pamphlet explaining that monarchs who had encouraged the drama had suffered violent deaths. Stripped of his degree and expelled from Lincoln's Inn, he had had his ears lopped off by the executioner while standing in the pillory. With Cromwell's accession to power, he was a scourge of the Catholics (both Roman and Anglican), but he also quarreled with John Milton in a pamphlet war, and, with the restoration, zealously pursued the regicides in the outburst of revenge that accompanied the restoration of the monarchy. He published some two hundred works, virtually all of them disputatious. Cobbett, like Prynne, had been both an ardent monarchist and a severe republican, and both he and Prynne were fluent and frequent writers. Unlike Prynne, Cobbett never was borne by the people over roads strewn with flowers, and he died with both his ears intact.

For Cobbett, grammar had a political purpose. In part he expressed this view through examples. For instance, in explaining the verb phrase, he offered two examples with a strikingly partisan flavor: "The borough-tyrants, generally *speaking*, are great fools as well as rogues" (144) and "The working-men, every day, *gave* money to the tyrants, who, in return, *gave* the working-men dungeons and axes" (147). In addition, he reached a much wider audience with the polemics that had appeared repeatedly in the *Political Register.*

> Another object in producing these specimens [of "false grammar"] is to convince you that a knowledge of the Latin and Greek languages does not prevent men from writing bad English. These languages are, by impostors and their dupes, called "the *learned* languages"; and those who [that] have paid for having studied them are said to have received "a *liberal* education." These appellations are false, and, of course, they lead to false conclusions. *Learning,* as a noun, means *knowledge,* and *learned* means *knowing* or *possessed of knowledge.* Learning is, then, to be acquired by *conception;* and it is shown in *judgment,* in *reasoning,* and in the various modes of employing it. What, then, can *learning* have to do with any particular tongue! Good Grammar, for instance, written in Welsh, or in the language of

the Chippewa savages, is *more learned* than bad Grammar written in Greek. The learning is in the *mind* and not in the *tongue*. . . .

The cause of the use of this false appellation, "learned languages," is this, that those who [that] teach them in England have, in consequence of their teaching, *very large estates in house and land,* which are public property, but which are now used for the sole benefit of those teachers, who are, in general, the relations [relatives] or dependents of the Aristocracy. In order to give a color of reasonableness to this species of appropriation, the languages taught by the possessors are called "the *learned* languages"; and [omit] which appellation is, at the same time, intended to cause the mass of the people to believe that the professors and learners of these languages are, in point of wisdom, far superior to other men; and to establish the opinion that all but themselves are *unlearned* persons. In short, the appellation, like many others, is a trick which [that] fraud has furnished for the purpose of guarding the snug possessors of the property against the consequences of the people's understanding the matter. (Cobbett, 165–67; the bracketed "improvements" are Osmun's)

Cobbett's purpose was to expose the "trick," to show that however firmly wrapped in "learning," aristocrats and their "dependents" were mired in bad grammar, weak logic, and worse reasoning. Even authorities on English (like Samuel Johnson) or on logic (like Isaac Watts) were capable of "doubtful meaning." The king's ministers, the future duke of Wellington, and a prominent bishop were all added, in subsequent editions, to the roster of shameful frauds who used English badly or deceptively.

Cobbett's idea in publishing an English grammar was to empower the "people's understanding" against the dishonesty of the elite. For him, grammar had little to do with etiquette or even fine writing; it had a great deal to do with dissecting the language in the search for truth. Cobbett's drift across the political spectrum from royalist toward republican did not change his mind about "understanding." In 1797 he had denounced Noah Webster as a "toad in the service of sans-culottism" and sneered at Webster's use of the word *revolutionize* ("a word entirely of his own disturbed imagination," Cobbett fulminated [*Porcupine's Gazette,* July 10,

1797], but one traced to British "disturbed imaginations" by the *OED*). When the apprentices and plowboys rose to his attention, he was equally vituperative about aristocrats and bishops. Consistently he urged action over reflection, application over theory, and grammar as a means of liberation. Though there were few like Cobbett to assist them, the apprentices and plowboys—at least in North America—emerged to positions of power and eloquence.

The best of the nineteenth-century schoolbook grammars repeated the idea that Cobbett had articulated: grammatical study was a gateway to learning. In the United States, Samuel Kirkham's *English Grammar in Familiar Lectures* (first published in 1829) asserted that grammar alone allowed the "unfolding and maturing of the mental powers" (2). Grammatical study had not only personal but also political purposes.

> You are aware, my young friend, that you live in an age of light and knowledge;—an age in which science and the arts are marching onward with gigantic strides. You live, too, in a land of liberty—a land on which the smiles of Heaven beam with uncommon refulgence. The trump of the warrior and the clangor of arms no longer echo on our mountains, or in our valleys; "the garments dyed in blood have passed away"; the mighty struggle for independence is over; and you live to enjoy the rich book of freedom and prosperity which was purchased with the blood of our fathers. (15)

Light, knowledge, science, the arts, freedom, and prosperity were all invoked as consequent on the study of English grammar, all of them obviously more important than carping verbal criticism or invidious social nuance. While it is impossible to measure the effects of such claims, it is worth noting that Kirkham's *Grammar* was the one Abraham Lincoln studied by the fireside deep in the Kentucky wilderness.

Hyperbolic as such claims for the liberating power of grammar may seem to be, they were a regular feature in the promotion of schoolbooks. The connection between grammatical study and national purpose was made vividly clear in a book published in the American Confederacy in the first year of the War between the States.

The only apologies offered for presenting a *new Grammar* to the public are—first, *that every independent nation must furnish its own literature;* and second, *that none of the works hitherto presented to the public are perfect.* The Southerners, in their previous history, have been content to have their books furnished them by the North. This not only *discouraged Southern authorship,* and *cramped genius,* but it allowed the North the *chief means of shaping national bias*—THE PRESS. But now that the Southern people have separated from the North, and established an *independent nationality,* she will, of course, hail with pleasure every industrious effort of *"her own sons"* to free her from *Abolition dependencies.* (Worrell, 1)

Such assertions may seem preposterous to twentieth-century readers; in the nineteenth century, they seemed entirely reasonable.

Unprecedented interest in grammar and near universal study of its rudiments in Britain and the United States emerged during the nineteenth century. Grand claims, like those made by Cobbett and Kirkham, are almost impossible to test, and the ideology of the Confederate States of America was certainly unaffected by the production of a homegrown grammar book. Many grammars fostered the idea that linguistic analysis would assist in the search for truth—though these claims are mainly found in the front matter and seldom exemplified in lessons and exercises. The main emphasis of these works was directed to the eradication of error, and in this effort they were almost entirely unsuccessful. The authoritative survey of the relation of grammatical precept to actual usage declares it to be "unmistakably certain that a whole century or even two centuries of laborious criticism and purism have produced no effect worth mentioning, if any at all" (DeKeyser, 276). In those few cases in which there is some statistically significant change in usage, it is the "incorrect" usages that prevail—for instance, "I'm sure there is a vast many smart beaux in Exeter" (Austen; "correct" usage mandates *are*); "But not so much so as to hinder us getting up this morning" (Keats; "correct" usage requires *our*). In these two cases—the use of *is* with a plural subject in extraposition and the use of objective rather than possessive pronouns before gerunds—the incidence of the "incorrect" form doubles from the first to the second half of the century (from 6 percent to 13 percent in the first case; from 22 percent to 46 percent in the second [DeKeyser, 273]).

All one can safely allege is that the rage of the pedants retarded linguistic change—that the popularity of the incorrect forms might have increased even more rapidly without their strictures and that the features where no significant change took place might have fluctuated even more widely without their attention. The pedants certainly raised doubts about usage, and these doubts instilled fear and silence in their pupils. Beyond an increased level of anxiety, it is difficult to attribute more to their efforts. At the end of the nineteenth century, educators were faced with the disquieting possibility that all the attention to grammar had made no difference whatsoever. Fred Newton Scott in 1900 expressed dismay over the "unsettledness" of English teaching. "*Are* our methods of instruction in English in harmony with the social demands of our great industrial community? I suspect that . . . our present ideals and methods of instruction are in large part remnants of an adaptation to a state of things which long since passed away" (293–94).

VOICES

CROWDING, AND THE RESULTING INTIMACY of people living close to one another, was normal for nearly everyone at the beginning of the nineteenth century. Huge families in tiny hovels characterized village life, and even the prosperous dwelt in houses small by modern standards. Artisans lived in extended families including apprentices; farmworkers slept in hovels or cramped lofts close to farm animals and to each other; many unmarried women spent years in domestic service living in garrets shared with other servants. Genteel life, whether on plantations in the Caribbean and the southern United States or in the stately homes of Britain, swarmed with people.

Here is Virginia Woolf's description of the house in which she lived as a child at the end of the century.

> It was a house of innumerable small oddly shaped rooms built to accommodate not one family but three. For besides the three Duckworths and the four Stephens there was also Thackeray's granddaughter, a vacant-eyed girl whose idiocy was becoming daily more obvious, who could hardly read, who would throw the scissors into the fire, and who was tongue-tied and stammered and yet had to appear at table with the rest of us. . . . There were chests of heavy family plate. There were hoards of china and glass. Eleven people aged between eight and sixty lived there, and were waited upon by seven servants, while various old women and lame men did odd jobs with rakes and pails by day. (160–61)

The Stephens were a prosperous middle-class family, and their cramped quarters were much more capacious than those of the classes below them.

With the explosive growth in population and with urbanization coerced by the privatization of common grazing lands in Britain, living conditions everywhere became ever more crowded, and people were forced into the company of others whether they liked it or not. Perhaps more important than the sounds of spoken English were the rules for silence.

The eighteenth century bequeathed to the nineteenth the idea of the inarticulate peasant. The "mute inglorious Milton" of Gray's "Elegy" was silenced by a lack of language. George Crabbe's poems of village life emphasized the brutishness of existence; mourners approached a funeral "sedately torpid and devoutly dumb" (7), and "vice and misery" produced their own language.

> Here, in cabal, a disputatious crew
> Each evening meet; the sot, the cheat, the shrew;
> Riots are nightly heard;—the curse, the cries
> Of beaten wife, perverse in her replies;
> While shrieking children hold each threat'ning hand,
> And sometimes life, and sometimes food, demand;
> Boys in their first stol'n rags, to swear begin,
> And girls, who heed not dress, are skill'd in gin. (10)

Gloom and sorrow found expression among the inarticulate, of course. Suffering, of which there was an abundance, was translated into stoicism, and stoicism often into silence. At the center of the anglophone world, quiet prevailed on occasions for which other cultures prescribed acts of speaking.

At the beginning of the century, social life still retained obvious traces of feudalism. Landowners in Britain and the southern United States exercised seignorial powers, while colonial proprietors and prominent local families controlled society on the frontiers. Landowners and property speculators in the newly opened "western reserve" of the United States had no compunction about appending *-ville, -burg,* or *-town* to their family names and ruling over those who settled in the resulting communities, and their elitism and relative wealth justified the adoption of their norms for English in the newly established schools (see Frazer).

With the development of capitalism and the growth of industry, *class-consciousness*—a term first attested in English in an 1887 translation of Marx's *Capital*—arose, and talk about social class became commonplace. While the words *order* and *rank* had previously been used in discussing social structure, the nineteenth century provided an abundance of terms—not only *upper class* (1836) and *working class* (1813), but a great variety of other terms as well. *Upper ten thousand* (coined in the United States about 1844) gave rise to an abbreviated form *upper ten* (1861) and the compounded word *upper-tendom* (1848). Sociology, with its obsession for classification, was very much a nineteenth-century science; it yielded dozens of compounds with *class* as the first element: *class barrier* (1889), *-bias* (1863), *-conflict* (1858), *-difference* (1879), *-distinction* (1841), *-feelings* (1839), *-hatred* (1851), *-interest* (1828), *-loyalty* (1899), *-morality* (1833), *-prejudice* (1861), *-spirit* (1840), *-struggle* (1850), *-superiority* (1859), *-system* (1877), and *-war* (1886). *Monster meeting* (compounded in Britain to deride rallies in favor of Irish self-rule, 1842) and *mass meeting* (the corresponding U.S. term for a huge public assembly, 1847) were other terms that submerged individuals in anonymous crowds.

The class consciousness reflected in these innovations in vocabulary produced a change in English. As the century progressed, people were more likely to speak and listen more and more exclusively to those of their own social class. The severe silences of nineteenth-century life survived into the mid–twentieth century, recorded, among other places, in the recollections of people in a small Suffolk village, gathered as oral history by Ronald Blythe in *Akenfield*. A laborer who had spent his youth as a gardener on a country estate recalled the values of speaking passed through the generations from his great-grandfather, who had been similarly employed on the same estate.

> As the years went by, we young men found ourselves being able to talk to Lordship and Ladyship. "Never speak to them—not one word and no matter how urgent—until they speak to you," the head-gardener told me on my first day. . . . We must never look at her [Ladyship] and she never looked at us. It was the same in the house. If a maid was in a passage and Lordship or Ladyship happened to come along, she would have to face the wall and stand perfectly still until they had

passed. I wouldn't think that they felt anything about their servants.
We were just there because we were necessary, like water from the
tap. (103–4)

Linguistic isolation, despite physical propinquity, supported
dialect divergence, with the regional differences that had united
landowner and peasant since medieval times being supplanted by
class-stratified ways of speaking and habits of silence. Upper-class
English became ever more national, and, with travel abroad and
the routine of home visits from the colonies, international. Lower-
class speakers who remained at home became more and more
localized and firmly fixed by place and by occupation.

Linguistic curiosity found much to celebrate in local speechways, and interest in peasant life was, at the end of the eighteenth
century, beginning to be satisfied by published accounts of "popular antiquities" and by a rage for collecting ballads, proverbs,
and lore representing folk wisdom. In 1765, Thomas Percy published a collection of such material—often "improved" by the
light of his own taste—and his example encouraged others to
gather stories and sayings from rural districts. In 1787, Francis
Grose published *A Provincial Glossary,* in which he recorded
regional vocabulary, listed proverbs, and compiled anecdotes of
"popular superstitions" (of which tales of ghosts, witches, and sor-
cerers provide the greatest number). The superstitions he gathered from "village historians" created a romantic picture of folk
life at a time when many cultivated people regarded the folk with
indifference.

> Other articles on this subject, and those not a few, have been col-
> lected from the mouths of village historians, as they were related to a
> closing circle of attentive hearers, assembled in a winter's evening,
> round the capacious chimney of an old hall or manor-house; for, for-
> merly, in counties remote from the metropolis, or which had no
> immediate intercourse with it, before news-papers and stage-coaches
> had imported skepticism, and made every plowman and thresher a
> politician and free-thinker, ghosts, fairies and witches, with bloody
> murders, committed by tinkers, formed a principal part of rural con-
> versation, in all large assemblies, and particularly those in Christmas
> holydays, during the burning of the yule-block. (vii–viii)

Such imagery reflects the wave of romanticizing peasant life that swept across the intellectual landscape of nineteenth-century Britain and North America. The idyll of innocence that Grose described was, in his day, being shattered by technology—here stagecoaches and newspapers. The "unspoiled" quality of rural life, with its characteristic vocabulary, was beginning to disappear.

In the preface to the *Provincial Glossary*, Grose justified his collecting on the grounds that such a work would be useful to "all persons desirous of understanding our ancient poets" (iii), thus placing his work in the context of antiquarian lexicography begun by John Ray (in his *Collection of English Words, Not Generally Used* [1674]). Grose had used Ray's dictionary as one of his sources, but the reviewers recognized in Grose's compilation a more important purpose, that of preserving rural speech against the encroachments of modern life.

> Provincialisms are the vestiges of older English, not quite worn out by additions, or polished by refinements: we should look at them with the veneration which we feel when we survey a Saxon arch mouldering to its ruin, or a Gothic window tottering at every blast. If not caught at this moment, they will be forgotten, since more frequent communications with the provinces, and more easy access will soon make little variety, except in the wilds of Exmoor, the barren heaths of Northumberland, or the sequestered mountains of Lancashire. (Review of Grose's *Provincial Glossary*, 285)

With the exception of the most remote parts of England, this reviewer opined, all "variety" would soon be lost. Looking at folk speech with "veneration" was, in the cultural context of the eighteenth century, decidedly a new idea that came to fruition in the century that followed.

Two eighteenth-century writers had provided the literary ground work for the flowering of "vernacular" writing in the nineteenth century: John Collier and Ann Coward Wheeler. Collier, who wrote under the name "Tim Bobbin," revived the ancient tradition of the comic debate. His *Tummus and Meary* went through nineteen editions between its publication in 1746 and the end of the century. (The number of editions gives no clue as to how many books were printed; the fact that the work continued to be reissued suggests that publishers repeatedly underestimated the demand.) Collier begins with a debate between "th'eawther an' his book." The author, Tim, displays his skill as a versifier in conventional English, but the "book" urges him to employ something closer to the vernacular.

T[im]. Whot te dule art' woode. Whot il't doo wi' this whiffo-whaffo stuff? dust think rhyme mun olis tawk stump Lankeshur?

B[ook]. Eigh, why not', let 'em speyke greadly as we dun i' God's-num.

T[im]. Nay, nay, ittleno doo; "tomitch ov owt's good for nowt."

[*Tim*. What the devil? Are you mad? What will you do with this trifling stuff? Do you think that verses must always speak in thick Lancashire?

Book. Aye, why not? Let them speak properly as we do, in God's name.

Tim. No, no. It won't do. "Too much of anything is good for nothing."] (4)

The "book" persuades Tim that he need pay no attention to the linguistic tastes of the "fawse Lunnoners" (crafty Londoners), and Collier went on, in addition to his exploration of "South Lancashire," to provide specimens of the vernaculars of Scots (for instance, *mind* 'remember'), Yorkshire (*t'Brigg* 'the bridge'), and Welsh (*Shustices Pace* 'Justices of the Peace'). Though it is difficult to determine the readership of Collier's vernacular compositions, Tim Bobbin must have engaged an audience far wider than the antiquarians. In addition to the London printings, editions published in northern cities—for instance, Manchester, Leeds, and Bolton—suggest that the book was read by persons personally acquainted with the regional speech he contrived to record.

Ann Coward Wheeler's *Westmoreland Dialect* first appeared in 1790, published in Kendal, the largest town in the county. A native of Lancashire, Wheeler spent eighteen years as a housekeeper in London before marrying and, on her prosperous husband's death, retired to a literary life in the north, where she became fascinated with English in Westmoreland.

> Struck with a dialect, which, to the Authoress, from her long residence in other parts of the kingdom, appeared quite novel, she was determined to try what kind of orthography could be formed from it, and accordingly wrote the Dialogue between Ann and Mary, without any intention of its ever appearing in print. (xi)

Hoping to "share the laurels with Tim Bobbin," Wheeler began her work, as Collier had done, with the theme of her reluctance to write in the vernacular.

> I kna mony of my readers will think, nay en say, I hed lile et dea tae rite sic maapment about nae body knas wha; I mud hev fund mitch better employment in a cuntry hause, tae mind milkiness, sarra th coafs, leak heftert pigs en hens, spin tow for bord claiths en sheets; it wod hev been mitch mair farently then riting books, a wark ets fit for nin but parson et dea; but en ea mud rite I sud hev meaad receits for sweet pyes en rice puddins, en taken mauls aut eth claiths, that mud hev done gud, but as tae this, nea yan knas what it means, it's a capper.
>
> [I know many of my readers will think, nay even say, I had no business to write such nonsense about nobody knows what; I might have found much better employment in a country house, to mind the dairy, care for the calves, look after pigs and hens, spin flax for table cloths and sheets; it would have been much more respectable than writing books, a work that's fit for none but parsons to do; but if I must write I should have made recipes for sweet pies and rice puddings, and how to take mud out of clothing, that might have done good, but, as to this, no one knows what it means. It's a puzzle.] (13)

Wheeler's characters are boisterous, given to drink, fornication, and fighting. (At a wedding, the parson looks grim when the bride is accompanied by her baby, thinking that an earlier marriage would have been proper. Wheeler's authorial stance puts the reader in sympathy with the mother's love rather than with the minister's censure.) Like Collier's, however, Wheeler's characters are all comic rustics, given to bickering rather than argument, communal joy rather than solitary reflection. The life they lead is identical to that of the villagers in Crabbe's *Parish Register,* with the striking difference that Wheeler's characters enjoy themselves— her characters are as loquacious as his were sullen.

Other eighteenth-century writers also took an interest in dialect, but most of their publications were not original compositions in the vernacular but unsystematic observations of what seemed to them exotic speechways—for instance, the glossaries found in William Marshall's books *The Rural Economy of Norfolk* (1787), *The Rural Economy of Yorkshire* (1788), and *The Rural Economy of the Midland Counties* (1790) or those in traveler's books like Thomas West's *A Guide to the Lakes* (1780). Other texts aroused antiquarian interest—for instance *An Exmoor Scolding* and *An Exmoor Courtship.* These two works (of uncertain authorship) had appeared in 1746 in the *Gentleman's Magazine,* and they attracted some scholarly attention and correspondence from persons allegedly knowledgeable about the English of Devon. Though endowed by some with considerable antiquity, these two works were almost certainly written not long before their first publication, but, most important for the articulation of rural voices, they were produced by a local writer for a local audience. They were reprinted some fifteen times before the end of the century, all in the district of their origin, and not until the seventh edition (1771) did anyone feel moved to append a glossary. The Victorian editor reprehended the "utter foulness of much of this dialogue" and sneered at publishers' "pandering to the taste of the class which delights to feed on garbage" (Elworthy, 13). (Only confidence that his own version would be read by scholars allowed him to "touch such pitch.") The consumers of these works certainly had a different view.

The two *Exmoor* dialogues are full of vulgar fun, and terms of abuse are heaped one upon another. In the courtship of Margery and Andrew, Margery finds occasion to criticize one of Andrew's female friends.

> Whot! marry to Earteen? —Es gee tha same Onser es geed avore, Es wudent marry tha best Man in oll Ingland.—Es eud amorst zwear chud never marry at oll.—And more and zo, Cozen Andra, cham a

told ya keep Company wey *Tamzen Hosegood,* thek gart banging, thonging, muxy Drawbreech, daggle-teal'd Jade, a zower-zop'd yer-ring, chokling Trash, a buzzom-chuck'd haggaging Moyle, a gurt Fustilug. Hare's a Trub! And nif ya keep hare Company, es'll hana no more to zey to tha.

[What! Marry all of a sudden? I give you the same answer I gave before: I wouldn't marry the best man in all England. I'd almost swear I'd never marry at all. And what's more, Cousin Andrew, I'm told you run around with Tomasin Hosegood, that great big ass-wag-gling, shit-clotted, mucky-hemmed hussy, that ill-natured loud-mouth, that cackling good-for-nothing, that red-faced filthy mule, that fat slob. She's a slut! And if you run around with her, I'll have no more to say to you.] (96)

The nineteenth-century editor of the *Courtship* seems to have missed the point when he wrote: "It is, however, quite absurd to maintain that such long strings of synonymous words as are here put into the mouths of different persons could ever have been heard in real life" (13). Both works were designed for entertain-ment and fun, and, if the "redundancy of epithet" lacks verisimili-tude, it does convey a roistering humor, though of the kind that creates its effects through dirty words forthrightly pronounced. Both dialogues maintained their popularity, and, more than a cen-tury after they were first published, they were available in "a cheap form at a railway book-stall" (as Skeat wrote in this preface to Elworthy's edition).

Dialect writing, even in forms lacking respectability, gives authority to the vernacular. All the more do serious compositions treating serious subjects. Another work from the Lake District of northwest England provided a more didactic view of village ethics than Wheeler's. In 1785, William Hutton—long the rector of a parish in Westmoreland—composed an instructive homily on Christian conduct in the local vernacular, *A Bran New Wark.* In his "prologue," Hutton offered a justification for his choice of lan-guage.

Excuse my provincial dialect? I only annex such words to my ideas as we and our fathers have used for ages past. When I reflect on the number of *men* which the north country produced, some of

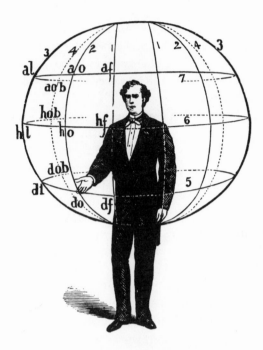

Oratory and declamation were popular public entertainments whether for politics, religion, or pleasure. Without artificial voice amplification, speakers were obliged to enunciate clearly, speak loudly, and employ broad gestures. Bacon's *Manual of Gesture* was designed to instruct would-be speakers in the last of these skills, and practice selections were keyed to the gestural sphere. (From Bacon, 70.)

whom even assisted in translating the bible and in composing our liturgy, I am not ashamed of it; I know them by their lingua, I trace them to have gone out from us. (185–86)

In the *Wark* itself, however, he employs a much more localized style.

Hes naane of ye seen a young thing, giggling and laughing at a firley farley? she quite forgat what the clark was saying, *Lord have mercy upon us!* dizened fra head to foot, she coud think of naught but her bran new bonnet. Her sawcy een were ticing fools, whilst the parson was converting sinners.

[Have none of you seen a young woman, giggling and laughing as some gee-gaw? She quite forgot what the reader was saying—"Lord have mercy upon us." Decked out from head to foot, she could think of nothing but her brand new bonnet. Her saucy eyes were enticing fools, while the parson was converting sinners.] (189)

As Skeat recognized in his editorial preface to the English Dialect Society edition, Hutton was localizing a literary work (rather than contriving a dialectal one), and he made no attempt to publish his *Wark* beyond the immediate district ("for use in the hamlet of Woodland," as the title page declares).

Eighteenth-century curiosity about the variety of English voices appeared as flickers of occasional interest in a prevailing pattern of indifference. From the philological perspective— curiosity about rural speech might illuminate "our ancient poets" (in Grose's words)—little was attempted. Pastoral poetry some- times was flavored by archaisms (in imitation of Virgil and Spenser) but seldom by the actual forms of speech used by living shepherds. Even the novelists and playwrights who created dia- logue for "low" characters seldom departed far from literary prece- dent, and Fielding, Smollett, and Sheridan (for instance) gave only occasional indications of a local flavor to English. Much more popular for literary humor were *malapropisms* (a linguistic category derived in the nineteenth century from Richard Brinsley Sheri- dan's character Mrs. Malaprop in *The Rivals* [1775]; see the *OED*, s.v. *malaprop* [1823], *malaproprian* [1860], and *malapropism* [1849]). Comic "misapplications" of words had their own literary tradition deriving from Shakespeare (in, for instance, Dogberry and Mistress Quickly), though verbal pratfalls of the linguistically ambitious certainly had a claim to reality.

Yet in this climate of indifference to folk speech, something was beginning to emerge that changed the culture of dialect and the perception of English voices. Rousseau's celebration of life untainted by civility is a usual landmark in discussions of this change in Europe and North America, and certainly British and American intellectuals were drawn into a sudden fascination with folk and even "savage" life.

Two authors who made their literary debuts at the end of the eighteenth century revealed differing and yet complementary views of people untainted by civilized refinement. The first was William Wordsworth and his declaration in the preface to *Lyrical Ballads* that wisdom, or at least sagacity, was to be discerned in the voices of "real" people (unexpectedly but profoundly in the leech gatherer, for instance). Despite his northwestern upbringing, however, Wordsworth did not represent his peasant savants in "dialect." As a poet, he "translated" folk speech into conventional English, the kind that one might expect of a shepherd who had idled away a few years at Cambridge and taken a pass degree. Yet his assumptions about the most "natural," and hence the best, in human life were profoundly influential for the literary creation of English voices in nineteenth-century fiction. In explaining the ideology of his poetry, Wordsworth in 1800 drew upon the conventional wisdom of the day in asserting that human language had begun in articulate sensation, in which the connection between word and feeling had arisen naturally. People whose lives remained close to the landscape were far more "primitive," and hence more authentic, than people who lived in cities or toiled at indoor occupations.

> The language, too, of these men [from "humble and rustic life"] has been adopted (purified indeed from what appear to be its real defects, from all lasting and rational causes of dislike or disgust) because such men hourly communicate with the best objects from which the best part of language is originally derived; and because, from their rank in society and the sameness and narrow circle of their intercourse, being less under the influence of social vanity, they convey their feelings and notions in simple and unelaborated expressions. (336)

Wordsworth's process of "purification" removed the foul-mouthed Margery from the imaginary rural landscape, and, despite his quarrel with poetic diction, Wordsworth had no argument with the consensus that had emerged about English spelling and grammar. Tim Bobbin's spirited advocacy of "stump Lankeshur" made no impression on Wordsworth, whose readers were not gathered round the "capacious chimney of an old hall or manor-house" (as were Grose's provincials) but were assembled in urban drawing rooms.

Far more important to nineteenth-century literary ideas about vernacular English was Maria Edgeworth. While Wordsworth had been satisfied to attend to the imaginary voices of rural people, Edgeworth's interest in Rousseau led her to coauthoring a volume titled *Practical Education,* published in 1798, the same year as the first appearance of *Lyrical Ballads.* In the appendix is a set of carefully transcribed conversations between teachers and children illustrating the growth of inferential thinking. These conversations, as well as the long introductory chapter on toys, show a characteristically empirical British reaction to French theorizing, and the dialogues record what was actually said rather than speculatively imagined. Edgeworth became an attentive listener and was skilled at re-creating individual voices, and not merely those of children. While she was English in taste and opinions, she lived much of her life in Ireland, and there she "acquired from her father the practice of collecting curious specimens of Irish speech" (M. Butler, 174). These she rendered in the first-person narrative of *Castle Rackrent,* first published in 1800 and the foundation for Walter Scott's uses of the vernacular in the Waverley novels.

Thady Quirk, the narrator in *Castle Rackrent,* was something new to English readers—not a comic rustic relegated to humorous speech and inept behavior but the central figure of Edgeworth's novel. In her preface, Edgeworth presented herself as both male and the "editor" of Thady's memoirs of the Rackrent family.

> For the information of the *ignorant* English reader, a few notes have been subjoined by the editor, and he had it once in contemplation to translate the language of Thady into plain English; but Thady's idiom is incapable of translation, and, besides, the authenticity of his story would have been more exposed to doubt if it were not told in his own characteristic manner. (ix)

The notes by the fictive editor align his views with those of the presumptive English reader. He confirms what might seem doubtful to that reader—for instance, that a wig might serve as a dust cloth (47n)—and directs attention to the glossary for the explanation of words presumed to be unfamiliar. Some of these linguistic notes provide legitimating etymologies for Irish English usage—that *gasson* 'little boy' derives from French *garçon* (35), that *tester* 'six-pence' was "used in Shakespeare" (67), or that *little* "is here used only as an Italian diminutive, expressive of fondness" (41).

Edgeworth thus provided a mediator between the articulately "authentic" peasant and the metropolitan reader. Unlike her eighteenth-century precursors in writing in dialect, she was not satisfied with reaching only a local audience, and her linguistic experiments in *Castle Rackrent* showed how local usages might be interpreted for and made palatable to a national audience. Of course the narrative itself mirrored the English sense of superiority to the Irish. The Rackrents are improvident bumblers, and Jason Quirk, Thady's son, is a scheming usurper. At the end of the tale, the "editor" explains that "all the features in the foregoing sketch were taken from the life, and they are characteristic of that mixture of quickness, simplicity, cunning, carelessness, dissipation, disinterestedness, shrewdness, and blunder, which, in different forms and with various success, has been brought upon the stage or delineated in novels" (69–70). Edgeworth's own novel arose among debates over the wisdom of unifying Ireland and England (ones in which her father played a prominent role and which resulted in the union of 1801), and her conclusion was that the salvation of Ireland lay in "the introduction of British manufacturers" (70). It was, however, her literary technique rather than her political views that made her novel so influential.

Scotland, rather than Ireland, was the arena in which vernacular literature first flourished. Writing in 1814, Walter Scott raised the question of the representation of speech that differed from the dialect of literary convention.

> It has been my object to describe these persons, not by a caricatured and exaggerated use of the national dialect, but by their habits, manners, and feelings, so as in some distant degree to emulate the admirable Irish portraits drawn by Miss Edgeworth, so different from the "Teagues" and "dear joys" who so long, and with the most perfect family resemblance to each other, occupied the drama and the novel. (Quoted by Tulloch, 167; Scott elaborated these ideas in his "general preface" to the Waverley novels in 1829—see Hewitt, 249)

Like Edgeworth, however, Scott used vernacular Scots for limited purposes, though without the intervention of an "editor." Scots-speaking characters tend to be aged, rural, and uneducated; upper-class characters, even ones from humble origins, are represented as speaking something much closer to English. Perhaps most important, the novels containing Scots are set in the past, at least a generation or two from Scott's own day. Scott himself, though educated for a year in Bath, regretted that he never "acquired a just pronunciation" in his efforts to eradicate his Scots and gain a mastery of English (Hewitt, 15). The vernacular of Scotland was, for him in both literature and life, the property of someone unlike himself.

Scott was swept up in the antiquarian interests that animated intellectuals in early-nineteenth-century Britain, and he corresponded with the Grimm brothers in Germany about early folk literature, for he had been impressed that they had included Scottish ballads in their inquiries (Scott, 3:434–39). *The Minstrelsy of the Scottish Border* (1802–3) was the first of Scott's literary productions, a collection of poetry of ancient lineage "improved," as the occasion struck him, by Scott himself. With the publication of *Waverley*, Scott opened possibilities for vernacular prose in a way that had been made popular by Robert Burns in vernacular poetry. The success of Scott's novel stimulated the publication of John Galt's *Annals of the Parish* (1821), a novel of rural life earlier rejected by a publisher with the explanation that "Scottish novels would not do" (Ainger, ix). Like Scott, Galt located his stories in an earlier time when the vernacular flourished. For both Galt and Scott, the vernacular was a variety of language descended from antiquity, and their writing made it possible for "dialect" speakers to be both authentic and heroic at the same time.

Significantly, Edgeworth, Scott, and Galt were not comfortable speakers of the vernacular. In the 1790s, Burns, who was, and whose origins were rooted in the peasantry of southwest Scotland, repeatedly alleged that he was not fluent in English: "I have not the command of the language that I have of my native tongue. In fact, I think my ideas are more barren in English than in Scottish" (quoted by J. Mackay, 545). But those who met him in Edinburgh drawing rooms recalled him as respectably anglicized, and at the beginning of his poetic career he wrote in the heroic couplets of Augustan England. In 1803, Galt described the prevailing customs of language use in Scotland.

> In polite companies a Scotsman is prohibited, by the imputation of vulgarity, from using the common language of the country, in which he expresses himself with most ease and vivacity, and, clothed in which, his earliest and most distinctive impressions always arise to his mind. He uses a species of translation, which checks the versatility of fancy, and restrains the genuine and spontaneous flow of his conceptions. (Quoted by Tulloch, 175)

Some of these claims were self-serving apologies, couched amid the terror of linguistic "vulgarity" that stifled so many in the nineteenth century. All three Scots writers—Burns, Galt, and Scott—set the language of their literature aside from themselves, making the vernacular the property of the folk and intelligibility to southern English readers the norm for selecting from it. One consequence of their popularity was to make the vernacular downright rather than eloquent, hidebound rather than innovative, and bucolic rather than industrial. It is no wonder that some twentieth-century Scots nationalists have seen them as the saboteurs of Scots rather than its saviors.

Edgeworth, Burns, Scott, and Galt were profoundly influential in setting precedents for the representation of speech in nineteenth-century fiction. The voices they created were imaginary ones, of course, and the depth of their representation was constrained by spelling and by the willingness of readers to confront the unexpected. Their example, however, fostered experiments with language unprecedented in earlier literature. Quite suddenly, the inarticulate peasant was replaced by the rustic sage. Critics of this new literary endeavor were quick to doubt the authenticity of the new voices. As early as 1792, a writer from Ireland addressed Burns.

> I'm thinking ye've been at the schools,
> Ye cou'd na just, 'mang countra fools,

Ye cou'd na, handling spades and shools,
Get sic knowledge;
Ye gat it handling ither tools,
In some college. (Fleck, 1)

But the appeal to real life seldom constrained authors or disappointed readers.

Vernacular writing flourished as never before and with a new-found sympathy for the speech of the uneducated. At the same time, antiquarians pressed forward with the collection of words and tales thought to be on the verge of extinction. Just as Francis Grose feared that the old ways of talking by the hearth side were being eradicated by education, transport, and technology, so, even in Scotland, did writers lament the presumed disappearance, particularly among the well born, of Scots and the lore it embodied. In 1822, Scott wrote to his publisher eulogizing the vanished generation of his parents.

> You remember how well Mrs. Murray Keith—the late Lady Dumfries—my poor mother & other ladies of that day spoke their native language—it was different from English as the Venetian is from the Tuscan dialect of Italy but it never occurd to any one that the Scotish any more than the Venetian was more vulgar than those who spoke the purer and more classical—But that is all gone and the remembrance will be drownd with us the elders of this existing generation & our Edinburgh—I can no longer say our Scottish gentry—will with some study speak rather a worse dialect than the Newcastle and Sheffield riders. So glides this world away. (7:83)

Nostalgia coupled with regret was an emotion felt by Scott and many of the other writers who exploited spoken English (and Scots) for artistic purposes.

A notable exception to the main line of development of vernacular fiction was James Hogg, well known for songs (and as a performer of Scots song). Like Burns, Hogg was self-educated, but unlike his influential predecessor he was unashamed of Scots ways of speaking and was even prepared to parody in English the improbable figures of Wordsworth's rural landscape and his humble occasions for exploring "the philosophic mind." (In

"Andrew the Packman," Hogg's walleyed poet is stimulated to speculation about "our beacon of Eternity" while contemplating a hatstand "after the manner of Wordsworth" [Groves, 163–68].) In the best of his fiction, Hogg created tensions between southern English and Scots, particularly in his *Private Memoirs and Confessions of a Justified Sinner* (1824). More than his contemporaries, Hogg explored linguistic variability, including the use of varying "editors" who mediate between the narrative and the reader. Scott asked Hogg, his protégé, if he were on "rather dangerous ground" in these experiments. Representing the conversation in a memoir, Hogg replied to Scott's anxiety that a magazine he proposed to edit would not stand up to the competition: "'No a bit!' said I [']I'm no the least feared for that. My papers may no be sae yelegant as their's but I expect to make them mair original' (Mack, 115; see also Letley). Here, as elsewhere, Hogg represents Scott speaking entirely conventional English and himself a vigorous vernacular.

"Originality" in vernacular writing never came so close to threatening the hegemony of southern English and of literary tradition as in the nineteenth century. Voices from the folk were increasingly represented, but they were represented as distinctly deviant. Nonetheless, there was a desire to make speakers of the vernacular articulate. In 1815, David Humphreys, famous in New England at the end of the eighteenth century as a member of the Hartford Wits, published *The Yankey in England: A Drama in Five Acts*. Part of his purpose in doing so was his recognition that the "character of the Yankey, from whom the play derives its name, is little understood in several parts of America; still less in Europe" (14). Doolittle, the Yankey, "may fairly be the subject of risibility on account of his dialect, pronunciation, and manners; yet his good qualities . . . will, doubtless, more than compensate for his singularities and failings" (14–15). As a member of the delegation sent to Paris and London to negotiate commercial treaties after the success of the American Revolution, Humphreys was well acquainted with London and with the emergent drama and fiction in which vernacular speakers were prominent. Doolittle's opening monologue provides the audience with the full blast of Yankee English.

Had that darned old vessel—that friggit there—bin a stun's throw furder off from land, I shood never have swimmed to shore, dead or alive, to all atarnity I swamp it. Oh, Doolittle! Doolittle! *(striking his forehead,)* you've brought your pigs to a fine market. Now, I guess, you'd better staid at hum, with mother, next time. She tell'd you all about the paerils of the salt sea: *(vexed with himself)* but you woodn't beleve 'em. No, no; you were too darned cute; to plaguey knowing in argufying the case, *(sobbing)* for poor mother: and you e'en-a-most broke her heart; you know you did: (bursting into tears) yes; yes; you were a nation deal wiser than brother Jonathan, brother Josiah, sister Deborah, sister Keziah, cousin Jemima, poor little Aminadab, and all the rest: (sobbing at every pause) not forgitting poor old granny, bent sumwheres about half dubble; and above all, my owny, towny, Lydy Lovett, the Deacon's darlin darter; with whom, both man and boy, I've sparked it, pretty oftentimes, so late. Well, well, I know it now—hum is hum, be it ever so humbly. (19–20)

Some of these spellings are merely phonetic representations of general usage (e.g., *friggit* for *frigate* or *staid* for *stayed*), but most are not (e.g., *hum* and *stun* representing the "New England short *o*"). In *I guess* and *well,* Humphreys hit upon expressions that would be stereotyped as American in the many representations of American English that appeared in the course of the century.

Traveler's reports published in Britain routinely contained remarks on American English, often with specimens attached. A representative one of these appears in Henry Bradshaw Fearon's *Sketches of America,* in a conversation collected during his visit in 1817; he reports a conversation with an African-American hairdresser "in Broadway, nearly opposite the city-hall."

And you come all the way right away from England. Well! I would not have supposed, I guess, that you come from there from your tongue; you have no hardness like, I guess, in your speaking; you talk almost as well as we do, and that is what I never see, I guess, in a gentleman so lately from England. I guess your talk is within a grade as good as ours. You are a mighty elegant gentlemen, and if you will tell me where you keep, I will bring some of my coloured friends to visit you. Well, you must be a smart man to come from England, and talk English as well as we do that were raised in this country. (59–60)

From "three American gentlemen," Fearon learned that the barber was not alone in his opinion about the relative merits of American and British English. Fearon packed his representation with features that readers in London would recognize as American—particularly *I guess* and *well.*

In literary works, vernacular speech was often the vehicle for comedy, and comedy often cloaked satire and social criticism. Vernacular humor was particularly popular in North America, and the first internationally known author in this genre was Thomas Chandler Haliburton, who composed a series of tales about a sharp-dealing Yankee peddler, Sam Slick, and published them beginning in 1837 as *The Clockmaker.* The son of a prominent Nova Scotia jurist and an ardent royalist, Haliburton followed the narrative method popularized by Edgeworth and Hogg; Sam Slick's "tales" were recounted to a "squire" who acts as an intermediary between the reader and the narrative.

In the opening story, the squire is approached by Slick, "a tall thin man, with hollow cheeks and bright twinkling black eyes."

> "I guess you started airly this mornin', sir?"
> "I did, sir," I replied.
> "You did not come from Halifax, I presume, sir, did you?" in a dialect too rich to be mistaken as genuine Yankee. "And which way may you be travellin'?" (1941, 31–32)

The squire soon realizes that Slick is "a Yankee, and a very impertinent Yankee too" (33). Through the squire's rendition of Slick's vernacular, Haliburton introduces readers to gullible Nova Scotians who are beguiled by Slick's "soft sawder" (flattery < *solder*). As the tales appeared, Haliburton presented African-Americans, Dutch-Americans, Native Americans, and a variety of others whose modes of speaking were presented in an amusing context. These characters were almost always swindlers, gulls, and buffoons—sometimes all three at once. Haliburton's purpose was to encourage virtue and to poke fun at democracy at the same time. The squire, and his English, are at the ethical center of the tales; Slick is a braggartly patriot who is indifferent to decorous English: "Our great a'mighty republic is the toploftiest nation atween the Poles"

FIG. 17 —WONDERMENT.
Sure enough, Santa Claus had come down the chimney

Public speaking was expected and enjoyed, particularly when performed by
schoolchildren. In the United States, the ideas of François Delsarte (1811–71)
were highly regarded. Central to them was the proposition that spiritual and
physical realms were connected through posture, movement, and succession.
Conventional expressions were carefully taught through illustrations. (From
Northrop, fig. 17.)

(195). In the decade of the 1830s, dozens of traveler's accounts of
North America were published in Britain; in many of them,
encounters were reported with citizens resembling Slick in beliefs
and in language.

With his literary success, Haliburton left North America in disgust at democracy and gained election as a Tory member of the
Parliament. In 1852, he published a three-volume compilation
titled *Traits of American Humour, by Native Authors*. In his prefatory
essay he presented his views undisguised by literary artifice.

A strange hybrid, indeed, did circumstances beget here, in the New
World, upon the old Puritan stock, and the earth never before saw

such mystic-practicalism, such niggard-geniality, such calculating-fanaticism, such close-fisted generosity. (1:ix)

Drawing upon John Russell Bartlett's *Dictionary of Americanisms,* a substantial volume published in London in 1849, a year after its appearance in New York, Haliburton distinguished the origins of American expressions and offered an unflattering picture of the "drawling pronunciation" of Yankees.

Most of the pieces compiled by Haliburton had appeared in newspapers, particularly in the *Sporting News* (published in Baltimore) and the *Spirit of the Times* (New York). Some had already been gathered into books, particularly the extremely popular, fabulous tales of "Colonel Crockett" on the frontier. The description of Crockett's engagement with a grizzly bear is representative of the genre.

> By this time I felt most inticingly wolfy and savagerous, and I jest giv him a hint that no man could neglect that it war best to turn in his tracks, and I waited for him jest on the edge of Little Great Small Deep Shallow Big Muddy. He pitched inter me like the piston of a steam-injin, and we both rolled into the drink together. Onluckily for him I didn't lose holt of Kill-devil [his rifle], and when he raised his head and tried to get over his astonishment, I clapt the barrel right across his neck to shove his visnomy under water. I'll be shot with a packsaddle without benefit of clargy if the ridiculous fool didn't help me himself, for he clapped both hands on the eends of the barrel and pulled away as if it war a pleasure to him. I had nuthing to do but hold on to the stock and float alongside of him till he war drowned. (Haliburton 1852, 1:300)

A variety of linguistic tricks were used to create the voices of this character, only a few of them designed to evoke a realistic vernacular voice. Phonetic spellings—like *inticingly* and *nuthing*—evoked the image of a speaker lacking in education even though they gave unambiguous clues to how these words were pronounced by everyone. Words like *savagerous* and *visnomy* (a blend of *visage* and *physiognomy*) reflect a different impulse, not the malapropisms used comically by Sheridan and his successors but a vigorous expression of linguistic creativity that found great delight in polysyllables with "learned" connotations.

High-flown vocabulary was a specialty of American humorists, particularly Bret Harte and Mark Twain. Pompous and abstruse words struck readers as intrinsically hilarious, and one writer, not intending to be humorous, mined exclusively in this vein, Samuel Klinefelter Hoshour. His *Altisonant Letters,* first published in 1844, presented domestic life in a way familiar from epistolary novels and specimen-letter books. The difference lay in outlandish words.

> DEBONAIR AND ALEGER MISS:—Desiderating not to be ambagious in the exordial part of this epistle, and waiving all polylogy, I will announce to you that I have a proclivity to assume the marital position; and that from our precedaneous and primal *tete a tete,* I have delapsed into a dilection which elicited this epistolography to you, and extorted the illation that you are the entity in consortion with whom the suavities and maritudes of my subastral vitality might be felicitiously sustained. (1870, 56)

Fortunately for Lorenzo Altisonant, the putative indicter of this epistle, his intended is suaded.

> CONCINNOUS SIR: . . . I accept your proffered "cincture of Hymen," with the esperance that our connubial adunation will be a delineament of the asperities incident of our terrestrial vitality, and aid us in the devitation of many of the tentatious in this immund and inquinated mundane extruction. (65)

So satisfactory a liaison can hardly be imagined, and readers must surely have been provoked to laughter, though risibility was by no means intended by the author. (For the studious, an exhaustive glossarial appendix was supplied; Hoshour's *Autobiography* reveals him to have been a solemn schoolmaster who thrashed his pupils into a knowledge of big words.)

Sam Slick's literary descendants were more likely to be homespun Yankees than polysyllabic pioneers. Though most of the newspaper fictions were written for and by men, women authors gained early entry into the field. Among the most prolific of these was Ann Sophia Stephens (1813–86), who drew upon Haliburton's popularity by creating the fictitious Jonathan Slick, Esq. in her *High Life in New York* (1843). Whereas Sam Slick had been a townsman, a sharper among innocent rural folk, Jonathan Slick was a rube in the city. The humor of his adventures lay in his ignorance of the mechanics of town life (for instance, how to use a bellpull at the entrance to a house) and his indifference to urban fashion (for example, failing to button his dancing trousers under the soles of his feet). Like Hoshour's Altisonant, Stephens's Jonathan wrote letters home, but, rather than grandiloquent pomposity, he employed the well-established spelling conventions for Yankee dialect: "Wal, you see I'm as good as my word. I hadn't hardly read t'other letter through, afore I sot right down and begun another right off the reel" (11). Such writing was regarded as amusing, and, like the other authors in this vein, Stephens was eager to have her works read aloud for the amusement of an audience larger than one.

A second woman humorist gained wider fame and national attention: Frances Miriam Whitcher (1812–52). Unlike most of her predecessors, she cloaked serious intentions in her humor. With the publication of the first of Whitcher's "Widow Bedott" sketches in 1846, the voice of the uneducated comic figure took on a new seriousness, and the opening line of the very first "sketch" showed a keen sense of idiom: "He was a wonderful hand to moralize, husband was, 'specially after he begun to enjoy poor health" (21). In these first-person narratives, Whitcher was able to critique the cult of gentility and the emergent ideals of "perfect" womanhood with the weapons of irony and satire. The immediate occasion for the following selection arises from the rage for racial classification and phrenology that rose to popularity in rural America in the 1840s. But her larger purpose was to expose narrow-mindedness and bigotry.

> What a curus consarn this phreenyology is, ain't it? What an age of improvement we live in! If any body'd a told us once how't in a few year we'd be able to tell egzackly what folks *was* by the shape o' ther heads—we wouldent a bleeved a word on't—would we? You remember readin' about old mother O'Killem, in that are book I lent you, don't you? Well, he's mistaken about one thing relatin' to her. He says she killed the nigger wench by choppin' off her head—now 't wa'n't so—she stomped on her—I remember just how 't was, don't you? Ain't his wife a turrible humbly woman? Her head looks jist like a punkin', and hisen looks like a cheese, don't it? You gwine to hear

her lectur to the ladies to-morrer? Guess *I* shall—if it's as interestin' a lectur as hisen, it'll be worth hearin'—though I don't think much o' these here wimmin lecturers, no way—the best place for wimmin 's to hum—a mindin' their own bizness, accordin' to my notions. You remember that one that come round a spell ago, a whalin' away about human rights. I thought she'd ought to be hoss-whipt and shet up in jail, dident you? (66–67)

Though personally shy and not directly engaged in the political arena, Whitcher created the Widow Bedott as a grotesque, given to every prejudice and fad the author found abhorrent (see L. Morris, 37). Raised in upstate New York, Whitcher became a faithful disciple of an evangelist who encouraged women to pray in the company of men (a step stoutly resisted by conservatives), and she lived near the Oneida Institute, where a national antislavery society had been formed and young African-Americans were educated on an equal footing with all others. When Whitcher was twenty-five years old, she became active in a circle of young men and women who met twice a month for music and entertainment, and to this group she contributed the first of her humorous poems and essays. Far from identifying with her character, Whitcher used the Widow's narrow-minded opinions as a comic foil to promote causes: abolition of slavery, human rights generally, and all the emergent conventions that kept women "to hum" rather than engaged in public life.

Whitcher's direct literary descendant was Marietta Holley (1836–1926) whose fictional narrator was "Josiah Allen's Wife," Samantha. (Like Whitcher, Holley began to publish anonymously and listed as author of her work "Josiah Allen's Wife.") Holley's political agenda shared many of the themes of Whitcher's: women's rights, temperance, and racial justice. Whitcher had died young; Holley continued to write well into the twentieth century and amassed a fortune as a popular author. Probably because her humor and her causes were presented much more transparently than Whitcher's had been, some critics have regarded her books as mere feminist tracts enlivened by rural humor. To counteract that objection, Holley early determined to provide a first-person disguise: "probably I thought it would soften somewhat the edge of unwelcome argument to have the writer meekly claim to be the wife of Josiah Allen and so stand in the shadow of a man's personality" (quoted from Holley's autobiography by K. Winter, 38–39).

Samantha Allen is not a comic foil but the spokesperson for her creator's views, and it is not surprising that her directness brought Holley to the attention and eventual friendship of nationally prominent advocates of her causes—particularly Susan B. Anthony, Clara Barton, Elizabeth Cady Stanton, and Frances E. Willard. Unlike most of her predecessors in the vernacular tradition, Holley revealed her absurd characters through her first-person narrator. The most famous of these grotesques was Betsy Bobbet, a middle-aged spinster who craves marriage and believes that a woman is unfulfilled unless she finds a husband.

> She thinks she talks dreadful polite and proper, she says "I was cameing" instead of "I was coming," and "I have saw" instead of "I have seen," and "papah" for paper and "deah" for dear. I don't know much about grammer, but common sense goes a good ways. She writes the poetry for the Jonesville Augur, or "Augah," as she calls it. She used to write for the opposition paper, the Jonesville Gimlet, but the editor of the Augur, a long haired chap, who moved into Jonesville a few months ago, lost his wife soon after he come there, and sense that she has turned Dimocrat, and writes for his paper stiddy. (1890, 28–29)

Betsy's "errors" are not those of ignorance so much as they are the result of striving for effect—generalization of *saw* in dread of "I seen her," use of *r*-less pronunciations in *paper* and *dear,* which, in the context of northern New York, evoked New England gentility. Samantha's own position is indicated by her bad spelling (e.g., *there* for *their, pole* for *poll, fantoms* for *phantoms,* and *beau knot* for *bow knot*) and her use of expressions that had become obsolete in respectable English (e.g., *hearn* for *heard, housen* for *houses,* and *obleeged* for *obliged*).

Holley followed Whitcher in mocking high-flown touring lecturers, in this case the utterances of "the noble and eloquent Prof. Aspire Todd Esq."

ON A LECTURIN' TOWER.

Women did not frequently appear as orators, and this illustration was, in its day, intended to be humorous. Even the distant trees at the right are crowded with cheering auditors. (From Holley 1890, 339.)

"Brotheren and sisters of Jonesville" says he; "Friends and patrons of Liberty, in risin' upon this aeroter, I have signified by that act, a desire and a willingness to address you. I am not here fellow and sister citizens, to outrage your feelings by triflin' remarks, I am not here male patrons of liberty to lead your noble, and you female patrons your tender footsteps into the flowery fields of useless rhetorical eloquence; I am here noble brothers and sisters of Jonesville not in a mephitical manner, and I trust not in a mentorial, but to present a few plain truths in a plain manner, for your consideration. My friends we are in one sense but tennifolious blossoms of life; or, if you will pardon the tergiversation, we are all but mineratin' tennirosters, hovering upon an illinition of mythoplasm. (1890, 164)

As a send-up of the Fourth of July oration, this opening could hardly be improved; Professor Todd is constantly interrupted by the affirming cries of a drunken and noisy spectator who obliges him to end abruptly and sit down "lookin' gloomy and morbid" (167). The subsequent speaker celebrates the modesty and delicacy of women, who would be imperiled by gaining "wimmin's rights"; his conduct as an unfaithful and indifferent husband subverts his message in just the same way that the affirmations of the drunk blunt the force of Professor Todd's mighty vocabulary. By such means Holley gave voices to her cause.

When she turned her attention to "the race problem," Holley was much more direct than Whitcher had been forty years earlier. As Samantha expressed the issue, the abolitionists had not thought whether "the white race . . . would at once forget its pride and its prejudices" (1894, 33). Sending Samantha on a tour of the southeastern United States, Holley provided an occasion for her to talk with a local African-American.

> And I akosted him, and asked him what wuz the meanin' of that big black chimbly a standin' up that curius way.
>
> He seemed awful ready to stop and talk. It wuz the hot weather, I spoze. And the mule had called for sights of labor to get him along, I could see that—and he sez:
>
> "De Cadimy used to stand dar."
>
> Sez I, "the school-house for the colored people?"
>
> "Yes," sez he.
>
> "How did it come to be burned down?" sez I.
>
> "De white folks buhnt it down," sez he calmly.
>
> "What for?" sez I.
>
> "'Cause dey didn't want it dere," sez he. "Dat's what I spoze wuz de influential reason" (1894, 169).

Such minstrel-show inspired stereotypes as *dere* for *there* were part of Holley's repertoire, but Samantha and the man she meets speak two forms of the same vernacular language. Later in the narrative, she meets a preacher who is represented with the same blackface English: "George Perkins am daid" (176). In private conversation with Samantha afterward, however, he speaks feelingly in a kind of English that is not only lacking in such features but is also far more "refined" than Samantha's own.

Of the vast crowd of humorous authors in nineteenth-century America, only a few paid serious attention to the vernaculars they represented. For most of them, plausibility rather than realism was the essential point; it did not matter much if people talked the way Samantha Allen did, only that they seemed to talk that way. An exception was James Russell Lowell, who combined the Romantics' belief in the vitality of "real language" with philological knowledge. In explaining his decision to undertake writing in the vernacular, Lowell laid out an ideology to vindicate his way of writing in defiance of oppressive purists.

> In choosing the Yankee dialect, I did not act without forethought. It had long seemed to me that the great vice of American writing and speaking was a studied want of simplicity, that we were coming to look on our mother-tongue as a dead language, to be sought in the grammar and dictionary rather than in the heart, and that our only chance of escape was by seeking it at its living sources among those who were, as Scottowe says of Major-General Gibbons, "divinely illiterate." . . . We use it like Scotsmen, not as if it belonged to us, but as if we wished to prove that we belonged to it, by showing our intimacy with its written rather than with its spoken dialect. And yet all the while our popular idiom is racy with life and vigor and originality, bucksome (as Milton used the word) to our new occasions, and proves itself no mere graft by sending up new suckers from the old root in spite of us. It is only from its roots in the living generations of men that a language can be reinforced with fresh vigor for its needs; what may be called a literate dialect grows ever more and more pedantic and foreign, till it becomes at last as unfitting a vehicle for living thought as monkish Latin. That we should all be made to talk like books is the danger with which we are threatened by the Universal Schoolmaster, who does his best to enslave the minds and memories of his victims to what he esteems the best models of English composition, that is to say, to the writers whose style is faultily correct and has no blood-warmth in it. (442)

Far more than Wordsworth and the other writers with an interest in the vernacular, Lowell was prepared to bring real voices to bear in his narrative discourse itself.

Lowell's *Biglow Papers* began to appear in a Boston newspaper in 1846, and the first series was collected in a book two years later. Increasingly popular, the papers were published in London in 1859, and, with the outbreak of the American Civil War, Lowell published a second series in *The Atlantic* between 1862 and 1866. Though it would be reductive to consider them only as political tracts, they were animated by two great national causes: the invasion of Mexico by U.S. troops and the struggle to abolish slavery and maintain the national government. Reflecting on their reception in later years, Lowell wrote: "The success of my experiment soon began not only to astonish me, but to make me feel the responsibility of knowing that I held in my hand a weapon instead of the mere fencing-stick I had supposed" (441). For all their humor and vitality, they were enlisted in the cause of moral earnestness.

Lowell, like Haliburton, provided his Yankee, Hosea Biglow, with an educated mediator, Homer Wilbur, A.M., "Pastor of the First Church in Jaalam, and (prospective) member of many literary, learned, and scientific societies." But Lowell disliked Haliburton and regarded Sam Slick as "a libel on the Yankee character, and a complete falsification of Yankee modes of speech" (457). Haliburton's "squire" had provided a reference point for moderation and linguistic propriety; Sam Slick was an extreme democrat who flouted good English. For Lowell, Biglow provided the moral center; Wilbur, the educated mouthpiece, was a fool. Biglow's English expressed for Lowell all the virtues that he and the other Romantics detected in untutored peasants, and he traced it "to long ago noonings in my father's hay-fields" where he heard the day laborers in conversation. The Rev. Mr. Wilbur, by contrast, was intended to "express the more cautious element of the New England character and its pedantry" (441). Both characters are rich in comedy. Wilbur purports to be the editor and explicator of verses sent to him by "my talented young parishioner, Mr. Biglow."

> I was at first inclined to discourage Mr. Biglow's attempts, as knowing that the desire to poetize is one of the diseases naturally incident to adolescence, which, if the fitting remedies be not at once and with a bold hand applied, may become chronic, and render one, who might else have become in due time an ornament of the social circle, a painful object even to nearest friends and relatives. (174)

Wilbur's old-fashioned, deeply layered grammar is ornamented with arcane vocabulary from classical sources, frequent Latin quotations, and occasional incongruity. The vernacular appears in the verse purportedly written by Biglow and inspired by the military exploits of his friend with the preposterous Puritan name Bird-ofredom Sawin.

> Afore I come away from hum I hed a strong persuasion
> Thet Mexicans worn't human beans,—an ourang outang nation,
> A sort o folks a chap could kill an' never dream on 't arter,
> No more 'n a feller 'd dream o' pigs thet he hed hed to slarter. (185)

The consequence of Lowell's selection was to provide for a linguistic middle ground, set between the vernacular of Biglow's verse and the school-mastered pomposity of Wilbur's prose.

Nineteenth-century American humorists often highlighted the contrast between the differing ideas about "proper" English articulated by the low-down and the high-flown. Perhaps the culmination of this line of development came in Mark Twain's *Roughing It* (1872). In Twain's travel narrative, he recalls the heyday of slang in the Nevada mining towns: "the slang of Nevada [was] the richest and the most infinitely varied and copious that had ever existed anywhere in the world, perhaps, except in the mines of California in the 'early days'" (298). To illustrate this claim, Twain imagined a conversation between a clergyman (the literary descendent of Lowell's Parson Wilbur) and a "stalwart rough," Scotty Biggs.

> "Are you the duck that runs the gospel-mill next door?"
> "Am I the—pardon me, I believe I do not understand?"
> With another sigh and a half-sob, Scotty rejoined:
> "Why you see we are in a bit of trouble, and the boys thought maybe you would give us a lift, if we'd tackle you—that is, if I've got the rights of it and you are the head clerk of the doxology-works next door."
> "I am the shepherd in charge of the flock whose fold is next door."
> "The which?"
> "The spiritual advisor of the little company of believers whose sanctuary adjoins these premises."
> Scotty scratched his head, reflected a moment, and then said:

"You ruther hold over me, pard. I reckon I can't call that hand. Ante and pass the buck." (299)

Here the comic misunderstandings do not validate either style of English, though Twain's sympathy clearly lies with Scotty's vigorous slang rather than the minister's stale metaphors of piety.

In the nineteenth century, vernacular literature flourished in those parts of the world remote from the influence of London— especially in Scotland, Ireland, and the United States. Anglophone enclaves in Africa, Asia, and the Caribbean were constantly refreshed with expatriate schoolteachers and were regularly improved by settlers and visitors who imposed London standards of linguistic propriety on alien soil. In these places, it was more difficult for writers to endow local speechways with great dignity. Only at the end of the century did a strong vernacular writer emerge in Australia, Henry Lawson (1867–1922). Lawson's sympathy for bushrangers and slum dwellers had a powerful effect on his fiction, and the method of representing their voices he borrowed from Bret Harte's tales of the American West. In Lawson's fiction, there is no educated narrator to mediate the language. His first-person narratives give only the voices of his characters.

> Well, we reached the pub about dinner time, dropped our swags outside, had a drink, and then went into the dinin' room. There was a lot of jackeroo swells, that had been on a visit to the squatter, or something, and they were sittin' down at dinner; and they seemed to think by their looks that we ought to have stayed outside and waited till they was done—we was only two rough shearers, you know. There was a very good-looking servant girl waitin' on 'em, and she was all smiles—laughin', and jokin', and chiackin', and barrackin' with 'em like anything. . . .
>
> We finished the first blanky course, and, while she was gettin' our puddin' from the side table, Dave says to me in a loud whisper, so's she could hear: "Ain't she a stunner, Joe?" says Dave; "I never thought there was sich fine girls on the Darlin'!" says Dave.
>
> But no; she wouldn't speak.
>
> Then Dave says: "They pitch a blanky lot about them New Englan' girls; but I'll back the Darlin' girls to lick 'em holler as far's looks is concerned," says Dave.
>
> But no; she wouldn't speak. She wouldn't even smile. (114–15)

Like virtually all nineteenth-century writers of vernacular literature, Lawson sustains most conventions of English spelling (hence
the page is scattered with apostrophes to show "missing" sounds)
and respects the taboos of respectability (for instance, the use of
blanky for the taboo word *bloody*).

Actual voices only approximated these literary creations, and
even those writers who most enthusiastically celebrated the English of the "folk" were anxious about how these voices could be
made acceptable to readers presumed to be ignorant of and
unsympathetic to them. Thus, when revising her lately deceased
sister's *Wuthering Heights* in 1850, Charlotte Brontë described her
eagerness to make the characters' voices intelligible.

> I should wish to revise the proofs, if it be not too great an incon-
> venience to send them. It seems to me advisable to modify the orthog-
> raphy of the old servant Joseph's speeches; for thus as it stands it
> exactly renders the Yorkshire dialect to a Yorkshire ear, yet I am sure
> Southerns must find it unintelligible, and thus one of the most graphic
> characters in the book is lost on them. (Wise and Symington, 3:165)

Other writers of midcentury England had the same anxieties, as
shown in a letter of 1858 from George Eliot to her publisher.

> I return the proofs by today's post. The dialect must be toned
> down all through in correcting the proofs, for I have found it impos-
> sible to keep it subdued enough in writing. I am aware that the
> spelling which represents a dialect perfectly well to those who know
> it by the ear, is likely to be unintelligible to others. Mr. Lewes is a good
> test, being innocent of dialects, and he is good enough to run over
> the proofs for the sake of checking unintelligibility. (1954, 500)

Such writers as found it difficult to practice self-censorship sought
others "innocent of dialects" to assist them. Everywhere the dead
hand of Lowell's "universal schoolmaster" grasped the throttle.

Authors wanted to convey the flavor of peasant talk without
too much of the reality. George Eliot summarized her practice in a
letter of 1877 to W. W. Skeat, who had written to inquire about the
dialects of her fictional characters.

> It must be borne in mind that my inclination to be as close as I
> could to the rendering of dialect, both in words and spelling, was

constantly checked by the artistic duty of being generally intelligible. But for that check, I should have given a stronger colour to the dialogue in "Adam Bede," which is modelled on the talk of N. Staffordshire and the neighbouring part of Derbyshire. The spelling, being determined by my own ear alone, was necessarily a matter of anxiety, for it would be as possible to quarrel about it as about the spelling of Oriental names.

The district imagined as the scene of "Silas Marner" is in N. Warwickshire. But here, and in all my other presentations of English life, except "Adam Bede," it has been my intention to give the general physiognomy rather than a close portraiture of the provincial speech as I have heard it in the Midland or Mercian region. It is a just demand that art should keep clear of such specialities as would make it a puzzle for the larger part of its public; still, one is not bound to respect the lazy obtuseness or snobbish ignorance of people who do not care to know more of their native tongue than the vocabulary of the drawing-room and the newspaper. (Skeat and Nodal, vii)

At the same time, Thomas Hardy expressed a similar view: "an author may be said to fairly convey the spirit of intelligent peasant talk if he retains the idiom, compass, and characteristic expressions" (688). Eliot and Hardy did not wish to cater to "lazy obtuseness or snobbish ignorance," though they certainly recognized that the people who would read their novels were not willing to make much effort to penetrate actual ways of speaking, particularly if the conventions of written English were challenged beyond what could be expressed by an apostrophe, a doubled vowel, or an unconventional spelling. The pedants and those under the sway of the universal schoolmaster could be tolerantly patient or patronizingly curious, but they were not willing to become deeply engaged with unfamiliar voices.

Another novelist, Elizabeth Gaskell, was a strong advocate of regional English, though she usually represented genteel voices. But she could give powerful utterances to characters whose expressions were in deadly earnest. In *North and South* (1854–55), she combined themes of regional and social conflict.

"Why, yo' see, there's five or six masters who have set themselves again paying the wages they've been paying these two years past, and flourishing upon, and getting richer upon. And now they come to us, and say we're to take less. And we won't. We'll just clem ['starve'] them to death first; and see who'll work for 'em then. They'll have killed the goose that laid 'em the golden eggs, I reckon."

"And so you plan dying, in order to be revenged upon them!"

"No," said he, "I dunnot. I just look forward to the chance of dying at my post sooner than yield. That's what folk call fine and honourable in a soldier, and why not in a poor weaver-chap?" (134)

In this extract, southern readers may have been unfamiliar with *clem,* but they could have no doubt of its serious meaning.

Encouraged by her experiments, William Gaskell, her husband, delivered and then published *Two Lectures on the Lancashire Dialect.* In them, he expressed the conventional opinion that distinctive forms of regional speech were rapidly dying out, but he also asserted that English in Lancashire retained features of early Celtic and Anglo-Saxon that had elsewhere been lost.

> There are many forms of speech and peculiarities of pronunciation in Lancashire that would yet sound strange, and, to use a Lancashire expression, strangely "potter" a southern; but these are often not, as some ignorantly suppose, mere vulgar corruptions of modern English, but genuine relics of the old mother tongue. They are bits of the old granite, which have perhaps been polished into smoother forms, but lost in the process a great deal of their strength. (13–14)

Gaskell's patronizing approval of survivals of "the old mother tongue" did not at all imply their use by educated people. *Clem,* for instance, had been used by Renaissance dramatists, and Gaskell gave its Anglo-Saxon derivation and Danish and Dutch cognates (28). Such words allowed him to declare that "on the whole, instead of saying that the Lancashire dialect is a corruption of English, it would seem truer to say that English is very often a corruption of Anglo-Saxon" (23). Though that may have been true in the past, it was no longer a consequential social fact, nor did Gaskell urge this point strongly. If "a southern" were *pottered* 'confused, perplexed' by a Lancashire voice, the southern was implicitly correct. Nonetheless, there was a literary tradition in the north of England that operated in self-conscious innocence of southern prejudices, writers who performed their own compositions in the tradition of Burns and Collier, the Lancashire schoolmaster who invented the debate between "Tim Bobbin" and his book quoted earlier.

Bringing his *View of the Lancashire Dialect* (1746) to a definitive edition in 1750, Collier had also thought as Gaskell did a century later that the rural people of his district had begun to "speak much better English. If it can be properly called so" (xxxii). By 1862, his editor thought fit to present some of Collier's work "rendered into simple English with the Idioms and Similes retained" (4), since the prior century had seen the increasing obsolescence of many expressions. Collier's successors in literary invention in the nineteenth century were Edwin Waugh (1817–90), Ben Brierley (1825–96), and John Hartley (1839–1915). Earning a scant living through the sale of pamphlets and occasional sales to newspapers, these writers were best known for readings among the people whose English was the basis for the pathos and humor of their stories and verses. Unfortunately, these writers accepted the evaluation of regional speech expressed in London salons, and comedy and sentimentality were the main veins in which they worked (see Vicinus, 192–95).

Arguments about the legitimacy of regional voices were vividly revealed in 1890 in a series of letters to the *Rochedale Observer* in Lancashire. J. H. Wylie, the inspector of schools for the region, had spoken at the annual presentation of school board certificates. As reported in the *Observer,* "He said he had lived long enough and had heard dialect enough, to know that a local dialect with local words was a valuable thing, and one they should preserve rather than eradicate" (Hollingworth, 15). Angry letters followed, including one from John Trafford Clegg, who wrote and performed under the name "Th'Owd Weyver": "Keep th'owd Lanky eawt o'th'schoo's Mesther Wylie, for aw want my childher to talk smart when they grown up" (17). Wylie proposed to produce a schoolbook edition of *Tim Bobbin* with apparatus to encourage its study through analytical grammar, an idea greeted with horror by those suspicious of humor and impropriety in classrooms. While the turmoil over Wylie's ideas soon died out, the correspondence concluded with an anonymous sympathizer writing under the name "Lancashire."

> Is it worth while causing the child to leave the speech entirely in which he can express himself most forcibly? What is language for? To express our thoughts, and the more expressive we can make the expression the better for us and our hearers. Yet "Th"Owd Weighver" and Mr. Greenwood [a prior letter-writer who had called the dialect "coarse and uncouth"] would practically take away from the child the ability to express himself in the most natural manner, for they would say to the teacher "reduce the child's vocabulary—make him write and speak only in a language fixed by southern writers and speakers who know nothing of his ideas, of his modes of expression, of the beauties of his everyday speech, and when you have done all that to the child, when you have given him only an artificial method of conveying his thoughts to others, say that you have done your duty to the child, that you have driven him from a dialect which abounds in vulgarities and expressions of bad breeding. (Hollingworth, 17)

"Talking smart" was perhaps desired by parents for their children, and "Lancashire"'s dire predictions were almost universally fulfilled as young northerners were hampered by artificiality and made fearful of vulgarities.

Even so, northern ways of speaking found other defenders. Richard J. Lloyd, writing for a German audience, commended northern English and derided some southern innovations. "[S]ome kind of *r*" was better than dropping it altogether, as Londoners were inclined to do (1895, 53). Lloyd further declared that, compared to London, the "North is much less tolerant of obscurations and elisions" (1899, 31), and he suggested that, on the whole, English for foreign learners should be based on an optimization of the best of several kinds.

> The aim of the student should be, not to follow implicitly either London or Liverpool or Boston or New York, but to choose a sound *via media*, and speak an English which will be recognised as pure and good everywhere. (1895, 52)

Such rearguard arguments were doomed from the beginning; London fashion and London English as expressed by "members of

the great Public Schools, and by those classes in society which normally frequent these" (Wyld 1934, 605), became, in the early
twentieth century, the only measures of what was "pure and good
everywhere."

Farther north, in Scotland, the linguistic environment was
more complicated. With an increasingly anglicized gentry, old
Scots forms of speaking were viewed as obsolescent. The acceler-
ated decline of Gaelic, begun in the eighteenth century, continued through urbanization and official action to extend education
in English to villages in the Highlands and Islands. As reported in
The New Statistical Account of Scotland, with information gathered
between 1834 and 1845 and compiled by the local parish ministers, Gaelic was giving way to English, and Scots to more anglicized
speech patterns. A few extracts from this rich source of information give a sketch of the language change in progress.

> *Dull, Perthshire.* Although almost all the people can both speak and
> understand the English language, still the generality of them have a
> decided predilection for the Gaelic. This appears from the fact that it
> is the ordinary medium of their daily intercourse, but it nowhere
> appears so evident as during public worship in church on the Sab-
> bath. While the common classes are apparently indifferent and
> unconcerned during the English service, they are all eyes and atten-
> tion during the Gaelic, and hanging with anxiety, as it were, on the
> lips of the preacher, thus indicating that it is by means of their ver-
> nacular tongue the voice of instruction can principally reach them
> "savingly and to profit." (Duncan Dewar, 10:770)

> *Caputh, Perthshire.* The Stormont dialect, of course, prevails, in which
> the chief peculiarity that strikes a stranger is the pronunciation of the
> Scotch *oo* as *ee,* poor being pronounced *peer,* moon *meen,* aboon *abeen,*
> &c. The Gaelic is not spoken by any of the natives; but not a few High-
> land servants have of late been engaged by farmers and others who
> understand the English or Scotch very imperfectly, and who thereby
> occasion some annoyance to the minister in his parochial rounds of
> visitation and examination. (Alexander Watson, 10:677)

> *Kenmore, Perthshire.* The language almost universally spoken is the
> Gaelic. It is likewise the language in which the greater part of the
> ministrations of religion is discharged. While I would say that, within

the last forty years, the language has neither lost nor gained ground, I would likewise say that the English language is becoming every day more generally familiar; for there is now hardly an individual who is not capable, more or less, of making use of it. How this invasion of the speech of our southern neighbors is ultimately to operate, seems not a very difficult thing to conjecture. At no distant period, it will, in all likelihood, so far prevail over its less potent associate, as almost entirely, if not altogether, to take its place. Nor does the substitution appear to be an event greatly to be deprecated. (David Duff, 10:471)

Redgorton, Perthshire. The language generally spoken in the parish is Scotch, which, as education advances, is receiving an admixture of indifferent English. None of the natives speak Gaelic, but some recent settlers are imperfectly acquainted with English, and some, as they express it, have the advantage of the "twa tongues." (William Liston, 10:183)

Bogart, Sutherlandshire. The Celtic, or Gaelic, language is spoken by almost all the inhabitants. There are a few shepherds who do not speak this language; but their families do. A considerable proportion of the inhabitants, however, can converse in the English language; and, in a few years[,] it is likely that none may be found who cannot do so. Their English, being acquired from books, and occasional conversation with educated persons, is marked by no peculiarity, except a degree of mountain accent and Celtic idiom; so that it is more easily intelligible to an Englishman than the dialect spoken by the Lowland Scotch. (John Mackenzie, 15:51)

Ettrick, Selkirkshire. The people speak the dialect of the forest, which is simple and soft in its tones, and, we should think, rather agreeable to the ear of a stranger. (John Smith, 3:69)

Eddlestone, Peebles-shire. The language generally spoken is a corrupt Scotch, with a barbarous admixture of English. A few only of the oldest of the people speak the Scottish dialect in its purity. These, however, are rapidly disappearing, and in a few years more in all probability there will not be one person alive who could have held converse with his grandfather without the aid of a dictionary. (Patrick Robertson, 3:149)

Hutton, Berwickshire. The language generally spoken is the Berwickshire dialect of the Scots, intermixed occasionally with the Northumbrian *burr.* The most remarkable peculiarities which distinguish this dialect are observable in the following words: fire, pronounced *feyre;* water, *wayter;* chair, *shire;* two, *twae,* church, *surch;* cheese, *sheese,* &c. There is no reason to suppose that any very material alteration in this respect has occurred within the last forty years. (John Edgar, 2:154)

These reports generally reflect affirmation of more anglicized varieties of English over more localized varieties of Scots. (The idea, still current, that Highlanders speak a variety of English "marked by no peculiarity" was also regularly expressed.)

The linguistic environment was rather more complicated than the *Statistical Account* allowed. Growth of shipbuilding and trade on Clydeside, and the accompanying crush of poverty in emerging slums in Gorbals, brought new urban dialects that were barely noticed by the respectable members of the Church of Scotland, or at least seldom reported. Within the cities, new voices emerged, but the market for imaginative literature was constrained by costs. Scotland was poor, and few of its people could afford poetry or fiction at the prices commanded by the products of London, much less the higher costs of small editions of locally produced work. While Charlotte Brontë, George Eliot, Elizabeth Gaskell, and Thomas Hardy were continually obliged to compromise regional voices to suit the prejudices of metropolitan readers of the mass market, writers in Scots were similarly constrained. Reviewing George Macdonald's *Malcolm,* Margaret Oliphant, though herself a Scot, raised the issue in *Blackwood's Magazine* in 1875.

> Why will Mr Macdonald make all his characters, almost without exception, talk such painfully broad Scotch? Scotch to the fingertips, and loving dearly our vernacular, we yet feel it necessary to protest against the Aberdeen-awa' dialect . . . which bewilders even ourselves now and then, and which must be almost impossible to an Englishman. So many beautiful thoughts, tender, and delicate, and true, must be obscured to the reader by this obstinate purism, that we feel angry, disappointed, and impatient at the author's perseverance in this mistaken way. . . . It is poor art, and not truth at all, to insist upon this desperate accuracy. Sir Walter's Scotch was never like this. (Quoted by Donaldson, 170 n. 9)

The economics of taste dictated that regional usage be lightly used and heavily glossed. The result was fiction of sentiment and nostalgia subsequently known as the "Kailyard School," J. M. Barrie being its most famous practitioner. (A *kailyard* is a kitchen garden.)

Just as the north of England supported such performer-writers as Hartley, Brierly, and Waugh, so did Scotland have many vernacular authors, though in Scotland they were less likely to attend to London tastes. A few of them knew what was demanded—S. R. Crockett said forthrightly of his own literary career: "The publisher tells you to cut down the dialect because the public does not understand it" (quoted by Donaldson, 147). Until nearly the end of the century, however, Scotland supported dozens of local newspapers directed at a local audience of middle- and working-class readers. In this environment, local writing could flourish. Among the most famous authors was William Alexander (1824–94), author of *Johnny Gibb of Gushetneuk* (serialized from 1869 to 1870 and published as a book in 1871). The following, from Alexander's short story "Baubie Huie's Bastard Geet," shows the uncompromising locality of this Scottish fiction.

> "Weel, weel, Jock'll get's nain o' 't lickly, honest man. It'll be a won'er an they hinna the tsil' to fesh up."
> "Ou weel-a-wat that's true aneuch; but there's never a hicht but there's a howe at the boddom o' 't, as I said to Eppie fan she first taul' me o' Baubie's misfortune; an' there's never a mou' sen' but the maet's sen' wi' 't." (Gifford, 192)

This story, from 1872, shows Alexander's sympathetic treatment of illegitimate births, a particularly acute social issue in northeast Scotland of the day, but it also reflects "a progressive urge to disrupt the monopolistic position of English as the language of authority" (Donaldson, 143; see also Leonard).

Alexander was by no means alone in his effort to make nuanced Scots, with distinctions of gender, region, and social class, an independent literary medium and thus to give authority to those who spoke it. Just as J. H. Wylie had used his position as school inspector in Lancashire to further the cause of the vernacular, so did a Scottish school inspector contrast the sterile image of

English with vigorous local speech. According to a report in 1876 by one Muir, English was associated with rote learning and Scots with thought.

> In one school I asked a junior class the meaning of the word "passenger" in the lesson before them. I was answered readily, "one who travels by a public conveyance." "Quite right," said I. "Now what is a public conveyance? Give me an example. Tell me any public conveyance you have ever heard of?" There was a painful silence.
>
> Far preferable to this are the rough and ready explanations in colloquial, or even vernacular speech I sometimes get. Of a history class I asked one day the meaning of the word "treason." "What do you mean by committing treason against the king?" "Gie'in him impudence," was the prompt answer of one boy. "Well, right so far, but tell me a little more accurately, what it is." "Speakin back to him." It is obviously more pleasant to get such answers than answers like those which define "invasion" as entering a country with hostile intentions. (Quoted without further documentation by Kay, 115.)

Like Wylie's, Muir's viewpoint was mostly ignored. The same process of anglicization took place as it had in the north of England; children, especially in larger towns and cities, were led to believe that they spoke "a dialect which abounds in vulgarities and expressions of bad breeding."

The more distant the voices from the moderating influence of London editors, the greater the difficulty in representing them and the less likelihood of their being received enthusiastically by educated metropolitan readers. In the first novel to represent village life in India, Lál Behári Day provided an abundance of Bengali words, all of them carefully glossed for the English-knowing reader.

> In the verandah of this little hut is placed the *dhenki*, or the rice-husking pedal. From this circumstance the little hut is called *dhenkisálá* (pedal-house), or more familiarly *dhenskál*. (29)

(It may not have been obvious to Day that *rice-husking pedal* would not be transparent to English readers.) How should the characters in this fiction be represented speaking? None of them would use any variety of English, but there were no traditions for Day to follow in capturing their voices.

> Gentle reader, allow me here to make one remark. You perceive that Badan and Alanga speak better English than most uneducated English peasants; they speak almost like educated ladies and gentlemen, without any provincialisms. But how could I have avoided this defect in my history? If I had translated their talk into the Somersetshire or the Yorkshire dialect, I should have turned them into English, and not Bengali, peasants. You will, therefore, please overlook this grave though unavoidable fault in this authentic narrative. (61)

Day did not find a solution for representing peasant voices, but only in the nineteenth century would he have felt obliged to address the problem as a serious one for authors contemplating a sketch of peasant life.

Fictional characters presented no serious threat to the status of conventional written English, and behind the vernacular in novels and poems was the sure hand of the puppeteer, the educated and omniscient author. Real vernaculars offered a much more unsettling challenge to the equanimity of the elite. When in 1803 the British acquired the colony of Surinam on the north coast of South America, they confronted a linguistic setting of considerable complexity. Of the European languages used in the region, Dutch was the most important, but French and Spanish were also spoken. During the seesaw struggle for possession with the Dutch, British ships sometimes stood offshore to load cargo at night in defiance of agreements with the Dutch authorities. In the port all ships were compelled to show the Dutch flag.

> Such was the nationality they were led to, that a poor negro captain one day, who after having passed the fort and anchored in the river, hauled his Dutch colours down, was taken on board the [Dutch] corvette, and severely punished for not keeping them flying until the sun set. I saw the poor fellow afterwards, and he told me that his schooner should not wear any colours in the river until the English took the colonies again; that he did not care for the Dutch captain, even if he flogged him every time he came in, he would have his own way; to use his own language—"Kie! massa Hendry, them Dutch colour no good, me schooner no shall wear flag in the river tae them English buckra come again, when me shall buy one English jack: me no mind suppose that Dutch officer flog me every time me schooner

come in; him no shall wear them colours." To me it was highly grati-
fying to observe how Englishly disposed all the negro interest is. Born
for the most part in the West India islands, these black sailors grow up
with a patriotic zeal for all who talk our language. (Bolingbroke,
195–96)

Of course it was typical for English and American voyagers to suppose that they were especially welcome and the local people "Englishly disposed." But this new contact was complicated by the fact
that Dutch missionaries had taken seriously the patois of the
area—"talkee-talkee," as it was called by English.

Devotional works had been produced earlier in the Dutch-
based creole of the Caribbean, and when the Danes came to control the Virgin Islands they too published for local use a *Creol
Psalm-Buk* (1834). Moravian missionaries in Surinam had translated portions of the Bible into "talkee-talkee" and used them in
services for the African-descended people of the country. Having
been cut off from their missionary activities, the Moravians
appealed to the British and Foreign Bible Society to publish their
carefully translated manuscript of the New Testament. After delib-
erations, the Society published an edition of a thousand copies,
925 of which were sent to Surinam, "where they proved highly
acceptable, and were received with great thankfulness"
(Greenfield, 5), though this handful of books can hardly have
been known to more than a tiny number of the ten thousand freed
and eighty thousand enslaved African-descended people of the
colony. A few of the remaining 75 copies provided the basis for
reviews, first in the church press (e.g., the *Edinburgh Christian
Instructor* in December 1829) and then prominently in the most
influential review of the day, the *Quarterly*.

The anonymous reviewer in the *Quarterly* was Robert Southey,
who noted that news of the translation had aroused a great outcry
against the Society (558). Southey declined to associate himself
with those critics who had selected specimens for ridicule, and he
wrote sympathetically of horrors of slavery and acknowledged that
talkee-talkee was the sole maternal tongue of great numbers of
people in Surinam. But he made a distinction between language

and a patois or lingo and applied the terms *patois* and *lingo* to
talkee-talkee. This distinction required some adroit logic since
English, he understood, was, like talkee-talkee, a mixed language.
Talkee-talkee suffered from "radical depravity"; that is, its root elements were intrinsically unworthy.

> Time and culture have softened, and regulated, and refined the var-
> ious languages which grew up during the wreck of the Roman
> empire, as in the various European kingdoms the conquerors and
> the conquered gradually became one people; and they are now noth-
> ing inferior to the Latin in perspicuity, nor in sweetness, nor in
> strength. But in all these cases the materials were good,—precious
> metals were fused into composites, differing rather in the proportion
> of their materials than in value; whereas the talkee-talkee is inher-
> ently, ridiculously, offensively, and incurably base. In its appearance
> as a written language there is nothing unpleasing, and in its sound it
> may be as agreeable as it is described to be; but it has been adapted
> in its construction by ignorant persons, of the vulgarest and coarsest
> minds, to the lowest state of human intellect. (564)

The metalurgical metaphor—the contrast of precious and base
metals—expressed conventional wisdom, some languages (and
their "roots") being inherently valuable, as Greek and Latin were,
and others from less worthy sources being riddled with dross.
Talkee-talkee was a "barbarous patois," different, in ways he did
not bother to explain, from other languages, like English, with
self-evidently mixed origins.

The controversy elicited a pamphlet from William Greenfield
(1799–1831), a polyglot who had acquired a mastery of languages
while apprenticed to a bookbinder and then become superinten-
dent of the editorial department of the Bible Society. (According
to the *Dictionary of National Biography,* "While nineteen months in
the society's service, Greenfield wrote upon twelve European, five
Asiatic, one African, and three American languages; and acquired
considerable knowledge of Peruvian, Negro-English, Chippeway,
and Berber.") Parallel word lists and extended selections from the
translation, carefully glossed, persuaded Greenfield that "Surinam
Negro English"—he declined to use *talkee-talkee*—was not made

from "base" elements or "depraved" roots but was constituted like all other modern languages.

> [I]t is thus that our own mother tongue has had its origin and formation. To originality it has not the slightest pretension, being evidently a compound language which has freely adopted words from every nation, at any time connected with our island by conquest, commerce, or otherwise. Upon its original Gothic base, the Anglo-Saxon, and a few British or Welsh words, was partially superinduced the Norman; and subsequently it has borrowed largely from the Latin, Greek, French, and other languages. All these languages must at one time have presented to those who spoke the languages from which they were derived in their purity, the same ludicrous appearance which the Negro-English now does to us. (50)

Greenfield, however, persuaded only a few of the small number who read his pamphlet; Southey reached a national audience, and his opinions were the source of subsequent commentary on the subject. In 1848, for instance, Matthew Harrison considered talkee-talkee and concluded: "The whole [language] is ridiculous, base, and shocking to the feelings" (115).

Deviant voices, particularly those speaking in "broken English," were scorned and suppressed. They could also be ridiculed as in Charles G. Leland's *Pidgin-English Sing-Song* (1876). The "China-English Dialect," Leland thought, "can present no difficulty to any one who can understand negro minstrelsy or baby talk" (9). Less censorious observers recognized it as the lingua franca of the Far East, and in his voyage around the world in 1872, William Simpson discovered that in China it was the only possible method of communication for the monolingual English visitor.

> It is usual to breakfast about twelve o'clock, and it is customary to have some tea, toast, and perhaps an egg served in your bed-room when you get up, and before dressing. The first morning I expressed my wishes on this matter in my usual way of talk, and the "boy" went off smiling, as if he understood my meaning; but as he did not come back, I made some inquiries of my friends in the house. They asked what I said to the "boy," and I repeated the words as nearly as I could recollect them, to the effect that I wanted some breakfast, and would

Stereotypes, both visual and verbal, emerged as sources of humor based on derision. (From Leland, cover.)

like it immediately. I was then told that I might as well have talked Greek to him, and that I ought to have said, "Catchey some chow-chow chop-chop." *Chow-chow* is understood in this as something to eat, and the last double word is equivalent to "quick-quick." Had I been a comic actor, and the ordering my breakfast been a farce, it might have been possible to feel that I should be saying the right thing in this way. That not being my "pigeon," I felt reluctant to do it; but when eating, drinking, and all your wants are found to depend upon its use, you soon give in; and here is the course of growth in the language, and the reason why it advances and spreads in China. (275)

Simpson believed that increased use of this kind of language would eventually "demand a translation of the Bible into this very vulgar tongue" (279), a book he had no wish to see in his lifetime. Partly because there were never any first-language speakers of this Pidgin, no such translation was ever called for, and hence no latter-day Southey was compelled to step forward to condemn it. For the same reason, there was no Greenfield obliged by his convictions to acknowledge the claims of its speakers to understandable religious instruction and even respect.

Learned philologists in Britain and North America paid little attention to Pidgin English, though a German, Karl Lentzner, thought it worth while to compile a glossary of some of its principal elements. The result was a naive treatment of words based on authorities far removed from its region of fluent use.

> *chow-chow*, to eat, or food of any kind. This is the chief definition, but the word is also specially applied to a kind of sweet preserve made of many things, and has thence been somewhat incorrectly taken to mean a medley of trifles of any kind. Also *chow-chow*, "to have a meal." In the Mandarin dialect, *chi-fan*, showing that the radical of the word means to eat, and not a mixture.

> "Littee Jack Horna,
> Makee sit inside corna,
> *Chow-Chow* he Clismas-pie;
> He puttee inside t'um."
> We ate *chow-chow* with chopsticks on the celestial restaurants.
> —*Mark Twain: Innocents at Home.*

> The word *chow-chow* is suggestive especially to the Indian reader of a mixture of things good, bad, and indifferent; of sweet little oranges and bits of bamboo-stick, slices of sugar-cane, and rinds of unripe fruit, all connected together . . . into a very tolerable confection.
> —*Bombay Quarterly Review,* 1858. (83–84)

Such a compilation was better than the stolid indifference of anglophone lexicographers, but there was no attempt anywhere to treat Pidgin as having even the modest claims of talkee-talkee to the status of a language, and no serious attempt to represent vernacular speakers of it (see Shi).

The missionary impulse—and the *joss-pidgin-men* 'missionaries' who covered the Orient—inspired thoughts of Bible translation nearly everywhere and produced an unprecedented explosion of creativity in the language of religious expression. In the nineteenth century, varieties of Christian expression were elaborated as never before or since. Voices of evangelists took myriad forms, many of them expressing reverence through archaism and formality of a highly conventional kind. Reflecting the language of the 1611 Authorized Version of the Bible, nineteenth-century religious ceremonies often drew upon vocabulary and grammatical structures long obsolescent in the language—for instance, the *-(e)th* endings for third-person singular present indicative verbs and the pronouns *thee* and *thou*. Not all the applications of archaic language were to religious matters, however. In 1844, Samuel F. B. Morse transmitted the first long-distance telegraph message in North America over a line raised between Washington and Baltimore; the content of the message was "What hath God wrought?"

If the dialects and broken varieties of English were seen as low forms of the language, religious English was taken to be the high form. Publishers were eager to print sermons, particularly those by preachers who attracted a considerable following for their eloquence. An excellent example of this genre from early in the century is the *Thanksgiving Sermon* preached by Absalom Jones, rector of St. Thomas's, the African Episcopal Church in Philadelphia. Jones (1746–1818) had been born a slave and, after immense struggles, was ordained priest and gained a considerable following. The *Thanksgiving Sermon* was preached in celebration of the abolition of the slave trade (though not slavery) by the United States in 1808. A typical passage shows how much Jones had mastered the approved forms of eloquence of his day.

> Fifthly, and lastly, Let the first of January, the day of the abolition of the slave trade in our country, be set apart in every year, as a day of publick thanksgiving for that mercy. Let the history of the sufferings of our brethren, and of their deliverance, descend by this means to our children, to the remotest generations; and when they shall ask, in time to come, saying, What mean the lessons, the psalms, the prayers and the praises in the worship of this day? let us answer them, by saying, the Lord, on the day of which this is the anniversary, abolished

the trade which dragged your fathers from their native country, and sold them as bondmen in the United States of America. (19–20)

Jones's discourse follows the conventions of sermonizing for nineteenth-century preachers: declaration of a biblical text to be expounded, numbered points highlighting the principal themes, frequent use of imperatives, a conclusion invoking God and seeking the assent of the hearers. In addition, Jones's voice exploits grammatical parallelism, occasional use of archaic language, and repetition of near synonyms to increase the power of the address. It was a powerful and compelling voice carrying forward the tradition of oratory in a way nineteenth-century listeners found both enthralling and satisfying.

During the century, some writers did more than interpret divine words; they received the words from a divine source. Perhaps the best known of these authors to experience revelation was Joseph Smith, founder of the Church of Jesus Christ of Latter Day Saints. Smith experienced a revelation in 1830 in which he was ordered to "translate" the Bible, a sense of *translate* understood by his followers to mean a "prayerful, analytical approach, in most places following the language form and arrangement of the King James version" (4). In the "translation," Smith did his nineteenth-century best to write seventeenth-century English.

> And it came to pass, that it was for the space of many hours before Moses did again receive his natural strength like unto man; and he said unto himself, Now, for this cause, I know that man is nothing, which thing I never had supposed; but now mine eyes have beheld God; but not mine natural but my spiritual eyes, for mine natural eyes could not have beheld, for I should have withered and died in his presence; but his glory was upon me, and I beheld his face, for I was transfigured before him. (7)

Of course this "translation" departs from the 1611 original in several linguistic ways—for instance, the pronoun *mine* appears in the seventeenth-century translation only before words beginning with *h* or a vowel in the same syntactic unit. Smith's words represent a nineteenth-century conception of the structure and sound of a holy voice.

Like Smith, Mary Baker Eddy proclaimed a revelation and expressed distinctly, though not in a manner so dependent on archaic English as Smith's had been, a vision of moral conduct and insight.

> Without a sense of one's oft-repeated violations of divine law, the individual may become morally blind, and this deplorable mental state is moral idiocy. This lack of seeing one's deformed mentality, and of *repentance* therefor, deep never to be repented of, is retarding, and in certain morbid instances stopping, the growth of Christian Scientists. Without a knowledge of his sins, and repentance so severe that it destroys them, no person is or can be a Christian Scientist. (107)

The texture of this voice, particularly in the interweaving of abstract nouns, compelled listeners to engage in serious and profound reflection. While Jones's stately parallelism evoked earlier styles based on symmetry and repetition and Smith's biblical vocabulary and archaisms even earlier discourse strategies, Eddy's loose syntax and periodic development of themes anticipate the more fragmentary and associative styles favored by the twentieth century.

Voices are often produced in one way and heard in another. Nowhere in the nineteenth century is this principle so clearly illustrated as in the case of Isabella Van Wagener, born a slave about 1797 in Ulster County, New York. In 1843, she changed her name to Sojourner Truth and became an evangelist and, increasingly, a nationally known speaker. In 1851, she appeared at a women's rights convention in Akron, Ohio; according to the earliest known version of her address, this is what she said.

> May I say a few words? Receiving an affirmative answer, she proceeded; I want to say a few words about this matter. I am a woman's rights. I have as much muscle as any man, and can do as much work as any man. I have plowed and reaped and husked and chopped and mowed, and can any man do more than that? I have heard much about the sexes being equal; I can carry as much as any man, and can eat as much too, if I can get it. I am as strong as any man that is now. As for intellect, all I can says is, if a woman have a pint and a man a

quart—why can't she have her little pint full? You need not be afraid to give us our rights for fear we will take too much, for we can't take more than our pint'll hold. The poor men seem to be all in confusion, and don't know what to do. Why children, if you have women's rights give it to her and you will feel better. You will have your own rights, and they won't be so much trouble. I can't read, but I can hear. I have heard the bible and have learned that Eve caused man to sin. Well if woman upset the world, do give her a chance to set it right side up again. The Lady has spoken about Jesus, how he never spurned woman from him, and she was right. When Lazarus died, Mary and Martha came to him with faith and love and besought him to raise their brother. And Jesus wept—and Lazarus came forth. And how came Jesus into the world? Through God who created him and woman who bore him. Man, where is your part? But the women are coming up, blessed be God, and a few of the men are coming up with them. But man is in a tight place, the poor slave is on him, woman is coming on him, and he is surely between a hawk and a buzzard. (*Anti-Slavery Bugle* [Salem, Ohio], 21 June 1851; from Ripley et al., 4:81–82)

Truth was illiterate, so these remarks did not appear in a written form carrying authorial endorsement, but they were powerfully influential both for abolition and suffrage, and doubtless she willingly repeated them when invited to do so.

In April 1863, Harriet Beecher Stowe published an essay in the *Atlantic Monthly* describing a visit from Truth (for whom she had earlier written a testimonial for the *Narrative of Sojourner Truth*, a pamphlet Truth sold to support herself). In Stowe's version, Truth spoke "with the strong barbaric accent of the native African" (477). As represented in the magazine, passages in common with the 1851 address appeared as full-blown "dialect."

"Well, honey, I 's ben to der meetins, an' harked a good deal. Dey wanted me fur to speak. So I got up. Says I,—'Sisters, I a'n't clear what you 'd be after. Ef women want any rights mor 'n dey 's got, why don't dey jes' *take 'em*, an' not be talkin' about it? . . .'"

"S'pose a man's mind holds a quart, an' a woman's don't hold but a pint; ef her pint is *full*, it 's as good as his quart." (479)

For all her fame as the author of *Uncle Tom's Cabin* (1852), Stowe was, compared to her contemporaries, remarkably incompetent in expressing the nuances of real life speech (see McDowell).

FREE LECTURE!

SOJOURNER TRUTH,

Who has been a slave in the State of New York, and who has been a Lecturer for the last twenty-three years, whose characteristics have been so vividly portrayed by Mrs. Harriet Beecher Stowe, as the African Sybil, will deliver a lecture upon the present issues of the day,

At   On

And will give her experience as a Slave mother and religious woman. She comes highly recommended as a public speaker, having the approval of many thousands who have heard her earnest appeals, among whom are Wendell Phillips, Wm. Lloyd Garrison, and other distinguished men of the nation.

☞ At the close of her discourse she will offer for sale her photograph and a few of her choice songs.

Lecturers drew huge crowds in both cities and rural towns, and from midcentury it was possible for inspirational or entertaining speakers to make a living from their performances. (Poster from the Berenice Bryant Lowe Collection, Bentley Historical Library, University of Michigan.)

Shortly after Stowe's essay appeared, Frances Dana Gage gave her own account of Truth's remarks, and her authority deserves special consideration since she had chaired the meeting in Akron at which they were delivered.

"Well, chillen, whar dar's so much racket dar must be som'ting out o'kilter. I think dat, 'twixt de niggers of de South and de women at de Norf, all a-talking 'bout rights, de white men will be in a fix pretty soon. But what's all this here talking 'bout? Dat man ober dar say dat women needs to be helped into carriages, and lifted over ditches, and to have de best place eberywhar. Nobody eber helps me into carriages, or ober mud-puddles, or gives me any best place," and, raising herself to her full hight, and her voice to a pitch like rolling thunder, she asked, "And ar'n't I a woman? Look at me. Look at my arm," and she bared her right arm to the shoulder showing its tremendous muscular power. "I have plowed and planted and gathered into barns, and no man could head me—and ar'n't I a woman? I could work as much and eat as much as a man (when I could get it,) and bear de lash as well—and ar'n't I a woman? I have borne thirteen chillen, and seen 'em mos' all sold off into slavery, and when I cried out with a mother's grief, none but Jesus heard—and ar'n't I a woman? Dem dey talks 'bout dis ting in de head. What dis dey call it?" "Intellect," whispered some one near. "Dat's it, honey. What's dat got do to with woman's rights or niggers' rights. If my cup won't hold but a pint and yourn holds a quart, wouldn't ye be mean not to let me have my little half-measure full?" and she pointed her significant finger and sent a keen glance at the minister who had made the argument. The cheering was long and loud. "Den dat little man in black dar, he say woman can't have as much right as man 'cause Christ wa'n't a woman. *Whar did your Christ come from?*" (1)

Compared to Stowe's minstrel-show dialect, Gage's version is distinctly more powerful, particularly the refrain "and ar'n't I a woman?"

But where is the authentic voice of Sojourner Truth in all these versions? It is impossible to say. Born into a family of Dutch speakers, she did not speak English until adolescence, and some commentators recalled her using a "guttural Dutch accent." Others viewed her as distinctively African-American, though not, as she would often urge, Southern. A British journalist, speaking to her during the Civil War, declared her speech as "correct and beautiful English" (when she chose to speak it). Frederick Douglass, himself famous as a former slave and author, regarded her as caring "very little for elegance of speech or refinement of manners" (quoted by Painter, 466). In fact, she seems to have delighted in her mastery of various styles and accents and to have used them to rhetorical advantage (see Mabee, 71–72). She invented herself and was, in turn, reinvented by others. For Stowe, attentive to the racial theories of her day, "she was evidently a full-blooded African" (473); for Gage, she had "the air of a queen" and was a powerful advocate for women. In the twentieth century, her refrain from the Akron convention has been rendered "And ain't I a woman," an expression described by one of her biographers as "more authentically Negro" (Painter, 464) and by another as, at the time, "the proper grammatical form for a negative interrogative in the first person singular" (Campbell, 444 n. 6). Both claims have little foundation in linguistic history. But the linguistic history is as elusive as Truth herself. Is not *ain't*, ascribed to Truth only in the twentieth century, the form used in the nineteenth century by such writers as Louisa May Alcott as an indicator of humble origins? Or is *ar'n't*, Gage's rendering, in fact, the more elegant form—since *are I not*, of which it is a contraction, was viewed the elegant alternative to *ain't*, however illogical? Or is *a'n't*, Stowe's form, not the proper contraction for *am I not*? All the labors of linguistic historians cannot recover the entire truth of what she said. Or Truth herself.

We mostly invent our images of the voices of the past. And even our best imaginative efforts and careful examination of the testimonies can scarcely bring them to life again.

Postscript

WHAT LINGUISTIC LEGACY did the nineteenth century bequeath to the twentieth?

Voices in English at the turn of the century were full of confidence. Economically, the anglophone world had dominated the globe, and its military forces were paramount in every significant theater of operations. Cecil Rhodes was on the verge of linking Cape Town and Cairo with British outposts, and the collapse of the Spanish empire provoked by the United States promised that America would extend its domain of influence from the Western Hemisphere to the southern Pacific and Southeast Asia. Diplomacy was increasingly conducted in English; international communications were more and more dominated by messages written in it. English expanded to accommodate the rhetoric of triumph.

Grammar had become a subject even more magical than before, with many methods of labeling and diagramming the structure of English to induct children into its mysteries. English grammar had been flattened in ways foreseen by Hester Piozzi: the age of nouns had dawned, and the plain style had triumphed over the orotund verbal felicities of balanced verbal phrases.

Slang signaled a cosmopolitan and racy kind of English in which the culture of youth began to be exalted over the solemnity of chaste and classical styles. Exuberance reigned; austerity and simplicity were seen as expressions of a dying age.

Words continued to flood the means of expression. Etymological harmony increasingly seemed to be an absurd prejudice of pedants. The idea that the language could be regulated and restrained gave way to the notion that new realities required new expressions. Science and advertising, in their separate ways, produced novelty for the sake of knowledge and of sales. Neologisms that formerly would have flourished briefly and died were preserved as curiosities in dictionaries. In the United States, especially, new immigrants brought with them a tapestry of words describing their cuisine and culture, and these gained wide currency.

Sounds in English were more various than ever. Though some lamented the loss of traditional dialects, new speechways emerged that added sounds to English—whether the melodic rhythms of south Asian English or the Scandinavian music of the upper Midwest of America. Urban dialects flourished in Glasgow, Liverpool, London, Boston, New York, Philadelphia, and the other cities drawing workers from agriculture to factory work. These sounds cemented deracinated people into new communities built around ways of speaking.

Writing was abundant and reading an expected skill. Cheap books and newspapers provided entertainment; sheet music and collections of poetry made it possible for communal oral traditions to be enriched through literacy. People found prosperous livelihoods in writing careers, not only those who were handsomely paid for journalism and popular fiction, but those as well who read, wrote, filed, and tallied business communications. Writing and reading became more than skills ancillary to real work; they often became the work itself.

There was a dark side to the legacy too.

Voices were parodied in cruel ways to lampoon the linguistically different, and popular entertainment in the music hall and in vaudeville made regular use of repugnant stereotypes to trivialize the English of rural people, racial minorities, and new immigrants.

Grammar acquired an array of shibboleths, fully documented and thoroughly anathematized. Testing for correctness became institutionalized, and admission to higher education and the professions was increasingly regulated by measurements designed to exclude people whose English was not regarded as worthy.

Slang vivified but also debased discourse, and public debate was increasingly marked by slogans, abbreviations, and boldness. Salacious and blasphemous English emerged from the shadows of Victorian propriety to form a staple of humor and abuse.

Words, as they increased in abundance, were no longer seen as neutral markers of expression but as indicators of intelligence. Knowing more of them was thought to be a sign of intellectual range and subtlety; parlor games and popular instruction combined to teach people words for which they previously had had no use.

Writing, and the schools that fostered it, encouraged greater class stratification. Artisans became operatives; clerks became stenographers. Large-scale enterprises, bureaucracies, and the development of suburbs separated managers from workers; distrust grew on both sides of the class barrier. Distrust gave way to doctrines justifying that separation, and these were fully supported in an ideology about English that smothered democratic optimism in linguistic anxiety.

Nineteenth-century English was part of a social transformation that changed the language and changed the world.

REFERENCES

A. C. C. 1829. "Corruptions of the English Language." *Gentleman's Magazine* 99:121–23.

Aarsleff, Hans. 1967. *The Study of Language in England, 1780–1860.* Princeton: Princeton University Press.

Abbott, Edwin A., and J. R. Seeley. 1881. *English Lessons for English People.* Boston: Roberts Brothers.

Ainger, Alfred. 1895. Introduction to *Annals of the Parish* and *The Ayshire Legatee,* by John Galt. London: Macmillan.

Alford, Henry. 1864. *A Plea for the Queen's English.* 2d ed. London: Strahan. Originally published in 1864 as *The Queen's English,* "the first three words being omitted by mistake."

———. 1888. *The Queen's English.* 7th ed. London: George Bell and Sons.

[Allen, Grant.] 1888. "The Great American Language." *Cornhill Magazine* 58:363–77.

Alston, R. C. 1971. *English Dialects, Scottish Dialects, Cant and Vulgar English: A Bibliography of the English Language from the Invention of Printing to the Year 1800,* vol. 9. Menston: Scolar Press.

Altenberg, Bengt. 1982. *The Genitive v. the "of"-Construction: A Study of Syntactic Variation in Seventeenth Century English.* Lund Studies in English, 62. Lund: C. W. K. Gleerup.

Anderson, Peter M. 1987. *A Structural Atlas of the English Dialects.* London: Croom Helm.

Andrésen, Bjørn Stålhane. 1968. *Pre-glottalization in Standard English Pronunciation.* Norwegian Studies in English, 13. Oslo: Norwegian Universities Press.

"Anglicus." 1818. "On Some Niceties in English Grammar." *Asiatic Journal and Monthly Register* 6:456–59.

[Anglicus, Ducange.] 1859. *The Vulgar Tongue: A Glossary of Slang, Cant, and Flash Words and Phrases used in London from 1839 to 1859.* 2d ed. London: Bernard Quaritch.

Anglo-American Code and Cypher Co. 1891. *The Anglo-American Tele-graphic Code* (1886). 3d ed. New York: Benjamin H. Tyrrel.

Angus, Joseph. 1866. *Handbook of the English Tongue.* London: Religious Tract Society.

Angus, William. 1800. *A Pronouncing Vocabulary of the English Language.* Glasgow: D. Niven. Facsimile ed., English Linguistics, 1500–1900, 164. Menston: Scolar Press, 1969.

Annan, Noel. 1984. *Leslie Stephen: The Godless Victorian.* London: Weiden-feld and Nicolson.

Annenberg, Maurice, ed. 1977. *A Typographic Journey through the Inland Printer, 1883–1900.* Baltimore: Maran Press.

Arnaud, René. 1983. "On the Progress of the Progressive in the Private Correspondence of Famous British People (1800–1880). In *Papers from the Second Scandinavian Symposium on Syntactic Varia-tion,* ed. Sven Jacobson, 83–94. Stockholm Studies in English, 57. Stockholm: Almqvist and Wiksell.

Atwood, E. Bagby. 1953. *A Survey of Verb Forms in the Eastern United States.* Ann Arbor: University of Michigan Press.

Austen, Jane [and Anne Telscombe]. 1975. *Sanditon.* Boston: Houghton Mifflin.

Avis, Walter S. 1967. *A Dictionary of Canadianisms on Historical Principles.* Toronto: W. J. Gage.

Ayres, Alfred [Thomas Embley Osmun]. 1881. *The Orthoëpist: A Pronounc-ing Manual.* New York: D. Appleton.

———. 1911. *The Verbalist* (1881). New York: D. Appleton.

Babbitt, E. H. 1896. "The English of the Lower Classes in New York City and Vicinity." *Dialect Notes* 1:457–64.

Bacon, Albert M. 1872. *A Manual of Gesture.* Chicago: J. C. Buckbee.

Badcock, John [Jon Bee, pseud.]. 1823. *Slang: A Dictionary of the Turf, the Ring, the Chase, the Pit, of Bon-ton, and the Varieties of Life.* London: T. Hughes.

Bagg, Lyman Hotchkins. 1871. *Four Years at Yale.* New Haven: Charles C. Chatfield.

Baker, Alfred. 1909. *The Life of Sir Isaac Pitman (Inventor of Phonography).* New York: Isaac Pitman and Sons.

Barisone, Ermanno. 1978. "Giuseppe Baretti and the Pronunciation of Standard English in the Eighteenth Century." *Bollettino dell'Insti-tuto de Lingue Estere* 11:72–88.

Barltrop, Robert, and Jim Wolveridge. 1980. *The Muvver Tongue*. London: Journeyman Press.

Barnes, William. 1869. *Early England and the Saxon-English*. London: John Russell Smith.

Barrère, Albert, and Charles G. Leland. 1897. *A Dictionary of Slang, Jargon and Cant.* . . . 2 vols. London: George Bell and Sons.

Batchelor, Thomas. 1974. *An Orthoëpical Analysis of the English Language* and *An Orthoëpical Analysis of the Dialect of Bedfordshire* (1809). Ed. Arne Zettersten. Lund Studies in English, 45. Lund: C. W. K. Gleerup.

Beecher, Catharine E., and Harriet Beecher Stowe. 1870. *Principles of Domestic Science*. New York: J. B. Ford.

Bell, James. 1842. *A View of Universal History, Literature, and the Several Schools of Painting* (1833). London: Robert Baldwin.

Blumenthal, Joseph. 1977. *The Printed Book in America*. Boston: David R. Godine.

Blunt, John Henry. 1874. *Dictionary of Sects, Heresies, Ecclesiastical Parties, and Schools of Religious Thought*. London: Rivingtons. Facsimile ed., Detroit: Omnigraphics, 1990.

Blythe, Ronald. 1969. *Akenfield: Portrait of an English Village*. London: Allen Lane.

Bolingbroke, Henry. 1813. *A Voyage to Demerary* (1808). Philadelphia: M. Carey.

Boone, Lalia. 1988. *Idaho Place Names*. Moscow: University of Idaho Press.

Booth, George G. 1902. *The Cranbrook Press*. Detroit: Cranbrook Press.

Bradley, Edward [Cuthbert Bede, pseud.]. [1853?] *The Adventures of Mr. Verdant Green, an Oxford Freshman*. London: James Blackwood.

Bradley, Henry. 1928. *The Making of English* (1904). New York: Macmillan.

Breen, Henry H. 1857. *Modern English Literature: Its Blemishes and Defects*. London: Longman, Brown, Green, and Longmans.

Bristed, Charles Astor. 1871. "Some Notes on Ellis's Early English Pronunciation." *Transactions of the American Philological Association* 114–37.

Bronstein, Arthur J. 1949. "The Vowels and Diphthongs of the Nineteenth Century." *Speech Monographs* 16:227–42.

Brougham, Henry Peter. 1835. "Taxes on Knowledge." *British and Foreign Review* 1:157–72.

Brown, Goold. 1850. *The Institutes of English Grammar*. New York: Samuel S. and William Wood.

———. 1851. *The Grammar of English Grammars.* New York: Samuel S. and William Wood.

———. 1868. *The Grammar of English Grammars.* Enlarged by Samuel U. Berrian. New York: Samuel S. and William Wood.

Burchfield, Robert W. 1987. "The *Supplement to the Oxford English Dictionary:* The End of the Alphabet." In *Dictionaries of English: Prospects for the Record of Our Language,* ed. Richard W. Bailey, 11–21. Ann Arbor: University of Michigan Press.

Burgess, Walton. 1856. *Five Hundred Mistakes of Daily Occurrence in Speaking, Pronouncing, and Writing the English Language Corrected.* New York: Daniel Burgess.

Burke, William Jeremiah. 1939. *The Literature of Slang.* New York: New York Public Library.

Burrows, J. F. 1987. *Computation into Criticism: A Study of Jane Austen's Novels and an Experiment in Method.* Oxford: Clarendon Press.

Butler, Benjamin F. 1892. *Butler's Book: Autobiography and Personal Reminiscences of Major-General Benjamin F. Butler.* Boston: A. M. Thayer.

Butler, E. H. 1951. *The Story of British Shorthand.* London: Sir Isaac Pitman and Sons.

Butler, Marilyn. 1972. *Maria Edgeworth: A Literary Biography.* Oxford: Clarendon Press, 1972.

Camden, William. 1984. *Remains concerning Britain.* Ed. R. D. Dunn. Toronto: University of Toronto Press.

Campbell, Karlyn Kohrs. 1986. "Style and Content in the Rhetoric of Early Afro-American Feminists." *Quarterly Journal of Speech* 72:434–45.

Catford, J. C. 1988. *A Practical Introduction to Phonetics.* Oxford: Clarendon Press.

Cavendish, Henry. 1879. *The Electrical Researches of the Honourable Henry Cavendish, F. R. S.* Ed. J. Clerk Maxwell. Cambridge: Cambridge University Press.

[Cecil, Robert.] 1860. "Competitive Examinations." *Quarterly Review* 108:569–605.

Champneys, A. C. 1893. *History of English.* London: Percival.

Clark, Stephen W. 1872. *First Lessons in English Grammar* (1854). New York: A. S. Barnes.

Clark, Thomas L. 1987. *The Dictionary of Gambling and Gaming.* Cold Spring, N.Y.: Lexik House.

[Clarke, Hewson.] 1811. *Lexicon Balatronicum: A Dictionary of Buckish*

Slang, University Wit, and Pickpocket Elegance. London: C. Chappell.

Cmiel, Kenneth. 1990. *Democratic Eloquence: The Fight over Popular Speech in Nineteenth-Century America.* New York: William Morrow.

Cobbett, William. 1911. *The English Grammar of William Cobbett.* Revised and annotated by Alfred Ayres [Thomas Embley Osmun] (1883). New York: D. Appleton.

[Collier, John.] 1854. *The Dialect of South Lancashire, or, Tim Bobbin's Tummus and Meary* (1746). Ed. Samuel Bamford. 2d ed. London: John Russell Smith.

———. 1862. *The Works of Tim Bobbin, Esq., in Prose and Verse.* Ed. Elijah Ridings. Manchester: John Heywood.

The Complete Art of Polite Correspondence; or, New Universal Letter-Writer. 1857. Philadelphia: J. B. Lippincott.

Cone, Carl B., ed. 1981. *Hounds in the Morning: Sundry Sports of Merry England.* Lexington: University Press of Kentucky.

Crabb, George. 1830. *English Synonymes.* New York: J. and J. Harper.

Crabbe, George. 1838. *The Village, The Parish Register, and Other Poems.* Edinburgh: William and Robert Chambers.

Craigie, William A., and James Hulbert. 1938–44. *A Dictionary of American English.* 4 vols. Chicago: University of Chicago Press.

Craik, George L. 1863. *A Manual of English Literature and of the History of the English Language.* London: Charles Griffin.

Creol Psalm-Buk. 1834. Copenhagen: P. T. Brünnich.

Curme, George. 1931. *Syntax.* Boston: D. C. Heath and Co.

Dana, Richard H. 1921. *Hospitable England in the Seventies: The Diary of a Young American, 1875–1876.* Boston: Houghton Mifflin.

Daniel, Evan. 1898. *The Grammar, History, and Derivation of the English Language.* Rev. ed. London: National Society's Depository.

Davitt, Michael. 1972. *Leaves from a Prison Diary* (1885). Shannon: Irish University Press.

Day, Henry N. 1843. "English Phonology." *American Biblical Repository.* 10 (second series): 432–54.

Day, Lál Behári. 1913. *Bengal Peasant Life* (1874). London: Macmillan. First published as *Govinda Sámanta; or, The History of a Bengal Ráiyat.*

Day, Lewis F. 1906. *Alphabets Old and New.* 2d ed. London: B. T. Batsford.

DeKeyser, Xavier. 1975. *Number and Case Relations in Nineteenth Century*

British English: A Comparative Study of Grammar and Usage. Antwerp: De Nederlandsche Boekhandel.

Dens and Sinks of London Laid Open (1848). 1971. Wakefield, England: S. R. Publishers.

DeWitt, Marguerite E. 1928. *Our Oral World.* London: J. M. Dent and Sons.

Dickens, Charles. 1986. *The Pickwick Papers,* ed. James Kinsley. Oxford: Clarendon Press.

Dickson, R. J. 1966. *Ulster Emigration to Colonial America, 1718–1775.* London: Routledge and Kegan Paul.

Donaldson, William. 1989. *The Language of the People: Scots Prose from the Victorian Revival.* Aberdeen: Aberdeen University Press.

Don't: A Manual of Mistakes and Improprieties More or Less Prevalent in Conduct and Speech. Ca. 1880. London: Field and Tuer. Facsimile ed., Whitstable: Pryor Publications, 1990.

Douglas, Sylvester. 1991. *A Treatise on the Provincial Dialect of Scotland* (1779). Ed. Charles Jones. Edinburgh: Edinburgh University Press.

Douse, Thomas Le Marchant. 1876. *Grimm's Law: A Study.* London: Trübner.

Dowling, Linda. 1986. *Language and Decadence in the Victorian Fin de Siècle.* Princeton: Princeton University Press.

Doyle, Brian. 1986. "The Invention of English." In *Englishness: Politics and Culture, 1880–1920,* ed. Robert Colls and Philip Dodd, 89–115. London: Croom Helm.

"Duncan, Professor." 1877. *How to Talk Correctly.* London: William Nicholson and Sons.

Dunglison, Robley. 1839. *A New Dictionary of Medical Science.* 2d ed. Philadelphia: Lea and Blanchard.

Duties of a Lady's Maid. 1825. London: J[ames] Badcock.

Earle, John. 1892. *The Philology of the English Tongue.* 5th ed. Oxford: Clarendon Press.

Eaton, Seymour. 1891. *Slips Corrected of Tongue and Pen.* New York: Hinds and Noble.

Eddy, Mary Baker. 1896. *Miscellaneous Writings, 1883–1896.* Boston: First Church of Christ, Scientist.

Edgeworth, Maria. 1903. *Castle Rackrent* (1800). New York: Century.

Edwards, Harold T. 1992. *Applied Phonetics: The Sounds of American English.* San Diego: Singular Publishing.

Egan, Pierce. 1812. *Boxiana; or, Sketches of Ancient and Modern Pugilism.* London: G. Smeeton.

———. 1821. *Life in London.* London: Sherwood, Neely, and Jones.

Eliot, George. 1954. *The George Eliot Letters.* Ed. Gordon S. Haight. New Haven: Yale University Press.

———. 1964. *Middlemarch: A Study of Provincial Life* [1872]. New York: Signet.

Ellis, Alec. 1985. *Educating Our Masters: Influences on the Growth of Literacy in Victorian Working Class Children.* Aldershot: Gower.

Ellis, Alexander J. 1869–89. *On Early English Pronunciation.* 5 pts. London: Published for the Philological Society by Ascher and for the Early English Text Society by Trübner.

Elworthy, F. T., ed. 1879. *An Exmoor Scolding* and *An Exmoor Courtship.* English Dialect Society, 25. London: Trübner.

Emerson, Ralph Waldo. 1883. *English Traits.* Boston: Houghton, Mifflin.

Errors of Pronunciation and Improper Expressions. 1817. London: Printed for the Author.

Esher, Viscount [Reginald Baliol Brett]. 1912. *The Girlhood of Queen Victoria: A Selection from Her Majesty's Diaries.* 2 vols. London: John Murray.

[Evans, Arthur Benoni.] 1808. *The Cutter: In Five Lectures upon the Art and Practice of Cutting Friends, Acquaintances, and Relations.* New York: D. Longworth.

Fallows, Samuel. 1883. *Hand Book of Abbreviations and Contractions.* Chicago: Standard Book.

Faraday, Michael. 1839. *Experimental Researches in Electricity.* London: Taylor and Francis. Facsimile ed., New York: Dover Publications, 1965.

Farmer, John S. 1900. *The Public School Word-Book.* London: Privately printed by Hirschfeld Brothers.

———, and W. E. Henley. 1890–1904. *Slang and Its Analogues.* 7 vols. Facsimile ed., New York: Arno Press, 1970.

Fearon, Henry Bradshaw. 1818. *Sketches of America.* London: Longman, Hurst, Rees, Orme, and Brown.

Finkenstaedt, Thomas, and Ernst Leisi. 1970. *A Chronological English Dictionary.* Heidelberg: Carl Winter.

Fleck, Jamie. 1792. "An Epistle to Robert Burns." *Belfast News-Letter,* March 27–30, 1.

Fonblanque, Albany de. 1881. "The English of America." *Tinsley's Magazine* 29:330–34.

Foucault, Michel. 1972. *The Archaeology of Knowledge* (1969). trans. A. M. Sheridan Smith. New York: Pantheon.

Fowler, H. W. 1927. *A Dictionary of Modern English Usage* (1926). Oxford: Clarendon Press.

Franklin, Benjamin. 1751. *Experiments and Observations on Electricity.* London: E. Cave.

Franklyn, Julian. 1960. *A Dictionary of Rhyming Slang.* London: Routledge and Kegan Paul.

Frazer, Timothy C. 1993. "The Language of Yankee Cultural Imperialism: Pioneer Ideology and 'General American.'" In *"Heartland" English: Variation and Transition in the American Midwest,* ed. Timothy C. Frazer, 59–66. Tuscaloosa: University of Alabama Press.

Fulton, George, and George Knight. 1821. *A General Pronouncing and Explanatory Dictionary of the English Language.* Edinburgh: Peter Hill and Company.

Gabriel, Virginia. 1868. *Voices Calling.* London: Charles Jefferys.

Gage, Frances Dana. 1863. "Sojourner Truth." *Independent* (Boston), April 23, 1.

Gaskell, Elizabeth. 1973. *North and South.* Ed. Angus Easson. London: Oxford University Press.

Gaskell, G. A. 1881. *Gaskell's Compendium of Forms.* Chicago: Fairbanks, Palmer.

Gaskell, William. 1854. *Two Lectures on the Lancashire Dialect.* London: Chapman and Hall.

Geikie, A. Constable. 1857. "Canadian English." *Canadian Journal of Industry, Science, and Art* 2:344–55.

Gellerman, Robert F. 1973. *The American Reed Organ.* Vestal, N.Y.: Vestal Press.

Gems of English Song: A Collection of Very Choice Songs, Duets and Quartets. 1875. Boston: Oliver Ditson.

Gifford, Douglas, ed. 1971. *Scottish Short Stories, 1800–1900.* London: Calder and Boyars.

Gilman, E. Ward. 1989. *Webster's Dictionary of English Usage.* Springfield, Mass.: Merriam-Webster.

Gilmore, William J. 1989. *Reading Becomes a Necessity of Life: Material and Cultural Life in Rural New England, 1780–1835.* Knoxville: University of Tennessee Press.

Goldstrom, J. M. 1972. *The Social Content of Education, 1808–1870: A Study of the Working Class School Reader in England and Ireland.* Shannon: Irish University Press.

Goodholme, Todd S., ed. 1882. *A Domestic Cyclopaedia of Practical Information.* New York: Henry Holt.

Goodrich, Chauncey A. 1864. *An American Dictionary of the English Language.* Springfield, Mass.: George and Charles Merriam.

Gordon, Elizabeth, and Marcia Abell. 1990. "'This Objectionable Colonial Dialect': Historical and Contemporary Attitudes to New Zealand Speech." In *New Zealand Ways of Speaking English,* ed. Allan Bell and Janet Holmes, 21–48. Multilingual Matters, 65. Clevedon: Multilingual Matters.

Gore, Willard C. 1895–96. "Student Slang." *Inlander* (University of Michigan) 6:59–67, 111–16, 145–53.

Gould, Edward S. 1880. *Good English; or, Popular Errors in Language* (1867). Rev. ed. New York: A. C. Armstrong and Son.

Grandgent, C. H. 1915. "Fashion and the Broad A." *Nation* 100:13–14.

Gray, Thomas R., ed. 1831. *The Confessions of Nat Turner.* Baltimore: Lucas and Denver. Facsimile ed., Ann Arbor, Mich.: Uniprint, 1967.

Greenfield, William. 1830. *A Defence of the Surinam Negro-English Version of the New Testament.* London: Samuel Bagster.

Greenough, James Bradstreet, and George Lyman Kittredge. 1923. *Words and Their Ways in English Speech* (1901). New York: Macmillan.

Grose, Francis. 1787. *A Provincial Glossary.* London: T. Hooper. Facsimile ed., English Linguistics, 1500–1800, 63. Menston: Scolar Press, 1968.

———. 1963. *A Classical Dictionary of the Vulgar Tongue* (1785). Ed. Eric Partridge. New York: Barnes and Noble.

Groves, David, ed. 1986. *James Hogg: Selected Poems and Songs.* Edinburgh: Scottish Academic Press.

Gwynne, Parry. 1856. *A Word to the Wise.* In *Conversation: Its Faults and Its Graces* (ca. 1850), ed. Andrew P. Peabody, 61–108. 2d ed. Boston: James Munroe., 1856. Peabody reprints the fourth English edition, "a few passages not applicable to the habits of American society being omitted" (8). The earliest London edition known to me is the third, published in 1852.

Haggart, David. 1821. *The Life of David Haggart.* 2d ed. Edinburgh: W. and C. Tait.

Haliburton, Thomas Chandler. 1941. *Sam Slick* (1836), ed. Ray Palmer Baker. Toronto: McClelland and Stewart.

——, ed. 1852. *Traits of American Humour, by Native Authors.* 3 vols. London: Colburn.

Hall, Benjamin Homer. 1856. *A Collection of College Words and Customs.* Revised ed. Cambridge, Mass.: John Bartlett.

Hall, Fitzedward. 1873. *Modern English.* London: Trübner; New York: Scribner, Armstrong.

——. 1882, "On the Separation, by a Word or Words, of *to* and the Infinitive Mood." *American Journal of Philology* 3:17–24.

——. 1893. "The American Dialect." *Academy* 39:265–68.

Hammarström, Göran. 1980. *Australian English: Its Origin and Status.* Forum Phoneticum, 19. Hamburg: Helmut Buske Verlag.

Hancock, Ian. 1974. "English in Liberia." *American Speech* 49:224–29.

Handover, P. M. 1965. "British Book Typography." In *Book Typography, 1815–1965, in Europe and the United States of America,* 137–74. London: Ernest Benn.

Hansard Parliamentary Debates, 1st ser., vol. 9. (1807).

Hardy, Thomas. 1878. "Dialect in Novels." *Athenaeum,* November 30, 688.

Harrison, Matthew. 1850. *The Rise, Progress, and Present Structure of the English Language* (1848). Philadelphia: E. C. and J. Biddle.

Hewitt, David. 1981. *Scott on Himself: A Selection of the Autobiographical Writings of Sir Walter Scott.* Edinburgh: Scottish Academic Press.

Hill, Geoffrey. 1902. *The Aspirate; or, The Use of the Letter "H" in English, Latin, Greek and Gaelic.* London: T. Fisher Unwin.

Hill, Thomas E. 1880. *Hill's Manual of Social and Business Forms.* 22d ed. Chicago: Moses Warren.

Hill, Thomas Wright. 1860. "A Lecture on the Articulation of Speech" (January 29, 1821). In *Selections from the Papers of the Late Thomas Wright Hill,* 8–34. London: John W. Parker and Son.

Hodgson, William B. 1882. *Errors in the Use of English.* American rev. ed. New York: D. Appleton.

[Holley, Marietta.] 1890. *My Opinions and Betsy Bobbett's* (1873). Hartford: American Publishing.

——. 1894. *Samantha among the Colored Folks: "My Ideas on the Race Problem."* New York: Dodd, Mead. First published in 1892 as *Samantha on the Race Problem.*

Hollingworth, Brian. 1977. "Dialect in School—an Historical Note." *Durham and Newcastle Review* 8 (autumn): 5–20.

Holmes, Oliver Wendell. 1896. *The Autocrat of the Breakfast-Table* (1858). Boston: Houghton, Mifflin.

Holt, Richard. 1989. *Sport and the British: A Modern History.* Oxford: Clarendon Press.

Horsley, J. W. 1879. "Autobiography of a Thief in Thieves' Language." *Macmillan's* 40:500–506.

[Hoshour, Samuel Klinefelter.] 1870. *Letters to Squire Pedant in the East, by Lorenzo Altisonant* (1844). 4th ed. Indianapolis: Printing and Publishing House.

———. 1884. *Autobiography.* St. Louis: John Burns Publishing.

Hotton, John Camden. 1882. *The Slang Dictionary: Etymological, Historical and Anecdotal* (1874). New ed. London: Chatto and Windus.

Hubbard, Elbert, II. 1927. *The Note Book of Elbert Hubbard.* New York: William H. Wise.

Hudson, James William. 1851. *The History of Adult Education.* London: Longman, Brown, Green and Longmans.

Humphreys, David. 1815. *The Yankey in England: A Drama in Five Acts.* Connecticut: n.p.

Hutton, William. 1879. *A Bran New Wark* (1785). Ed. Walter W. Skeat. English Dialect Society, 25. London: Trübner.

Ihalainen, Ossi. 1991. "A Point of Verb Syntax in South-western British English: An Analysis of a Dialect Continuum." In *English Corpus Linguistics,* ed. Karin Aijmer and Bengt Altenberg, 290–302. London: Longman.

Jackson, George. 1830. *Popular Errors in English Grammar, Particularly in Pronunciation.* 3d ed. London: Effingham Wilson.

Jeans, J. H. 1920. *The Mathematical Theory of Electricity and Magnetism* (1908). 4th ed. Cambridge: Cambridge University Press.

Jespersen, Otto. 1913. *Lehrbuch der Phonetik.* 2d ed. Leipzig: B. G. Teubner.

———. 1961. *A Modern English Grammar on Historical Principles* (1909–49). 7 vols. London: George Allen and Unwin.

Johnson, John. 1824. *Typographica; or, The Printers Instructor.* 2 vols. London: Longman . . . & Green.

Johnson, Samuel. 1755. *A Dictionary of the English Language.* London: W. Strahan et al. Facsimile ed. London: Times Books, 1979.

———. 1790. *The Idler.* 6th ed. 2 vols. London: J. Hodges.

Jones, Absalom. 1808. *A Thanksgiving Sermon.* Philadelphia: Fry and Kammerer.

Jones, Charles. 1991. "Some Grammatical Characteristics of the Sierra Leone Letters." In *"Our Children Free and Happy": Letters from Black Settlers in Africa in the 1790s*, ed. Christopher Fyfe, 79–104. Edinburgh: Edinburgh University Press.

Jones, Stephen. 1810. *Sheridan Improved: A General Pronouncing and Explanatory Dictionary of the English Language* (1798). 19th ed. London: Cuthell and Martin.

Kay, Billie. 1986. *Scots: The Mither Tongue.* London: Grafton Books.

Kelly, Rob Roy. 1969. *American Wood Type, 1828–1900.* New York: Van Nostrand Reinhold.

Kemble, John Mitchell. 1834. "Analecta Anglo-Saxonica." *Gentleman's Magazine* 156:391–93.

Kennedy, Arthur G. 1941. "Odium Philologicum; or, A Century of Progress in English Philology." In *Stanford Studies in Language and Literature,* ed. Hardin Craig, 11–21. Palo Alto, Calif.: Stanford University Press.

Kenner, Hugh. 1995. "In Memory of Fanny Fern." *Times Literary Supplement,* November 24, 8.

Kington Oliphant, T. L. 1886. *The New English.* 2 vols. London: Macmillan.

Kirkham, Samuel. N.d. *English Grammar in Familiar Lectures* (1829). 11th ed. New York: Robert B. Collins.

Kökeritz, Helge. 1932. *The Phonology of the Suffolk Dialect, Descriptive and Historical.* Uppsala: Uppsala Universitets Årsskrift.

Krapp, George Philip. 1919. *The Pronunciation of Standard English in America.* New York: Oxford University Press.

———. 1960. *The English Language in America* (1925). 2 vols. New York: Frederick Ungar.

Kruisinga, Etsko. 1932. *A Handbook of Present-Day English.* 5th ed. 3 vols. Groningen: P. Noordhoff.

Lang, Andrew. 1890. *Life, Letters, and Diaries of Sir Stafford Northcote.* 2 vols. Edinburgh: W. Blackwood and Sons.

Langker, R. 1980. *Flash in New South Wales, 1788–1850.* Australian Language Research Centre, University of Sydney, Occasional Paper no. 18.

Laqueur, Thomas W. 1983. "Toward a Cultural Ecology of Literacy in England, 1600–1850." In *Literacy in Historical Perspective,* ed. Daniel P. Resnick, 43–57. Washington, D.C.: Library of Congress.

Lass, Roger. 1987. *The Shape of English: Structure and History*. London: J. M. Dent and Sons.

Latham, Robert Gordon. 1875. *Handbook of the English Language*. London: Longmans, Green.

Laudermilk, Sharon H., and Teresa L. Hamlin. 1989. *The Regency Companion*. New York: Garland Publishers.

Lawson, Henry. 1972. *Short Stories and Sketches, 1888–1922*. Ed. Colin Roderick. Sydney: Angus and Robertson.

Leigh, Percival. 1840. *The Comic English Grammar*. London: Richard Bentley. Facsimile ed., London: Bracken Books, 1989.

Leland, Charles G. 1900. *Pidgin-English Sing-Song* (1876). 5th ed. London: Kegan Paul, Trench, Trübner.

Lentzner, Karl. 1892. *Dictionary of the Slang-English of Australia and of some Mixed Languages*. Halle-Leipzig: Ehrhardt Karras.

Leonard, Tom, ed. 1990. *Radical Renfrew: Poetry from the French Revolution to the First World War*. Edinburgh: Polygon.

Letley, Emma. 1988. "'The Management of the Tongue': Hogg's Literary Uses of Scots." In *Papers Given at the Second James Hogg Society Conference (Edinburgh 1985)*, ed. Gillian Hughes, 11–23.. Aberdeen: Association for Scottish Literary Studies.

Lewis, Matthew Gregory. 1834. *Journal of a West Indian Proprietor*. London: John Murray.

———. 1845. *Journal of a Residence among the Negroes in the West Indies*. London: John Murray.

Leyburn, James. G. 1962. *The Scotch-Irish: A Social History*. Chapel Hill: University of North Carolina Press.

Li, Dun J. 1969. *China in Transition: 1517–1922*. New York: Van Nostrand Reinhold.

Liebling, A. J. 1956. *The Sweet Science*. New York: Viking.

Lighter, Jonathan Evan. 1994–. *Random House Historical Dictionary of American Slang*. 1 vol. to date. New York: Random House.

Lindstrom, Edwin, ed. [1941.] *Penmanship and Alphabets: Reproductions of Plates Engraved and Printed in the Eighteenth and Nineteenth Century*. New York: Irving Zucker.

Lloyd, R[ichard] J. 1895. "Standard English." *Die Neueren Sprachen* 2:52–53.

———. 1899. *Northern English: Phonetics, Grammar, Texts*. Leipzig: B. G. Teubner.

Lockridge, Kenneth A. 1981. "Literacy in Early America, 1650–1800." In

Literacy and Social Development in the West, ed. Harvey J. Graff, 183–200. Cambridge: Cambridge University Press.

Lounsbury, Thomas R. 1908. *The Standard of Usage in English.* New York: Harper and Brothers.

Lowell, James Russell. 1896. *The Complete Poetical Works.* Boston: Houghton, Mifflin.

Mabee, Carleton. 1988. "Sojourner Truth, Bold Prophet: Why Did She Never Learn to Read." *New York History* 69:55–77.

Mack, Douglas S., ed. 1972. *James Hogg: Memoir of the Author's Life and Familiar Anecdotes of Sir Walter Scott.* Edinburgh: Scottish Academic Press.

Mackay, Charles. 1867. "Inroads upon English." *Blackwood's* 102: 399–417.

Mackay, James. 1992. *A Biography of Robert Burns.* Edinburgh: Mainstream Publishing.

MacMahon, M. K. C. 1985. "James Murray and the Phonetic Notation in the *New English Dictionary.*" *Transactions of the Philological Society,* 72–112.

Maitland, Frederic William. 1906. *The Life and Letters of Leslie Stephen.* New York: G. P. Putnam's Sons.

The Manners of the Aristocracy, by One of Themselves. [1881.] London: Ward, Lock.

Mathews, William. 1882. *Words: Their Use and Abuse* (1876). Chicago: S. C. Griggs.

Matsell, George W. 1859. *Vocabulum; or, The Rogue's Lexicon.* New York: George W. Matsell.

Matthews, Brander. 1893a. "The Function of Slang." *Harper's* 87:304–12.

———. 1893b. Letter to the editor. *Dial* 15:108.

Matthews, William. 1938. *Cockney Past and Present: A Short History of the Dialect of London.* New York: E. P. Dutton.

Maxwell, J. Clerk. 1883. *Theory of Heat.* 7th ed. New York: D. Appleton.

———. 1910–11. "Michael Faraday." *Encyclopaedia Britannica.* 11th ed.

———. 1990–. *The Scientific Letters and Papers of James Clerk Maxwell.* Ed. P. M. Harmon. Cambridge: Cambridge University Press.

Mayhew, Henry. 1861–62. *London Labour and the London Poor* (1851). 4 vols. Facsimile ed., London: Frank Cass, 1967.

McArthur, Tom. 1981. *Longman Lexicon of Contemporary English.* Harlow: Longman.

McCabe, James Dabney. 1868. *The Secrets of the Great City: A Work Descriptive of the Vices, Mysteries, Miseries and Crimes of New York City.* Philadelphia: Jones, Brothers.

———. 1879. *National Encyclopedia of Business and Social Forms.* Chicago: G. W. Borland.

McDowell, Tremaine. 1931. "The Use of Negro Dialect by Harriet Beecher Stowe." *American Speech* 6:322–26.

McKnight, George Harley. 1928. *Modern English in the Making.* New York: Appleton-Century.

McLachlan, Noel. 1964. *The Memoirs of James Hardy Vaux.* London: Heinemann.

McPharlin, Paul. 1941. "The Cranbrook Press." *Dolphin* 4, no. 3:268–78.

Mencken, H. L. 1967. *The American Language.* Ed. Raven I. McDavid Jr. New York: Alfred A. Knopf.

Meredith, L. P. 1877. *Every-Day Errors of Speech.* Philadelphia: J. B. Lippincott.

Michael, Ian. 1987. *The Teaching of English from the Sixteenth Century to 1870.* Cambridge: Cambridge University Press.

Moncrieff, William Thomas. 1820. *Modern Collegians; or, Over the Bridge, a Half Hours Comic Sketch before Dinner.* London: J. Lowndes.

Moore, John. 1961. *You English Words.* London: Collins.

[Morgan, Thomas Charles.] 1842. "Contributions to a Fashionable Vocabulary." *New Monthly Magazine* 66:213–21.

Morison, Stanley. 1926. *Type Designs of the Past and Present.* London: Fleuron.

Morris, Linda. 1992. *Women's Humor in the Age of Gentility: The Life and Works of Frances Miriam Whitcher.* Syracuse, N.Y.: Syracuse University Press.

Morris, William. 1898. *A Note by William Morris on His Aims in Founding the Kelmscott Press.* Hammersmith: Kelmscott Press.

Mugglestone, Lynda C. 1988. "Prescription, Pronunciation, and Issues of Class in the Late Eighteenth and Nineteenth Centuries." In *Sentences: Essays Presented to Alan Ward on the Occasion of His Retirement from Wadham College, Oxford,* ed. D. M. Reeks, 175–83. Southampton: Bosphoros Books.

———. 1995. *"Talking Proper": The Rise of Accent as Social Symbol.* Oxford: Clarendon Press.

Murray, James A. H. 1873. *The Dialect of the Southern Counties of Scotland.* London: Asher.

Murray, K. M. Elisabeth. 1977. *Caught in the Web of Words: James Murray and the "Oxford English Dictionary."* New Haven: Yale University Press.

Murray, Lindley. 1816. *English Grammar, Adapted to the Different Classes of Learners.* [1795]. "From the twenty-third English edition." Cooperstown, N.Y.: H. and E. Phinney.

My Secret Life. 1966. New York: Grove Press.

Napier, E. Elers. 1849. *Excursions in Southern Africa.* 2 vols. London: William Shoberl.

Nares, Robert. 1784. *Elements of Orthoepy.* London: T. Payne and Son. Facsimile ed., English Linguistics 1500–1800, 56. Menston: Scolar Press, 1968.

Nash, Ray. 1969. *American Penmanship, 1800–1850.* Worcester, Mass.: American Antiquarian Society.

The New Statistical Account of Scotland. 1845. 15 vols. Edinburgh: William Blackwood and Sons.

Nichols, Ann Eljenholm. 1987. "The Suasive Subjunctive: Alive and Well in the Upper Midwest." *American Speech* 62:140–54.

Niles, Norma A. 1980. "Provincial English Dialects and Barbadian English." Ph.D. diss., University of Michigan.

[Nordhoff, Charles.] 1864–65. "Thieves' Jargon." *Harper's* 30:601–7.

Northend, Charles. 1862. *Exercises for Dictation and Pronunciation.* New York: A. S. Barnes.

Northrop, Henry Davenport. 1895. *The Delsarte Speaker, or Modern Elocution.* [Chicago: Monarch.]

Ogilvie, John. 1850. *The Imperial Dictionary.* 2 vols. Glasgow: Blackie and Son.

Olsson, Yngve. 1961. *On the Syntax of the English Verb, with Special Reference to "Have a Look" and Similar Complex Structures.* Gothenburg Studies in English, 12. Göteborg: Almqvist and Wiksell.

Osselton, N. E. 1994. "Dr. Johnson and the Spelling of *Dispatch.*" *International Journal of Lexicography* 7:307–10.

P. 1834. "Inaccuracies of Diction: Grammar." *New-England Magazine* 7:467–70.

P22 Type Foundry. 1995. *Arts and Crafts Type and Ornaments for Windows.* Buffalo, NY.

Page, Norman. 1988. *A Dickens Chronology.* London: Macmillan.

Painter, Nell Irvin. 1994. "Representing Truth: Sojourner Truth's Knowing and Becoming Known." *Journal of American History* 81:461–92.

Palmer, Abram Smythe. 1876. *Leaves from a Word-Hunter's Note-Book; being Some Contributions to English Etymology.* London: Trübner.

Paz, D. G. 1980. *The Politics of Working-Class Education in Britain, 1830–50.* Manchester: Manchester University Press.

Peabody, Andrew P., ed. 1856. *Conversation: Its Faults and Its Graces.* Boston: James Munroe.

Pegge, Samuel. 1844. *Anecdotes of the English Language.* Ed. Henry Christmas. 3d ed. London: J. B. Nichols and Son.

Penzl, Herbert. 1940. "The Vowel Phonemes in *Father, Man, Dance* in Dictionaries and New England Speech." *Journal of English and Germanic Philology* 39:13–32.

Perrin, Noel. 1969. *Dr. Bowdler's Legacy: A History of Expurgated Books in England and America.* New York: Atheneum.

[Perry, William.] 1818. *The London Guide.* London: J. Bumpus.

Peterson, William S. 1991. *The Kelmscott Press: A History of William Morris's Typographical Adventure.* Berkeley and Los Angeles: University of California Press.

Pettman, Charles. 1913. *Africanderisms: A Glossary of South African Colloquial Words and Phrases and of Place and Other Names.* London: Longmans, Green.

Philipson, Uno. 1941. *Political Slang, 1750–1850.* Lund Studies in English, 9. Lund: C. W. K. Gleerup.

Phillipps, K. C. 1970. *Jane Austen's English.* London: Andre Deutsch.

———. 1984. *Language and Class in Victorian England.* London: Basil Blackwell.

Phyfe, William Henry P. 1926. *Putnam's 18,000 Words Often Mispronounced.* New York: A. L. Burt. This was the culminating edition of a series beginning with 7,000 words in 1889.

Pickering, John. 1816. *A Vocabulary; or, Collection of Words and Phrases, which have been Supposed to be Peculiar to the United States of America.* Boston: Cummings and Hilliard.

Piozzi, Hester Lynch Thrale. 1794. *British Synonymy.* 2 vols. Facsimile ed., English Linguistics 1500–1800, 113. Menston: Scolar Press, 1968.

Pound, Louise. 1914. *Blends: Their Relation to English Word Formation.* Anglistische Forschungen, heft. 42. Heidelberg: Carl Winter.

———. 1915. "British and American Pronunciation: Retrospect and Prospect." *School Review.* 23:381–93.

Poutsma, Hendrik. 1914–28. *A Grammar of Late Modern English.* 4 vols. Groningen: P. Noordhoff.

Pratt, T. K. 1988. *Dictionary of Prince Edward Island English.* Toronto: University of Toronto Press.

[Preston, Thomas. Ca. 1880.] *A Dictionary of Daily Blunders.* New York: Frederick A. Stokes. Though this scarce volume has a U.S. publisher, the books were printed in London and the contents have a decidedly anti-American flavor.

"The Projector." 1804. "Essay on the English Language." *Gentleman's Magazine* 72:816–19.

Quirk, Randolph, Sidney Greenbaum, Geoffrey Leech, and Jan Svartvik. 1985. *A Comprehensive Grammar of the English Language.* London: Longman.

Ramson, W. S. 1988. *The Australian National Dictionary.* Melbourne: Oxford University Press.

Randall, Henry S. 1863. *The Practical Shepherd.* Philadelphia: J. B. Lippincott.

Raymond, Darrell R., ed. 1987. *Dispatches from the Front: The "Prefaces" to the Oxford English Dictionary.* Waterloo: University of Waterloo Centre for the New Oxford English Dictionary.

Read, Allen Walker. 1963. "The First Stage in the History of 'O.K.'" *American Speech* 38: 5–27.

Read, Hollis. 1849. *The Hand of God in History.* Hartford, Conn.: H. Huntington.

Reeves, Arthur Middleton, Samuel Thurston Ballard, and Robert Augustus Parke. 1877–78. *The Cornelian.* Ithaca, N.Y.: Norton and Conklin.

Remy, Charles F. 1900. "Where the Best English is Spoken?" *School Review* 8:414–21.

Review of Anglicus's *Vulgar Tongue.* 1859. *Athenaeum,* January 1, 17.

Review of Grose's *Provincial Glossary.* 1788. *Critical Review* 66:282–85.

Ripley, C. Peter, Roy E. Finkenbine, Michael F. Hembree, and Donald Yacovone, eds. 1985–91. *The Black Abolitionist Papers.* 5 vols. Chapel Hill: University of North Carolina Press.

Robbins, Keith. 1988. *Nineteenth-Century Britain: Integration and Diversity.* Oxford: Clarendon Press.

[Roebuck, John Arthur.] 1831. Review of *Society for the Diffusion of Useful Knowledge* (Reports and Prospects, 1830). *Westminster Review* 14:365–94.

Rydén, Mats, and Sverker Brorström. 1987. *The "Be/Have" Variation with Intransitives in English.* Stockholm: Almqvist Wiksell.

S. H. 1853. "Jacob Grimm on the Genius and Vocation of the English Language." *Notes and Queries* 7:125–26.

[Sala, George A.] 1853. "Slang." *Household Words* 8:73–78.

Sampson, Henry. 1874. *A History of Advertising from the Earliest Times.* London: Chatto and Windus.

Savage, W. H. 1833. *The Vulgarisms and Improprieties of the English Language.* London: T. S. Porter.

Schele de Vere, Maximilian. 1867. *Studies in English; or, Glimpses of the Inner Life of Our Language.* New York: Charles Scribner.

Schofield, Robert S. 1981. "Dimensions of Illiteracy in England, 1750–1850." In *Literacy and Social Development in the West,* ed. Harvey J. Graff, 201–13. Cambridge: Cambridge University Press.

Schopenhauer, Arthur. 1974. *Parerga and Paralipomena: Short Philosophical Essays.* Trans. E. F. J. Payne. 2 vols. Oxford: Clarendon Press.

Scott, Fred Newton. 1900. "The Report on College Entrance Requirements in English." *Educational Review* 20:289–94.

Scott, Walter. 1932–37. *The Letters of Sir Walter Scott.* Ed. H. J. C. Grierson. 12 vols. London: Constable.

Shaw, George Bernard. 1946. *Six Plays.* New York: Dodd, Mead.

Sheridan, Thomas. 1967. *A General Dictionary of the English Language* (1780). Facsimile ed., English Linguistics, 1500–1900, 50. Menston: Scolar Press.

Shi, Dingxu. 1991. "Chinese Pidgin English: Its Origin and Linguistic Features." *Journal of Chinese Linguistics* 19:1–40.

Shoemaker, Charles C. 1915. *Choice Dialect and Other Characterizations.* Philadelphia: Penn Publishing.

Silva, Penny. 1996. *Dictionary of South African English.* Cape Town: Oxford University Press.

Simpson, William. 1874. *Meeting the Sun: A Journey All Round the World.* London: Longmans, Green, Reader, and Dyer.

Skeat, Walter W., and J. H. Nodal. 1877. *English Dialect Society: A Bibliographical List.* London: Trübner.

"Slang." 1893. *Atlantic.* 71:424–26.

Smart, B. H. 1849. *Walker's Pronouncing Dictionary of the English Language, Adapted to the Present State of Literature and Science* (1836). London: Longman, Brown.

Smith, Harold. 1974. *The Society for the Diffusion of Useful Knowledge,*

1826–1846: A Social and Bibliographical Evaluation. Dalhousie University, School of Library Service, occasional paper no. 8.

Smith, Joseph. 1974. *The Holy Scriptures (Inspired Version).* Independence, Mo.: Herald Publishing House.

Smith, William. 1795. *An Attempt to Render the Pronunciation of the English Language More Easy.* London: T. Gillet. Facsimile ed., English Linguistics, 1500–1800, 182. Menston: Scolar Press, 1969.

Society Small Talk; or, What to Say and When to Say It. 1879. 2d ed. London: Frederick Warne.

Soule, Richard, and Loomis J. Campbell. 1873. *Pronouncing Handbook of Words Often Mispronounced.* Boston: Lee and Shepard.

———, and William A. Wheeler. 1872. *Manual of English Pronunciation and Spelling* (1861). Boston: Lee and Shepard.

[Southey, Robert.] 1830. Review of *Da Njoe Testament. Quarterly Review* 43:553–64.

The Stag Party. [1888? Connecticut?]: n.p. This clandestinely published book is apparently very rare; the copy cited here is from the Yale University Library.

Stenhouse, Thomas. 1928. *Lives Enshrined in Language.* 2d. ed. Newcastle-upon-Tyne: Andrew Reid.

Stephens, Ann Sophia. 1843. *High Life in New York, by Jonathan Slick, Esq.* 2d ed. New York: Edward Stephens.

Stephens, F. G. 1860. "American Humorous Poetry." *Macmillan's* 1:203–11.

Story, G. M., W. J. Kirwin, and J. D. A. Widdowson. 1982. *Dictionary of Newfoundland English.* Toronto: University of Toronto Press.

Stowe, Harriet Beecher. 1863. "Sojourner Truth, The Libyan Sibyl." *Atlantic* 11:473–81.

Straumann, Heinrich. 1935. *Newspaper Headlines: A Study in Linguistic Method.* London: George Allen and Unwin.

Sundby, Bertil, Anne Kari Björge, and Kari E. Haugland. 1991. *A Dictionary of English Normative Grammar.* Amsterdam and Philadelphia: John Benjamins.

Suplée, Thomas D. 1889. *Suplée's Trench on Words* (1877). 20th ed. New York: A. C. Armstrong.

Surtees, Robert Smith. 1968. *Jorrocks' Jaunts and Jollies* (1838). London: Cassell.

———. 1981. *Mr. Sponge's Sporting Tour* (1853). London: Batsford.

Sweet, Henry. 1877. *A Handbook of Phonetics.* Oxford: Clarendon Press.

———. 1958. *A New English Grammar, Logical and Historical* (1898). 2 vols. Oxford: Clarendon Press.

Tabbert, Russell. 1991. *Dictionary of Alaskan English*. Juneau, Alaska: Denali Press.

Talmage, T. DeWitt. 1884. *Perfect Jewels: A Collection of the Choicest Things in the Literature of Life, Love and Religion*. Adrian, Mich.: Mills, Dodge and Pomeroy.

Taylor, Dennis. 1993. *Hardy's Literary Language and Victorian Philology*. Oxford: Clarendon Press.

Taylor, Geoffrey. 1969. "Amateur Scientists." *Michigan Quarterly Review* 8:107–13.

Teall, Edward N. 1937. *Meet Mr. Hyphen*. New York: Funk and Wagnalls.

Tooke, John Horne. 1857. *Epea Pteroenta: or, The Diversions of Purley* (1840). Enlarged and corrected by Richard Taylor. London: William Tegg.

Treasures of Use and Beauty. 1883. Detroit: F. B. Dickerson.

Trench, Richard Chenevix. 1860. *On Some Deficiencies in our English Dictionaries* (1857). London: John W. Parker and Son.

———. 1891. *The Study of Words* (1851). New York: Macmillan.

Tulloch, Graham. 1980. *The Language of Walter Scott*. London: Andre Deutsch.

Twain, Mark. 1972. *Roughing It* (1872). Ed. Franklin R. Rogers and Paul Baender. Berkeley and Los Angeles: University of California Press.

Twyman, Michael. 1970. *Printing, 1770–1970: An Illustrated History of Its Development and Uses in England*. London: Eyre and Spottiswoode.

Tylor, E. B. 1873–74. "The Philology of Slang." *Macmillan's* 29:502–13.

Updike, Daniel Berkeley. 1927. *Printing Types: Their History, Form, and Use*. 2 vols. Cambridge, Mass.: Harvard University Press.

Van Riper, William R. 1957. "The Loss of Post-Vocalic *R* in the Eastern United States." Ph.D. diss., University of Michigan.

Vicinus, Martha. 1974. *The Industrial Muse: A Study of Nineteenth Century British Working-Class Literature*. London: Croom Helm.

Vincent, G. Robert. n.d. *Hark! The Years: A Scrapbook in Sound about America from 1890–1933*. East Lansing, Mich.: National Voice Library. Michigan State University (sound recording).

Visser, Fredericus Theodorus. 1963–73. *An Historical Syntax of the English Language*. 3 pts. Leiden: E. J. Brill.

The Vulgarities of Speech Corrected: with Elegant Expressions for Provincial and

Vulgar English, Scots, and Irish; for Those Who are Unacquainted with Grammar (1826). 1829. London: F. C. Westley.

Walker, John. 1807. *A Critical Pronouncing Dictionary and Expositor of the English Language* (1791). 3d American ed. New York: Samuel Stansbury et al.

Ware, J[ames] Redding. 1909. *Passing English of the Victorian Era: A Dictionary of Heterodox English, Slang, and Phrase.* London: George Routledge and Sons. Facsimile ed., Wakefield, Yorkshire: EP Publishing, 1972.

Webster, Noah. 1789. *Dissertations on the English Language.* Boston: Isaiah Thomas. Facsimile ed., English Linguistics, 1500–1800, 54. Menston: Scolar Press.

———. 1828. *An American Dictionary of the English Language.* New York: S. Converse. Facsimile ed., New York: Johnson Reprint Company, 1970.

———. [1880?] *The Elementary Spelling Book.* New York: American Book.

Weekley, Ernest. 1952. *The English Language.* London: André Deutsche.

Welcome, John. 1982. *The Sporting World of R. S. Surtees.* Oxford: Oxford University Press.

Wellman, Francis L. 1962. *The Art of Cross-Examination* (1902). New York: Collier Books.

Wells, J. C. 1982. *Accents of English.* 3 vols. Cambridge: Cambridge University Press.

Wells, James M. 1966. "Book Typography in the United States of America." In *Book Typography, 1815–1965, in Europe and the United States of America,* ed. Kenneth Day, 325–70. London: Ernest Benn.

Whalley, Joyce Irene. 1980. *The Pen's Excellencie: Calligraphy of Western Europe and America.* Tunbridge Wells, England: Midas Books.

Wheeler, Ann Coward. 1840. *The Westmoreland Dialect in Four Familiar Dialogues* (1790). London: John Russell Smith.

Wheeler, Paul, and Anne Broadhead. 1985. *Upper Class Rhyming Slang.* London: Sidgwick and Jackson.

[Whitcher, Frances Miriam]. 1858. *The Widow Bedott Papers.* New York: Derby and Jackson.

White, J. F., and W. F. Parsons. 1882. *Parsons' Hand-Book of Forms.* Battle Creek, Mich.: J. E. White.

White, James. 1969. *The English Verb* (1761). Facsimile ed., English Linguistics 1500–1800, 135. Menston: Scolar Press.

White, Richard Grant. 1872. *Words and Their Uses: Past and Present*. Rev. ed. New York: Sheldon.

———. 1880. "English in England." *Atlantic* 45:374–86, 669–79; 47:697–707.

———. 1908. *Every-Day English* (1880). Boston: Houghton Mifflin.

Whitford, Helena Wells. 1799. *Letters on Subjects of Importance to the Happiness of Young Females*. London: L. Peacock.

Whitman, Walt. 1969. "Slang in America" (1885). In *The English Language, 1858–1964,* ed. W. F. Bolton and David Crystal, 54–58. Cambridge: Cambridge University Press.

Whitney, William Dwight. 1871. Review of Richard Grant White's *Words and their Uses. New Englander* 30:305–11.

———. 1874. "The Elements of English Pronunciation." In *Oriental and Linguistic Studies, Second Series*, 202–76. New York: Scribner, Armstrong.

———. 1877a. "Cockneyisms." *Transactions of the American Philological Association*, 8:26–28.

———. 1877b. "Grimm's Law." Review of *Grimm's Law: A Study,* by Thomas Le Marchant Douse. *Nation* 25:75–76.

———, ed. 1889–91. *The Century Dictionary*. 6 vols. New York: Century.

Williams, Ralph Olmsted. 1897. *Some Questions of Good English*. New York: Henry Holt.

Williams, William P. 1979. "Some Notes on ſ and s." *Analytical and Enumerative Bibliography* 3:97–101.

Willis, Robert. 1830. "On the Vowel Sounds, and on Reed Organ-Pipes." *Transactions of the Cambridge Philosophical Society* 3:231–68.

Winer, Lise. 1993. *Trinidad and Tobago*. Varieties of English around the World, T6. Amsterdam: John Benjamins.

Winter, Kate H. 1984. *Marietta Holley: Life with "Josiah Allen's Wife."* Syracuse: Syracuse University Press.

Wise, Thomas J., and J. Alexander Symington, eds. 1980. *The Brontës: Their Lives, Friendships and Correspondence* (1933). 4 vols. in 2. Oxford: Basil Blackwell.

Woolf, Virginia. 1976. *Moments of Being: Unpublished Autobiographical Writings*. Ed. Jeanne Shulkind. New York: Harcourt Brace Jovanovich.

———. 1990. *Mrs. Dalloway*. London: The Hogarth Press.

Worcester, Joseph Emerson. 1876. *A Dictionary of the English Language* (1830). Boston: Brewer and Tileston.

Wordsworth, William. 1952. Preface to the second edition of *Lyrical Ballads* (1800). In *Criticism: The Major Texts,* ed. Walter Jackson Bate, 335–46. New York: Harcourt, Brace.

Worrell, A. S. 1861. *The Principles of English Grammar.* Nashville, Tenn.: Graves, Marks.

Wrench, R. G. K. 1891. *Winchester Word-Book: A Collection of Past and Present Notions.* Winchester: J. Wells; London: D. Nutt.

Wright, Albert D. 1872. *Elements of the English Language; or Analytical Orthography.* New York: A. S. Barnes.

Wright, Arnold. 1891. *Baboo English as 'tis Writ, Being Curiosities of Indian Journalism.* London: T. Fisher Unwin.

Wright, Joseph. 1905. *The English Dialect Grammar.* Oxford: Henry Frowde.

———. 1963. *The English Dialect Dictionary* (1896–1905). 6 vols. New York: Hacker Art Books.

Wroth, Lawrence C. 1939. "Book Production and Distribution from the Beginning to the War between the States." In *The Book in America,* ed. Hellmut Lehmann-Haupt, 3–111. New York: R. R. Bowker.

Wyld, Henry Cecil. 1914. "Class Dialect and Standard English." In *A Miscellany Presented to John Macdonald Mackay, LL. D.,* ed. Oliver Elton, 283–91. Liverpool: At the University Press.

———. 1934. *The Best English.* Society for Pure English, tract 39. Oxford: Clarendon Press.

———. 1936. *A History of Modern Colloquial English.* 3d ed. Oxford: Basil Blackwell.

Yule, Emma Sarepta. 1927. "The English Language in the Philippines." *American Speech* 1:111–20.

Yule, Henry. 1886. "Hobson-Jobsoniana." *Asiatic Quarterly Review* 1:119–40.

———, and A. C. Burnell. 1903. *Hobson-Jobson: A Glossary of Anglo-Indian Colloquial Words and Phrases.* London: John Murray, 1903. Rev. 2d ed. by William Crooke. Facsimile ed., New York: Humanities Press, 1968.

Zachrisson, R. E. 1914. "Northern English or London English as the Standard Pronunciation." *Anglia* 38:407–32.

SOURCES OF ILLUSTRATIONS

The typeface of this book is Baskerville, an eighteenth-century design much admired and imitated by nineteenth-century printers. Chapter headings and other types found here come from the following sources.

INDEX.

cabby, 153
café noir, 162
Cairo, 66
calcite, 147
calf, 112, 114, 115, 117, 122
call, 193
calm, 113, 115, 119
calorie, 151
Cambridge, University of, 12, 111, 115, 131, 185, 210–11, 255, 274
Cambridge Philosophical Society, 115
Camden, William, 5
camisado, 112, 121, 158
camp, 114
Campbell, Karlyn Kohrs, 316
Campbell, Loomis J., 85, 90
Campbell, Thomas, 254
Canada, 4, 20, 99, 108, 125, 126, 150, 169, 170, 282–84
Canadian English, 202–3
canal, 120
cannot, 118
canophilia, 142
Cant, 19–20, 177–78, 195–98, 204–5
cant, 77, 101
can't, 119
cantabile, 121
cantata, 121
canteen, 207
canticle, 121
canto, 121
car, 112, 126
carbohydrate, 151
carborundum, 149
card, 100–101
cardigan, 158
cards, 196
card sharp, 200
Caribbean, 78
Carlyle, Thomas, 44, 165
carman, 117
carpet bag, 230
Carroll, Lewis, 154
carrot, 117
cashmere, 158

cask, 113
cast, 111
castle, 118
catawampously, 200
catch, 119
Catford, J. C., 116
Cato, 84
cattle, 120
caucus, 199
Cavendish, Henry, 240
Caxton, William, 44
Cecil, Robert, 39
celery, 64
cent, 202–3
century, 134
Century Dictionary, The, 174, 185
certainly, 77
chain-lightening, 200
chaise longue, 158
chamber-pot, 168
chamois, 161
Champneys, A. C., 134
chance, 112, 118
chapter, 111
Charley Lancaster, 196
chattermag, 154
Chaucer, Geoffrey, 10
cheek, 201
cheese, 209–10
chiacking, 201
chic, 158
chiffonier, 158
chignon, 158
Children's literature, 8
Chilton, Stephen N., 44
China, 5, 7, 69, 308
Chink Gulch, 169
chisel, 202
chitterlings, 191
chloride, 147
chlorine, 147
chlorite, 147
chloroform, 149–50
chlorophyll, 151
chow-chow, 309–10
Christian Science, 313
Christmas, Henry, 97

Crimean War, 84
Criminals, 179–83, 204–5, 212. *See also* Cant
Crockett, Davy, 284
Crockett, S. R., 303
Cromwell, Oliver, 257
croquet, 189
crosstown, 169
crouton, 159
Cruikshank, George, 193
Cruikshank, Richard, 193
Cuba, 69
cucumber, 64
cundum, 186–87
Curme, George, 250
currant, 94
current, 94
curse, 99
cuss, 99
cycle, 153
cyclometer, 145
cyprian, 193

Daily Mail, 26
Daily Telegraph, 140
dam, 120, 209–10
Dana, Richard H., 91
dance, 112, 115, 116, 118, 126
dandy, 191
dandyism, 191
dandymania, 180, 191
dandyzette, 191
Daniel, Evan, 253
danna-drag, 181
darwinite, 147
dashed, 187
daughter, 75
Davitt, Michael, 183
Day, Henry N., 116
Day, Lál Behári, 304
dead, 200
decimated, 143
decrescendo, 160
Defoe, Daniel, 222
DeKeyser, Xavier, 260, 261
Delsarte, François, 283
demagoguery, 19

demand, 110, 120
demi-rep, 177
democratometer, 145
Denmark, 306
dentistry, 164
depot, 169
Derbyshire, 296
Derivation, 140, 147, 150, 156, 163, 199, 205, 211, 228–30, 265
De Vinne, Theodore Low, 44, 174
Devon, 270–71
DeWitt, Marguerite, E., 90
dhenki, 304
Dickens, Charles, v, viii, 20, 68, 132, 155, 164, 180–81, 187, 207, 241–42
Dickensesque, 156
Dickensian, 156
Dickensiana, 156
Dickensish, 156
Dickensite, 156
Dickensy, 156
dicycle, 153
dietetics, 151
digamy, 142
dilapidated, 143
dilemma, 167
Diminutives, 205
ding bat, 200
dining table, 231, 233
dinner table, 231, 233
Discourse margin, 239–40
dispatch, 84
distanceometer, 145
disulphobenzoic, 148
ditto, 236
ditty bag, 230
doddie, 172
dodger, 187
do in unemphatic present, 221
dolichocephalous, 141
dollar sign, 56
domestic science, 150
Don't, 107, 119
don't, 77
Donaldson, Willliam, 20, 302–3
donder, 206

gentoo, 206
genus, 134
German, 6, 145–46, 159
German flutes, 196
German scholarship, 14–16, 141, 146, 151
Gesture, 272, 283
get, 221–22, 227, 247–48
Gibbon, Edward, 232
Gibbs, J. W., 223
Giddy, Davies, 29–30, 32
Gifford, Douglas, 303
Gilbert, Davies. See Giddy, Davies
Gilbert, W. S., 121
Gilman, E. Ward, 250, 252
Gilmore, William J., 32
giraffe, 121
girl, 99, 101, 136
give, 228–29
Gladstone, William Ewart, 90
gladstone, 156
glance, 112
Glasgow, 77
glass, 112, 113, 116, 118, 123, 136
glengarry, 158
Glottal stop, 76–79
go-cart, 233
goal, 190
God, 82
godemiche, 186
gold, 84
goldarn, 188
Goldstrom, J. M., 39
goniva, 207
good-for, 207
Goodholme, Todd S., 159
gooseberry puddin', 196
G. O. P., 155
Gore, Willard C., 211
got, 77
gotten, 221–22
Gould, Edward S., 82, 87, 232
gown, 95
gowner, 190
graffiti, 161
graft, 116, 122, 198
Grammar, 10, 51–54, 214, 215–61,

319, 320
gramophone, 146
Grandgent, C. H., 125
Granger, James, 47
grangerize, 47
grant, 111, 112
-graph, 145–46
graphite, 147
grass, 112, 118, 122
Gray, Thomas, 264
Gray, Thomas R., 30–31
Greek, 79–80, 141–48, 152, 216, 254–55, 307–8
green, 192
green apple quick step, 202
Greenfield, William, 306–8, 310
Greenough, James Bradstreet, 214
greens, 186
Greenwich, 73
Grimm, Jacob, 16, 134, 277
Grimm, Wilhelm, 277
grinder, 39
grisaille, 161
Grose, Francis, 177–78, 266–67, 273, 274
Groves, David, 280
guess, 281
Guild, James, 62
Gurney, Thomas, 68
Gutenberg, Johannes, 44
guy, 172
Gwynne, Parry, 94

ha, 115
habit, 127
habitation, 127
habundance, 127
Haggart, David, 181
hair, 135
half, 112, 113, 114, 117, 124
half bath, 170
Haliburton, Thomas Chandler, 20, 178, 282, 292
Hall, Benjamin Homer, 210–11
Hall, Fitzedward, 217–18, 222–24, 226, 249
halve, 112

Oxford English Dictionary, 2, 19, 139,
    148, 152, 162–63, 164, 174, 185
oxide, 147
oxygen, 147
oyster social, 203

paillette, 161
Painter, Nell Irvin, 316
Painting, 160–61
pal, 171
palm, 115, 116, 119
Palmer, Abram Smythe, 173–74
Palsgrave, John, 127
pan, 114, 115, 116
pants, 153
papa, 112
papadom, 159
Paper, 40–41
Paradise, 169
paragraph, 95
paramatta, 158
parcel, 99
pard, 172
parka, 163
Parke, Robert Augustus, 211
Parliament, 29–30, 114, 131, 283
parlor organ, 160
partan, 172
Participle, 228
Participle, dangling, 241
participled, 188
partridge, 64, 125
pass, 111, 115, 123
passable, 117
passel, 99
passible, 117
Passive voice, 217, 245–48
past, 111, 114, 115, 116, 118
pastor, 123
Past tense and past participle,
    219–21
pasture, 111
pat, 110
paternal, 134
path, 110, 111, 112
Pat Malone, 205
patois, 307

Paz, D. G., 39
p-deletion, 80
Peabody, Andrew P., 84
pearl, 101
Peculiar, 169
Peebles, 301
Pegge, Samuel, 17, 95–96, 127, 132
peg off, 207
Penmanship, 60–62, 65
Penzl, Herbert, 124
per, 236
Percy, Thomas, 266
Perrin, Noel, 187
Perry, William, 79, 83, 177
personality, 217
Personal names, 170
Perthshire, 300–301
Peruvian, 154
Peterson, William S., 34, 41
petrol, 150
Pettman, Charles, 206–7
Philippines, 5, 69
Phillipps, K. C., 85, 227
Philipson, Uno, 199
Phillips, Edward, 236
Philology, v–vi, 3, 12, 15, 39, 86–87,
    207, 213, 291–93
phiz, 153
phone, 160
Phonetics, 67, 73, 75
Phonograph, 72
phonograph, 146
phosphate, 149
phosphoric, 147
phosphorous, 147, 150
photographer, 165
photography, 146
Phrasal verbs, 230
Phrenology, 181, 286
phrenology, 141
piblokto, 163
Pickering, John, 252
pidgeon, 192
Pidgin-English, 7, 75, 212, 308–11
Piozzi, Hester Lynch, 228, 319
piss-pot, 168
Pitman, Isaac, 57, 66